# A NEW DESIGN PHILOSOPHY

**Dr Tony Fry** is Australia's leading design theorist, an educator and a consultant. He has written numerous influential books, essays and articles, and has lectured at universities in Europe, Asia and the United States. Tony Fry was formerly Senior Lecturer in Design and Associate Director of the National Key Centre for Design Quality at University of Sydney. He is the founding Director of the EcoDesign Foundation, Sydney.

# A NEW DESIGN PHILOSOPHY

## AN INTRODUCTION TO DEFUTURING

*Tony Fry*

UNSW PRESS

**A UNSW Press book**

*Published by*
University of New South Wales Press Ltd
University of New South Wales
Sydney 2052 Australia
www.unswpress.com.au

© Tony Fry 1999
First published 1999

This book is copyright. Apart from any fair dealing for the purpose of private study, research, criticism or review, as permitted under the Copyright Act, no part may be reproduced by any process without written permission. Enquiries should be addressed to the publisher.

National Library of Australia
Cataloguing-in-Publication entry:

> Fry, Tony (Anthony Hart).
> A new design philosophy: an introduction to defuturing.
>
> Bibliography.
> Includes index.
> ISBN 0 86840 753 4.
>
> 1. Design — Philosophy. 2. Design — History — 20th century.
> 3. Design — Social aspects. 4. Change. I. Title.
>
> 720.1

*Printer* Griffin Press, Adelaide

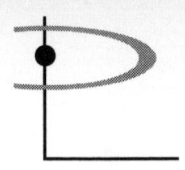

# CONTENTS

| | |
|---|---|
| Preface | vii |
| Introduction | 1 |
|     An introductory lexicographical review | 3 |
| | |
| PART 1   AN OPENING | 19 |
| Chapter 1 Technology, warring and the crisis of history | 21 |
|     Technology in flux | 22 |
|     From structure and from *techné* | 32 |
|     From war to warring | 38 |
|     The crisis of the crisis of history | 47 |
| | |
| PART 2   HISTORY, MODERNITY AND DEFUTURING | 59 |
| Chapter 2 Made in America: a world production | 69 |
|     America | 74 |
|     Then and now | 90 |
|     Productivism and a history of world making | 95 |
| | |
| Chapter 3 Dwelling in streamlined America | 105 |
|     Streamlining design | 115 |
|     The New York World's Fair | 120 |
|     Utopia: a designing idea | 129 |

Chapter 4 Total design: Europe . . . . . . . . . . . . . . . . . . . . 146
   The Bauhaus, as told . . . . . . . . . . . . . . . . . . . . . . . . . . . 151
   The Vkhutemas postscript . . . . . . . . . . . . . . . . . . . . . . . 161

PART 3   ONE POINT: FOUR LOCATIONS . . . . . . . . . . 171
Chapter 5 Design and the body of competition . . . . . . 173
   The body . . . . . . . . . . . . . . . . . . . . . . . . . . . . . . . . . . . . 178
   Bodies of the body . . . . . . . . . . . . . . . . . . . . . . . . . . . . . 186
   The measured that measures the standards . . . . . . . . . 195
   Openings as endings . . . . . . . . . . . . . . . . . . . . . . . . . . . 200

Chapter 6 Time and China . . . . . . . . . . . . . . . . . . . . . . 205
   Time . . . . . . . . . . . . . . . . . . . . . . . . . . . . . . . . . . . . . . . 206
   The years of 1926 . . . . . . . . . . . . . . . . . . . . . . . . . . . . . 210
   China: four perspectives . . . . . . . . . . . . . . . . . . . . . . . . 213

Chapter 7 Televisual in-human design . . . . . . . . . . . . . 227
   The televisual . . . . . . . . . . . . . . . . . . . . . . . . . . . . . . . . 229
   Perspectives and horizons . . . . . . . . . . . . . . . . . . . . . . 238
   Ecology of the image . . . . . . . . . . . . . . . . . . . . . . . . . . 241

Chapter 8 The autonomic technocentricity of
computers . . . . . . . . . . . . . . . . . . . . . . . . . . . . . . . . . . . 252
   The reason machine . . . . . . . . . . . . . . . . . . . . . . . . . . . 254
   The force of design . . . . . . . . . . . . . . . . . . . . . . . . . . . . 264
   Reiterations towards making decisions . . . . . . . . . . . . 273

Concluding impressions . . . . . . . . . . . . . . . . . . . . . . . . 283

Select bibliography . . . . . . . . . . . . . . . . . . . . . . . . . . . . 291
Index . . . . . . . . . . . . . . . . . . . . . . . . . . . . . . . . . . . . . . . 296

# PREFACE

Felix H Mann's 'Stahlwerk', 1929 (San Francisco Museum of Modern Art, Byron Meyer Fund Purchase)

The claim of the title of this book immediately generates a question: What is a new design philosophy? Briefly, the direct answer is: a philosophy that delivers a new foundation of thought and practice. This philosophy is here to be discovered — it is not formulated as a philosophical system, although it does draw heavily on the ontological tradition and demonstrates an ontological theory of the agency of design. The motive for doing this is not to complement existing design thinking but rather to confront and hopefully displace it. Indeed, the text is intended to touch a chord with the existing design community while also reaching people for whom design has not so far been an object of serious concern or study

What is written here is aimed at creating a new understanding and useful knowledge. It will also strive, without idealist and utopian self-deception, to create reactions, altered perceptions, and offer a confrontation with negatives that engender a resolution to act.

The book has its genesis in series of public lectures at the Faculty of Design, Architecture and Building, of the University of Technology in Sydney. More substantially, in common with the thinking of many to whom it owes a debt, it arrives from living with, and working on, a particular problem for a very long time. The problem it confronts always expresses itself in terms of a question that continually changes, but ever remains the same, a question that gets constantly clearer but still stays ill defined:

> How is it possible to gain that ability to act to sustain what needs to be sustained in conditions that devalue and negate that with sustaining capability for the sake of short term gains and immediate gratification?

Living this question has meant working in and on design and technology; studying culture and analysing cultural technologies, like television; politicising that which is not normally deemed as part of the political sphere; reading philosophy; teaching; creating organisations; writing books, and more. The journey towards the question has been long, and a good deal of baggage has been accumulated: yet one ever remains at the beginning.

The implication of accepting this challenge is that finding an answer becomes an exploration and act of labour, rather than being the product of a sudden moment of insight or protracted contemplation. The answer thus has to be made and demonstrated, rather than just reasoned and espoused. Such a task demands conceptual tools, critically reflective thought, design, construction, testing and remaking. One of the major elements of this process is being able to adequately define the problem. Explicitly, the ability to sustain cannot be gained without problems of unsustainability being defined, fully understood and appropriately dealt with. 'Defuturing' is introduced into this critical setting to precisely provide the kind of conceptual tool needed to define the unsustainable, and identify how it takes the future away. As a sensibility, carried by a particular mode of reading, it directs our attention to how the unsustainable is historically constituted and how it functions.

Defuturing is a new naming, it is not of the mindset of conventional thought, and neither is it a fellow traveller with either environmentalism's biocentrism or ecological design's technocentricity. Defuturing delivers another agenda of thinking, making and living which recognises that the future is not a vast void, but a time and place constituted by directional forces of design, set in train in the past and the present, and which flow into the future. This reveals that the historical is as much before us as it is to our rear. As will be shown, to introduce defuturing necessitates a rethinking of 'sustainability' as the ability to sustain. The shift of understanding that this produces is to be signalled by the word 'sustain-ability'. The use of the term is not merely a gesture, for it is able to be given significantly new connotations, uses and inflections.

Defuturing, as will be shown in the coming pages, is an idea of a form of negation that assists in defining, confronting and disclosing the temporality of unsustainability. Learning to think, hear and feel how the unsustainable defutures effectively installs a literacy, as a thinking, seeing and touching, that turns defuturing into a tool able to help create sustain-ability.

Involvement in the formation in 1991 and subsequent work of the Sydney based EcoDesign Foundation has been significant as a place of such learning. At its simplest, sustain-ability and defuturing are works in progress, time markers, that come out of the indivisible relations between: study; labouring to advance both material and immaterial means with the ability to sustain that which needs to be sustained; reflections on failures; and thinking in practice. They are not abstractions offered up for use but the used offered up for appropriation via abstraction.

The EcoDesign Foundation set out to bring research, education and commercial consultancy together as reciprocal activities. Existing between the academy and industry, it has used design, in all its complexity, as its primary agent of change. Design, in its widest sense, provides the basis for dialogue on sustain-ability and the form of the future with government and professional practitioners in areas such as architecture, construction, engineering, industrial design, management, as well as with students and educators across various disciplines. Bringing design and sustain-ability together also provides the basis for tertiary and professional development education, curriculum development, educational materials development and event presentations. Additionally it has formed the focus for research projects and writing.

Working within the EcoDesign Foundation has meant trying to succeed while working against the grain. While the Foundation has undertaken many projects and a good deal of research, worked with industry and government, educational institutions and professionals, especially architects and engineers, often on major projects, it constantly confronts the negation of sustain-ability by the efforts of 'the mainstream' to sustain the unsustainable. With the rise of 'sustainability' as a mainstream concern, the task of establishing difference, and a place from which to speak it, ever remains.

ACKNOWLEDGMENTS

Help and encouragement has come in various forms and from a number of people. I particularly wish to thank Geoffery Caban, Clive Dilnot, Keith McMenony, Tim Marshall, Tigger Wise and Michael Zimmerman. I am especially indebted to my EcoDesign Foundation comrades Abby Mellick-Lopez and Cameron Tonkinwise. The greatest debt is without doubt the one I owe to my partner Anne-Marie Willis, whose solidarity, insight and practical assistance is long-standing, unwavering and valued beyond measure. Finally, the excellent support of the publisher Robin Derricourt, the book's editor James Drown and all the staff at UNSW Press has been truly appreciated.

*Tony Fry*

# INTRODUCTION

'Now' (author's collection)

As the 'telling' of defuturing, this text arrives as something confronting an impossibility and a necessity. What is impossible is the telling of the story, for once one understands the nature and magnitude of the defutured, how one accounts for the history and making of the material world dramatically changes. In this respect it is a way of seeing, remaking and making anew — hence it delivers a new foundation of design which radically transforms what design is and does. Defuturing is thus the generator of a new design philosophy, the character of which will emerge shortly.

The full story of the defutured can never be told, for it requires the rewriting of everything. However, demonstrating that one understands the method of telling is essential. Defuturing is a necessary learning that travels before any design or constructional action if any effort is to be made to acquire the ability to sustain. The fact that so far the defutured and defuturing (the method by which the defutured is understood) has not been learnt means that even the well intentioned go on sustaining the unsustainable.

While design history is employed by this text, what is written here is not itself design history, and it is not intended to add to this body of knowledge. What it does do though is to use historical material on design to expose the archaeology of another ground, the ground of the negation of the future — defuturing. The history of what has been made present by design is employed parasitically to expose what design has taken away. History is thus employed against history, and out of this reconfiguration the entire frame of reference of design and designing shifts. The deconstructive move is accompanied by a reconstructive one, with the re-assembled forming a new pattern. Such an exercise in 'applied theory' is no naive lapse into instrumentalism. If it had to be defended it would be on the basis of being a critical practice that is critical.

The making of a future, against forces that defutured, demands the identification, judgement, selection and clearing of what this negation puts in place. To do this does not amount to wholesale destruction of the forms of our materialities, neither does this clearing proclaim the past as a block to the future (which is the way the Italian futurist movement in the early decades of the twentieth century viewed it). Rather, embracing defuturing means confronting and removing the authority of the foundations of thought, upon which the narratives of the like of 'world', 'future', 'production' and 'progress' stand — this in order to make things otherwise. This means, in effect, undercutting the authority of the designing, making, technical functionality and modes of occupation of the multiple worlds of everyday life.

What is essential to grasp about the point of doing this kind of deconstructive exercise is that it is not being negative for the sake of it, but rather it is something vital in the gaining of new knowledge and active capabilities able to contribute to advancing an ability to sustain what needs to sustained. Such change cannot arrive without such transformations of knowledge and action. As will be shown, current understandings of what 'unsustainability' is are completely inadequate: to date, our notions, assumptions and understandings of unsustainability have been woefully inadequate. To find and adopt a better comprehension of the 'nature' of unsustainability is a major and longstanding intellectual enterprise, one which is a necessary accompaniment to a learning of defuturing.[1]

## AN INTRODUCTORY LEXICOGRAPHICAL REVIEW

To assist the reader a small number of key concepts need putting forward and disposing in relation to each other. While all the concepts have a rich intellectual history, for the sake of brevity the origins and evolutions of the terms will not be unpacked (notwithstanding a certain unavoidable nominalism, they are no nominalist indulgence).

Five concepts are reviewed: design, sustain-ability, unsustainability, defuturing, and relationality. Two other concepts, productivism and utopianism, will also be reviewed at length later, and in context. However, a few comments drawn from the review of utopianism will be added at the end of this particular review, this so as to counter any assumptions that what is being put forward subscribes to this disposition.

### DESIGN

While the nature of the defutured and of defuturing needs to unfold with care and detail, and in a way that makes its relation to design, structuring and complexity clear, it is also most important that we put the idea confrontationally before the dominant historical narrative and characterisation of design. In particular, the history of design and technology beg to be directly confronted with a theory of unsustainability that undermines existing narratives. In doing this it then becomes possible to read the history of design and technology as a history of error and unthinking at the very centre of a progressive advancement toward unsustainability. While the many attainments of design are acknowledged, so too are its massive number of unrecognised failures and contradictions.

In general, and notwithstanding the efforts of some, design, as object, process, history and theory, has not arrived to date as a generally recognised area of critical study or action outside of design education and practice. Once the question of design is looked at with any degree of seriousness it becomes apparent that it is more important and more complex than even designers and design scholars acknowledge. This not least because it is inseparable from setting directions and making decisions which determine either unsustainable or sustainable forms of the future. What follows from this perspective is the realisation that design's agency does not usually come from it being mobilised with a clear vision of consequences, but rather from its power as an unrecognised structural inscription.

Writers on design, in their vain, essentialist quest for the perfect, totalising and definitive definition, constantly trip over how they define what should be a compound term. For all the efforts of modernists to impose it, there is not even a universally agreed category 'design', thus there is no single frame of interpretation. As we can see, for instance, in the work of historians of technology like David Noble, the history of the design of machines in industrial culture can be told in various terms of the global 'evolution' of technological systems and mechanical forms, the transfer of human knowledge to inanimate objects, the designer's and design's implication in the structures of power and knowledge of the forces of production.[2] Certainly no common understanding is in use. It is not our aim here to seek to secure an unambiguous meaning for the term 'design'. The chances of establishing and holding a hegemonic meaning are negligible. Rather, what is put on offer is a relational and generic understanding of design that can be taken to any design practice or product.

It should be said that the term 'design' occupies an uncomfortable place, certainly in the English language. It lacks any discursive convention to produce and hold a correspondence of evoked signifier or signified between subjects in linguistic exchange. Put simply, no common meaning exists or is likely to get consensual agreement. An understanding of design will never be theoretically secured, simply because design gets configured so differently in the relations of varied discourses of its practice, presentation and economic exchange. Object, form, appearance and process, individually or in various permutations, all get designated as what design is. What results is seemingly commonly agreed understandings that are in fact misrecognitions predicated upon the differently adopted referents.

Design is prior to, within and independent of, both the sciences and humanities. Although we, and the worlds we occupy, are significantly determined by design it has never actually arrived as a serious object of inquiry — the study of design is a marginal activity of the academy, it does not attract the best minds, gain significant research support or generate general interest. The project of trying to create 'design studies' stalls on the ambition of disciplinary recognition, because of its failure to engage foundational thought and its proximity to contemporary 'low rigour' interdisciplinary thought (the fate mostly of cultural studies). Even those institutions where people are taught to be designers — industrial, architectural and visual — fail to comprehend the importance of design. While there is a philosophical tradition of the study of the social, the subject, mind, ethics, language, meaning, science, technology; while there are the established disciplines like classics, sociology, psychology, economics, geography, history and modern languages as well as new areas like contemporary culture, media, conflict studies and feminism; and while there is the full weight of mathematics, the sciences and technology; and further despite the fact that design is universally everywhere — it remains intellectually nowhere. As a specialism it is weak and locked into a service relation to vocational education. As curriculum content in all the domains of knowledge that it could inform, if it were treated seriously, it is all but non-existent.

The question of design is always an ontological question, which is a question of what it does in the ways that it acts. Equally, design is also a domain of metaphysical knowledge. Design always arrives as the way something acts as, in and on the world, and as a learnt thinking (theory) that informs practices which bring something into being. It is always more than its reified forms, immediate applications or applied functional acknowledge. What the relational ensemble that is design actually determines, what it actually sets in motion as an assemblage, goes unseen. Design is everywhere as the normality of the made world that is rendered background as soon as 'design' becomes an individuated object of focus. There is not a single thing around us that is not designed — door, walls, ceiling, window, curtains, desk, lamp, computer, books, bookshelves, chairs, pens, radio, clock, pictures, waste bin, carpet, heater and a myriad other things. Thus the world of designed objects and processes that are present for us constitute the designing environment. This pre-designed environment over-determines the designing of design processes and the products of design, all of which are deeply embedded in a circular process. The operational world, design process, designed objects, the agency of the designed and world creation constantly flow into and transform each other. To reify design, which is to present it in an objectified form removed from its dynamic in process, is to misconstrue the very nature of what design is.

There are three points of focus for this presented understanding of the design complexity:

1. the designed object that results from the design act or process (be it a city, building, industrial product, dress, visual image or garden)
2. the design agency: that is the designer designing, or the designing tool created by a designer for the design act (software, a pattern, a drawing, instructions, specifications)
3. design in process, which is the on-going designing that is the agency of the designed object as it functions or dysfunctions.

Of the third point it can be elaborated that all designed objects have determinate consequences, which may be great or small, as they constitute active environments and impacts. This is to say, all design in process futures or defutures, and that the environment out of which designing and the designed object come is a designing that prefigures the design act and the design form. Put succinctly: designers design in a designed world, which arrives by design, that designs their actions and objects, or more simply: we design our world, while our world designs us.

From what has been said, it follows that the way in which a new philosophy of design is manifested is not via an articulated system or theoretical framework but by an ontological shift that transforms how design is viewed, heard, felt, thought, understood, explained and done. Philosophy comprehended in this way is an embodied change that can only think the old through to new.

This meta-view of design (hereafter capitalised as Design) then is that which gathers the expressed particular forms of design, as object, agency and process as they exist conjuncturally and relationally in a specific time and space. Overlayed and underpinning the disposition of all elements of Design is its non-neutrality. Whatever we say Design is, it is also direction, force, power, imposition. This is why, in its omnipresence, it begs to be taken so seriously and is so implicated in, and between, the plurality of sustain-ability, the pluralism of the unsustainable, and the concealment of the crisis of unsustainability as it is misrepresented as a desirable standard of living, quality of life, needed economic growth and the like.

Anthropologically, designing is able to be recognised as omnipresent and integral to every intentional act we take. It is therefore elemental to our being and, as such is one of the defining qualities of what we are. In this respect we are all designers. We live in and by Design — our choices, be they of homes, lifestyle, dress, actions, perceptions, employment practices or environments are directed by the employment and consequence of Design. Its non-discreteness makes it seem an impossible object of study, and so legitimises its oversight.

Design always strays across fields, it always bleeds into, and travels with, the banners of work/labour/production, and consumption/culture/pleasure/lifestyle. Here is the impossibility of a history of design, since its options cover everything, or scattered fragments existing outside any regime of meaning.

No matter what its character, the activity of Design (and its application to structures, objects, forms, functions or appearances, as well as Design as thinking) has predominantly concerned itself with 'being-in-space'. In contrast, defuturing as a mode of inquiry, takes temporality as its major preoccupation, not on the basis of a wish to create the 'timeless' but rather the 'timemaking' that is bonded to the project of sustain-ability.

Restating — a critical engagement with unsustainable Design, as it defutures, has the ability to expose the profound dysfunction of the seeming functionality of now. A frontal encounter shows how Design is inscriptively posited in forms of power, exercised operationally as technology and implicated in those social, political and economic forms of industrial, post-industrial and consumer culture, which have made unsustainability a structural feature of the environment of the making of our 'natural' world.

The kind of thinking about Design exposed above will be developed in various ways later. What, however, we especially want to emphasise is that gaining an understanding of Design is of enormous critical importance to understanding how unsustainability has been created, how it defutures and what one needs to think if one is to work to create an ability to sustain. Approaching Design in this way by implication undercuts, and thus deconstructs, the agency of its existing foundations of authority in designer education, practice and scholarship. What is learnt in this exposé demands that we gain a far better grasp of how to make sense of our world, its un-freedoms and the impacts of our actions. This in turn implies that designing across the board itself be re-designed. But of course to be able to do this will require a mixture of abstraction, theory and concrete illustration, as well as a much clearer view (via the illumination of defuturing) of Design's attainments and errors.

At the most general, this text leads to a total revision of the way in which designed modern material and immaterial culture and economy have been, and are, regarded and engaged. More than this, and linking back to the question of ambition of this book, the knowledge and understanding aimed for here sets out to liberate a new way to know, think, theorise, remake and practice design that can help rupture it from unsustainable foundations and make 'it' otherwise.

## SUSTAIN-ABILITY AND UNSUSTAINABILITY

'Sustainability' is regarded as neither knowledge, knowable nor an end point. It is not as if there is a definable condition to name or put in place. Just at a physical level, as the second law of thermodynamics makes clear in defining the inherent entropic process of a dying universe, it is never possible to establish a permanent condition wherein everything is sustained, for every system of order becomes disordered over time. Moreover, because of circumstantial material differences and processes of perpetual change, the 'nature' of that designated to be sustained can never be universally uniform or fixed. In contrast to environmentalism's projection of 'sustainability' as an empirical endpoint condition, or its employment as a loose term by journalists or in economic and political rhetoric, 'sustain-ability' is to be used to designate the agency of a process (which evokes all connotations of ability) for a process (which evokes all connotations of sustaining). Sustain-ability is no less and no more than 'the ability to sustain'. This is to say it is an ability to constantly learn, work on and improve that which is vital to, and for, the 'being of being'. This is especially so as the impacts of human being ever extend the unsustainable.

In the light of the qualifications made, it is evident that the political discourse of 'sustainability', and the actions that flow from it, do not equate with sustain-ability. One of the most obvious manifestations of the political discourse of 'sustainability' is expressed by the rhetoric and politics of Ecologically Sustainable Development (ESD) as it was given momentum by the World Commission on Environment and Development (the Brundtland Report) of 1987. Out of this setting, ESD posits economic development (in other words, economic modernity) as the agency of delivery of sustainability. In doing so the logic and direction of economic growth was not contested. In contrast, sustain-ability acknowledges the need for change, based on the growth of the 'development of ecological sustainment' (DES). Such 'development' implies the adoption of fundamental directional change, the creation of new economies and a rejection of a 'steady state' model as the other of existing forms of growth.

Currently, there are three ESD positions toward (ecological) sustainment, each of which has a different history. Firstly, there is the reformist position that emanates especially from the institutional perspective of the United Nations (with its universal imperative to modernise, to create a value system of the universal human rights of 'one world order', and to continue the 'development process', be it modified by environmental concern and sought for control). The second position is the utopian one, which puts forward the view, expressed in various forms from various sources that 'development', as progress and growth, is fundamentally at odds with ecological sustainment. The 'Limits to Growth' thesis of the Club of Rome, which predated the arrival of the term ESD by well over a decade, was one of the main statements of this. Position three is the pragmatic, radical and contemporary one of the environmental crisis being linked to far more than just ecological problems; that the ecological is not just what development threatens but is equally what development has created materially, socially and culturally. Its focus shifts away from saving (Earth, the planet, life) to the production of the conditions of sustainment that create, gather and conserve.

On examination, the first two ESD positions are predicated upon sustaining the unsustainable. It follows that a comprehension of unsustainability is not just a precursor to moving onto a theory and practice of sustainability, rather it is the primary ground that makes the ability of sustain-ability possible. Again we insist sustain-ability is always posed in relation to, and against, the unsustainable (the latter being comprehended by its product: the defutured). To acquire the ability to sustain requires that the ground of the unsustainable be learnt. Unsustainability, as the condition of the defutured, arrives out of defuturing-in-process.

Sustain-ability is diversity, it is difference, it is a 'being-toward' the constant creation of a chain of finite sustainments (means with sustain-ability). As this, it is the dispositional quality of an agency, be it inert or organic, mechanistic or human. Sustain-ability can only come into being by a design-in-learning that has learnt how 'the different' can constantly return as 'the same'. (The more familiar metaphor of this return is 'life'. What needs to return is however always more than what we mean by life.) Thus for sustain-ability one has to learn the ability to create a world of things and processes with the ability to sustain. This kind of learning clearly exists in contrast to academic disciplines, and their often monocultural, restrictive world views, their tendency to function through exclusions, and their rejection of connections deemed outside their disciplinary terms of reference. Above all such learning confronts the designed, manufactured and lived unsustainability of education in error, for unsustainability is not only a product of habit, unthinking, myopia, ill-informed practices and inappropriate methods, but also of misconceived, uncritically adopted and misdirected education. It follows that it is quite impossible to adequately think or pursue, let alone realise, sustain-ability unless unsustainability is understood and engaged.

Sustain-ability is an anthropocentric construct in so far as it depends upon values and judgements that are always centred on the human. However, this does not mean that it is predicated upon the dominantly dualist and humanist character of Western metaphysics. The familiar and dominant binary schema makes divisions like those between the organic and inorganic, the animate and inanimate, the natural and the unnatural, the human and animal. In contrast to this binary schema the difference and diversity of sustain-ability requires the grasping of variable relations of complexity. These relations transcend the systems-thinking that underpins ecological precepts, such as the distinction between ecology and environment, the view of 'life' that rests on a biology, or the human as a universal category.

Sustain-ability begs the question of what is to be sustained, rather than assuming it. Answering this question hereafter becomes not a matter of naming an essential condition but rather requires gaining an ability to identify options, and judge what is appropriate and responsible action in ever-changing relational circumstances. As this, it is a learning to think, analyse and act in the face of unsustainability. Invariably this will mean engaging that which has changed 'unnaturally' by Design — even in the frame of what seems fundamentally natural: air, water, earth, wilderness. Quite clearly, on the basis of what is being said, sustain-ability cannot have an available representational form. Sustain-ability, is a learning that creates new grounds, therefore it does not have an existing history, philosophy or a science. Defuturing, as a new design philosophy, is one contribution towards this learning of sustain-ability. As an imperative to think, create, act, become, overcome and 'dispose in difference', the emergent practices of sustain-ability (including defuturing) are not reducible to utility or instrumental action. Nor can they be predicated upon a monocultural perspective (for cultural singularity is simply another name of the unsustainable).

Above all, sustain-ability demands an ethically managed responsibility that is able to over-ride a misplaced faith in 'natural evolutionary processes', science and techno-fixes. Sustain-ability equally demands a confrontation with the dominance of the synthetic environments into which we have become 'naturalised' — homes, workplaces, schools, cars and myriad other locations of our post-natural lives. Yet we actually still do not have the language to speak the ecologies of these synthetic environments. As the text will show, the metaphysical foundations of science and Western philosophy conceal the very possibility of knowing (but not inventing) life in these ecologies. To illustrate, just consider a few examples from the multitude that surround us. Where, for instance, is the technological/biological division for the dairy cow that has biologically adapted to the designing of the milking machine, or of a human being living with the support of a pacemaker, or a crop that will grow on land providing it has a constructed irrigation system and is regularly chemically fertilised, or a cloned fish in a fish farm?

Obviously in such situations the gap between that which we have to judge and our available means of judgement ever widens, and while much could be said on the problems of judgement, one particular caveat is now immediately needed. There are many way of thinking about judgement — it travels under the guise of lots of other terms such as bias, evaluation, moralism. Its determinations are inescapable, we have no options but the available options, for we cannot act without cultural imposition, we cannot *not* be anthropocentric nor without values. What we can do, however, is bring our actions before ourselves and judge them from those values that can arrive from our knowledge of imperatives. Postmodern culture passed judgement on those who judge: for to judge is to take a position from which to judge. To do this is taken as an imposition, for with the adoption of a position comes values, imperatives, limitations and loss of freedom. The entire enterprise of bringing oneself into a confrontation with defuturing, and thereafter acting on this knowledge, rests on judgement. This is accepted, made explicit, offered for critique, made available for modification and advocated for mobilisation. The basis of this judgement is an elaboration of sustain-ability. The key issue here is whether one's position for judgement is undogmatically adopted with knowledge and responsibility as a position from which to learn.

In the context of what has been said here, sustain-ability cannot be created without a learning of defuturing.

## DEFUTURING

Defuturing, 'the new naming', as a mode of inquiry, seeks to disclose the bias and direction of that which is designed and how it is totally implicated in the world we conceptually constitute, materially produce, waste (rather than consume) occupy and use as an available material environment. More specifically, defuturing, as a learnt act of critical deconstructive reading, is able to trigger an unmaking of the ground of thought and 'logic' of fabrication, form, utterance and image, upon which present worlds, and world-makings, stand. Defuturing effectively exposes the negation of world futures for us, and many of our unknowing non-human others.

We need to remind ourselves that the future is never empty, never a blank space to be filled with the output of human activity. It is already colonised by what the past and present have sent to it. Without this comprehension, without an understanding of what is finite, what limits reign and what directions are already set in place, we have little knowledge of futures, either of those we need to destroy or those we need to create. Without a knowledge of defuturing, from the perspective of Design, we have little comprehension of what designs, the agency of the already designed or the consequences of designing.

The price of myopic market-driven pragmatism, as it delivers short-term gains and profits, is massive mid- and long-term losses of diverse and structurally critical means of planetary sustainments. Such a mindset and its institutions cast the future into the unknown, and then disregard it, claiming 'one cannot know the future'. That the future is made by actions in the past and present, and is then destined to travel towards us, escapes consideration. Thus, in contradiction, the future is neglected and negated by the very way short-term futures are created and rushed towards. The unsustainable is the familiar way in which these defutured future conditions are named. What the practice of defuturing exposes is that the processes and consequences of the unsustainable are far more foundationally and actively inscribed in the material and immaterial 'nature' of our worlds than the rhetoric of unsustainability reveals. Rather than just argue this proposition in the abstract, this text will make its case by reading a range of contemporary and historical examples against the grain of established history and assumed common sense.

In can be argued that defuturing is a key characteristic of our anthropocentricity. It is that self-centredness of actions that have come to be a defining quality of our species. However, with the numbers that we now are, with powers we have amassed and mobilised for ourselves by design, technological extension and fabrication (which has underpinned our rise to domination), our self-interest has started to turn back upon itself. Fundamentally, we act to defuture because we do not understand how the values, knowledges, worlds and things we create go on designing after we have designed and made them. Bringing this last comment back into more familiar language, what is being said is that we have very little comprehension of the complexity, on-going consequences, and transformitive nature of our impacts.

Defuturing arrives out of an attempt to speak about that which is present but unrepresented. As this it is a recognition that our interpretative relation to our world is always partial, culturally framed and linguistically restricted. It seems that we are always trapped within limited options of understanding. For example, and just at the level of language, we can try to speak the new in familiar terms, in 'plain language' or 'plain English', which carries the logic of the same and thus returns us to familiarity. To do this negates the dynamic and transformative potential of language and thereby subordinates it to the functionality of the status quo. In contrast we can try to create and speak a new language that defamiliarises the familiar. Unavoidably we slide between these culturally relative options in the attempt to produce the activity of effective exchange. Such a view recognises that communication is a process of labour rather than a correspondence of meaning. These remarks on language run counter to the current 'transparency thesis' of 'the republic of information' constituency of information technology cultures. In terms of writing and other forms of communication, the common assumption is almost always that efficacy depends on 'reaching' as many people as possible. In contrast to this mass communication/mass entertainment model, this text is based on giving the reader work to do. In this respect, its success will be measured by the extent to which it brings active readers into being who accept responsibility for finding ways, in their own circumstances, of taking appropriate action.

RELATIONALITY

Relationality is a key concept for understanding the various ways in which sustain-ability, unsustainability, defuturing and Design are dynamically articulated with each other. But it is also much more than this. Relationality is at odds with the model of 'cause and effect' that has been at the very core of the Western metaphysical tradition since its inception two and a half thousand years ago. Relationality is a way of thought which is not based upon cause-effect relations but on correlative processes and structures, and as such draws on the correlative thinking of the ancient Chinese. Yet this thinking, as we shall show in a later chapter, has been powerfully present in the West, if nurtured in the shadows. This presence has, for instance continually refused the dominant Western dismissal of traditions like Taoism as pure mysticism. Moreover, relationality has been recognised as being of major importance by significant scholars past and present.[3]

Relationality provides a means to think modes of being-in-the-world in relation to the being-of-the-world as a condition of involvement. It recognises that all we designate as 'life' is actively involved in given and made environments for life itself to be. At the same time, life as a condition of change is environmentally constitutive. Specifically, in relation to human life: the relations of the produced environment or lifeworld into which we are born produce us; while at the same time our 'being-in-the world' acts on the-world-of-our-being transformatively. Obviously the way Design was explained above conforms to this indivisible and reciprocal model of exchange in being.

As a concept, relationality speaks to the inseparability of material and symbolic exchange. It makes no appeal to a higher being or category of knowledge of a transcendent authority. Flow overrides arrival, and essences are not claimed to be lodged in things, or able to be captured and held, rather they are understood to arrive out of conjunctural relations between things material and immaterial. Relationality is time and movement; it is dynamic. As well as this, relationality is the way of language. Equally, it is a comprehension of information, the animate, the inanimate, exchange, transformation and a finitudinal limit beyond the biocentrism or stretched metaphorics of ecological thinking or modelling.

Even from the perspective of this briefly sketched account we can comprehend that unsustainability and sustain-ability, defuturing and futuring (the project of future-making that the recognition of defuturing clears the path for) are not merely opposite binary terms. Each only arrive out of a relation to another, neither can be characterised by reference to single form, the one always exists implicated in a struggle with an other. In this context Design and learning arrive to alter the balance in an unbalanced situation, to swing the balance toward sustainment and a futuring future. In this contest there can be no victory, just conflict: affirmation requires negation, sustainability requires imbalance.

The relational approach adopted understands that unsustainability cannot be reduced to a singularity. From this viewpoint, it is not worth trading in a history of names — be they of movements, designers or validated designed objects. In actuality, the incoherence and difference of the unsustainable is to be found everywhere. In the coming chapters, Design will be disclosed as being at the very core of unsustainability, as it undoes the very fabric upon which the modern world has been built, both metaphorically and literally. At the same time it is posited with a potential sustain-ability.

## GUIDED READING

As stated, to rethink Design within the telling of the story of defuturing is an impossibility and a necessity. Clearly there is too much to tell, too many ways to tell it, too much to understand, too many problems to make sense of to be cajoled into a seamless account. At the same time one of the aims of this text is to create a sense of just how much there is to understand, in order to open a way into a needed and extremely large intellectual enterprise, one to which many heads and hands could contribute over an extended period of time.

The ambition is to create a sensibility able to inform a process of thinking and acting in whatever the context the reader finds him- or herself. It is not a matter of presenting a more elaborate, more complex, theoretical picture of the concept. Rather it is a question of demonstrating a learning against what has already been accepted. Here is a particular conflict, a struggle to take an idea into ownership to displace already established ways of thinking.

We have learnt to read, think, organise and function within linear structures (the notion of beginning, middle and end that is narrative of course illustrates this fact). At the same time we are able to gain an ability to make more complex associations and connections. We ever live trying to find ways of showing, saying, reading or hearing that which we can barely grasp. And yet we have the ability to think within and across rule-governed structures. We make leaps, insert knowledge from our own experience, construct other patterns, view things in their circumstances of encounter. This text in fact invites a relational reading of its problems, complexity, arguments, invisibilities, and insights as they run in, between and constantly across the formal disposition of the chapters.

There are many problems and pitfalls on the path before us. Metahistory and metanarrative present two linked problems that will be confronted (in Part 2). Both constructs are discredited, yet defuturing appears to speak as a metanarrative, and deal in metahistory. The way both terms travel in this text carry unambiguous deconstructive lessons. While this has been learnt from writing, it will hopefully become available to the reader on reading.

A caveat should therefore be made in relation to defuturing and metanarrartive or metahistory. Its important to emphasise that while defuturing is put forward with a certain overarching meta-claim it is not offered up as a universal totalisation, nor does it imply ideological uniformity. It is redolent with difference and begs a great deal more questioning and elaboration. The ambition is to install a first word on the topic rather than the last.

Obviously, the kind of questioning being opened up here is within a structure that arrests relations in flow. However, as we learn from Niklas Luhmann, structure is always the appearance of the arrest of fluid relations within a system.[4] At the same time relationality undermines the integrity of systems models. With these qualifications said we can proceed.

The complex picture to be assembled stands for more than the sum of its content. Each chapter works as an incremental exposure and qualification of defuturing. The ambition is to demonstrate a way of a learning to see and think the familiar differently, so as to inform transformative action that can become a transportable method. Such action is effectively a remaking of 'worlds', not however by a literal material reconstruction (although material change has to occur) but by the creation of a perceptual shift so that the meaning of one's world and actions alters, which in turn changes one's being-in-the-world and the 'nature' of the world for others. In this context the work of the text is not just to put the reader before something new to be thought, but to produce an alteration in thinking.

Specifically the chapters are grouped into three parts. Part 1 comprises of a single chapter which sets up the entire project in two ways: firstly by grounding defuturing in technology and war, both of which are deeply embedded in ways of world-making; and secondly by using the material of the chapter to illustrate the book's method — which becomes reflected upon immediately afterward.

Part 2 confronts the problems of history and narrative as they impinge upon how it is possible to address the relations between defuturing, Design and the grand narratives of 'design history'. It also explores, by the accumulative story that is built by its three chapters, the means by which defuturing became a global impetus and presence. Chapter 2 addresses the rise of the power of industrial production in nineteenth- and early twentieth-century America. Chapter 3, staying in America, looks at the consequences of how the productive power of the American economy was brought into a direct relation with the design ideology of 'streamlining' at a particular historical moment in the 1930s, in order to deliver a 'solution' to an economic crisis. Particular attention will be given to the rise of consumer society, the New York World's Fair of 1939, and the place and problems of utopianism in the making of the modern world. Chapter 4 moves to Europe between the wars to show how Europeans, especially in Germany and the Soviet Union, established total design cultures whose theories and practices also inform the story of defuturing.

Parts 3 consists of four very different chapters that move to a thematic approach which undercuts the sufficiency of history. This enables a greater scale and complexity of defuturing to be put in place, as well as bringing our confrontation with it to the present. Thematically, the chapters speak to the body, material and immaterial, as a site of relational connections and intersections from which we are able to view our immediate placement in the defutured (Chapter 5). The way time and space (Chapter 6) and cultural technology (the televisual: Chapter 7) are examined make evident what the televisual is and does and how human beings live as much in immaterialised environments as they do material spaces. Lastly, the presentation of computer technology in Chapter 8 exposes that the emergent 'nature' of technology is far more complex than our descriptive language is able to articulate and that major questions of sustain-ability need to be put into the 'technosphere'.

The conclusion reconnects with the style and content of this Introduction, so as to complete this first gathering and opening onto defuturing.

\*\*\*

Although this text cannot realise its full ambition (the impossible) or completely meet its imperative (the need), and is undoubtedly flawed, there is the sincere hope that every reader will open themselves to embracing the critical importance and inseparable relation between design, defuturing and a making otherwise.

### NOTES

1. In terms of modern thought the opening move of this enterprise would be a negotiation of Immanuel Kant's *Critique of Judgement* of 1790.
2. See David Noble, *America by Design*, Alfred A Knopf, New York, 1977; and *Forces of Production*, Oxford University Press, Oxford, 1986.
3. Leibniz is one significant historical example, while the work of David Hall and Roger Ames (in a series of books starting with *Thinking Through Confucius*, SUNY Press, Albany, 1987) is a contemporary one.
4. Niklas Luhmann, *Social Systems* (trans John Bednarz Jr and Dirk Baecker), Stanford University Press, Stanford, 1995, pp. 282–85.

# PART 1
# AN OPENING

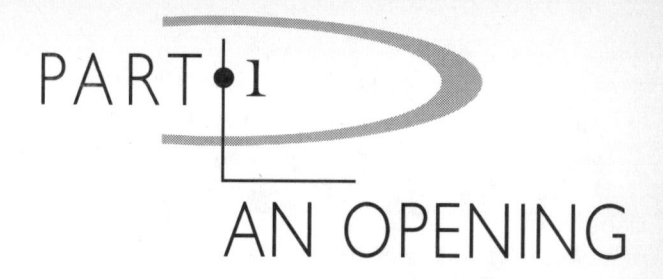

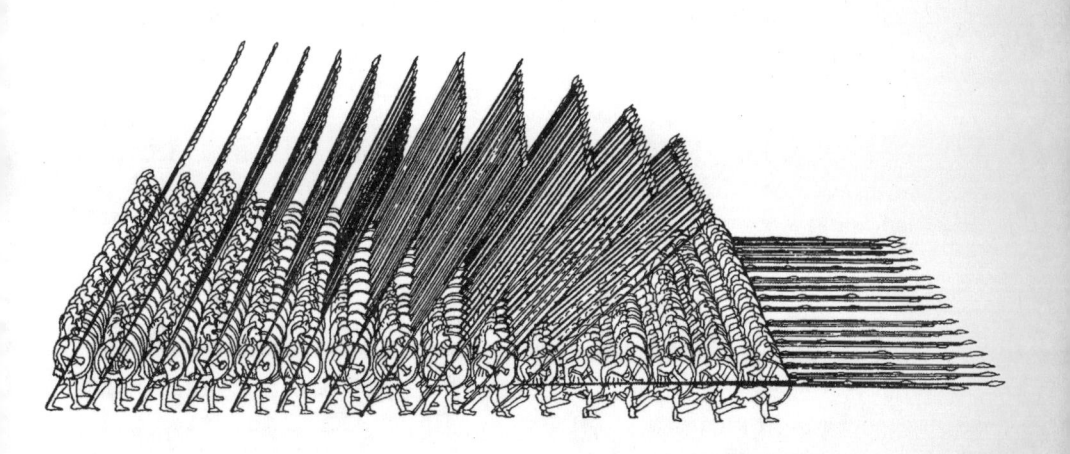

The Macedonian phalanx in its fighting formation of 256 men (author's collection)

We all live with our own seeing, hearing, feeling and thinking that to us seems individual, natural and owned. We know we come from a culture, have been shaped by our education and differ in our interests. We realise the world we occupy has problems, but nevertheless are at home in this world — it is familiar. What is strange is 'elsewhere'. The story of the defutured upsets these sets of assumptions: it exposes so many of our self- and world-formations as deformations; it tells us that much of what we believe to be supporting us, is in fact undercutting our being as beings; and it reveals that the unfamiliar is not elsewhere but within and everywhere around us.

So often we look for obvious differences, when the dramatic change often arrives by small inflection. In the main, defuturing is about reading these inflections of the familiar. However, this reading opens onto an entirely new way of understanding the worlds that humans have made, and what humans do, hence its link to the new philosophy. We are in many ways surrounded by a hostile environment of our own making, but in which we feel safe. In the epoch of our present existence (which is in fact a plural moment), and in order to take care of ourselves and the things we need and value, we, as a diverse species, need to change direction: to continue to be, 'our' being-in-the-world has to become other than it is. For the few this means a new thinking and a remaking (mostly of meaning, partly of matter); for the many, as ever, it means living the change with what has been changed.

The argument of the chapter that makes up the first part of this text illustrates much of what has just been said, by denaturalising how we think about technology, and war. In so doing it will expose the fact of our living in the midst of much which defutures. This telling also starts to demonstrate that defuturing can be a thinking in practice towards change. More theoretically, it can be the very basis of a non-instrumental, but materially positive, application of a deconstructive strategy. As a mode of inquiry, defuturing is a crucial tool to turn the acceptedness of unrecognised but omnipresent unsustainability into a foundation to make things otherwise. In a world of constant change, obsessed with change, and ever creating images and rhetoric promoting change, the encounter with the defutured tells us what should and should not change, where responsibility rests and what it means to confront the imperatives upon which a future with a future might mean.

# 1

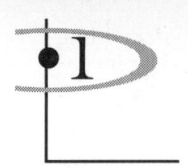

# TECHNOLOGY, WARRING AND THE CRISIS OF HISTORY

A small Gatling gun (Charles Pelham Mulvaney, *The North-West Rebellion of 1885*)

This chapter aims to inform a way reading the defutured that forces it to disclose itself. To assist in this task the most available form of that which defutures, which is war, will be employed, but only after a critical relation to technology has been established. The fundamental proposition is that war, in its familiar and unfamiliar manifestations, is deeply embedded in world unmaking — 'deworlding'. As this, war is confronted as both the designed and a designing.

Design, as indicated already, is not just a way of talking about one organisational activity, the prefiguring of objects, or the directing of aesthetics. Rather, taking the wider view of Design, it is one of the most powerful ways to understand how a world is prefigured, made and acts. Yet neither society at large, the intellectual community nor 'the design world' seem to recognise this. There is in fact a general failure to understand the complexity which is Design, and the extent to which Design is implicated in forming the ground of the unsustainable, all of which thereby acts to advance the defutured. Also unrecognised is the impossibility of sustain-ability without a fundamental reconstruction of design theory, thinking and practice.

To be able to read the relation between the defutured and Design requires not so much a method but a sensibility, or better still an attunement to the discovery of a diversity of signs of destruction. By looking at and learning from war, as a techno-ontological domain, the intention is to inform a nascent 'literacy' that can be brought to the reading of defuturing in general. Our encounter is not a characterisation of war as just a violent historical event. War is viewed as being more fundamentally within a vectorial designing of forces that exceeds any possibility of bounded event. The resonances of war — 'warring' — will be shown to be both a product and generative force of design and technology. So while the immediate hostilities and overt signs of war may be spatially and temporally contained, the flow of design, technology and pain in and out of warring cannot be.

War is a primary agent that defutures, not just through its obviously quantifiable damage to life, limb and material environments, but more substantially (if less dramatically) as it creates 'closure' of potentialities, including the potentialities of what design and technology might have been.

## TECHNOLOGY IN FLUX

Technology is ever changing and never able to be adequately identified reductively. While technology is addressed here it will invite continual comment throughout the text. While Design gets named from time to time, its presence should be understood as structurally omnipresent: technology arrives by design, is applied by design and, in its form and use, technology itself designs. It follows that in the historicity of modern worlds, technology importantly exposes the phenomenology of Design (and vice versa) as the intentionality of an act, the intention of what the act produces, and the experience of a product in action.

A consideration of technology generates a whole range of issues. There are, however, four which will especially concern us. The first issue is to re-emphasise that technology is not a fixed phenomena — it ever changes and it is ever generative of change, this in constantly proliferating material and immaterial forms. The second is to acknowledge that the division between it, us and our environments is no longer easy to make (we exist as much in it, as with it). The third issue is a qualification of the second in so far as divisions between technology, knowledge and culture become increasingly hard to identify. Issue four, simply asserts the long and established relation between design, technology and war. While these four issues are all profoundly implicated in the defutured (as we will show in this and other chapters) what we immediately want to draw attention to is the complexity of our 'proximity' to that complexity we name technology.

Technology is present for us in a number of ways. It has an existence, it has being, as 'a thing', an object and process, which is not to say it can just be reduced to material substance. This means that no matter what the technology is, that it has ontological status and agency. Next (and leaving the question of the use of tools by animals for future consideration), all technology, both in order to come into being and for use, requires knowledge and new technology frequently becomes knowledge (software). On this latter point, a claim can be made that any, and all, technologies gain an epistemological status. Finally technology becomes environment. It becomes a place of dwelling, in some instances one of absolute dependence (like for the pilot of an aircraft).

Being able to make such distinctions about technology does not mean the question of proximity to it is solved. To recognise we have a proximity to something is not the same as knowing what it is we are near. Although we are able to make and use technologies, this does not mean we fundamentally understand their agency (not least because we understand so little about the designing of productivism).

Dwelling as we do inside technology, one has to work within the movement of the machinery of technology's heterogeneous parts. This requires appropriating and assembling as one's conjuncture, needs, desires and demands change. Quite simply there is no position available for an over-reading of technology that is outside technology's reach. It is just not possible to step outside its design. The key issue of proximity then is one of no critical distance, no gap and potentially induced alienation.

In one direction, technology appears to have been developed by man (which in this case perhaps almost totally equates with men) as an instrument to make 'a world'. However, as this making evolved, the technological remaking of 'the world' by technology, including the remaking of technology itself, has become more evident. Historically, technology has been dominantly projected as a human-directed tool created to tame, exploit or re-fashion 'nature'. What is now becoming clearer is that it also acts to reshape its maker and user as much as, and perhaps more than, that which it is presented as making. Moreover, in the present manufactured environment of human and inhuman technological dwelling, a point has been reached whereby technology constitutes its own designing ground of auto-creation. Technology, de facto, has taken on a life of its own, a development of itself that brings into question the basic assumption that a division exists between technology and 'life', the 'organic' and the 'inorganic'. Exactly if, where, when and how such a change occurred is clearly not self-evident. Conspiratorially, our being and technology seem to evoke each other.

One indistinct moment can be identified as profoundly redefining the relation of what is usually deemed the animate and the inanimate. This was when technology fused with information, and in so doing connected itself to the cognitive core of culture. This fusion arrived long before 'information technology' was invented or named as a technological domain. This indistinct moment was a moment of absolute transformation in two ways. Firstly, the coming of the tool re-designed pre-human being: it was the agency of a pre-human becoming human. (Here 'the tool' is cast as the means by which animal passed to *animal laborans* and then to *homo faber*.) The second transformation was the tearing, the cut, and the creation of the abyss wrought by the coming of the tool as it effected an instrumental division from, and thereafter an eternal mediation of, the environment. (The coming of the tool was thus the coming of the world, its first reified making.)

The first cut of the tool totally transformed the existent being-of-being and the being-here (*dasein*) of being. Quite simply the fundamental nature of dwelling changed. To talk of a moment in this context is to evoke an unplaceable but temporally extended time (definable as the sum of a continually repeating moment over a protracted period of time, and across a dispersal of spaces of difference). The crucial focus here is phenomenological rather than archaeological change, the facticity of which is 'being-present-now' rather than the representational claim of artifactual evidence.

'Worlds' were created by the tool's turning of 'the world' into a standing reserve for making and then by learning from the feedback from the tool. The sound of stone against stone, the feel of the strike made, the look of the material after being struck and opened up, broke the hermeneutic limit of hunting with, and for, whatever was to hand. Suddenly the interpretative space of being-in-the-world was expanded, and with every expansion the informational ecology grew. (It was the knowledge-designing of this ecology that divided 'human' from a tool-using animal.) Thus the indistinct moment of absolute transformation of the animal arrived not just because tools were materially transformative but because they expanded and changed the 'world of information', how information was acquired and the conditions, content and application of directly engaged empirical learning. With the coming of the tool the die was cast for direct empirical observation having to give way to a 'truth' not just mediated by technical mechanisms, but created by them. That science failed to reflect upon the designing of its instruments of mediation meant that realist knowledge was taken as if it were empirical.

What has just been characterised is that human life is itself not only mediated by technology but implicated in ontological circling. This fact, which is but another expression of the designed designing, will constantly return, for the moment it is perhaps illustrating the point more simply.

Data from measured lifespans, recorded body height, weight and age, the health of our bodies as gauged by testing the composition of blood and urine, strength testing and the measurement of intelligence by IQ testing — these are but a fraction of the constructs that designs data that locks us into designing our selves by the designing of the 'things' that deliver or respond to this data. Food, clothes, sports equipment, transport are just a few of the reactive, and then directive, 'mechanisms' of the metaphysics of our ontological designing. Thus, the mediated knowledge from feedback information 'throws us into things'. Without us realising it, the measured has became unbounded. Equally, the conceptual and technical means to measure, as well as the knowledge of the measured and the 'fact' of the measured, have become inseparable.

Modern economies, be it on the back of anthropocentric and productivist thought, have manufactured 'reality' as a technologically registered outcome. The 'proof' of this 'reality' is delivered by the compound knowledge of science — knowledge which, as indicated, itself depended upon the 'true' data arriving via technological instruments and methods of measurement. More than this, and by the greatest possible conceit of reason, science, in the name of particle and astro-physics, claims that the creation of everything (the cosmos and God, as force) is knowable. At the extreme, with a massive dose of myopic metaphysics and vast amounts of research funding, science set itself the challenge of finding a way to be able to eventually measure and 'prove' the mechanism of the origin of the universe.

Over the course of the Enlightenment 'the world' was brought into being as an abstracted object of view — this via theory and practice which produced the quantification of space, the measured grid, the map, the power of what the lens exposed and the authority of the picture. Through the development of these means, there accrued a massive agency of calculation, and its representational forms. These forms put into place those knowledges that established perceptions of the real and truth. But more than this, they also underpinned the proliferation of applied knowledges of world-making (and unmaking) that profoundly altered the relation between metaphysical and ontological modes of being-in-the-world. So, for instance, once building became presented and directed by calculation, and realised by a technology, perceptions of dwelling and dwellings were to significantly change. Increasingly, technology acted as a world inscriptive instrument that both embodied theory, instrument and action.

Picturing the world, when 'world' was presented through representation, was fundamentally a projective act. What was 'seen' represented a thinking, constructing, picturing — the conversational sharing of thought with picture being constitutive of both a self and culture. It has been in large part by these means that technology has actually acquired its accumulative authorial function. In this way it has always authored more than the forms of its apparent artefacts or effects show. Moreover, operationally, this authorial character of technology makes no separation between material and cultural production. Separation occurs; it arrives as a result of an interpretative error, guided or misguided by reason. It follows that while always being functional, even in a state of dysfunction, technology is never just instrumental. However, this is the way it is mostly treated.

Having registered this, an encounter with the understanding of contemporary technology can tell the inquirer something even more confronting. Namely, that humanity knows no more about the 'nature' it has made (as and by its technologies of 'discovery') than about the 'nature' that it discovers (which is elemental to the made) — we know no more about the artificial (our nature) than we do of the 'natural'. At this point we should remind ourselves that being able to explain how something works is not the same as knowing what it is, why it is or what it does beyond its directly observable functions.

Philosophy has from its beginning recognised a disjuncture between 'what is' (that which Western culture has named, like a 'world, 'cosmos', 'universe' or even 'nature') and 'what is known' (astronomy, geography, biology). While knowledge is taken to be the consequence of an act of revelation, it transpires to be as much, if not mostly, an act of invention. While we can be brought to such a recognition, we ever live in the vast gap between 'what is' and 'what is known'.

Technology did not arrive with the birth of the first machines — usually designated by the history of technology as war engines — but as a materialised idea of structured directional thought (productivism), which itself was the outcome of constructing a knowledge of the world based on order/ordering/categories/classification. (From such a beginning we need to reassert that technology is not reducible to objects, the mechanistic, hardware or software.) Moreover, technology not only became an instrument of constructing a world but also a mediating force that equally constructs the mode of observation — as cognition and perception. Technology thus no longer has an essential form or essence, it is not just matter rather than mind, or the self-evident 'other' of the human. Instead we find ourselves modified by the symbolism of its projected meaning, its mode of physical and mental extension and its operational performance.

Technology, as we have come to know it in its most easily identifiable forms, was both heralded by and facilitated, a particular moment — the Enlightenment.[1] Within this moment the ways of making sense of the world were instrumentalised to advance the means of taking, appropriating and making a world and its subjects (retrospectively, we name this process as 'development'). This trajectory still totally infuses our daily lives, expands the domain of the artificial and further establishes 'man made' nature in the technological.

In actuality, the situation is far more complex than one of life among technologies. Rather, it is one of life by technologies. For instance, the world we inhabit is measured by chronometric technological norms. We are located in measured time in ways that prefigure an encounter with the temporal. From this perspective, a clock, as well as being an object composed of ordered technological functional parts (clockwork or electronic), is also a mechanism which designs perceptions, thinking, working life, everyday actions and more. The structure of technological time has become part of us, our biorhythms have been altered by its regulatory regime.

To reinforce the point: we rise in the morning from a bed, not waking naturally but naturally waking by the call of the alarm clock. Listening to the events of the world as they arrive by the radio or via the unwatched television, we stand before the sink, cooker, toaster, teapot, coffee grinder, oblivious to the long and complex history of their cultural and technological development and the vast global network of manufacturing from which they and their components arrive. Our concern becomes with the time we have, the time of travel, the time of the working day and the volume of our leisure time. Our acceptance of technological time never becomes critically exposed. In this regulated functionality, the impact of our actions upon time (as the finitudinal variant of planetary temporality) never comes to mind. We do not have time to confront the unsustainable way that we are, how we live, and how our individual and collective actions are articulated to our place of dwelling; that increasingly 'freedom' and continuity will be predicated upon accepting the imperative to conserve, to materialise care, and to recognise the value of what is to hand. All this passes us by as we seize the moment and overlook the future.

An idealist call to ethically command and redirect technology will, however, not get us very far. We techno-dependent beings who live in a technologically omnipresent lifeworld have neither the motivation, awareness nor agency to directly resist technology. In the face of this situation, the extraordinarily difficult task of identifying the changing state of being human and of new needs imposes itself. We lack the directional pointers: if evolutionary process were ever in command it is certainly no longer the case (as the exposition of autonomic technocentrism in our final chapter will show). The one directional pointer, figure of judgement and imperative that we can recruit is sustain-ability. It is not a condition of existence, but a means of decision: this is its power. The key to being able to exercise decision for sustain-ability is the ability to recognise what defutures. Action to sustain, in the face of technology and the unsustainable, absolutely requires the ability to read defuturing in a particular relational conjuncture. (In this context decision cannot claim certainty, but it can assert judgement.) Such action can only arrive by educated effort.

We might start by trying to understand the metaphysics of technology in terms of how it directs a compliance with a disembodied 'logic' — which means a non-human technically inscribed thinking that is directive of human action (again to be explored as the autonomic). Thereafter, to turn this thinking toward an ability to sustain, needs to be contemplated as a redesigning technology. The ambition here is the creation of a critical knowledge of the multiple choices, which do not defuture, that can become technically embedded as sustainments (time-making relations, products or processes).

Historically, the notion has been that technology is a unified domain that can be used for good or bad. If taken up to a level of high performance, and used for good, it could liberate humanity. The 'peaceful' use of nuclear power and the 'spaceship earth' techno-fix concepts of Buckminster Fuller are contrasting examples of this.[2] What is being proposed here does not conform to the residual mind-sets of such dispositions. Rather, technology is recognised as not being a coherence (in spite of the commonality of structure), and it certainly is not viewed as a neutral force that enlightened beings can simply mobilise as a tool. That technologies came out of various theories of knowledge, Eastern and Western, would suggest that they can be created by ontological and metaphysical projects.

The challenge is thus not so much to reform existing technology but to confront it with another technological modality of being that goes unrecognised within its current system of reference. Crudely, sustainable technologies need to be created and brought into confrontation with the unsustainable technological norm. The site of engagement, the contestational ground, is the performative demand for sustain-ability. The inchoate designing of this ground of confrontation can, for example, be seen to come after the failing language of 'ecologically sustainable development' (ESD) and its implications in sustaining the unsustainable.

In putting forward a critique of ESD we note that the word is always the first act of design. ESD is a contestable first designing. Its thinking came out of an economistic modernist reformism that retained the agenda of the restricted economy of late capitalism. Its ambition was to secure on-going global modernisation, but to remove those actions of ecological damage that had the potential to undermine the prospect of the realisation of its goal. Most ecological design simply falls in behind this rationale. As stated, ESD can be turned in a totally different direction by being redesigned against itself, by becoming DES (developing ecological sustainment). In this inversion DES expresses an economy predicated upon restructuring for wealth creation through ecological sustainment, while ESD is simply about securing the future of the current restricted system of the non-relational global economy. ESD is thus based on the contradiction of trying to subordinate sustain-ability to development, while DES is about the developing sustain-ability.

The practical task of design and technology bonded to DES would be to 'seek and destroy' technologies that are destructive of that which sustains life. This implies discarding some technologies, deflecting the performative qualities of others (the proposition here is that radical change is frequently not a matter of dramatic intervention but strategically chosen small modification) and invention. There is, of course, an urgent need to conserve that knowledge and those materials and techniques that already have the ability to sustain.

## FORCE-FIELD TECHNOLOGY

It is perhaps worthwhile reiterating that technology carries brute power and has been celebrated as such. One can, for instance, evoke Macauley's claim of the 1830s that Britain was the greatest nation in the history of the world because its navy could 'annihilate in a quarter of an hour the [pre-industrial] navies of Tyre, Athens, Carthage, Venice and Genoa together'.[3]

The power of applied technology produced not only the ships, navigation aids (especially the compass and chronometer) and weapons that enabled the European heartland of proto-modernity to colonise the world but also, as said, the system of classification which mapped and named the world. In this frame 'the world' was not discovered by exploration but was a discourse that was invented by science, enabled by technology, and managed and presented by design.

The claim is always that it is by design that the power of technology is directed and is subjected to control, whereas what design actually does is to enable the structure of power (the economy, state, industry, institution) to determine the forms of the exercise of power, and the point of its application (which may or may not deliver the sought determinate outcome). In other words, power is extended by design. The design of a machine tool is, for instance, never just the design of a machine, a tool. It is also the mechanism by which a power to control is moved from the designer/manufacturer to the worker/user/product. However, the product of the machine tool designs the form and the performance of the machine, as well as the actions of the machinist. Thus the design of the field of power of a machine is always greater than its immediate process or product, for it is also a designing of a set of relations. It designs, and often mediates a relation to, its immediate environment by restricting and extending the machinist's sensory field, speed of movement and bodily disposition. Just think of driving in these terms. It is never just a question of pushing pedals and pointing horsepower, for we drive in a sensory field of information feedback. We see the road in the frame of the windscreen, a projection screen. As the road appears on the screen it is read, while our ears and our bodies tell us something about the road and mechanical performance. We in fact drive with our whole being. As Don Ihde argues of this technology — its body extends our body.[4]

## A HISTORY OF THINKING ON TECHNOLOGY

It is important to recognise that technology as a subject of study has a long history of inquiry and literature attached to it, be it not always critical. In the modern epoch, two traditions cross each other's path:

the history of technology and the philosophy of technology. In both cases, these traditions recede back into Western classical thought, into Eastern ancient philosophy and merge with economic, political and cultural domains.[5]

What one gets from this literature is a view of technology that is quite contrary to its reification as simply technique, machine, process or thing. Rather its character emerges as an ever changing complexity, manifesting a constant power of transformation (of being, world and exchange) and itself. As we shall draw attention to in numerous ways, the more one learns of technology the more difficult it is to draw the line between 'it', us and what we designate as 'natural'.

The crisis of unsustainability is not of course a consequence of technology, rather it is the displacement of an anthropocentric appropriation of 'world' into instrumental forms. This crisis is the result of the use of the tools and products of a human-centred world-making. Technology in this context is the materialisation of alienated being — making it that outcast progeny, one that always returns classified as the non-human. The alienated is alien, through technological mutation and what it engenders. Far from the science fiction image of cyborg, or any mechanical or electronic fusion with the biological, the technological mutation talked of here is a software-engineered entity, or put another way, it is the flesh of a metaphysical fabrication.

Yet within intellectual culture, while the loss or failure to arrive of the totally human can be acknowledged and felt, and a 'correct' posthumanist line espoused, there remains a repressed assumption of a division between the human and the technological. Moreover, an accompanying feeling of the human still being under threat lingers. The erasure of such an assumption and feeling operates in a stark manner within popular culture. Remembering that culture has become technology — a technology culture — it is possible to state that the alien feels and thinks nothing that is not technologically implanted. For instance, while it has become prosaic to say that technology invades and exploits biology, it has also transmogrified itself into information, has disembodied memory, conducts much of our routine thinking, watches us, co-opts science and mediates the environment we inhabit. It is now appropriate to say that, in the current epoch, for most people in most places, not only has the full scope of the technological not yet arrived as knowledge, let alone passed into understanding, but 'now' it never will. Even the question of what is technology?, or a counter question of what now is not technology? appear to be totally redundant today.

Three linked preoccupations reassert themselves: the first is a concern with technology as 'enframing';[6] the second is a concern with it as danger; and the third is 'the nature' of technology. What links these preoccupations is a concern with, and approach to, technology as being ontological. From this perspective the basic question is what has technology done, and what does it do to the being of all things, including to human being? The answer to this question enfolds some of the oft asked questions, like: can technology save?; can 'it' be subordinated to human willing?; is technology understandable in itself?; and equally, is something new happening in this epoch? Perhaps now overarching all of these questions is whether technology is 'other' than what we continue to cite as 'life'.

From the ontological viewpoint, what technology does is deflected from view by the visibility of its specific functionality. This masks its general relational performance. The ontological concern brings us to technology's general performativity rather than merely its instrumental operation — and here it becomes possible to focus on the agenda that an ontological approach to technology delivers. There is a line — technology is on it, and so are we. On one side, the defutured which has been technologically empowered, on the other, a future with technology subordinated to futuring. The contest of design, and our proximity to it, now becomes paramount, for design draws the line and determines on which side we fall.

## FROM STRUCTURE AND FROM *TECHNÉ*

The application of technology, contrary to many latter-day appearances, and its on-going preoccupation with measure and ordering, was not, in the first instance, guided by reason. Rather it was guided by 'know-how' (by *techné*), that knowledge of the hand tutored by experience, and inscribed in memory of the making. The disorder, which is crisis, arrived out of that order installed by reason as it recruited and subordinated *techné*, as well as instrumentalising productivist thought. The history of modern world making is therefore a history of unmaking the already made.

### TOTALITY AND FRAGMENTATION

Technology manifests apparent contradictions, but mono-plurality is the key one. As earlier comments indicate, technology is now only knowable as a realised metaphysics, and as an unknowable totality (it cannot be fully made present, not least because it is its own mode of presencing). At the same time it is an everyday thing of continual phenomenal encounter. We encounter technology on multiple levels as both the object and the means of perception. Existentially, technology arrives for us in several forms: as instrumentality (the use that we use and that use that uses us); as mechanistity (the functionality that structures function as well as the structure that performs); as measure (the interval of order that orders interval); as a metaphysics at the end of metaphysics (that disembodied hermeneutic structuring of mind and picture of the world that the mind comes to know); and as system (the economy and ecology that has the ability to function in the present, but without the means or intention to sustain itself in the future).

Technology is without a directing human subject. It now exists and functions independently of any subject's overall direction. This is to say that technology has taken on a 'life' of its own. It has become something to react to, rather than direct — just try directing your latest word processing package outside its parameters, setting up a new television set without its pre-loaded instruction, or servicing your own brand new car. Such technologies have been designed with an embodied 'will' of their own that designs the users' and the technicians' relations to them.

The character of technology, as world-making, has brought and is still bringing all peoples into the same functioning dysfunctional structure. As this, technology provides an operationality beyond cultural difference. It is a commonality of function without meaning which allows exchange without understanding, which makes it an ecology. The universal subaltern class of techno-culture is the technician. Economic and philosophical modernity truly manifest themselves here, for while a functional world culture of sorts has been created — a culture in which people around the world can perform the same tasks, in the same way for the same economic reasons — this 'world culture' operates without any constructed ability of people to understand each other's world views, to communicate or share values. The anti-humanism of the instrumentalism of technological functionalism has in actuality acted to conceal difference by the ontological character of the things it does.

Technology's designing of 'the same' (as an on-going transfer from an embodied to a disembodied metaphysics) and the concealment of this process delivers several problems. For example, there is a misreading of identity whereby 'the other' is taken as if it were 'the same'. Conversely, there is a misreading of difference that reduces it to just a difference of style or performance. In both cases what goes unrecognised is the ontological designing that comes from the replication of the same foundation. The third problem is to recognise that technology transforms one's proximity to others, one's place in a world and one's world itself, all in ways that reconfigure the qualities and dynamics of space, temporality, speed and sustain-ability. These problems constitute a 'bifrontality' — a term employed to indicate that technology functions with an essential capacity to both threaten and save.[7] To come into a technologically hegemonic world is to be fully 'enframed'. Subject formation and deformation thus occur by and within particular forces of world or object form-giving. These forces govern what is to be known, thought, calculated, done and valued. The sovereign power of '*techné-logos*' (the know-how of technology that acts and speaks as reason) is not domination or conformity, but something far more basic. It is the violent establishment of a ground of being. So even to resist is to function on this ground. Our hermeneutic entrapment within the always already enframed imposes a perception which can only see and feel as 'that which is'. It is our absolute horizon. To achieve a limited condition of alienation, that makes the familiar strange, in this enframed state means remaking a self/world construction. It means coming into a world again by discovering the concealment of the futuring in the creation of the activities and pleasures of our everyday life. This condition is one of proximity to the concealment: there is a world which comes closer and there is a world that withdraws.

But alienation must not be taken as an affirmation of humanist expression: as a rupture riven from the world being mediated by the capitalist mode of production; or as a cry from the heart of a centred, suffering and estranged subject. Rather alienation is the means of the subject's mutation. Kinetically, alienation is force without attachment to a singular or identifiable form. It is a recoil to 'being-in-the-world' as it is made to appear and is available to be lived.

This alienation requires a language that can denaturalise the language upon which the technology of language rests. Its aim is not the speaking of an alternative world (madness), or a utopian world (dream or art), but a pain (an unavoidable focus) that forces critical examination. The sensibility of defuturing arrives in this pain as it screams what is seen and felt. For what defuturing allows to appear is the suffering of dwelling on the ground of technological world-making. It is a suffering that exposes that the current form of so of many 'things' are diseased beyond recovery and are spreading the condition of the defutured. This implies that sustain-ability can be driven by pain to create functionalist and pragmatic demands, with transitional force, that can recast and redirect technology. The pain of alienation casts itself against how technology rules, appropriates, is applied and destroys — but for all this it does not proclaim any possibility of technology's abandonment.

## EDUCATION

There are many things to learn in the unfolding epoch. There is a learning to recognise what defutures and makes 'otherwise'. There is a learning to give way to a recognition of being delimited; a learning to alienate, and to be alienated; a learning to mis-calculate; a learning to recognise the sustainable limits of existing technology and metaphysics. All of this leads to a learning to sustain by learning to learn another technology as a 'care structure'.

The action that speaks in learning sustain-ability, as an informed practice, has retro-actively already been given a name: *phronésis*. *Phronésis* is Aristotle's notion of practical philosophy, wherein action, theory and practice function together with foresight. *Phronésis* can be taken to be *praxis* ahead of itself. While Aristotle's idea was posed in the infancy of technology, it now re-arrives in the imperative of its remaking as redirective practice. In the context of sustain-ability, it is that action being acted upon as one acts in giving way to that which has to be sustained. Action here is thus not just kinetic, rather it is that which enables an ontological learning, in the immediately to hand, that informs what has to be done in order to secure sustainment. Action so posed is a basic political comportment that gives way to the essence of dwelling — with sustaining-ability.

## THE GRIP OF FUNCTIONALISM

Technology, social existence, sustain-ability, subject — all presume system, and thereby 'function'. The history of thinking on function manifests itself in different discourses, all of which, however, proclaim an analogical relation between biological, social and mechanical-electronic systems.

Functionalism — be it expressed in biological, sociological, architectural, cosmological, or philosophical theory — constituted the 'how' of the operationality of the 'nature of things'. Functionalism thereby became a surrogate framework of meaning that formed the very basis of meaning itself for Western metaphysics. In the human perspective, life, especially human life, was understood according to a directional model of function whereby it evolved towards a higher form. Meaning thus became both operation and destination. The structure that functioned was of course mostly based upon an organic and presumed universal model that transposed a model of nature from 'natural' to 'artificial' systems. From this point of view, functionality presumed order across both the given and the constructed, and thereby was posited as a transcendental agency. At the same time the positing of order should be regarded as an act of force — one which itself authorises function by the provision of an epistemological commonality across seemingly different expressive domains. Functionalism provided, for instance, a way for biology, technology and aesthetics to become harmonised in the one condition —

culture. Equally, the full force of function could be and was positioned by the way an onmipotent power — God, Darwinian evolution, technological determinism or whatever — was projected as the directive of all and everything in a functioning whole.

Lest the impression be given that functionalism represents a single coherent theory, it is important to note that while social and design theories of functionality do have a common point of origin in a Platonist cosmology of final order, they developed in very different ways, and were attached to very different projects. At the same time, a certain convergence arrived between the social functionality of culture, communication and biology — the city as 'organic structure' — and the aesthetic and practical functionality of architecture. There is perhaps nowhere where these convergences are more apparent than in the intellectual and design cultures of Chicago. In the late nineteenth century Chicago was not only one of the birthplaces of functionalist urban sociology, which itself was informed by the rise of structural functionalist anthropology, but also and at almost the same time it was the place out of which the American tradition of functionalist architecture emerged (which, especially via Louis Sullivan and then Frank Lloyd Wright, had a major impact on the rise of the Modern Movement). Later into the twentieth century it became the locus of the 'Chicago School' of communication.

Clearly, as the briefest sojourn into the literature of sociology and architecture will reveal, there are far more complex accounts of functionalism available than this quick sketch. The issue is, however, to acknowledge the history of the agency of functionalism as it became inscribed into common sense practice and the operational world views of many professional practices. This identifies a condition of possibility as much as it does a problem for the functionalist discourse, as well as the designing power of the causal model of rationality on which it rests. Functionalism's dominance also provides an opening for a counter-discourse that travels under the flag of hyper-functionalism. This potential can be found in the work of a number of people, especially Niklas Luhmann.

For Luhmann 'function' is what connects system with environment.[8] Luhmann managed to turn a functionalist account from an operational observation of elemental relations to a means for identifying problems as 'system problems' that cannot be addressed and resolved by their being extracted from their context. In other words he refused to reduce functionality to mechanisity and acknowledged relationality.[9] While his approach elevated the complexity by which causality is understood, it is not predicated upon the privileging of causes, rather his functional analysis is an observational perspective to 'ascertain the relations among relations'.[10] This needs to be put in stark contrast to the functionalist imperative that, in silence, asserts that to explain how something functions is sufficient knowledge — a position which effectively reduces the question of why something exists to its function. 'How' and 'why' of course presume meaning, and for Luhmann meaning is a consequence of system: it is a closure within a closure, produced by the eradication of difference, by its own processing of itself, that has the ability to form a world and thereby overlap 'the difference between system and environment'.[11] What Luhmann actually did was to attempt to resolve the problematic of functionalism by the creation of a hyper-functionalism, within which 'how' or 'why' can only ever be questions that arrive out of the functioning of a specific meaning system. As he was well aware, and attempted to practise, there is also a necessity to explain the position of observation and speech that is always located as a self-referential framework of distinction that produces the self that observes.[12]

Returning to the dominant understanding of the functional: it has, as indicated, moved well beyond the academy. In fact it has acquired an operational, and mostly silent status, as a foundational reference for the fabrication of meaning, order, system and harmony in the common sense of numerous professions. Perhaps currently its most overt expression is 'economic rationalism', with its assumption of the economy as a system of functional integrity. Functional 'qualities' are, of course, deemed to be either good or neutral. Again here is the weakened echo of the cosmology of Platonism and its modernist manifestation in a social and economic determinism towards an idealised whole. Function, so approached, was the sign of the evolutionary dynamic towards a transcendental realisation of unification (historically and differently configured as God, freedom, cosmos). As this, function was a marker of the good and the moral. For instance, the *polis* — the good city, the fully planned city, the moral city — was one that functioned well within, and as, an integrated economical, social, cultural and political system so as to deliver a civil subject who was a perfectly operative atomic element.

The entire edifice of functionalism was built upon a productivist foundationalism which posited two moments. The first moment projected an imagined unity and balance of structural elements making up an aesthetic, spiritual and physical whole, which predated the agency of 'man' as fabricator. For the West this became the back projection of 'nature', as Eden, before the fall of 'man'. The second moment was the arrival of the idea of making an ideal world, the modern utopia, in which, under God, 'man' ruled as a master of 'nature'. The tools of this construction were: a vision, the resources of the earth, science and technology. While the misguided utopian end was slowly abandoned (as the spirit of the industrial age withered), the means, process, and destructiveness of the functional systems ran on.

Functionalism, as the projection of a particular mode of productivist cognition, thus made a world making, and a world knowledge, that rendered everything functional (or deemed others useless) within the schema of a forgotten vision, the defutured and destruction.

## FROM WAR TO WARRING

Man lives in war. As Heraclitus put it: 'War is the father of all, and king of all. He renders some gods, others men, he makes some slaves, others free.'[13] Whoever we are, wherever we are from, we have all been touched by war: its historicity is, in variable proximity, equally ours. As we reach back into time, we find we are all unavoidably either the conquerors or the conquered, the colonisers or the colonised. War is always before us: as ideology, the threat of an other, the pressure of constrained populations, a contest of resources. The reasons for war are ever proclaimed to remain present, as are the reflexes towards force. The image of war constantly assaults us, and we call it news, drama, pleasure, play. We constantly function within its shadow. Even in the most peaceful of social environments — whether as fiction, fear, image, style, rhetoric — war still designs the emotional topography of men and women.

One and the other, beginning and ending, inside and outside, subject and object and that whole raft of binaries, not least war and peace, seem so 'natural' and so 'given'. Our language, its categories and our thinking belie the existence of the most intimate of couplings and the absolute perspectival problem of our position of observation and proximity to the 'observed'. The violence, disruptions, forces and extremes that are war, alter points of view and perspectives, which means that war always brings much more into feeling, hearing, touch and sight than just itself. War continually begs address beyond a 'violent historical event' or as a vectorial designing force that goes well beyond any possibility and means of bounding an event.

***

The links between military and civil research, the arms trade and national economies, the technological spin off from weapons development and military technologies are all taken as read. Our position is the claim that war is the defutured inscribed in us, our technology, and our world.

> Machine 1: The Macedonian phalanx
>
> The machine is an organisation of a system of interactive parts into a functional operational whole, and therefore requires an understanding of structure. The first machines were war engines — weapons — and weapons as we know them are prehistoric. The spear is at least 40,000 years old; the bow about 15,000.
>
> Some of the most organised war machines were human. Refined from 500 years of development that stretched from the Assyrian technologies of war to the hoplite phalanx of Classical Greek warfare, the Macedonian phalanx, created in 360 BC, under Philip and Alexander, was both machine and machine part. It was formed from a square of 256 men, called a *syntagma*, that was arranged into a *taxis* of six syntagma. Each armoured man was armed with a four and a half metre long *sarissa* pike. Each syntagma was precision-drilled in side and arc movements. The enemy was not attacked by the phalanx, rather it was the anvil that the hammer, the cavalry, drove the enemy onto.

Besides acknowledging the environmental and ontologically designing condition of war we need to ask, following on from the discussion of technology above, what war has to do with functionalism and technology beyond the obvious relation between innovation and fighting machines. Why raise the question of war at all? First of all, as a practice predicated upon destruction, nothing is as unsustainable as war. Second, in an endeavour to grasp the nature of ontological designing, it will be argued that the question of war is unavoidable, for it is the perhaps the most overt instance of such designing.

War is the starkest site of technology, but equally it is also the starkest expression of the human's constant return to the non-human. It is in war that we discover that the non-human both pre-dates and post-dates 'man'. Moreover, as indicated, war is the absolute other of sustain-ability, not only in terms of the destructive consequences of weapons, or war's ability to produce social and psychological devastation or its desensitisation of concern for environments (given or fabricated) but also in its total disregard for the consequences of the depletion and loss of potential human, material and immaterial resources. In this respect destruction always travels two ways — forward into the war zones and back into the ecologies from which the resources come, be they used or not. The concern registered here is not so much about design for war but rather design by war.

The power of war — as a disposition of human-constructed force over time — is beyond calculation. This is to say, and to say so in such a way as to invite plural interpretation, that the form that human life has taken cannot be separated from war as its very agency, technology and event. Neither the histories of the artefacts nor the narratives of war ever get anywhere near war's actual historicity or ontological designing. The claim being made is fundamental: war is the most extreme case of ontological designing.

> Machine 2: The stirrup
>
> Stirrups came into use in the third century AD by Chinese cavalry, and the four centuries later in the West. They turned man and horse into a single machine unit. Combined with a saddle built up at either end to restrict longitudinal movement the stirrup enabled the rider armed with a lance, controlled with one arm, to function from a semi-rigid platform that had the ability to absorb a shock force while guiding the horse's reins with the free arm. The result was great mobility and an ability to transfer the force of the body weight and speed of a charging stallion to the point of a weapon with unprecedented violence.

Ontological designing (the designing of the designed as it acts in and on the world) at its most general, has been exposited as 'worlding' — the undirected world-making of the directional agency of the created world, including its designed forms and processes. At its most specific, ontological Design is the directional consequence of the 'thing-ing' (the on-going effects and environmental impacts) of some 'thing' designed. There is no condition more violent or dramatic in which things and worlds meet and clash than war. While every war is not a world war, every war is a war of worlds. War is being cast here as the name of an unsustainment between things and worlds that perpetuates the defutured well beyond any contained event. At the same time, war starkly discloses the ontological character of Design in the way it exposes its agency as directive of events, technologies, forms, relations, experience, knowledges, subjectivities, imaginations, psyches and memories, but with a very limited degree of directive or design control. War manifests the full mobilisation of instrumental reason in the service of designated causal outcomes, and the standing of all that is mobilised upon the unreason of unpredictable and untraceable consequences. The history of a war culminates in a moment of victory or defeat, whereas the historicity of war is its unnarrated continuum as it violently transformed and transforms conditions of being and beings.

## REFRAMING AS ENFRAMING

War, as an absolute preoccupation, is an unthinking. War is a closure of horizons, it is occupation by instrumental aim, an enframing powered by 'total mobilisation' in which everything (mind, body, matter, spirit, energy, love, ethnicity, gender and labour) is totalised. War, by image, design, technology and action, negates a developmental notion of human being, while the rhetoric of humanism conceals the loss.

War as a festival of excess and sacrifice always exceeds itself. One problem of thinking war is thinking its delimitation, finding an edge. Where is that line that divides war from that shadow of destruction out of which all life comes? We ever live on this line, as it both divides and connects creation and destruction. Here is the line to think the relation between war and the crisis that is the defutured. Crisis and the defutured are, however, no easier to delineate than war.

War, as it imposes itself on Earth, acts with total disregard, and in so doing exposes the frame of 'our' anthropocentrism like nothing else can. Its destruction arrives to continually reimpose our original moment of forcing our being into being. Certainly from the Western perspective, and echoing Hegel, war makes visible that 'force is everything': it brings everything into being and takes everything away. But more than this, war has also become that place that 'shows forth' the inseparable 'other than humanity' (itself a designation of ethnocentric force) within and between the human. Rather than it having a given and secured condition, 'being human' is a relative and mostly unstable state that humanist discourse misrepresents by universal and essentialist claims. Being human, in those cultures in which this mode of being is designated, always hangs in the balance. War tips things either way. Selves transcend their individualisation and become a species being together with and for an other, they also degenerate to instinctive creatures without value or reference. In war it is possible to see more overtly than in any other circumstance that unsustainability does not just centre on modes of actions of beings in their worlds but just as much upon the particular mode of the being of a being. In other words sustain-ability exposes the limits of the abstract division between self, ecology and environment.

War was always and remains deeply implicated in the extension of productivism. This is seen most starkly across the West's five-hundred-year (and more) employment of force and deployment of the technological tools and forms of war all to clear a space, install and expand the structuring of productivism in its global meta-infrastructural form — modernity. In the name of lawful appropriation, the removal of the obstacles to trade, acceleration of economic development and the need to impose 'enlightened' ideologies, force was employed as 'right and just'. Here is the inter-national competitive historicity of war as a means to force 'a' world into being, to draw colonised space as a map of worlded imposition and to break 'beings-together' away from the cultures of their own creation, and transform them into subjects and nations.[14]

> Machine 3: Mechanical vision
>
> The telescope was invented in the Netherlands at the start of the seventeenth century. Not many years after the semaphore was invented. By the late eighteenth century semaphore towers were in use with signal arms that could be arranged in the order of 200 configurations. These enabled complex messages to be sent and were viewable by telescope up to 10 kilometres apart. This meant a message could be sent about 400 kilometres in a day. No horse-mounted dispatch relay system could get near this distance. Machines with power to extend human vision have continued to be developed from this moment. The strategic target finding eye, an eye that images or informs, is a key war machine. This is the machine that enables an aircraft laser weapon to shoot down an air to air missile travelling toward it at 3500 kilometres per hour, or a smart bomb to reach its target.

The violence of productivism was not simply a matter of its explicit manifestation but also the imposition of its regulatory order on the mind of an other.[15] Order and organised matter were emplaced as the order of 'man' and one God. The worlding of all other determinate powers and gods was to be materially and immaterially destroyed, usually by war.

The rise and arrival of Eurocentrism authored a particular anthropocentric human being who was to become a global sign and agent of the unsustainable. Being human, violence, unsustainability and warring are clearly always implicated in each other. If this point is recognised the agenda of environmentalism, design, aesthetics, ethics and politics radically changes.

The most confronting result of such a recognition is that we are ever locked into anthropocentrism and while not able to be both human and free, there is a great deal of difference between being interpellated by the anthropocentric drive and confronting it in such a way as to live, by decision and by design, in a disposition of accepted responsibility (This is an ontology rather than a condition of enforced consciousness.)

The destructive impetus of war, especially when technologically assisted, converges in many ways with the unsustainable character of 'consumption' which is one of the general features of the system of dysfunctional exchange that is economic modernism. Both the economy of peace and the economy of war of modernity have treated resources as infinitely disposable. That war had the ability to consume/dispose so voraciously meant that the war and arms economy became an integral element of the modern economy. Making (for) war was one of the fastest ways to get rich. In this context, it is worth remembering the cybernetic principle that life systems not only can tolerate some destruction but depend upon it. When, however, destruction goes over the line, when it no longer fuels creation, then a terminal condition sets in.

War, as a functional system, destroys before a single shot is fired. Its agency has always been activated prior to the sighting of an enemy. Equally, its destruction continues well beyond the final silence of the battlefield. War has been extended ecstatically, the battle ground is substance, image, everywhere, electronic and smart.

While war is brutal, strident and overt, it can also insinuate its way into our lives in the most concealed manner. War can be both the most intolerable conditions and a tolerated backdrop. In extremes, it can be all consuming action or an unnoticed televisual image. Meanwhile, war also becomes woven into being in-human as the sensibility of 'the metaphysic of living by command' which produces inhumanism. There is that 'carrying on as normal' against the everyday presence of war in close proximity, which in the age of the televisual — which has made the theatre of war the world stage — it always is. Moreover, be it on the streets of Kabul, Jakarta, Sarajavo, Tel Aviv, or wherever it is on the day where the camera and conflict converged, we have all got used to seeing people going about their daily lives amid the activity of declared or undeclared urban warfare. This is part of the image of war we see, or directly encounter, almost daily.

War has imploded as grand causes have fragmented and 'the enemy' has proliferated. We lie in bed at night in the knowledge that somewhere urban warfare is always going on. In such settings, the lines between public and private police forces and the military are now very thin. Compound living, with razor wire, high fences, guard dogs, human activity detectors, video camera monitoring, armed guards and fortress mentalities, are now 'normality' for the wealthy and for corporate interests in many and diverse parts of the world. South Africa and Brazil boast some of the most extreme examples of this, as does Papua New Guinea. There is, of course, another trend for the wealthy to live in walled, electronically protected and patrolled spaces. Here is an architecture of emergency.

> ### Machine 4: The tank road
>
> The Reichsautobahnen was formed as a corporation in 1933 to construct the autobahn system which, as far as Hitler was concerned, was to be the best motorway system in the world. The layout, design, strength and construction of the system, which has been claimed as the most impressive of all the achievements of the Third Reich, was for military rather than civil needs. This motorway system copes with the weight and volume of today's traffic because it was built to transport tanks. Moreover, its layout was not based on linking major urban centres but on a grid to take troops to and up and down Eastern and Western borders. As a United States post-script: the post-war American highway program of linking individual states into an interstate system was funded as a defence measure.

### RE-TURNING

We have already noted that modern war stands on a structure of modernity, and that both modernity and war stand on the production of structure — productivism. There is always that erasure in the beginning which accompanies whatever is brought to presence.[16] At the same time, one is ever caught out by finding oneself back at the beginning. These philosophically inflected observations may seem far distant from the 'reality of war': they are not.

> ### Machine 5: Pre-loaded logistics
>
> As a result of its 'Mechanisation and Modernisation' plans of 1960, the United States Navy introduced containers and container ships. This push by the military, combined with the Vietnam War, powered the international shipping container revolution.

War produces breakdowns which defuture, but war is increasingly driven by techno-cybernetic systems that 'get the result', while at the very same moment installing dysfunction. Productivism increasingly meets its own dysfunctional product. Techno-cybernetics are, in fact, profoundly lacking in the self-sustaining qualities that define ecological cybernetic structures. Here is the return to destruction, and the finitude of life, in the failure of 'our mode of being here' to secure that (the 'here') upon which it, and other forms of life, depend. Power, violence, force, order, politics all get cited in some way or another as the structural components in the making and conduct of war. Yet these figures explain little in themselves, they all beg close interrogation. More than this, there is a structure of structure of war that a phenomenology of war has the ability to uncover. This goes to the violence of design as forced direction, imposed knowledge and universal time.

The necrological call of war, as the experience of heightened authenticity, still resonates. War destroys community but it also creates a surrogate bond after its loss. Additionally, in an epoch of the deepening dysfunctionality of community, as yet another face of unsustainability, there are new and residual desires for other ways of being together that deliver a certain internal social cohesion within a group, but at the price of broader social damage. The gang can be the extreme social expression of this. While it is a manifestation of breakdown, it also transposes the conflict models of unity against the enemy and solidarity in war into the condition of dysfunction that is a response to, and thus accelerates the situation.

## REFRAMING IN THE LIGHT OF MODERN WAR

The form of war has, and continues to, change. There are certainly three trends that warrant identification.

Firstly the spatiality of war has become far more complex. While wars are still geographically delineated, and formally declared, they also proliferate as fragmented conflicts. We see this not least in parts of Africa, Asia and Eastern Europe, where the structure of a nation disintegrates and repressed social formations reassert themselves. Here is a breakdown of the designing of the map and its accompanying political matrix of colonialism. In these circumstances lines of demarcation are unclear, there is no clear single cause of conflict, but a series of agendas flowing from a 'return of the repressed'; there is no defined war zone; no distant semiological separation between the terrorist, the soldier and the criminal; no defined division between the military and the civilian (or even between soldiers and children); no unambiguously military targets; no legible event structure of battles but often totally unpredictable outbursts of violence; and no containment of conflict within event time (while a moment of origination may be identifiable there is no certainty as to when conflict is terminated, rather it just smoulders and flares up from time to time). In these circumstances military planning shifts from the disposition of large standing forces to the creation and use of rapid deployment forces and small irregular units working outside 'rules of engagement'. Such circumstances dramatically alter how a target is identified and engaged. The way unsustainability is manifested in these conditions is of course not the ground zone obliteration of warfare of mass destruction but rather a continual environmental degradation that follows from the dysfunction of infrastructure (the breakdown of water systems, power supplies, road systems and so on).

The second point is directly linked to the first. Modern war has in significant part been dematerialised. This means it is not contained in just one space of conflict. From Vietnam onward, war has been waged in the space of the televisual as well as on the ground. This takes us to designed and designing forms, such as the image of war where a 'theatre of war' is constituted as a television set upon which events unfold with the audiences becoming players in the action of staged events. There are many examples, like the set piece battles organised for video recording by the Mujahideen in Afghanistan, IRA bombings in Ireland, United States military press corps officially distributed film footage during Gulf War, and Hamas auto-destructive human bombs in Israel. People die for the image: making it, trying to obtain it, as a result of an interpretation of it, and in wishing to live up to it. Equally, people are being made in the form of the image, they are born into it. The control of the image, its management, is now a major feature of the politics and conduct of war.

Image relations have now become absolutely integral to the technology of 'smart weapons'. The image takes the future away. War imaging now flows across conflict zones, time, space, subject, memory, desire and media. The war 'machine' is now far more than functional systems complexity in the immaterial space of televisual media. The images of reported conflict flow along with historical and fictional images to constitute the warscape of public perception in which the psychology of warring becomes naturalised. The image of war has simply become one more visual element of everyday life that folds into the normalisation of unsustainability by worlding it as 'reality'. The genres of news media divide the picturing of crisis between 'ecological disaster' and 'conflict crisis', yet such a division actually fuels crisis by its de-relationalisation. Picturing the news of separate crisis events, that themselves are often staged and almost always edited, in fact conceals the crisis — it creates a 'crisis of crisis', as will be dealt with in more detail in Chapter Seven. The televisual experience confirms that the slippage between 'being at' war and 'being in' war is no simple division. These experiences are not the same but they do implicate each other in action, memory and dream.

The third change is the imperative for forward planning of the use of rapid deployment forces arising out of the spectre of future 'eco-wars'. With increasing demands on earth's resources from unevenly distributed and rapidly growing populations, the availability of fresh water, oil, fertile soil and forests, are increasingly becoming strategic concerns. It is around the disjuncture of supply and demand of these staples of nations that many future conflicts are being anticipated. The notion of eco-wars has arrived, and water is now deemed an inflammatory liquid. The theology of productivity that stems from productivism, and the associated aspiration to a universal high standard of living, promoted by economic modernism, drive this situation. In its condition of silent expectation, the inhumanity of humanism awaits another of its disasters. The crisis of crisis ensures that with the arrival of every disaster, the accumulative crisis, that begs the naming of a state of emergency to prevent the emergency, never gets named. The dangers unconsidered by anthropocentrism and the limited temporal horizon of human beings ever press. On the latter point one can say that in the scale of movement of geophysical events, human-induced climate change is travelling at the speed of light whereas from the myopic human perspective there is all the time in the world! There is almost no sense of the historicity of crisis, not least because science deludes itself with facts while looking in the wrong place for the truth (it has not learnt the first lesson of the confrontation with anthropocentrism).

## THE CRISIS OF THE CRISIS OF HISTORY

History reveals itself as that indurated fabrication and orderly presencing that silences the past. The latent disappears with history, meanwhile historicity runs on. History interpellates subjects in its schemas of authored structural causal relations that so often not only block an understanding of the past by turning it into a parade of significant events, but more importantly prevent an understanding of the future as an already filled space that has to be contested. Sustain-ability cannot arrive or be maintained without the destruction of the unsustainable. In this sense it is at war with war, while also making no division between war and other definable figures of the defutured in action. Sustain-ability turns on learning how to choose between what is created, conserved or destroyed. In this condition of ethical demand the relation between doubt, time and observation begs reworking.

If the inability of 'the media' to picture crisis beyond disarticulated fragments is one registration of the crisis of crisis. The concealment of the past and the future by the discourse of history is another. For all the talk of endings accompanying the arrival of postmodernist thought, the notion of the end of history is not new. This can be seen at its most general in the *telos* of the Enlightenment, which presumed that there was a conditional point of arrival at which the historical journey ended.

Violence is deeply embedded in the discourse of history as one of the principal means by which change was created. As Michael Roth points out, in a world where violence is affirmed, and thus where particular forces rule, no free historical choice exists.[17] It follows that the nature of the form of a projected future, its design, as a particular desired destination, can only be reached in and by contestation. This observation leads to a broader recognition of the designing agency of the relationality of war, violence and history as they are mobilised as grounds of action in narratives of Western humanist culture. The direct and indirect major influence of the ideas of Emmanuel Kant and GWF Hegel illustrates this powerfully.

Enlightenment, as the discovery and path of reason, was for Kant the means by which 'man' was liberated 'from his self-incurred tutelage' — a condition he considered as fundamental to emergent human nature.[18] Reason, he claimed, was born out of nature but it transcended its origins as it accumulated substance in the historical passage of the Enlightenment.[19] Kant asserted that 'Nature has willed' the use of reason and free will to express and deploy a transcendental purpose that was grounded in nature itself 'man accordingly was not to be guided by instinct, not nurtured and instructed with ready-made knowledge: rather, he should bring everything out of his own resources.'[20] Kant's motor of history, which drove the ascent of reason, was presented as antagonism: 'By "antagonism" I mean the unsocial sociability of men, i.e., their propensity to enter into society, bound together with a mutual opposition which constantly threatens to break up the society'.[21]

Conflict is posited as the agency which awakens the power to both conquer and advance the development of the world, the 'human race' and the self. The destination of history (its designing power), which Kant presents in the ninth thesis of an 'Idea for a Universal History' is a realisation of a natural plan 'directed to achieving the civic union of the human race'.[22] This is the arrival of a state of political and social grace (peace) where change is no longer necessary. It is by a 'cunning of nature' that human destiny is fulfilled 'here on earth'.[23] At this point the Enlightenment is realised and history ends. (This did not imply for

Kant, however, that the end of writing the history of the history of how the end of history came to be would occur.[24])

Antagonism and violence, put forward as the means which brought about a capacity for social development, were not primarily resting upon being at war with nature (a secondary effect). Rather, what was marked was the conflict between the individual and the collective subject. Such a view of aggression is implicit in Kant's anthropology:

> Without those in themselves unnameable characteristics of unsociability from whence opposition springs — characteristics each man must find in his own selfish pretensions — all talents would remain hidden, unborn in an Arcadian shepherd's life, with all its concord, contentment, and mutual affection. Men, good natured as the sheep they herd, would hardly reach a higher worth than their beasts; they would not fill the empty place in creation by achieving their end, which is rational nature. Thanks to Nature, then, for the incompatibility, for heartless competitive vanity, for the insatiable desire to possess and rule! Without them, all the excellent natural capacities of humanity would forever sleep, underdeveloped.[25]

So while war, as the most extreme expression of aggression, was viewed by Kant as the greatest of evils, he also regarded it as, once gained (if need be by force) indispensable to the development of human culture, and to the extension of this enlightened condition.

To end history, Kant argues, requires the universalisation of Enlightenment by the enlightened peoples going out into the world to conquer it with reason. Here then is the basis of the inhumanism of humanism — as expressed by, for instance, the ethnocentric postulate of the idea of the 'just war'. For Kant war was natural: it was the means by which nature continues to create the conditions reason had to overcome. It was design by nature and, for him, ultimately God (the God of forgiveness thus was equally the God of war). The effects of the Enlightenment were, to quote Kant in manifesting the most overt of Eurocentric statements, to 'spread from the centre, like a beehive, sending everywhere as colonists men already civilized. With the epoch, too, human inequality began, that rich source of so many evils but also of everything good. Later on inequality increased.'[26]

The evolution of reason for Kant, equally implicated in the 'evolution' of modernity, moves on two convergent axes: the one of global expansion; and the other of generational accumulation. For Kant, such movement gives history its project, moral imperative and rationalised worth.

The tautology of Kant's proposition of reason becomes evident when he calls up the Idea of 'nature' as a category. Like all other categories, it is apparent that nature is a product of culture: 'nature' is reason's designation.

As Yirmiahu Yovel says of Kant's argument:

> According to this theory, nature itself, even without the rational will, is working to a hidden design, bringing about political pressure by means of violence and passion. It is through wars, exploitation and calculated self interest that new political institutions, domestic and international are created, which in effect serve the goals of reason and freedom.[27]

The evolutionist character of Kant's ideas not only puts a theory of history and reason in place but also a theory of the subject. The subject was proclaimed as coming into being through a rupture from 'nature' and advanced by the commanding of its force. Humanity not only elevated itself above 'creatures with no plan of their own' but asserted, by mind, to know that which mind has classified and named 'nature'. 'Nature' was placed, before and after Kant, on one side of the line while humanity was placed on the other, as its product or master, with a nature of its own. 'Nature', for all the explorations of the 'natural sciences', and assumed as given, was thus the unknowable, the ontic, and a posited presence.

Hegel countered Kant's notion of the location of reason in nature by his placement of it in history, which he punned as the 'cunning of Reason'. This view asserted that history was a regime of directional sense which 'can remain hidden beneath events'.[28] The movement of history, for Hegel, was a passage toward its end. At this point reason would have arrived and be in full command and embodied in the state — understood as the 'End State', the term Hegel used to name the loci of fully developed reason (absolute spirit) and realised freedom.

Hegel's teleological philosophy of history has been enormously influential. It powerfully underscored a belief in the capability of history to be able to relentlessly deliver continual progress towards a final goal.[29] Here then is a registration of one of the most powerful foundational designing ideas of modernity in its every guise. It was generative of a theory of social development which transposed Enlightenment thought from being lodged in the power of the discourse of reason to the structural power of the state.[30] Hegelian thought has been enormously significant, to the extent that it has become elemental to Western rationalism. Although most people would perhaps be unaware, his ideas partly shaped accepted knowledges of the modern Western mind.

Hegel's philosophy of nature dialectically drove the fabricated division of the human from 'nature' to new extremes:

> Nature for Hegel is the Idea in the form of pure externality, the negation of the Idea which is subjective existence or spirit ... . To be a sheer

natural being is to exist unreflectively. Nature is spirit's sacrifice of its primal unity in the interest of a freedom to be achieved by Spirit in the process of its becoming.[31]

As a sphere of becoming, 'nature' for Hegel is configured in time and space — the latter an 'immediate externality' while the former is its proof as confirmed movement.

Clearly many instances of the illusion of a human command of 'nature' can be cited. Briefly, two particular examples come to mind. The first is the rhetoric of the unfolding atomic age of the 1950s: a moment of full intoxication in capturing force, not least to create vast destruction. The second, more recently, is the designing power of genetics to invent and let loose organic processes with no real understanding of eventual outcome and relational impacts. It seems the more natural science advances, the less it knows what it is doing. One can observe that science is contradictorily smart, myopic and nihilistic. The question here is, can there be a science of another direction, speed and time, a science that knows at what to direct violence and aggression? A science that recognises, as Michael Roth puts it 'When the goal of all human effort is the triumph over nature, victory removes the very ground of the human'.[32]

Technology, as instrumental means and metaphysics, is becoming a tool of the subject's auto-destruction as it evermore arrives at the fingertips of agents without judgement — agents who act under instructions from the instrument they appear to employ. Hegemonically, technology has become implicated in a culture of seduction and fascination through which it has arrived as an obsession. Notwithstanding the utterances of the afterlife of humanism, the onward march of productivism, in the form of contemporary technological systems, continues to remove all non-instrumental values and the need to remember. That there was any fear of technology has been forgotten. In the human's becoming other, its being-here forgets what it was. Memory now divides the human from the inhuman. The animal rationale has become the rationalised animal.

In the company of just a few other thinkers, Hegel's philosophy erected a great edifice of directional reason which brought the (newly arrived) modern rational subject and ordered state into convergence. In contrast with Kant's placement of violence in nature (as a generative force out of which reason arrived), one can note that for Hegel violence was elemental to history and history was reason thus violence was also elemental to reason. Moreover, as the state was both a carrier, resting place and agent of reason, it must also be the case it was equally the *habitus* of violence. Extrapolating further: violence was rationalised in, and exercised by, the state as it was developed by the development of the machinery of war. Hereafter, for Hegel, war was able to be viewed as 'the slaughter bench of history'.

Violence can be viewed as both an eruptive expression of force without mind or the outcome of a calculated willed mobilisation. No single form or causality can be reductively disclosed. The primary issues of violence are 'what directs it' and 'to what is it directed'. This takes us to the question of force.

Productivism designated everything that design directed and that technology produced. It brought the world to hand, but by force.[33] As reiterated in the utterances from Heraclitus to Heidegger and beyond, everything moves and force animates the character of everything.

Nothing arrives without force: everything created requires the transformative force that both takes away and brings into being. Creation is ever co-joined to destruction. While this statement has an obviousness about it, it does not mean that it is generally recognised and comprehended. Modern human beings have not learned to confront the implications of the fundamental, inseparable and inescapable relations between creation and destruction. While we live immersed in these relations they elude everyday consciousness; our sensibilities are oriented elsewhere. The *telos* of dynamic forces of modernity were ever projected forward and in so doing failed to glance back at the havoc, ruins and wreckage of the world left in its path. This failure, as a failure to take account of and responsibility for, what is destroyed, is at the very core of unsustainability — it is its basis. This is not to say that destruction can be avoided. It is to say that the choice of what is destroyed, how it is done and who takes responsibility is critical (in a life or death sense).

At its simplest it can be observed, as the history of technology illustrates, that there is currently an enormous imbalance between a capability of constituting instruments of force and an ability to appropriately employ and manage them. Nowhere is the problem greater than when there are attempts to control force by the exercise of violence. The breakdown of the line of demarcation between war and peace is one significant instance of this problem when it turns critical. Many people, in many places, neither live in the one state or the other. Rather, the force of war, its directional drive, increasingly folds into a condition that Paul Virilio has called 'pure war': 'Pure War is neither peace nor war: nor is it, as was believed, "absolute" or "total" war. Rather it is the military procedure itself, in its ordinary durability.'[34] Pure war is the full militarisation of the anthropocentric agency of everyday life in which everything is sought to be brought under bio-technological and socio-political control. It is a war against the integrity of fundamental cybernetic process, in which the accelerated violence of technology impacts with already delivered accumulative biophysical damage and social destruction.

## SPACE, TIME AND WAR

Modernity, in its economic, political and cultural forms, drew a map, claimed a space and totally filled it with its projections. In difference, it expanded beyond just physical territory: from the topography of place it moved across the grids of the body, screen, mind and time. We now live physically and electronically in the fracturing of this space. War is now not only conducted in this space but contributes to its break up. It calls up the past as battleground. Meanwhile, missiles fly towards a point, viewed on a radar screen as a point of departure, a point on the move, a pin point, a point of impact, a point that disappears at the point of arrival. Every punctum marks an end. Equally, the time and space of war is not discrete. War exists in real time, simulated time and electronic time, the time of the pulse, the wave. There no longer a single 'field' of battle.[35] War has let loose the warring of a technology of the invasion of the instant, the future, the image, language, mind, spaces of everyday life. and the very environment of our being-in-the-world.

As already discussed, wars are not contained by the state, a territory, a mode of combat, international convention or law, rules of engagement, or even the trace of morality. Mostly they have no declared start, clear aim, status or ending. The combative life of the normalised everyday, the fight to survive, runs a nomadic line that marks everywhere as competitive and conflictive. War is presenced by the camera. In the absence of the formalities of political and military protocols, the image makes the declaration of war. The event now only exists for us if imaged. The consequence of this image, a fiction of fact and a force, is the production of interest, then invisibility and finally indifference. Memory arrives and blurs.

Unsustainability, like war, is disposed towards indifference. Crisis has no one place of confinement, it respects neither the division of map nor flesh — it is omnipresent. Crisis is our historicity: ours is a condition of running out of time from its start. In this situation it is not possible for the human being to remain, and remain the same. Anthropocentric being, however, still continues on (be it as an ontologically designed entity that is often technologically inscribed) in ways that no longer depend upon the projected or recognised identity of a centred subject. The directional impact of technology, initially by human design, has not run full circle. Rather than just being directed by human agency it now, in significant part, directs 'our' fate. In doing this, technologically imposed modes of being fail, and are unable to acknowledge and respond to the functional relationality of existent systems of life. The result of this situation is that the 'nature' of life itself is not a constant, but ever an object of destruction and remaking by technology and technological modes of being. Clearly life defined in one paradigm does not necessarily recognise life in another. Here is yet another instance of indeterminacy and the unavailability of a category of universal transcendental resolution (like 'god').

Four observations can be made in relation to this lack of recognition. Firstly, it is apparent that this situation resulted from the disembodied thinking of productivism, which itself never lets 'life' simply be in process.

Secondly, that a new kind of structural conflict (war) between pre-technological and technologically engineered life is emergent. (Cloning is one overt instance of this. Whatever evolutionary changes have occurred in the past, there has never been an intervention of one species in the system of reproduction of others to create genetic auto-reproduction, thereby making the 'normal' system of reproduction redundant. It is now in prospect that a woman will be able to bear from her own womb a genetically engineered clone child from her own genetic material.)

Thirdly, it can be seen that the entire relation between technology, imagination and fiction is undergoing a profound change. The world is now being inscripted, and writing (which always has been a technology) is now becoming totally integrated with designing and biology. As was seen with genetics, a human-extrapolated symbolic code gets used to author qualities of a life form. Science/fact is no longer the other of fiction, and a humanist notion of 'creativity' looks increasingly outmoded.

The final observation is the most profound. What is now evident is that we are moving into a circumstance in which what is, needs to be and what has to be sustained, cannot be taken as given, but rather hinges on our imposition of ethical knowledge and practice. The 'nature' of the human, of life, the nature of power, 'neo-biological technological determinism': a whole space of conflict that will spill into other places is being opened up. The revenge of humanism's designation of the 'other' as 'non-human' may well be returning as the creation by humans of a species of 'human' clones. What is the space between this prospect and the kind of genetically engineered combat troops of science fiction?

The death of God (the Western metaphysically constituted giver and taker of life) was followed by the death of the illusion of universal meaning (the epistemological ground upon which transcendental categories, such as life, God and reason, stood). As technology expanded, it inducted the 'natural' sciences, and 'life' was literally increasingly taken into our own hands. What this means is that we accelerate, with ever greater speed, towards a situation of conflictive decision over who, or what, designates the meaning of what is life itself. In this setting a binary picture of survival unfolds: from one perspective, the survival of the process of transformation and mutation of 'life as we know it'; from the other, life's survival by its re-engineering, a remaking from both available and new life materials. The second scenario is effectively a discontinuity, for what 'survives' is more than a transmutation of what was. It also implies a technologically adaptive life, able to be designed to emergent circumstances. The current disjuncture between the speed of environmental change and the 'natural' ability of an ecological system to adapt would thus be broken. Such a techno-fix disposition will always generate unplanned effects and directions. Equally it also renders the techno-scientific making of the problems, to which such adaptation has to react, even less visible than they are now.

***

Viewed from the aspect of continuity or discontinuity, sustain-ability increasingly looks like it will depend upon bringing value to 'life', rather than just anthropocentrically acting to ensure human life's intergenerational continuity. It follows that the 'nature' of unsustainability is as unstable and problematic as that of sustain-ability. That this is undoubtedly the case in no way negates a vital engagement. Rather than trying to metaphorically close the door on war, unsustainability and the defutured, it has to be forced open — there is no other way forward. Sustain-ability unflinchingly demands this stepping through.

NOTES

1 Francis Bacon asserted that man could conquer nature, this with the aid of the 'mechanical arts' as they act as an extension of the human hand and mind. These comments he put forward with great influence in *The New Organon; or, True Directions concerning the Interpretation of Nature* of 1620. By the eighteenth century one finds a celebration of what Bacon could only dream of, for example, Jean D'Alembert an editor of *Encyclopedie*, a massive compendium of eighteenth-century knowledge, writes of natural science in dramatic terms: 'Spreading throughout nature in all directions, this fermentation has swept with a sort of violence everything before it which stood in its way, like a river that has burst its dams': cited by Michael Adas, *Machines as the Measure of Men*, Cornell University Press, New York, 1989, p. 72.
2 See for example Buckminster Fuller, 'Prime Design' in James

Meller (ed), *The Buckminster Fuller Reader*, Pelican Books, Harmondsworth, 1972.
3  Cited by Adas, *Machines as the Measure of Men*, p. 136.
4  Don Ihde, *Technology and the Lifeworld*, Indiana University Press, Bloomington, 1990, p. 74; Martin Heidegger, *The Question Concerning Technology and Other Essays* (trans William Lovitt), Harper and Row, New York, 1972.
5  For example Michel Haar says 'Through Technology man is reconnected and once more linked with the whole History of being since the Greek'; in *The Song of the Earth* (trans Reginald Lilly), Indiana University Press, Bloomington, 1993, p. 89. More generally, to cite just two very different and significant survey texts that give a sense of critical reflection of this field: Carl Mitcham, *Thinking Through Technology: The Path Between Engineering and Philosophy*, University of Chicago Press, Chicago, 1994; and Arthur M Melzer, Jerry Weinberger and M Richard Zinman, *Technology in the Western Political Tradition*, Cornell University Press, Ithaca, 1993.
6  Enframing is a translation of Heidegger's term *gestell*. It is discussed at length in his 'The Question Concerning Technology' in *The Question Concerning Technology and Other Essays*, pp. 3–35.
7  Reiner Schürmann, *Heidegger On Being and Acting* (trans Christine-Marie Gros), Indiana University Press, Bloomington, 1987, p. 207.
8  Niklas Luhmann, *Social Systems* (trans John Bednarz Jr and Dirk Baecker), Stanford University Press, Stanford, 1995, p. 176.
9  *Ibid.*, pp. 52–58.
10  *Ibid.*, p. 54.
11  *Ibid.*, p. 61. The account of function, structure, environment and meaning given by Luhmann is far more complex than is indicated above, not least because they are accounted for as they function in relation to each other. Anything other than a full account will thereby always be transformative.
12  *Ibid.*, pp. 437–77.
13  Fragment 53, *Heraclitus Fragments* (trans TM Robinson), University of Toronto Press, Toronto, 1987, p. 36. A modern return of this articulated spirit of war was the German anarcho-fascist writer Ernst Jünger who respoke Hereclitus in his evocation of war as 'the father of all things', as cited by Michael Zimmerman, *Heidegger's Confrontion with Modernity*, Indiana University Press, Bloomington, 1990 p. 51.
14  One can note as an aside, that all contemporary searches for national identity come down to a picking through the ruins of colonisation, devastation and occupation. Here is the condition of mutual non-recoverability. Neither the coloniser nor the

colonised can recover this history, this because, for the one, identity cannot come out of darkness and, for the other, because it cannot arise from the unrecoverable. The only possibility of invention is the return of the same.
15 Within the narrative of Western thought, the moment when productivism began to bring almost all we know into presence (while unknowingly driving that which had to be fundamentally sustained into concealment) has been assigned to the pre-Socratic period of Greek culture. The crucial 'fact' here is not the truth, or otherwise, of this moment but rather the actuality of its occurrence. Most significantly, the consequence of this rupture was that in establishing the very foundations of Western (and thus modernist) thought, the essential grounds of sustaining being were concealed. The implication of the production of this concealment was that the very thing that now gets called unsustainability arrived not as a consequence of the effects of modernity but as part of its causality. Moreover, sustainability, from the very birth of reason, has been there as a question of thinking, of ethics as much as one of biology. Certainly it is possible to read the entire works of Aristotle as a expression, and at times an almost direct statement, of acknowledgement of this observation.
16 See Jacques Derrida, 'Violence and Metaphysics' in *Writing and Difference* (trans Alan Bass), University of Chicago Press, Chicago, 1978, pp. 79–153.
17 *Ibid.*, p. 160.
18 See LW Beck (ed), *Kant on History* (trans LW Beck, RE Anchor and EL Fackenham), Bobbs-Merrill, Indianapolis, 1963, p. 3.
19 *Ibid.*, p. 13.
20 *Ibid.*, p. 14.
21 *Ibid.*, p. 15.
22 *Ibid.*, p. 23.
23 *Ibid.*, p. 25.
24 *Ibid.*, pp. 25–26.
25 *Ibid.*, pp. 15–16.
26 *Ibid.*, p. 64. It can be noted here that the narrative of breaking away from, but being guided by, nature, the rise of the sovereignty of reason and the dawning of the journey in search freedom, as a universal unfolding, all get separated from the narrativisation of how the designated conditions came to be.
27 Yirmiahu Yovel, *Kant and the Philosophy of History*, Princeton University Press, Princeton, 1980, p. 8.
28 This term is delivered by Roth in his reading of Hegel: see *Knowing and History*, Cornell University Press, Ithaca, 1988 p. 120.

29 *Ibid.*, pp. 32.
30 GWF Hegel, *Philosophy of Right* (trans TM Knox), Oxford University Press, Oxford, 1975, pp. 155–223.
31 Edith Wyschograd, *Spirit in Ashes: Hegel, Heidegger and Man Made Mass Death*, Yale University Press, New Haven, 1985, pp. 107–108.
32 Roth, *Knowing and History*, p. 132.
33 Heidegger actually poses the question: 'What is the pervasive character of the World?' and he answers force. He goes on to reject the explanation of force offered by physics by calling up Nietzsche's notion of the will to power. Force then is registered as a fundamental of Being: see Heidegger, *Nietzsche Volume 2* (trans David Farrell Krell), Harper Collins, New York, 1991, p. 86. On Heidegger's thinking about the relation between force and metaphysics see the influence of Hegel's, 'Force and Understanding' in *Phenomenology of Spirit* (trans Parvis Emad and Kenneth Maly), Indiana University Press, Bloomington, 1988, pp. 97–126.
34 Paul Virilio, *Popular Defence and Ecological Struggle* (trans Mark Polizzotti), Semiotext(e), New York, 1990, p. 35.
35 Paul Virilio, *Speed and Politics*, Semiotext(e), New York, 1986, p. 138.

# PART 2

# HISTORY, MODERNITY AND DEFUTURING

A wartime aside: A German-built observation tower at La Corbière, Jersey, meets Frank Lloyd Wright's Guggenheim Museum started in 1943 in New York (author's collection)

In watching we surrender to what we see. Film is perhaps the best example of this, for it has had an entire environment of submission created for it — the scale of the screen image, colour, movement and narrative, the darkness, the use of sound, the seating, all seductively combine to erase critical distance. In contrast, theory, mental and bodily discomfort — the 'pain' of the defutured — can all combine to re-establish a proximity that allows the seen to be viewed and reviewed. Even when we are well prepared and practised we ever catch ourselves out being drawn into that which we are encountering. Many issues flow from these observations, but the one most relevant to the content of this part of the book is the power and problem of narrative.

So much of what is being attempted here goes to the ambition of de-familiarising the familiar in order for it to become reviewable. This means being forced to work with what seduces, but we have to transform our disposition towards it. In this respect, learning is an ability to mobilise a disposition alienated from, but interested in, what it encounters. Certainly to learn defuturing is to acquire agency: it is to learn to destroy one designing, making and dwelling, in order to create some thing other (sustain-ability).

These somewhat oblique remarks are directed at the way the narratives of history, especially design history and histories of modernity and technology, are being used in this text in order to say something through, rather than about, their respective narratives. In doing this, the extent to which the defutured is deeply inscribed in the making of the modern world will become clearer.

## ON HISTORY

George Orwell's famous lines from *Nineteen-Eighty-Four* ever resonate: 'Who controls the past', ran the Party slogan, 'controls the future: who controls the present controls the past'.

While debates about history are long running they have, however, intensified considerably during the last few decades. We need to remind ourselves that history has became a discipline of contested epistemological and socio-cultural assumptions, methodological paradigms, interpretative practices and narrative forms. The contested appearances of history have either a historicity (the named recognition of something existing in a historical condition but of having no acknowledged presence because of the absence of appearances, values and meaning brought into being by narrativised history) or a historiography (a history of a history). For the West, the dominant notion is of history having function and direction, that it leads to end points and conditions (be they civilisation, Enlightenment, the modern).

This was the product of a particular theory of history resting on particular metaphysical claims. Immanuel Kant and Francis Fukuyama, for instance, illustrate convergent positions at the opening and closing of this teleogical model.[1]

Historiography has become an area of intense critical inquiry in recent years, with the basis of the truth claims, forms and genres of history (official discourse, science, social, political, economic, military and so on) all having become contested.[2] This led to a full recognition of the degree to which history writing is a literary construction, from an always biased perspective, that translates various forms of historical materials into a usually academically validated narrative. Design history, it should be said, stands on the margins of these developments.

History can be neither objective, neutral, nor total. Again a great list of proper names could be marshalled to support the point, however, we will let but one major contributor to the debate, Hayden White, stand for all.[3] Against the backdrop of this field of inquiry several problems become necessary to confront — in particular, the interlinked problems of metanarrative and metahistory and their associated relation with politics and ethics.

For White, metahistory is an over-determination of historical interpretation by a 'web of commitments' to what is in effect a taken-for-granted aesthetic, cognitive and ethical ground of thought. Metahistory thus both rides on the back of, and writes, metanarratives.[4] The metahistorical is argued by White as an extension of the 'superhistorical' modality of thinking history, constituted in and by an Enlightenment metaphysic, which claimed its authorial status by appearing to occupy a position of observation outside and above history. This position created a contradiction between an appearance of disinterest, judgement and objectivity, and the production of what were actually value-biased accounts.[5] The implicit narrative strategy of metahistory then is to make a subjectively inflected view of the past seem objective through an ability to create and adopt a discourse having the authoritative style of objectivity. The most overt statement of this strategy is the claim of history as a science, and the most trenchant critical retort is to return all history to a first history — mythology (which in a contemporary characterisation removes the distinction between history and literature).

Jean-François Lyotard moves the political frame of reference by viewing metahistory as over-determined by metanarrative. Perhaps more than any other work, Lyotard's *The Postmodern Condition: A Report on Knowledge* (which first appeared in French in 1979) announced the arrival of postmodernism as a 'crisis of narratives'.[6]

He presents science/philosophy as a metadiscourse that functions to legitimise by 'making appeals to a grand narrative' that writes 'the rules of its own game'.[7]

While not referring to White's argument, lines cross. The consequence of the White/Lyotard axis (along with other long-standing and varied assaults on the foundations of Western thought that can be headlined by the passage of the ideas of Nietzsche, Heidegger and Derrida) was to create an extremely constructive 'self-awareness' of writing and its mobilisation of history and narrative by a great swathe of the international intellectual community. But equally, a massive inhibiting force was let loose that paralysed generalisation, claims to universality, and of course metadiscourses. The story of the 'crisis of the university' of the last two decades could be told in terms of a lacuna created by those who behaved as if 'business as usual' were possible, and those who retreated into either the particularist, the literary, or both. Effectively, a vacation of knowledge as politics was installed by the coming of postmodernism in association with, and out of, the debacle of intellectual politics of the 1960s.

The problematic of the commentary above, as its form manifests what its content speaks, provides the hinge around which defuturing turns. Although 'one's back is exposed', the reader is to be spared a detailed justification of how one gets from the situation sketched above to the position stated below. It's another long and complex story that is not the one we have set out to tell. What needs to be registered is that there is a great deal of difference between an unknowing and a knowing employment of metadiscourse, metahistory and metanarrative. Once these figures are made present, they are felt, expressed, engaged and rendered critical as untranscended and inescapable problematics. While this suggests that no historical conversation can be free from a metahistorical or metanarrative voice, to deal with history with the knowledge of such speaking creates the need for an ability to make a difference to its appearance, application and possibility. From such a situation claims of historical truth are displaced by a recognition of history's social construction and the need for interpretative effort.

It is against this backdrop that defuturing is knowingly offered up as a counter metanarrative within the upcoming 'histories'. Defuturing is thus a constructed meta-object with heuristic value, rather than a claimed truth, and as such it needs grounding, rather than being a ground. This means defuturing exists to bring what has to be learnt into being, as an obligation to find a way to act: it is not what has been learnt. Defuturing is acknowledged to be a biased, objectified critical figure that is not asserted as objective. As this it is a decided point of view that invites correction in work (the 'remaking of practical reason' can stand for all the ways that this conclusion could be expressed). More than this, the learning of the defutured is a form of judgement appropriate to the present epoch.

The whole point of these remarks is to set up this part of the book, in which a good deal of historical material appears, in such a way that it can be read with a deconstructive sensibility that both undoes the authority of the history, while enabling the reading of historical content. Quite simply defuturing invites reading history in a new way, one that comprehends the defutured.

ON MODERNITY

For some, modernity may well be familiar conceptual territory. Even so the orientation offered is significant in striving to build conditions of cultural exchange between reader and writer.

What is now taken to constitute 'modernity' emerged out of discourses constituted by the Enlightenment over a 500-year period.[8] Modernity, from its unfolding from the sixteenth century, became a contradictory mixture of the plural and the enclosed, the ordered and disordered. The philosophical and political manifestations of modernity were generative of the modern individuated social subject, civil society and the nation state. They were also formative of that thinking from which modern modes of inquiry and institutions arrived. This is marked especially by Descartes' force of doubt, together with the rise of influential dualist modalities of thought (like the mind/body split), linear causality, dialectics, and the hegemony of a subject who viewed liberation as the freedom to realise the self (as the romantic individual) as a right of a subject free under the law.[9]

The formative power of economic modernity, and its ideological agent (modernisation), was extended by a theory and practice of economic liberalism, which also needs acknowledgement.[10] This theory was to underpin the rise of free trade, and of the free market as a justification for colonisation, war and the subordination of other values, and the people who held them. In the more recent past, modernisation has travelled under the tag of 'world development'.

Another facet of modernity that emerged in the nineteenth century was the project of creating and expressing a modern cultural sensibility ('modernism'). Here, ways of life, values, ways of seeing and taste were all appropriated and re-shaped by the colonising force of an aesthetic regime that extended the forms and concerns of the romantic subject, and which ultimately flowed effortlessly into postmodernism's absolute aestheticisation of everything. The impetus of cultural modernisation was propelled by a variety of agencies, technologies and cultural forms, not least the novel, the painted or photographic image, cinema, architecture, fashion, and all the other designed appearances of modern life. Thereafter, everything in and of the material environment was rendered as potential raw material for the content or expression of a 'work of art' and the cultivated perception of individuated sensibilities. This milieu relationally intersects with the rise of the rationalised worker, technocentricity, the modern consumer, the power of the media, the social psychotic obsessed with self-appearance, the ocularcentric modern spectator, the modern ego, as well as to the colonial/colonised subject.

The historicity of the onward progression toward ever more individuated or atomised subjects — often living an instrumentalised existence in proximity to materialised forms of the modern state, economy and culture — has led to a proliferation of fragmented and metaphorically homeless selves living in ever more conjuncturally dispersed ways across multiple locations in time and space. We almost all live the contradiction between the elevation of individualism and the loss of the authority of the narrative of individual identity that is confronted when we become aware of the multiplicity of our subject positions. In actuality we are treated (and end up viewing ourselves) as individuated multiple subjects, rather than unique singular individuals.

During the past 150 years, at least within Western intellectual culture, there has been a pre-occupation with seeking to understand modernity. Again, like history, this enterprise has become more intense over the last few decades — not least because the viability of the project of bringing the world into one moment of time, culture, economy, political system, and world view has come to be seen as an ever more impossible goal. The rise of 'the postmodern' is a certain recognition of this situation. Specifically postmodernity and postmodernism (the latter an accompanying but not altogether corresponding cultural condition) mark the loss of power of the discourses of modernity to deliver a universal identity, sense of direction and historically assured destination. This breakdown of the universal project was a rupture of a variety of forces that never cohered as a whole but were often projected, or assumed to be, unified. Crudely what has arrived in the wake of the rupture is an acknowledgement of what was always present in the elemental forces of modernity, but repressed by its utopianism and the fiction of linear and uniform progress.

Four undercurrents beg naming: 'difference' (as incommensurate world-formation, world-occupation and understanding); 'fragmentation' (of structures that were, and still are, taken to be the means of social cohesion: identity and cultural tradition, religious belief, local economies, and family); a very expedient form of 'pragmatism' (currently evident as 'globalisation': a traffic in labour, power and commodities without any attachment to anything that does not serve its expedient ends); and the reality of 'regress' (that individuals, cultures and nations go backwards as well as forward, or sometimes nowhere). Additionally we note that for all the apparent advancements delivered by cultivation, education, science, technology, and notwithstanding the legitimising rhetoric of humanism, war and the myriad other ways of damaging lives and the fabric our planet continue as constant reminders of humanity's failure to become humane, responsible and ethical.[11]

Stepping back, we can see that the initial moment of inquiry into the modern sought to comprehend how this 'development' created the modern human being (Freud, Durkheim), a new social and economic order (Marx), and its institutions (Weber). The mountain of literature of contemporary debate stands on this foundational work. However, there are a few additional observations to make that take us beyond this tradition of critique, and its postmodern extension.

Particular elements of the metadiscourse of modernity were implicated in the instrumentalisation of the Enlightenment under the banner of 'modernisation'. This carried an enthnocentric, humanist assumption of the 'family of man' being on an evolutionary path to universal realisation and perfectability. This assumption was enacted through a variety of instrumental and institutional forms (like UNESCO) and is now clearly discredited. A universal notion of the form of the human is breaking down. Moreover, the content of the lives, worlds and futures of a vast number of people is becoming less certain. In the difference of our circumstances, we are increasingly finding ourselves living in a state of caution and anxiety. One can claim that most people live in a gap between the knowledge of the functional inadequacies of their lifeworld, and a sense of being unable to do anything about its determinate structures. In this setting, a sense of identity, of having a place in the world and of having an ability to direct (or to at least have some control over one's life) all become undermined.

This situation is not exactly new. Yet something else is arriving for us more dramatically than at any time before: time is shrinking, in the sense that the image we have of the finitudinal horizon of being (and our being) ever moves toward us. This image of a process of diminishing time is in fact the defutured, also in process. Existentially, defuturing is experienced as living with a felt knowledge of unsustainability, as it results from the defutured as damage and on-going results. While this may be explicitly confronted, living unsustainability is mostly enacted as unconsciously living the error of a striving to gain, or retain, 'the quality of life of a standard of living' that has been taken to be a right, all with no regard for the consequences. Error here thus means living in the belief one can secure individual means of future well-being independently of the care for the general condition. It is to live without a sense of the defutured. These comments equally apply to the myopia of individuals, government and corporations. In the face of this situation the anomic are helpless and the privileged have a choice — resignation or striving to find a way to learn, think, act and make otherwise. It is into this context that the counter metanarrative of defuturing is introduced. It exists to contribute to a thinking and acting otherwise.

Reiterating, there is no metadiscourse available with the authority to constitute, let alone, speak for all modernity. No single knowledge rules. Modernity is now, in its specificities, inherent in the multiplicities of the worlds we know, but inseparably we are also it. Through the diversity and contradictions of modernity, we are the human being that the Enlightenment brought into being (which is not to say we are enlightened beings). In this, we present ourselves as rational beings, members of civil society, productive, educated, cultivated and so on.

Quite clearly it is impossible for us to be outside of the modern: we cannot be pre-modern. No matter what our lifestyle or however we try to reconfigure our world view, we cannot expunge how we have been socialised as modern subjects, we cannot change the already designed designing of our being of a particular epoch. Even as it manifests a terminal condition, modernity still has, as we shall see, enormous force in bastardised and perceptibly dysfunctional forms. In a dis-unified way, the agents of modernity are fighting to survive, they are transmuting — again in contradiction. Eurocentric values as a world view are, for example, still implicated in exporting global unsustainability, while at the same time starting to claim leadership in addressing its causes.

We would remind ourselves here that unsustainability is not reducible to just an environmentalist view of the problem. Our crisis goes much deeper than this. Fundamentally it is not those biophysical problems that seem most threatening or that bring the greatest danger. Rather it is living without, or in a diminished state of, belief and meaning. Put bluntly, sustain-ability has to confront and overcome the meaninglessness of life which hides in making life 'meaningful' as an unchecked advancement of a 'standard of living' (which in no way suggests that a sound economic foundation is not an essential condition of sustainment) and in the shallowness of aesthetic totalism. This can only happen if the authority of belief can be reinvented, for without belief and a critical facility we are unable to destroy that which threatens what is essential for sustainment. There can be no future for us without belief, and its interlocutor, value. The key question this leaves us with is 'In what do we believe?' In this setting, the fabrication of metadiscourse returns not as recovered truth, but a contingent need. The 'history' of mythology/science tells us this has ever been so.

Notes

1   Kant, late in the eighteenth century, writes of the 'end of history' in his essay 'Conjectural Beginning of Human History': see Beck, LW (ed), *Kant on History* (trans LW Beck *et al.*), Bobbs Merrill, Indianapolis, 1963, pp. 63–66; and Francis Fukuyama, *The End of History and the Last Man*, The Free Press, New York, 1992.
2   EH Carr's *What is History* (Macmillian, London, 1961) is a popular and well cited example of this kind of writing.
3   Hayden White, *Tropics of Discourse*, John Hopkins University Press, Baltimore, 1978.
4   *Ibid.*, p. 71. White cites Northrop Frye as the creator of the term metahistory in 1963. *Ibid.*, p. 72, n. 2. White's concern with metahistory was first influentially registered by *Metahistory: The Historical Imagination in Nineteenth Century Europe*, John Hopkins University Press, Baltimore, 1973.
5   *Ibid.*, p. 136–37.
6   Jean-François Lyotard, *The Postmodern Condition: A Report on Knowledge* (trans Geoff Bennington and Brian Massumi), Manchester University Press, Manchester, 1984, p. xxiii.
7   *Ibid.*
8   Modernity was manifested in specific discourses that travelled with, and was expressed as, unified transcendental theories that became the ground of thinking God, world, the East, the West, the human and certainties like time, space, power, reality, art, truth, ethics, meaning, communication, politics, philosophy, history, reason, nation, community, nature and so on. All these totalities, like modernity itself, and the example of history above, have now been exposed as either culturally relative pluralities or as discursive colonising fictions that are no longer able to retain their former authority. Clearly, however, what is common currency of the academic enclaves should not be taken as the general views. As far as popular consciousness is concerned the profound consequences of the force of the forms of modernity and 'the endings' of the modern epoch have hardly been recognised.

Linguistically the concept of 'modernity' is the product of the contradictions of a universal discourse (the Enlightenment): it is ever disarticulated from the idea, and constantly shifting signifier, of what is 'modern' from a specific cultural point of view (the only point of view there is), and the slide between its employment as a naming of an historical period and its form, while what is modern remains ever mobile, perspectival and often created by the appropriation and reworking of that taken from the past (often no clear-cut binary exists between the old and the new).

9   With the emergence of the mind of political philosophy we are of course in the company of Hobbes, Locke, Rousseau, Machiavelli *et al.*

10  Intellectually, 'the debt' here is to the thinking of Burke, Condillac, Smith, Ricardo and others.

11  The Eurocentric call in recent years by some academics, most notably Jürgen Habermas, for the project of modernity to be completed is laughable. There was never a coherent and unified project to complete: formation was always accompanied by deformation and breakdown.

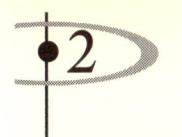

# 2
# MADE IN AMERICA: A WORLD PRODUCTION

Dreamlined progress (The Austin Company)

For the West, America arrived with modernity and became the most dynamic nation in its advancement. It follows that to comprehend modernity, in all of its manifestations, one has to engage America. More than this, once one sees the attempt to universalise the modern — as economy, political formation and culture — and also acknowledges the intimate relation between modernity and America, then one has to recognises that, interchangeably, the universalisation of the one became the universalisation of the other (although neither totalised each other). Once we see that America was both a specific place and a global projection of the modern world linked to forces of modernisation, we can make two further pertinent observations.

The first observation is that the creation of America as a nation was equally the making of an image. While this image instrumentally functioned in the nation's formation it also was employed as a powerful projection of the modern to the rest of the world which, by degree, was deemed to be less modern. In turn, the external projection fed the internal perception.

The second observation points to the relation (and relationality) of the images of America as having a long-standing, if inchoate, history of being recognised and mis-recognised. One term especially expresses this well — 'Americanism'. The term not only names Americanisation as forming a 'somewhere' and an 'everywhere', but also suggests the agency of a cultural, political and economic ideology. One particular text that clearly illustrated the point well is Antonio Gramsci's seminal essay 'Americanism and Fordism' in his prison notebooks of 1929–35.[1]

Our argument is of course that American modernity (in its fragmented and contradictory specificities) was deeply implicated in the growth and global expansion of defuturing. So, in highlighting the rise and establishment of mass production and consumption in America, we are also registering the future-making forces of a large part of the rest of 'the world'. At the very moment when progress was being celebrated, a regress in human well-being was being installed as the unsustainable inscription of unaccountable production and unforeseen impacts. However, as implied when introducing Part 2, we are not able to take the idea of 'world' for granted. Thus, before going further it needs to be qualified.

## WORLD[2]

Inhabiting the same planet does not, of itself, constitute the basis for a commonality. Moreover, nothing obscures what needs to be sustained more than the image of this planet as an object to save. This is a view from an elsewhere that hides what needs to be seen with 'the world' as Idea and idealisation. Unless the agents and agency of defuturing can be imaged, grasped and engaged, remaking the means of sustainment is impossible. World-making, as thinking, building and dwelling sustainments by design, is antagonistically at odds with the displacement of world by that image of 'the world to save'.

Most of us bandy the word 'world' around with ease. We have the image, we have the object, we know what we see. Yet all we really have is but another projection that acquires its meaning from a 'world view' that is formed out of a particular cultural location. The way the world is thought or viewed is always predetermined by a culturally authored perception and naming. In this respect Americanism and modernisation are metanarratives that aim to authorise a world view which seeks to displace a pre-existing view of 'world'. For us, in 'our world', 'the world' as idea or image comes before us as that which cannot be experienced as a 'thing-in-itself', thus it always remains as an abstraction that mediates a designated entity by word or image. In this context we live the historicity of our culture, in common with every culture, imposing 'its' world on 'the' world. The links between a concept of world, an image of world, the world of our experience and the empirical world are thus all much weaker than we think.

The material consequences of the metaphorics of world clearly envelop everything for us: they gather and hold our sense of the physical totality of all things and all knowledge, they secure the boundary of our experience, the geography we have knowledge of, the commonality of understanding we function with. The sensibility of our perceptions and images, our comprehension of our culture, work, things, relationships, pleasure, and imaginaries are projected and ordered as elements and levels of an inhabited larger whole that inhabits us. This world, constituted by objectivation, involvement and imagination that makes and unmakes all other worlds we know for us, is vulnerable — for worlds shatter as cultures or minds are destroyed; likewise worlds arrive as cultures are created.

The ground of 'being human' arrives when a human is 'thrown' into being-in-a-world of made meaning that is other than 'world' as a thing-in-itself. It follows that 'human' is not a fully secured universal being but the being of a culture that has acquired the power to designate the universal being named human. In this respect 'the human', as now understood, is not a neutral biological classification, but a product of philosophical modernity arming modernisation with a discourse able to globally totalise, and then accommodate, the entirety of the species. One clear illustration of this is the notion of 'universal human rights' which completely rests on the hegemony of the ideal of a universalised human.

In bringing 'world' and 'human' together, as we know them, what we confront are productions and unmakings. Whatever we now know and think arrives by constructed means, and at the price of other ways of knowing. The violence of modernisation was that, in the main, it either discounted what its 'others' made and knew, or more overtly set out to destroy what it sensed or partly recognised. All of this is obviously counter to the impression that the natural sciences have given us of the world and the human as entities ever being disclosed to us from a point of origin.

While such observations are familiar fare in contemporary thought, they are not embraced — a schism exists between knowledge and understanding. In this situation, ethics and responsibility (which now rest inseparably between the spaces of the indivisibility of the animate and inanimate, the given and the fabricated, the organic and the synthetic, design and chaos) fail not only to re-examine, embrace and mobilise an appropriate remaking of themselves, but remain silent on the absolute unsustainability of unconfronted anthropocentricity. This is the silence of defuturing in being.

For things (whether us or a world) to be other than they are, an unmaking and remaking is unavoidable. While this has material implications, what it fundamentally implies is an ontological transformation of the present ground of knowing and acting to change a disposition to every thing and every body. Such a deconstructive exercise is equally a reconstructive one. To use the argument already posited: one cannot act to make things otherwise without understanding how a world is made by modes of dwelling in, and things of, the world. For all our inescapable involvement, and irrespective of our understanding of world, we can never simply occupy our world, it can never be just a dwelling place. For we are of it, partly as makers, partly as content. In a sense we are the world we invent — it is both our project and our projection of meaning, it is our discourse — and it is nothing without us.

## WORLD DESIGNING

In every sense 'being here' as 'being-in-the-world' has always transformed where we are.[3] While the issues of sustain-ability and unsustainability have always essentially accompanied human beings, as concerns anthropocentrically negated, they have now asserted themselves as the future arrives as a question for the species. As indicated, the need for the species to gain the ability to confront anthropocentrism is an essential task for human sustainment (with consequences also for non-human others) as it faces its variable finitudinal horizon. This is not a vain and misguided hope of overcoming anthropocentrism but a recognition that what has to be learnt is how to conserve (including conserve time) rather than taking away. Design has to be turned (by becoming informed by defuturing) from being the unwitting tool of unsustainability to become the means of making the sustainments that make time, and so serve futuring.[4]

In order to move from the way design is presently constituted as an object of inquiry and practice, an ontological theory of design (Design) is needed. Such a theory allows questions about the consequences of the design of things and worlds (past, present and future) to be asked, and for Design, as an agency and site of a practical philosophy, to be constituted, in ways that are in accordance with how Design was presented in the Introduction.

An ontological theory of Design is not confined to ontological questions of philosophy or to questioning existing professional design practices. On the contrary, it presumes that thinking about and engaging with Design has to spill over into every situation in which it is possible to embrace responsible action. In sum, ontological Design is a theory and a practice concerned with the being of things (designed objects, environments, processes, texts or appearances) and the way these things create and sustain the time of the future.

Ontological Design brings into question the very division between embodied and disembodied matter by an exploration of reciprocal relations. It renders problematic the separation between us and things, subjects and objects, designing and being, world, self and others. Quite clearly, Design can make no appeal to the essential being of a thing. It cannot appeal to a ground upon which the essence of a thing can be disclosed, for it is the world rather than the thing that conceals essences. The being of a thing has no beginning, original form or foundation outside the explanatory framework of the world that its maker makes present.

'The product' (the produced thing) acts as the causal and directional focus, and limit of view, of existing design thought and practice. In contrast, Design foregrounds the relationality of the designed material or immaterial thing in or as process. However, Design does not pose itself as an absolutely determinate model able to understand or mobilise design. At the same time the relational complexity it can muster is able to shatter the frame of containment of design action, its institutional underpinning, professional application and economic direction. Such a theory exposes the limited capabilities of reason to control designing, and as such it goes well beyond current ecological design thinking and practice. What it does is to broaden views of fields of actions, effects, structures, time and objects to allow a contemplation of circumstantial remakings of 'the thing' as it changes by being in use, exchange, process, system and environment. Design, when linked to sustain-ability, does not function with certainty but with learning to change. While all design (and designing) is directional, ontologically biased Design comprehends direction. It is always multiple, relational and within a field of force: it knows everything is force (from Hegel), and power is everywhere (from Foucault).

## AMERICA

We now come back to America's leadership in the making of modern industrial culture (which transpired to be the culture of defuturing). The conventional form of this history has been recounted many times before. The point of its retelling is not to celebrate it (although achievement is not denied), nor to claim another interpretation or to revise it. Rather, the aim is to expose that almost all that we manufacture as history conceals the historicity of the error that negates the future. The essential task is not one of getting the history right (the 'right', the correct and truth do not in fact converge), but rather to obstruct the prospect of returning to the same path of error that history inscribes as a disposition. The implied proposition is that modernised cultures make the world an unsustainable place largely because of determined habits of making, using and disposing in ways which are inherently unsustainable. The problem of unsustainability thus needs to be understood to dominantly rest with the designing power of this habit to defuture, rather than resting with products in themselves.

The story opens by recognising some of the problems that flowed from the ambition to colonise North America. At its simplest, the colonisation of the land mass of North America required a critical mass of people and considerable material resources. This was not possible until a colony had established a secure foothold, reached a sufficient size and acquired the means to both support and extend itself. This took from the opening of the seventeenth century to almost the end of the eighteenth to happen. During this period, viewed in the frame of a modern map, colonies were established from Massachusetts in the north to Georgia in the south, and to just beyond the borders of Pennsylvania and Virginia in the west. The explorations of Lewis and Clark (1804–06) mark the moment from which the west was opened up. Most significantly, however, it was the occupation of the Great Plains in the 1830s, as well as the construction of canals and railways from the mid-1820s, that established the conditions that enabled and induced larger numbers to venture westwards. The realisation of this colonial expansion was symbolised by the completion of the transcontinental railway in 1869.

It was the combination of the organic and mineral wealth of the land, technology, a pioneer culture and the creation of a canal, rail, road infrastructure that enabled the mining of coal and iron ore, the bulk manufacturing of goods, the growing of food stuffs and the raising of livestock in vast numbers. Thereafter, transportation of these commodities to markets made the modern American economy possible, dynamic and large. Such development and the making of a nation came, however, at a high human and environmental price: native peoples were slaughtered from the initial moments of land clearance to the cultivation of the Great Plains and the occupation of the west; a bloody history accompanied the establishment of national independence and national unification; and there was the enormous destruction of flora and fauna (not least the native bison).

As intimated, the move westward, and the bringing of the vast land resource of the Great Plains into the farming economy, required not only a transport system but also a whole array of technical means. To give some measure of the significance of technology to this moment of national expansion, consider that in the 263 years between the settlement of Jamestown in 1607 and the east being joined to the west in 1869, there were 186 million hectares (408 million acres) of land brought under cultivation. In contrast, in just the next 30 years (1870–1900) another 196 million hectares (431 million acres) were added to the agricultural economy.[5]

Western culture became very familiar with the narrativised adventures of colonising the New World and the winning of the west. These narratives became the mythologised and universalised fodder of print and, later, moving image media — they spawned a whole genre of popular culture. However, apart from gun, telegraph and railroad, the significance of the rise of technology and science in the making of America's rural, urban, agricultural, industrial and cultural environments did not feature centrally in the popular appearances and projections of American mythology. Yet technology and science need to be understood as being totally implicated in the formation of a profound relation between conquest, industrial culture and biological 'nature'. Perhaps the most lucid account of this relation so far has been Leo Marx's *The Machine in the Garden*.[6]

Marx tells of a view which developed in American intellectual circles from the eighteenth century onwards. This constructed a unity between the machine and a mechanistic view of the universe, functioning as a cosmic operational structure. In this social milieu, a perception arrived which posited the machine as a means to harness, draw out and extend 'the power of nature'. A romance with 'nature' and technology was formed out of this culture which, rather than seeing them as difference and in opposition, saw them as existing in harmony. This romance deepened the symbolic place given to land, as the locus wherein a harmonisation of God, man, nature, culture and technology occurred. The expressive product of this unification was, Marx argues, the arrival of an ideology of national identity. In this ideology, the triumph of a technically equipped 'new world man' was projected as if it were at one with the spirit of the first settler, the back woodsman, the frontiersmen, the militia who gained the nation's independence, and with all other colonists whose blood was spilled in conquering the 'hardships of nature' (a condition into which, anthropocentrically and ethnocentrically, all native peoples were conflated). A mythology emerged in which the sum of all human courage, inventiveness, applied instrumentation and endeavours were unified in a grand narrative in which everything appeared to be harnessed to the common project of taming the land. It was the agency of this mythology that constituted a community that symbolically posited American soil as sacred. The tools and exercise of labour, the blood rites of war, individualistic overcomings of nature, the surmounting of the hardships of the frontier all combined to create an emotional and political geography of identification and attachment, expressed in the notion of 'the land of the free'. Thus an American ideology was born. Out of this context, moreover, popularist ideas and beliefs emerged which fused with technology, which was then seen as naturalised, as a sign of progress, as a force unified with spirit, and as an essence of the American culture.

Viewing nature as a mechanism was, and is, of course not unique to American culture. In fact the idea has a long history that takes us back to Descartes, then further back to Plato and then to the first Greek models of structure and function. The fusion and confusion of nature and technology was to become implicated in many facets of American life. Again as Leo Marx observes, the American Constitution itself was structured by the metaphor of a self-regulating machine, that 'like an orrery' (a mechanical model of the universe whereby when one celestial object moved so did all else) operates with 'checks and balances' that function across the three structures of government.[7]

The importance of technology for American culture did not arrive of its own accord. It had some powerful ideologues behind it from the eighteenth century onward. These included campaigners like Tench Coxe, who gained the ear of government, and Harvard academic Timothy Walker. Walker wrote an influential critique of Thomas Carlyle's 'Life of Schiller', a philosophical essay in which the modern age and the machine were attacked. Writing in 1831, Walker argued that technical progress was a means for man to gain knowledge of God's divine plan.[8] As has been indicated, the establishment of this kind of thinking fused gradually with the national culture, and so became part of the psyche of many Americans. The extension from, and conflation of, a national ideology to world view (evidenced, in the mid-twentieth century, as the global modernisation goal of American foreign policy) is summed up in a comment from Thomas Hughes, who pointed out that 'Men and women assumed, as never before, that they had the power to create a world of their own design'.[9]

The cultural and economic project of making the New World invited extreme judgements that truly exposed the full contradiction of human existence. On the one hand the project manifested a level of determination, application and courage of enormous proportions; on the other, it exposed all the horrors of anthropocentric and ethnocentric brutality, the consequences of which are visible as the 'conquest' of nature and the mass destruction of an other deemed sub-human. This genocide happened, as it did in the colonisation of many other nations including Australia, in the name of progress. Designated 'sub-humans' were of course eliminated with the help of technologies of destruction in the belief that actions which 'tamed nature' were ethical. The result of this enacted ignorance and extreme myopia clearly tarnishes the view of 'human' attainments. More starkly, it can be read as a massive directional error; one that, via desire and habit, maintained America (and later other 'advanced' nations) on a path toward an increasingly unsustainable future.

Such a path was complex, unseen as it was created and is only partly visible with hindsight. To fully explore every twist and turn would be a major exercise of critical inquiry. What can be done, however, is to give some sense of it by looking at two moments.

MOMENT ONE: TECHNOLOGY AND LABOUR POWER

The settlement of New England and Pennsylvania was based on the scale of a model of European rural and urban development. Change was rapid after significant numbers moved westward, which started immediately after the gestural war against Canada in 1812. Leaving the security of established settlements in the east, settlers confronted a long-standing, but increasingly pressing, need for manpower to bear arms and to do skilled and manual labour. They set about farming on a scale previously unknown, herding animals and transporting goods vast distances. The national economy was also viewed as having to deliver a labour force able to create the goods and services that could support expansionary activities. This demand was in the face of existing material problems, not least a lack of unskilled and skilled labour, as well as the high cost and logistical problems of importing large volumes of manufactured products from Europe. This latter problem obviously became more extreme once settlement moved ever further from the ports of the eastern seaboard. Solutions had to be, and were, found. Out of these conditions of necessity, the fundamental features of modern American culture were forged. These features slowly emerged from a unification of circumstantial pragmatism with an absolute social and economic investment in the agency of technology. (In part, this pattern of 'development' has been characterised by the 'frontier theory'.)

The labour power of technology is predicated upon its ability to function in ways that replace, or extend, human skill, but with far higher levels of output. Instead of skilling workers, skilled machines were created. In America this move was part of an enormous effort towards a national base of invention.

America's enthusiastic adoption of technology had a profound impact. It provided the fire power of the weapons of genocide, compensated for the small size of the skill base, brought many new products into being which did not require highly skilled craftsmen to make them, and enabled a large civil infrastructure to be built at speed. The nation learned that a small technologically literate cadre could make a very large economy function and have major material impact.

American industry grew in significant part from the efforts of a relatively small and unco-ordinated body of designers, inventors and craftsmen whose innovatory approach to problems of circumstance drove the re-invention of work, work process and products. This was done with sufficient momentum to eventually transform the economic, cultural and social environment of the entire modern world. At the centre of this developmental impetus was the creation of new technologies and work methods. These innovations were initially demonstrated by the quality of products and volume of outputs of the light engineering factories, as well as the establishment of major machine tool industry, that grew up in the north-eastern states.

These events were happening at the same time as a national civil infrastructure was being put in place. The eastern seaboard was linked to the Great Lakes, by the 560-kilometre (350-mile) long Erie Canal in 1825. Immediately after this a of a railway network was established. From the 1830s, this enabled the transport of cattle driven up from Texas; grain grown on the Great Plains; coal mined from Pennsylvania, Kentucky, Tennessee (and thereafter the mid- and north-west); and iron from Indiana, Ohio and Pennsylvania to arrive in those industrial cities established on the shores of the Great Lakes and the ports of the east.[10] It also meant a constant flow of materials to the factories of the north-east and conversely an ever-growing market for their products.

Whether in transportation, mining, slaughtering cattle, sawing timber, smelting iron, farming, making machinery, manufacturing arms or any other of the emergent industries, the expertise of limited numbers of craftsmen became directed towards the creation of machines that could embody and generalise their skills. In turn the mechanised labour power dramatically powered the economic and technological development of America. The example of the agricultural industry makes the point.

The business potential of farming the Great Plains on a vast scale would not have been possible without the recognition of what a small labour force, supported by mechanised farm machinery, could do. The ability of an already established engineering industry to create a farm machinery industry enabled the growth of this whole sector of the national economy. This technologicalisation of large-scale farming had major consequences, not just in America but world-wide. From the American perspective it enabled the nation to become both a food and farm machinery producer and exporter on a vast scale.

Although the statistical evidence of the national economic performance of America showed that agriculture dominated manufacturing for many decades, it should be remembered that this output depended upon the mechanised giant farms of the mid-west. Farm machinery — ploughs, harvesters, reapers, harrows, fertiliser spreaders, drills, pumps and then traction engines[11] — represented a constantly evolving and expanding area of technology. By 1880, for example, 80 per cent of all wheat grown in America was being harvested mechanically.[12] Science also made a significant contribution to increasing productivity by applying new knowledges of plant biology and agricultural chemistry to the development of standardised seed stock, and factory-produced fertilisers and later insecticides.

The rise of the farm machinery industry also contributed to the nation's manufacturing base by adding to the stock of newly invented, or improved, machine tools and providing opportunities for the arrival of new technical knowledge on manufacturing methods. Additionally, this sector of the economy created the conditions out of which a modern industrial working class emerged. Farm machinery also made a significant contribution to America becoming a global manufacturing nation, and while in the mid-nineteenth century industrial manufacture was only a small part of the national economy, it was, even by 1860, generating an output that was only exceeded by one other country: Britain. The speed and scale of industrialisation during this period is well illustrated by the volume of farm machinery produced. By 1858, for example, the McCormick Company of Chicago were producing over 4000 reapers per year. This output represents not just very large production numbers for the day, more evidence of the mechanisation of farming, or an indication of the scale of operation of the largest exporter of farm machinery of the time: but the extent to which traditional craft-based farming had been transformed in agricultural business in America by the mid-nineteenth century.

With hindsight, these innovations bring to light technologies, chemical products and methods that established what have transpired to be very unsustainable practices. Specifically, these products (such as pesticides) and their associated practices, have taken vast tracts of good land out of productive use, turned them to desert (both in America and many other parts of the world), reduced biodiversity, and damaged human health and the health of other species by the use of various toxins.

Prior to the establishment of a mechanised farm machinery industry, an even more advanced engineering sector of the economy was already well established — the arms industry. This was important not just because of the impact of what it produced but because of its centrality to the establishment of advanced technical knowledge, new production skills and workplace methods.

Like others in the arms industry, Eli Whitney, one of its leaders, did not confine his active technological leadership to that industry. Whitney was also a leading pioneer in many other technologies, including the invention of the cotton gin. He developed and adopted technologies based on making machines that made things with the subordinate help of men (rather than the European tradition which was the inverse of this relation). What he put in place was to be one of the main designing forces of industrial production in America. His aim was to substitute:

> correct and effective operations of machinery for the skill of the artist which is acquired only by long practice and experience; a species of skill which is not possessed in this country to any considerable extent.[13]

Whitney was among a cluster of gun-makers such as Simeon North, John Hancock Hall, the Remington Company, Sharps Rifle Company, Robbins and Lawrence, and George S Lincoln and

Company, who all figured in making the mechanisation of arms an extremely important development in the industrial history of America. Less recognised in this history has been the role of the United States Ordnance Department. This department, especially at its Harpers Ferry and Springfield armories, undertook engineering research, metallurgy, testing, design, and technological education. It also led the way to the establishment of standardisation. Moreover, it created the most system-organised work places of the time. Rather than operating in the climate of secrecy that is such a feature of contemporary governmental arms manufacture, the influence of the department was due to its policy of openness. As Merritt Roe Smith writes:

> As early as 1815 the chief of the ordnance and his staff had recognized the importance of disseminating new techniques. Without the rapid assimilation of machine and gauging processes, the coordination and control necessary for uniform production would have proved well-nigh impossible. Continual communication and cooperation therefore became essential elements in the department's strategy. Resultant information transfers soon manifested themselves in published reports of tests and experiments and in the day-to-day operation of the armaments network.[14]

In the formation of an engineering industry in America, the Department of Ordnance not only provided a major portion of the knowledge base for industry but also set the highest standards in technical performance (including an ability to manufacture parts that had interchangeability). It also provided the most highly trained pool of mobile labour.

The most famous name of all the arms manufacturers was Samuel Colt. Colt's .36 navy revolver captured much attention when it was presented at the Great Exhibition at Crystal Palace 1851. It put America at the fore in the global leadership of industrial manufacturing systems. Colt's system, which was named the 'American system of manufacture', had one key characteristic — the creation of precision-machined, interchangeable components of standard tolerances to ensure the standardisation of fit.

Nowhere was the impetus to create accurate and rapid-fire small arms greater than in America where the threat of native peoples was ever present. The large-scale destruction of these people, and their subordination by small armies, totally depended upon the maximisation of fire power. The same logic was applied to the ability of the nation to defend itself from without. One can note, be it ironically, that the death of animals, Indians and other colonists was mechanically delivered by some of the best small arms ever, to that point, invented. As an indicator of the inseparability of modernity and war, it can be observed that the ability to mechanise mass death was the first major achievement of mass production technology. This achievement was epitomised by the machine gun, which first made its appearance on the battlefield in the American Civil War (1861–65).

By the early nineteenth century, a highly developed industrial infrastructure had been developed in New England, mostly based on light engineering, an established skill base and a small number of industries, especially for the manufacture of small arms. After a reduction in the level of demand for weapons, after the west had been 'won' and the Civil War ended, there was an increase in momentum towards product diversification. A pattern became established: the design of systems evolved by the American Government Armories were passed to industry as the 'American system'. This not only established methods and standards that enabled component interchangeability but also made precise measurement by precision gauges a central element of engineering practice. It also put the invention of specialised machines for specific tasks into a key position within the manufacturing system. Moreover, men trained in the high standards of the armories became a labour pool, after the demand for weapons fell off, for both private arms makers and other new industries.

The result of the convergence of invention, advanced skills, high standards and the requirement for precision was the rise of the modern American machine tool industry (which made high quality machine tools, like lathes, milling machines, planers, pillar drills, presses, gear cutters, universal grinders and so on). These machines were what enabled the mass production, at affordable prices, of many products that were to become part of modern life: the already discussed farm machinery, factory-made clocks, the bicycle, railroad equipment and then later the safety razor, the typewriter, sewing machine, telegraph, vacuum cleaner, phonograph and so on. These new products are part of the story of the mechanisation of the home and the office. Not only were such products sold worldwide (which made their manufacturers giant companies), but at the same time the machines that made the products themselves were sold worldwide as products, (which also made their manufacturers giant companies). This machinery is not only deeply implicated in the globalisation of mass production but also in the designing of the infrastructural conditions of unsustainability.

Two others United States government agencies beg address: the Topographical Bureau, and the Corps of Engineers, both of whom played a major role in exploring and surveying the west geodetically. The engineers were also responsible for the construction of a large number of civil works.[15] They were especially important in the establishment of a railroad system, through surveying and engineering, as well as in creating systems of management. Army engineers actually served directly with some of the nation's railroad companies between 1827 and 1850.[16] Bringing the highly organised army administration system to these entrepreneurial companies created a management model for American business per se. In many ways the military provided both the technical and organisational structure for American industry; as contemporary researchers, like Seymour Melman have argued, this relation in fact became elemental to American capitalism.[17]

There is yet another factor in the globalisation of technological militarised modernity led by America — the rise of mass technical education. This instrumental form of education was promoted by Benjamin Franklin in 1749, established in the City of Philadelphia in 1756 in a public academy and registered at Harvard in 1815, with the establishment of a chair in 'utility and useful arts' (first held by Jacob Bigelow, the man credited with the invention of the modern use of the term 'technology'). Technical education was fully institutionalised by the 1840s at both Harvard and Yale, in 1862 the Massachusetts Institute of Technology was founded, and by 1880 there were 85 engineering schools such as Columbia, Cornell, John Hopkins, Michigan, Illinois at major universities in the country.[18] Graduates increased from 100 in 1870 to well over 4000 by 1914: making America, without question, a world leader in this field of practical knowledge.[19]

In a nation that, by large degree, was 'opened up' by the gun, the railroad and the farm machine, the engineer was, and still is, a cultural hero. The engineer was ever found, and again still is, on the new frontier — the space of the unknown. This romance with technology, its folding into nature and its moral claim of acting in God's name, is integral to American culture. The steam train embodied this more than anything else:

> By 1844 the machine had captured the public imagination. The invention of the steamboat had been exciting, but it was nothing compared to the railroad. In the 1830s the locomotive, an iron horse of fire Titan, is becoming a kind of national obsession. It is the embodiment of the age, an instrument of power, speed, noise, fire, iron, smoke — at once testament to the will of man rising over natural obstacles, and yet, confined by its iron rails to a predetermined path, it suggests a new sort of fate.[20]

The railroad filled media of the day, it was a political preoccupation, a major figure in all forms of popular culture, a poetic celebration (not least by Walt Whitman) and above all, as it raced forward, the symbolic icon of 'progress' as system and object.

The romance with technology was established as an inscriptive of power within America which has left a major mark on economic and cultural forms: ranging through technically complex rule-governed sports, technique-based formalist art, youth car and motorcycle subcultures, the popularism of the American space program, the constant stream of gizmo products, and a population that embraces anything automatic. Technology became naturalised as part of the normality of the everyday American lifeworld. Social, economic and cultural life was thus lived, both on the land and in the city, in the nature of technoculture. As the international critical concern with 'Americanism' and 'Fordism' over the past sixty years indicates, this lifeworld has long since become universalised.

What is the issue here is not found by revisiting the debates in which 'Americanism' and 'Fordism' surfaced but rather how they stand for a disposition towards technology that itself needs to be understood as a designing of the unsustainable, not least because the more technology arrived the more its designing became concealed (which is another way of saying the more it became taken for granted as 'naturally' there).

More specifically, from a disposition formed out of the inscriptive power of pragmatic technical action there was a calling up, designing, 'making' of a world of dynamic productivism. This meant that the world was rendered as a resource available for use, reassembly and organisation. Structures and modes of thinking were put in place to sustain the evolution of a technocracy, and to extend and conceptually legitimise instrumental action (this was to lead to the American philosophical tradition of pragmatism, with John Dewey at its highest point). Modes of education were put in place that ensured the basis of arts and sciences were united by a technological sensibility. (This can be seen, for example, in dominance of rule-governed methodologies and in the hegemonic establishment of positivism in the natural, physical and social sciences as well as in philosophy and history.) Certainly the famous 1930s proposition made by the British writer CP Snow of the academy having two cultures — the arts and science — stands on far more shaky ground in America than in does in Europe.

The consequence of the formation of a techno-instrumental ontology — a human being who acts in, and on the world from the perspective of the technological — has been profound, especially as this way of being was, and still is, universalised by American technoculture and its global offspring, be it with the background support of other nations who, while having a technological tradition, also had other well-established traditions before and alongside it. These traditions in America, rather than predating technoculture, feed off it. As has been suggested, America spawned a technoculture which constructed a world view, which became world-wide as a feature of the culture of economic modernity. 'Americanism', however, was not just an economic project — nor a cultural one, although it displayed both economic and cultural features — rather it was an ontological project which centred around 'being-with-American-things' (be they sound, image or object) that made the world act in a particular way. This designing environment of material and immaterial forms constituted beings who felt, and acted, as if almost every problem — social, biological, environmental, organisational or physical — was available to be resolved by technological means.

## MOMENT TWO: THE AMBIGUOUS FORCE OF FORDISM (AND THE QUIET ACT OF GENERAL MOTORS)

This moment seems to offer both a continuity and something new — things are always more complex than they appear.

Formal histories of design and technology present mass production as having three fundamental components. Firstly, the ability to assemble a product from standardised interchangeable parts (the American system of manufacture outlined above that de facto became a global system). Secondly, the setting up of an 'in-line' assembly system, in which parts are organised into managed inventories which are then designed into a moving production line (major product components, or the total product, are moved down the line by a conveyor system and incrementally assembled as they passed by assembly workers stationed at particular inventory and production line intersections). And, thirdly, the adoption of Frederick Winslow Taylor's methods of 'scientific management', which pulled together live labour, the assembly system and inventory as one managed structure of time, speed and movement.[21]

The historical focus on the technology of mass production centres predominantly on Henry Ford and his plant for the Model T set up in Highland Park, Michigan in 1913, just prior to World War I.[22] Ford's technology meant that a Model T could be assembled in 93 minutes, in contrast to the previous time of 840 minutes. This 'progress' ensured that a car left the line every ten seconds. By 1916, Ford factories were producing a staggering 600,000 Model Ts per year, and by 1920 half the cars in the world were Fords.

Reviewing the Ford phenomenon in brief, we can note the following:

- the organisational principle of 'in-line' assembly, and disassembly, had historical precedents prior to Ford[23]

- 'interchangeable parts inventory management' was already a well systematised practice before Ford adopted it
- the actual design of the system was not done by the man himself, but by his team
- that Ford's system was not the only 'viable' mass production method. General Motors employed many of the same methods as Ford, but with a greater degree of diversity and flexibility, including product diversity and a gang system whereby work was organised around clusters of teams competing with each other on productivity (this mostly on a piece-work model). The ruthless productivity and profit-driven philosophy of General Motors, under the direction of Alfred Sloan, was to lead to it overtaking Ford by the early 1930s. Sloan ruled the company for over six decades, over half of these as chairman. His reputation was as the most ruthless, impressive and influential industrial manager of the twentieth century. Sloan basically lived by one rule: the maximisation of profit.
- the trade off of a higher wage for less individual control over the nature and speed of work. This was a major feature of the Ford system, and effectively shifted qualitative considerations of the nature of, and type of, work to disposable income and purchasable lifestyle. The key moment in the advance of this philosophy was the introduction of the $5.00 day in 1914 (this was over double the prior wage of $2.30).
- that Fordism was neither confined to the motor industry nor to the United States. It became an international paradigm of industrial production across a whole range of commercial and domestic products and appliances.

Ford's real innovation was to bring together a concept of a product, the management of resources, and the design of work — he was a systems builder. To a significant degree his operation was based on applied militarisation, in the sense that it was a designed regime of order and discipline. This was because it was grounded in the militarised character of a good deal of nineteenth century American engineering culture (recall the role of the Department of Ordnance). The influence of Fordism cannot be overestimated, and not only as an ideology of production, which sometimes delivered economic gains and always restructured the nature of work and its social relations. It has equally significant status in advancing a technology of mass destruction. The relational flow of environmental impacts stemming from the material inputs and outputs of Fordism, across industrial culture per se, make it a major contributor to the on-going proliferation of the defutured. Fordism conjuncturally impacted with a number of other key elements in advancing humanity towards the pleasure of the modern world within the frame of a culture of mass destruction.

The nineteenth century also saw the rise of mass communication (the newspaper industry, for instance, had gained the technical ability to print and distribute vast number of papers), and mass distribution of goods in volume, facilitated by modern shipping and railways, while mail order catalogues (mostly the products of department stores) were printed in their millions and sent around the world. The purchase of goods was of course enabled by the system of distribution of the department stores, who themselves were vast, spectacular and systematised structures that delivered 'lines' of goods in highly organised work environments. Named 'palaces of consumption' they became cultural machines which put modern domestic life on show as an array of available commodities. Department stores exhibited, and instructed on, modern life on a epic scale, and in forms that made them very powerful instruments both in the creation of mass consumption, and its accompanying negatives. Resulting from their self-creation, as enclaves of desire within a market economy, they were able to mobilise product, staged as signs of style and taste, in ways that displaced shopping to meet needs grounded in utility.

Many histories of mass (proto-defuturing) culture converge at this point. Modern consumerism, mass production, mass markets, mass media and the like all fuse with a technology of fetishisation (advertising), the generation of modern quantities of waste, and the unthinking, uncaring and myopic self-interest that is at the core of unsustainable lifestyles. Notwithstanding what economic determinism told us, culture became deeply implicated in replicating and deepening the problems of the world that economy appeared to sustain. Remembering the ambiguity of 'world', we note that this moment was one when a new world in formation not only aimed to displace the old but unknowingly negated the conditions of both the old and the new — in the name and image of progress, economy and culture merged as they defutured what was and needed to be.

Fordism advanced defuturing beyond the ways already outlined, for it was also associated with technologies of mass death. While the broader issues of the relations of the creative and destructive force of modernity, technology and war, have been discussed elsewhere, there is a need to identify connections between the American system of manufacture, 'in line' assembly and Fordism in the context of our argument.

As has already been indicated, the ability to create weapons that enabled a small number of men to mobilise enough firepower to overcome much larger numbers was an important imperative of the American arms industry. The Colt revolver and the Remington repeating rifle are both examples of this imperative realised. More significantly, and more centrally within a battlefield environment, there was one weapon which delivered more on this score than any other. This was the machine gun, which created the ability to kill en masse to the extent that it actually transformed war. As has already been noted, the machine gun first arrived during the American Civil War (actually in 1862, its second year). The first machine gun was of course the Gatling gun, invented by Richard Jordan Gatling. In an uncanny recognition of the very argument on the significance of in-line production (and destruction), as is being rehearsed here, its inventor said 'It bears the same relation to other firearms that the McCormick's Reaper does to the sickle, or the sewing machine does to the common needle'.[24] This multiple-barrelled gun was hand cranked and had the ability to deliver 200 rounds per minute. While it was superseded by more sophisticated machines its mechanical principle was very sound and provided the basis for more recent re-engineering of the technology to create the modern version — with a mechanism powered by an electric motor and a rate of fire 6000 rounds per minute. The gun which displaced the Gatling was the Maxim, first demonstrated by its inventor Hiram Maxim in 1884. This extremely reliable gun reloaded automatically and was to become the basic model in its British licensed form (by Vickers) and in the German (by Krupps).

The Maxim was followed by a medium machine gun, the Browning, in 1890 and a light machine gun, the Lewis, in 1913 (just in time for World War I). All of these guns were American inventions. These weapons are paradigmatic of 'in-line' destruction: they mark the industrialisation of war delivered by industrial process. They maintained a constant stream of fire against a line by ammunition being fed 'in-line' (this was, and is, variably done by a round of pre-loaded chambers, a charged magazine or a belt feed system). The ammunition was mass produced, as was the gun, and so also was death. Such weapons not only changed the nature of war, they also changed how it was perceived and what it meant to die in war — in large part they 'killed' valour and the virtue of the heroic act. They changed the fundamental character of the battlefield, the duration of the battle, the image of the enemy, the human scale of war, and the speed of death of the masses.[25]

To wage 'world war' demanded a vast landmass, armies of the masses, mass destructive weapons, mass movement, and it all produced mass death. Such wars generated massive logistical problems; to move men, weapons and provisions on the scale of an event like World War I required mass transport. Of course war not only destroyed human life, but also all the objects of war, including vehicles. As was made clear when addressing war in Chapter 1, nothing compares with it as a mechanism for the production of consumption by destruction: nothing defutures like the relational cycles of destruction of war. Now re-enter Henry Ford.

Fordism (which from 1913 to 1923 was the dominant name under which 'mass production' travelled), as we have noted, arrived as a system just before World War I. The war created enormous demand for vehicles and multitudes of other industrially manufactured goods. Ford was in a position to service this need. Orders for trucks and cars for the war made a very substantial contribution to the growth of the Ford company. More importantly, as far as the designing power of Americanism and the inscription of unsustainability were concerned, the internationalisation of the company and the globalisation of Fordist methods were very much accelerated by the war. Again, this is in keeping with the whole history of war as an accelerator of research, development and mass production.

> ### A postscript on the nature of Fordism, by Henry Ford
>
> Almost anyone can think up an idea. The thing that counts is developing it into practical products. I am now interested in fully demonstrating that the ideas we have put into practice are capable of the largest application — that they have nothing peculiarly to do with motor cars or tractors but form something in the nature of a universal code. I am quite certain that it is a natural code and I want to demonstrate it so thoroughly that it will be accepted not as a new idea but as a natural code. (*My Life and Work*, 1922, p. 3)

The histories of the two moments outlined above have been researched, studied and worked over, in great detail, by many people over a considerable expanse of time. The brief overarching remarks here will add nothing to this history and its extensive literature. The way this history is read is, however, open to fundamental revision. Certainly, the characterisation of all these 'developments' as actual development, progress and attainment needs to be contested. This re-reading is the point of this immediate exercise, it also articulates with the rest of the project of uncovering and confronting defuturing, as presented by this book.

As an object authored by its interpretative framing, history has the ability to tell us many things. The history touched on here tells us something very particular — it exposes a great deal about how the condition of universal unsustainability was inscribed into the modern world as a future designing.

## THEN AND NOW

The economy and culture of America followed a direction, set by the pattern of its own internal colonisation, towards continual expansion. This directional designing was powered by the desire — of government, corporation and individuals — for growth, wealth, recognition and power. It was not informed by foresight, critical reflection or impact assessment. In this way, as suggested, America became the world's 'leading' modern industrial culture and economy. From its industrial foundations of the 1830s to its peak in the 1960s, the disposition was towards high output, resource negation, disposability and environmental irresponsibility. While the contemporary condition of unsustainability is still unfolding, it is quite clear, with the wisdom of hindsight, where the ground of its thinking (productivism) and making (mass production) came from. Working even with our still limited understanding of the unwarranted damage done by human habitation and habits, the damage that has been done is staggering and ongoing. There is an enormous gap between how such problems are quantified, and their consequences. There is almost no tradition of projective thinking about what design designs. It has become normal to dismiss responsibility by just asserting that in is not possible to foresee the future. This perspective rests on a 'logic' of short-term returns and an absolute inability to recognise that the future is not a void but rather a space already filled by the past and the present. While certainty is not available, a great deal can be gathered from simply extrapolating from the ongoing designing of the 'what is'.

The history of the motor car is an example that powerfully illustrates the point. One does not have to exercise too much brain power to decide how many of the creators of motor cars remotely considered its impact upon the world's climate, trauma medicine, wildlife, house design, urban form, cultural values, road construction, waste generation and so on. While one is never going to 'get it right', every invention of consequence should pass through an impact evaluation before it goes into production. What this adds up to is a projective impact statement, and what it puts in place is not a science but a learning towards responsibility. From this viewpoint on products, not only does their world-designing become ever more apparent (even a cursory consideration of a brief list of common objects — like a car, television set, washing machine, computer, fridge, electric lamp and aeroplane — makes the point dramatically, for here are transformative forces of cities, knowledge, image, food, time, movement, resources: worlds) but, even within the horizon of instrumental pragmatic thought, an amazing poverty of mind is exposed. There is simply no philosophy, no methodology, no science, no tradition, no instruction, no intellectual tools, no cultural imperatives that invite, assist or impose a planetary environmental impact assessment of what we make or mean to make.

There are of course some standards. Things do get tested in relation to functional properties and safety. It is possible to calculate, via tools like 'life cycle analysis', a relational picture of total energy and pollutants invested in a product. But there are no means to evaluate what it will do. In Australia, Environmental Impact Statements (EIS) are required for major construction projects. Notwithstanding the gesturalism and limitation of these instruments of planning law, at least an EIS does allow the question of the future to be posed: there is an object of critique and development. Whereas for products, whose impact can be world-changing, there is nothing at all.

That industrial culture has not been critically reflective is at the core of why it ever travels towards crisis. In fact, industrial culture thrives on perceptual failure: it conceals crisis and converts its appearance into 'needs' to be met for or by the market. For instance, how is the greenhouse problem being confronted? Does responding to it change habits, realign demands, creating new cultures? No. The imperative of existing industrial culture is to find new ways to generate wealth, new technologies, new products and new markets that deflect the problems in order to keep things the same: so, for example, the electric car arrives rather than the problems of population growth, cities and transport being addressed. It is not that the solutions to the problems are so hard: vast numbers of people drive cars in cities simply because public transport systems are so poor. Anyone who has experienced those few cities that do have a fast, clean, regular, cheap and comprehensive public transport system do not have to be convinced of the merits of taking a train, tram or bus; everybody in one enjoys a city designed for walking; and there is no public resistance to renewable energy, other than cost, for there is no difference once it arrives as a standard unit of supplied power. The issues of cost here are as much structured by the size of, and protection given to, existing fossil fuel suppliers; the amount of foreign exchange that coal and oil exports earn; and the power of the organisations selling these commodities to lobby governments. Certainly in Australia (in contrast to Japan, some European countries and to a degree the United States) restricted research funding and limited general support for renewable energy prevents the coming of an economy of scale that would reduce prices, generate large numbers of jobs and displace the domination of non-renewable forms of energy production.

What is being said is that, against the assumed benefits of late industrial culture (which themselves beg questioning), there is clearly the need to assess and address the negatives in a far more rigorous and comprehensive way. Moreover, this activity needs to be, in large part, elemental to the future of design.

There is a backdrop to work against. There is, for example: the 'fall out' of the way that industrial society has used fossil fuel; climate damage; the destruction of forests; the destruction of rivers by pollutants; the squandering of water; the over-fishing of the world's oceans; the destruction of habitats; the destruction of soil by the way land has been cleared and over-farmed; the bio-genetic damage done to almost all life forms by chemicals introduced into environments by the manufacture and disposal of plastics; and the way in which so much is produced is discarded as waste. Such listings run on and beg detail, however, the point to be made is that one has to read the generative source of these problems (the specificity of unsustainable desires), read the directional trends that they set and act without having a full sense of the relational consequences of the destruction set in train. That we cannot reach the truth of what will be defutured by the consequences of the agency of the unsustainable is no argument against acting and learning as much as possible across a broader base and with more rigour than is currently the case. At the most basic level, just to reduce damage, to create sustainments, to make otherwise or to learn sustain-ability, a far more developed understanding of causality and impact needs to be created. To do this is not simply a matter of the application of existing Eurocentric and mostly positivistic knowledge but, as the argument of this text seeks to show, rather a task of unmaking and remaking 'knowing'.

The kind of biophysical problems listed, and there are many more, provide what is currently the dominant focus of the 'ecological crisis'. As argued, the material and cultural impact of products needs to be added to this picture, with the consequence that the environment and environmentalism has to be moved well beyond the agenda of the environmental movement. Even so we are still only registering part of the story.

As was shown by the universal directional designing of patterns of American development, industrial society and its cultures created numerous environments of creation and destruction. Every environment arrives by, and functions in, the elements and relations of a world making system (an ecology). The systems identified when looking at America can be understood as worlding an ecology that goes well beyond any organic model of ecology or environment. Although not the aim, the accounts given here expose the fundamental limits of naturalistic models of understanding environments and ecologies. Moreover, bringing the historicity of the unsustainability of American industry and culture to light exposes a need to totally rewrite all American history (and indeed the history of everywhere else), this not least because of what the narratives of history omit. More significantly, the available metanarratives do not consider the conflictual grounds of world making as the very ground of historical events. It is not an exaggeration to say that more than any other rupture of the grand narratives of teleological history, the exposure of the historicity of unsustainability, as anthropocentrically led defuturing, marks the end of history by showing the need for an absolutely other telling.

American industry and culture, and its globalisation (Americanism), more than any other culture, made the world an image of projection. And then, Americanism, more than any other culture, became implicated as image and object, form and relation, in every other world culture (where is this not the case?). America, in its designing, as it has escaped the confines of place and history, became elemental in the relations of the material, social, cultural and psychic ecologies of the modernised, desiring human being. What its culture and economy activated, as a relation of image, product and felt-to-be-needed futures, was an unmaking of other (often more sustainable) worlds. Countering the recognition of the presence of this particular face of defuturing has been the dominant representation of biocentrically constituted ecological problems and unreconstructed notion of 'environment'. The imaged and felt world in crisis (the world 'to save') transpires to be a concealment of the worlds of crisis.

Americanism has also been complicit with a massive error of ontological Design leadership — it set the example and led the way to the unsustainable like no other mass culture before. What gets celebrated as the success of America is thus exposed as a fundamental failure. There is, however, no subject of condemnation. To try to apportion blame would just lead to that stasis vested in the Judeo-Christian tradition. If a culpability needs identification then let us place it with that unknowing that rests within the foundations of the metaphysical construction of a world making animated by productivist thought. The basic point is not to morally judge but rather to ethically learn. Where condemnation is appropriate is where knowledge of foundational flaws exist and are not acted upon in an attempt to make otherwise (which is the only site of action wherein the learning for an other foundation can arrive).

## AN AUSTRALIAN POSTSCRIPT

Australia is a place of erasure and appropriation. Its pre-colonial past was a world to destroy. (Aboriginal cultures at best have no more than fragments of this lost world: a trace is not a culture.) Its colonial making was first a European affair and then much later an American import.

In the nineteenth century the industrial development of Australia was dominated by the European tradition of industrial craft work, which was organised around the skilled craft worker and fitter. Machines were employed to support this mode of working, rather than to replace it. In terms of the scale of production, in a conventional sense Australia's industrial base worked quite well. It even gave manufacturers a sense that they could actually compete in overseas markets. The prospect of Australia rising as a small but significant industrial nation on the back of its primary industry sector was entertained, and fuelled a certain mood and optimism in the mid-nineteenth century.

By the 1890s the picture, mood and economy had changed. The power of America was becoming clear, the market power of resource appropriation by European, especially British, companies was substantial. The economy became depressed. The rise of mass production technology within leading industrial nations further weakened Australia's position as a proto-industrial power, not least because the small local market meant that the economy of scale of mass production could not be realised, thus capital expenditure was not justified. Equally, ramping up production to compete for overseas markets required getting product unit costs on a par with overseas competitors, while at the same time operating from a far weaker economic platform, with a far less developed and substantial manufacturing infrastructure, and with high transportation costs to market delivery. Equally significant was the afterlife of the mindset of colonialism, as it blocked the possibility of new kinds of relationships. The ethos of mass production did, however, arrive in Australia as outposts of international companies, especially American, and not least Ford and General Motors.

Ford, as a product, arrived in Australia in 1904 (one year after the company was established). Commercially the Model T was imported from 1909. As a result of a corrupt and badly organised distribution system, the Ford company cut off supply and set up their own offices and distribution network in 1925. In the same year they set up a plant in Geelong (although Fordist methods had already been established by a Sydney-based manufacturer of compressors in 1924).[26] General Motors arrived in Australia in 1926 and set up their head office in Melbourne. In the next few years they were to also set up a number of assembly plants around the country, and then in 1931, in the shadow on the depression, they were to take over Holden.[27]

What is interesting, from the perspective of proto-ecological sustain-ability, is that Australia had, in its modernised industrial craft sector, partly developed the driver of an environmentally low impact economy without ever realising it.[28] How is it possible to learn from lessons of the past? Certainly it is clear that we cannot put the past behind us, nor view it nostalgically with added utopian embellishment.

## PRODUCTIVISM AND A HISTORY OF WORLD MAKING

It may appear that a massive shift in focus, concern and analysis is about to occur, but this will be no shift at all, for everything about to be said was already inscribed in what has already been registered.

Our understanding of unsustainability and defuturing rests with reason, function and structure. The making of the modern world stands upon the ground of Western metaphysics, which is a standing upon structure. Structure is a product of a particular kind of projection of mind which produces a certain sense of, and instrumental relation with, 'the world', viewed in terms of function and consequences (hence the notion of 'productivism'). Structure was not discovered, but invented.

While the Western mind finds it so hard to think outside structure, this does not mean that no other way of thinking is possible, but rather that the grip of this way of thinking is extremely powerful and perhaps impossible to fully erase once established. The way the Western mind thinks and its relation to the world of its existence (as it is mediated via specific thoughts and action) has a history. It is suggested here that this history is the history of productivism, which in turn is deeply implicated in the historicity of defuturing.

### PRODUCTIVIST METAPHYSICS

The productivist metaphysic is at the very core of Western metaphysics. It is the transcription from a way of knowing a world by lowering the idea of structure upon it (number, grid, pattern, causal chain and so on). Productivism has been a foundational and deep structure for us that has acted as an ontological meta-designing. As this, it has been the taken-for-granted knowledge of 'a world' that the knowing and making of 'our world' took as given. To be able to see world as structure, to treat it as such, and then make an other world from and as structure, all stood upon a thinking of structure that productivism installed. All other thinking, made other worlds.

To face productivism's impetus towards the defutured requires that we take responsibility for its making as negation, which means taking responsibility for how and what we are, what we do, what we have made as mind and matter, and what this making makes. This includes recognising that modern being both instrumentalises and is instrumentalised. Moreover, the disclosure of the authorial agency of productivism — as a ground for the formation of thought, idea, image, action — considerably undercuts notions of human-centred creation, for while we may be producers we are also products of its Design.

The history of productivist metaphysics turned, to a great extent, upon a movement in how causality was understood and engaged. This marked a shift from concerns with 'what is' to 'what can be'. It thus indicates a passage and extension of metaphysics from knowledge to its becoming a produced ground of Design.

Prior to the shift was the pre-Socratic context. Philosophy before Socrates was concerned with questions of existence (what ontological philosophy calls 'the questions of being'): what the Earth is, how it came into being, what life was/is and how it evolved. Such questions were formed in the founding moment of Western thought, and have remained on its agenda ever since. The very moment when these questions were first asked can be understood as that moment in which the very ground of thinking reflectively on 'what is present' arrived. Embedded in this first thinking are some lines of thought that travelled with time and remain elemental to whatsoever is the latest thinking. For instance, Anaximander's notion of evolution, formed over two and a half thousand years ago, or Parmenides' notions of the disjunction between 'what exists' and 'what is experienced', almost seem uncanny in their contemporary resonances.

However, the post-Socratic context was concerned with how 'what exists' was produced, and how it functioned. Here is the shift: away from the questions of why, and the manner in which, something exists; to questions that foreground the function and operational manner of existence. Modern thought derived from how these later questions were answered, and in so doing many of the other fundamental issues of earlier thought became concealed.

One of the major figures at the point of turning was Pythagoras (who lived about 100 years after Anaximander). Although he wrote nothing, at least nothing that survives, his thinking was extremely influential. His ideas were mostly promoted through a community of learning which he formed. Beyond the contribution that he made to thinking about 'immortality', Pythagoras postulated a theory of numbers which we would now characterise as an atomic theory of structure. This stated that any whole was constituted from an assembly of individual units configured in a particular order, and for him this ranged from music to the universe. For Pythagoras, number was the basis of nature and beauty. Moreover, his notion of harmony, ordering and beauty was taken as the basis of a claim of unity between rational thought and the sacred. While his thinking now seems to fold into the history of mathematics and geometry, it also has to be understood as a dynamic and more general force of productivism. Certainly the addition of Plato's cosmology — which brought structure, aesthetics, the good and function into a transcendental holism — added a very long-lasting and increased impetus to this dynamic.

Productivism functioned projectively to construct the 'nature' of whatever was discovered. It was in fact a designing of how the world appeared. Interpretation, from this contextual moment onward, does not translate the observed into knowledge, but rather knowledge is mobilised, by interpretation, to projectively form the observed, out of which arrives what is known. The idea of structure thus articulates with the idea of order, and thereafter reason, and thus is produced the (designed) ground upon which reason, and reason's others, stood. In this respect 'structure' was a bridge (an *arché*) from the unthought to a thinking that became subordinated to what it helped create (that is, reason). So for us, what was before reason can only arrive via it. To use an analogy: although a foundation is prior to a built structure, that which is built upon it becomes totally incorporated into the logic of the total structure. However, neither the foundation nor the built form are understandable as a structural relation without the idea of structure preceding them.

There is another factor. From the moment of the unfolding of Western thought a particular mode of gaining knowledge dominated: visual observation. Thereafter, knowledge was predicated upon seeing and interpreting the object of sight. The key assumption here was that the 'world' was available simply to see: everything just appeared and knowledge could thus be extracted by engaging appearances in a condition of illumination. Truth and sight were conflated, and became inscribed in our language — 'enlightenment', 'bringing to light', 'shedding light on', 'revelation', 'exposure', 'disclose', 'show up' and so on. Equally, 'I see' became one of the primary metaphors for 'I understand'. The image became the proof, the established fact. In almost all modern discourses, such as the law and medicine, the eyewitness account, the photograph, the x-ray was assured not to lie. Of course, the rise of science was implicated in this history. A great deal of the knowledge of science is based upon observation via the optical magnification or electronic amplification of sight. This modality of gaining knowledge is now naturalised and is thus totally embodied in our being. (This is explored in greater depth in Chapter 7.) A sight-centred (ocularcentric) disposition is therefore now a part of our being. It thus cannot be simply wished, nor thought, away. As the principal means of gaining modern knowledge, technologies of sight, and the represented 'seen', need to be understood as an historically created way of seeing which we take for granted.

From this, it becomes possible to understand how our ways of seeing are deeply implicated in the creation of the modern world, and its 'myopia'. One can get some measure of this by the act of acknowledging that ignorance exists, not just against the backdrop of what we do not know when we encounter the unknown, but against the unquantifiable mass of all that we cannot make appear. What we know is in actuality not predicated upon appearances but upon projections; we make things appear by the presence of what we know: being is presence presented. Sound becomes the viewable sound wave, the landscape becomes the map, atomic structure becomes a three dimensional model, the elements become the symbolic form listed in the periodic table, the digestive system becomes a diagram, God becomes an icon. Such a listing clearly heads off into an uncontainable exercise. The point it makes is to confront us with the vast and unquantifiable void which stands for everything we do not see, or do not transcribe into the visual and its linguistic surrogate.

Representational theory of 'the world' and its objects — as a theory of knowledge of the observed as represented in and by mind (which then get transformed into other symbolic forms) — folds into the analysis being outlined here. What is seen, what appears, is actually the product of projected knowledge. What you see is thus prefigured and limited by what you know. Plato was one of the first thinkers to recognise and state this, insofar as he noted that 'we see with our minds, not our eyes': the mind thus circumscribes seeing and sight. Many issues cluster around these comments, but the one of greatest relevance to our argument is this: how a world is seen is directly implicated in how it is made, unmade and dwelt in.

Why was it that Greeks did not produce a world of technological artefacts?, or alternatively, why was it that modern technology was born out of the Enlightenment, which itself rested on a great deal of Greek thought? These questions give us a number of problems to pose and answer that will advance our understanding of productivism.

One answer to the questions presented by philosophers over

time has been that the Greeks did not develop technology because they failed to create an experimental science and a theory of progress. For all the concern with 'demonstration', as the counter to rhetoric, Greek productivist thought did not deliver a practice of applied science. For this humanity, en route to enlightenment, had to wait for the physics of Copernicus, Galileo, Newton and others, and the idea of utopian progress as delivered by Francis Bacon. Once productivism shifted from mainly being a way of knowing to becoming a basis of making, the 'world' became an instrumentalised structure.

What this moment registers then was the arrival of a way of seeing (reason), which saw the world as a structure of many structures, which could be exposed (by science) and employed (via an economy) as a standing reserve (an inventory) to build other worlds and other futures (design). The historicity of productivism is therefore able to be narrated as the history of the end of 'nature' and the birth of defuturing by anthropocentric beings installing a causal trajectory, still in play, that constituted knowledge, unknowingly, to displace the given world with constructed worlds. This was a one-sided ability: a great deal of knowledge was gained on creation and making, while very little knowledge was acquired on concomitant destruction and unmaking. What the Enlightenment marked was the major development and acceleration of the forms and forces of change in flight. This moment gave rise to world making as a proto-universal system, underpinned by a theory of world construction able to inform processes of fabrication.

As indicated, in the course of the coming of the Enlightenment, productivism moved from being just an epistemology to becoming a theory of production. Technology arrived, and was made possible, by this way of thinking as it brought a particular view of the world into focus as a picture to change. The anthropocentric character of productivism was manifest in a world making — projected variously in time as enlightened, modernising, advanced, civilising — which centred human being in ways which led to a thinking that installed a conceptual separation between human life (and 'human nature') and 'the world of nature': all worlds were rendered the dominion of man. Thereafter, 'the natural world' became a site of resources for human needs and an object of sought control. But, as suggested, action was not informed by a comprehension of consequences. That human beings live in ignorance ever became obscured by the one-sided generation of knowledge and by an arrogance that erased important things learnt. Technocentric civilisation is barely aware of its forgetting and abuse of the wisdom of the ancients.

Science was posited by the Enlightenment as the means to bring truth: a truth based upon, and a construction of, an ocularcentrically observational — and therefore enlightened — subject who was able to bring the fact, and meaning, of structure 'to light'. This subject lacked, and still lacks, a critical knowledge of what is critical. One can ask, for example, what does 'natural science' know of the soul, or, while these sciences can cite Aristotle as a founding figure, how many of their community recognise that in certain vital respects some of the most important things Aristotle knew are yet to be discovered (the issue being the quality of Aristotles thought rather than his proto-science).

We might note that structure and system, the turning of disorder into order in operation in fact, presumed the presence of design. For the Greeks we find reference to *eidos*, meaning shape or form. The concept travelled into modernity as, for example, plan, style, *Gestalt*. It could be said that productivism led from thinking the world as structured product to a prefigurative model, in which making was predicated upon a structural fabrication of elements or components, ultimately leading the making of the product world we are so familiar with. Here is the trajectory which created the synthetic ecology that ever breaks down the opposition between natural and artificial. We live in an ecological fusion and confusion: this is our world; it is a world resulting from the consequences of structural designing; a world we continually visualise, but which we are still almost totally unable to see as unsustainable. This means we, as well as what we make, defuture.

Productivist thinking was transported by *logos*: as reason, logic and sensibility within structurally inscribed modes of thinking, acting and speaking. What all of this implies is that being born into, and formed within, Western culture meant being born into its *logos*. Hence we reason, and even seek to explore, unreason from the given ground of reason. Language, image and making sense of the world are thus actual productions that produce a world as a perception, designed prefiguration, instrumental form and lived environment. De facto, *logos* naturalises constructed thought. Therefore to be able to rationalise is to live with reason as a given condition of thinking — thinking that makes sense and judges non-sense as an auto-reflexive reflection. Again there is a need to re-affirm: 'we' cannot think without reason, for it is with reason that we think everything we think. Everything other than reason thus exists on the grounds of a referential relation to reason, which means that reason, once you have it, constitutes the point of view and seat of judgment of thinking the value and validity of all other thinking. All the questions we might have, our very notion of mind, thus come out of this enframing — its *logos* stamps the form of thought: it is both frame, statement and appearance.

The *logos* of *logos* implies that there was and is no universal mind, while the project of the combined forms of modernity — the exercise of Eurocentrism — was precisely to create this universal condition. It follows that Eurocentric thought was also *logos*-centric — the place from which the world or universe was constructed was a place where the mode of observation prefigured the object of observation, not least by its system and structure of classification. Its universalism was blind to difference. That it was possible to create a being-in-the-world without reason was beyond the cognitive scope of the rational mind. Cultural difference, as it arrives in its trivialised populist forms of expression, seriously fails to recognise this, not least because 'man' is an invented discourse of reason.

* * *

In summary: post-Socratic Greek thought set the stage for the formation of the questions that were to become the principal concerns of Western knowledge, especially in terms of philosophy, science and technology. In each case the proposition of structure was employed in order to invent the problems, methods and solutions of the field of knowledge. Such a lineage of instrumentalised thought returns us to the ascent of America and the American pragmatic tradition. This latter day tradition is important to embrace in its full ambiguity: it certainly assisted the means of making unsustainable worlds. However, it also carries a philosophy that thinks conjunctural problems contingently. It is thus a thinking, if fused with the imperative to learn sustain-ability, that is capable of thinking otherwise.[29]

Equally, and leaping to the present, the post-structural thus arrives not without structure, for the very recognition of the invention of structure means that truth is always bound to the structure that constitutes its ground of knowing. Moreover, language structures what we know and thus folds back into *logos*. In this context, post-structuralism arrives as a questioning and a contestation of the structures of structure: it rests on the indeterminate line between the given and the constructed, world and image, language and subject, being and non-being.

Finally we must note in this account (which has sought to make a point rather than tell the full, long and complex story) that at almost the same time as Western metaphysics were in formation in Greece a philosophical tradition was being established in China. This tradition cannot be simply designated as culturally different from the world views constituted in the West, which of course it was. What the example of Confucianism points to is a totally different cosmology that in turn produced a totally different world and disposition towards the cosmological.[30] In other words, a different metaphysics constituted a different being-of- and being-in-the-world. While each metaphysic may no doubt view its structure as universally authoritative, there is in fact no overall authority, only contests of power (which from the perspective outlined above have been named from the West as modernity). We will, however, return to China at length later.

**NOTES**

1. Antonio Gramsci, *Selections from Prison Notebooks* (ed and trans Quintin Hoare and Geoffrey Nowell Smith), Lawrence and Wishart, London, 1978, pp. 277–316. Interestingly Gramsci quotes a newspaper interview with Luigi Pirandello in the last section of the essay: 'America is swamping us. I think that a new beacon of civilisation has been lit over there. ... The money that runs throught the world is American (?!), and behind the money (?!) runs a way of life and culture.' p. 316.
2. Without making matters any more complex than they already are by starting another long and complex philosophical discussion we should acknowledge that the way 'world' is treated owes a great deal to Martin Heidegger's understanding of world as plural, active (worlding), and as something one has, rather than simply something that just is. See especially, *Being and Time* (trans John Macquarrie and Edward Robinson), Basil Blackwell, London, 1962 and *What is Called Thinking*, (trans J Glenn Gray), Harper and Row, New York, 1968.
3. 'Being here' is a loaded term. It echoes the concept of *dasein* that occupied such a central position in Heidegger's argument in *Being and Time*.
4. What 'futuring' stands for here, as action informed by the deconstructive power of defuturing, is a term elemental to a language we currently just do not have, one that fuses ethics and responsibility as sustain-ability.
5. Carl N Degler, *The Age of Economic Revolution 1876–1900*, Scott, Forman Co., Glenview, 1977, p. 65.
6. See Leo Marx, *The Machine in the Garden*, Oxford University Press, London, 1964, p. 162.
7. *Ibid.*, p. 165.
8. *Ibid.*, p. 185.
9. Thomas P Hughes, *American Genesis: a Century of Invention and Technological Enthusiasm*, Penguin Books, New York, 1989, p. 7.

10 Eric Homberger, *The Penguin Historical Atlas of North America*, Penguin Books/Viking, London, p. 66.
11 In 1840, by which time large farm machines had started to be invented, only 10 per cent of the labour force was in manufacturing. This situation was to start to change dramatically from 1850 onward. See Craig R Littler, *The Development of Labour Process in Capitalist Societies*, Heinemann, London, 1982, p. 161.
12 Degler, *The Age of Economic Revolution*, p. 66.
13 Cited in John Ellis, *The Social History of the Machine Gun*, John Hopkins University Press, Baltimore, 1986, p. 22.
14 Merritt Roe Smith, 'Army Ordnance and the American System of Manufacture, 1815–1861' in Merritt Roe Smith (ed), *Military Enterprise and Technological Change*, MIT Press, Cambridge (Mass), 1985, p. 76.
15 See especially William H Goetzmann, *Army Exploration in the American West*, Yale University Press, New Haven, 1959.
16 Charles F O'Connel Jr., 'The Corps of Engineers and the Rise of Modern Management' in Merritt Roe Smith, *Military Enterprise and Technological Change*, pp. 88–90.
17 Seymore Melman, *The Permanent War Economy*, Simon and Schuster, New York, 1974.
18 For a detailed account of the rise of technical education in America see David F Nobel, 'The Wedding of Science to the Useful Arts I–III', in *America By Design*, Alfred Knopf, New York, pp. 3–49.
19 *Ibid.*, p. 24.
20 Leo Marx, *The Machine in the Garden*, p. 191.
21 For an account of Taylorism see Craig R Littler, *The Development of Labour Process in Capitalist Societies*, Heinemann, London, 1983.
22 See Huw Beynon, *Working for Ford*, EP Publications, Wakefield, 1973; and David Harvey's discussion of Ford in *The Condition of Postmodernity*, Blackwell, Oxford, 1989.
23 Assembly and disassembly methods were used, for example, in the nineteenth century in chain making and in the slaughter and butchering of animals.
24 Cited by John Ellis, *The Social History of the Machine Gun*, p. 16.
25 *Ibid.*, pp. 9–46.
26 Tony Fry, 'A Geography of Power' in Victor Margolin and Richard Buchanan (eds), *The Idea of Design*, MIT Press, Cambridge (Mass), 1995, pp. 213–214.
27 LJ Hartnett as told to John Veitch, *Big Wheels and Little Wheels*, Landsdowne Press, Melbourne, 1964, pp. 59–66.
28 The reinvention of industrial craft, as a basis of more sustainable

production and longer life products, is explored at length in Tony Fry, *Remakings: Ecology, Design, Philosophy*, Envirobook, Sydney, 1994, pp. 79–86.
29 Yet again we note the presence of another project that begs our attention.
30 See David Hall and Roger Ames, *Anticipating China*, State University of New York Press, New York, 1995.

# 3
# DWELLING IN STREAMLINED AMERICA

The building of Fort Loudoun Dam, 1943 (author's collection)

Modernity, in the sum of its differences, tried to make a world in its projected image via the mobilisation of its reified instruments: war, the nation state, political ideology, trade, law, technology, education, culture and more.

Completely entwined in the historicity of this history was the modern social subject as product and producer; as a constructed interiority and an external agent. While we can recognise ourselves as the offspring of this subject (be it via an acknowledged family lineage or as abandoned bastards) we are still only dimly aware of our inheritance. We especially have a problem in confronting the contradictory status and consequence of our modes of existence: we are at once victim and transgressor; colonisers and colonised; world constructors and self-constructions; and sustainers and the unsustainable.

This chapter will focus on more American narratives that inflect defuturing. As will be seen, these narratives circle and occasionally collide. Our starting point is that space where our inner selves and outer being meet — the place we call home. This will lead to a consideration of dwelling, and thereafter how economic and cultural modernity propelled us to dwell more unsustainably. This will be done by looking at a key relational intersections of design, the home, dwelling, modernity and America (again, as somewhere and everywhere). The moment of this intersection was the decade of the 1930s, marked by the birth of a new profession — industrial design — and by the rise of the power of 'style' — which at that time travelled under the banner of 'streamlining'. Nationally, this profession represented a strategic deployment of design against economic depression, but its agency was to become far more than this. What was created in this moment was what we now know as 'consumer society': a socially, culturally and economically propulsive force with such a dynamic that it has transformed human life and the planet itself. Here was a momentary formation of America as that universal utopia which still has an afterlife. With the exception of the industrial revolution, nothing before or since has had such a consequence in bringing about the defutured. The New York World's Fair will be taken as the iconic focus of this moment.

In making judgements about this moment, the intention is not to moralise but to learn to be otherwise: as Mayakovsky said, 'It would be useless making a list of who did what to whom'. Learning to be otherwise means we learn to break a pattern of thought and action that accepts that the more of us there are, the more resources we will squander and waste, the more we will continue to act in ways that damage the environments of our dependency, and the more the possibility of a future is sacrificed to the unsustainable desires that drive our actions in the present. This is not because what we are doing now is 'wrong' but because being otherwise is pragmatically essential to sustain all that we, in our anthropocentric preoccupations, value.

HOME SWEET ... AND SOUR

As we have seen in the industrial development of America, and its leadership in technologically advanced society, the development of design, machines, war and farming all played significant parts in establishing the modern conditions of tension between creation and destruction. Streamlining sped up this dynamic, and made the home a more powerful force of both sustainment and unsustainability, along with these agents of change. Thus before coming to streamlining, how the 'home' is to be viewed requires comment. This is done in terms of 'dwelling'. Although this approach delays encounter it does enable streamlining to be read beyond the limits of a constituted history.

We live the disjuncture between the comfort of the notion of home, and its violence. Modern cultures treat home metaphorically, as the fabricated womb, the place of care, restoration and shelter. It is viewed as a retreat, safe from the vagaries of the world. Home has emerged as that place into which the idea of private space is publicly projected, and wherein individuality is moulded (albeit with the help of mass produced cultural commodities). Home is affirmed as a space, an almost sacred space, in which a secret life and true persona can blossom.

Home can, however, be viewed very differently from the way it appears in economic, socio-cultural or political debate. Understood from the viewpoint of sustain-ability it can appear as a hostile environment, for after the battlefield, the home is in the front line of destruction. Contrary to its aura and image as a shelter from the storm, the domestic domain was and is, from the perspective of a market economy, a vital site of conflict between the forces of supply and demand. In this context, the home can be viewed as that site to which so many other economies of destruction were and are subordinated. The home has thus been turned into a vast sink hole for the continuous supply of goods, information and services, all of which arrive at its front door, while a continual stream of waste departs at its rear. The metabolism of this machine is in contrast to Le Corbusier's modernist 'vision' and 'dictum' of the home as a 'machine for living'.[1]

As the domestic labour debates of modern feminism made clear, home-making became fully implicated in the systems of modern production, as a site in which the workforce was sexually reproduced, physically maintained, and positioned as the purchasers of manufactured goods. Moreover, the home, and the family, was and is an essential element in the creation and operation of the modern subject.[2]

The mechanisation of the household, for instance, became a complex mix of the development of mechanical services, the rise of domestic technologies and the arrival of factory-processed or produced foodstuffs that often required another technology to store or cook (for instance ice cream demands the refrigerator, tinned soup needs a cooker). The impact of these technologies has been profound: mains sewerage systems transformed public health; piped potable water enabled laundry to be done at home, while water heaters changed bathing habits; domestic refrigeration changed the patterns of food marketing, storage and purchasing. In turn, piped gas and then mains electricity created new domestic cultures via the technologies of lighting and cooking. Then there have been all the consequences of the rise of radio, television, video, home computers and a whole host of domestic appliances — vacuum cleaners, sewing machines, washing machines and so on. These technologies were forces that transformed not only the home but the very nature of the fabric of social and community life.[3] In many respects, these technologies worked, and still do, to atomise social life and individualise domestic labour: they altered, and still alter, temporal and spatial existence.

While 'modern rich world consumers' buy a great deal, they only consume a small proportion of whatever they purchase. Although the language of economics calls this activity 'consumption', be it enacted materially or immaterially, the term really is a misnomer. More accurately, the activity identifies an economy of destruction. While its detritus spreads everywhere it centres on one convergent point: the home.

The picture of 'unconsumption' is a familiar one and not hard to conjure up in outline. The economic expenditure of the home feeds a constant stream of 'unconsumed matter' (which may or may not be 'waste') into the black hole of unsustainable capitalism that no amount of cleaner production, environmental standards or ecodesign can sort out. This matter flows to the dump, land fill and incinerator. Old mattresses, busted chairs, the darkened screens of television sets, pots and pans, plastic carrier bags full of packaging, busted heaters, old tyres, cracked plastic buckets, discarded shoes: here is an unending list that writes the concrete poem of the habit of the unsustainable.

Day in day out and year in year out this overt form of unsustainability, the material evidence of unconsumption, amasses. Over time, as this litany of metabolic failures has grown, it has moved from the classification of wasted materials, squandered resources, incidental rubbish and environmental damage, to the more abstract registrations, like greenhouse gas tonnage, toxic waste volumes, and air and water-borne emission levels. Yet there is still little acknowledgement of the very ground upon which the unconsumption of unsustainable living is constructed, not least because Design is not generally acknowledged. This means there is little recognition of negated use value, misformed and misplaced desires, expended sign value, market-manufactured destructive values, and the irrationality of the status of economic growth.

The extreme perspectives outlined above strive to make sense of why dwelling and the home figure so strongly in all the ways of thinking about design, as it has been, or will be. Turning the home from a figure of social inquiry, cultural study and design history into an overt driver of the narrative of unsustain-ability clearly opens up other ways of reading the familiar.

For instance, Henry Ford, with an inchoate sense of the power of design, saw the significance of bringing production, products and the home into a far more managed structure. In this he grasped that, in changing the nature of work, he was also changing the nature of the home. In many ways he relocated the perceived place of the home in everyday American life. He did this first of all through the reduction in the status of 'meaningful' work, by adopting production methods that replaced craft skill with machine function, and by paying high wages for an output of standardised volume rather than for individually crafted product. His second move was to elevate the importance of the link between disposable income and leisure in the worker's life-world — the motor car being the object that absolutely epitomised this link. In this move the home came to be viewed as an increasingly 'meaningful' place to 'make' from purchasable commodities, which were readable as the signs of modern life and its forms of leisure. Ford contributed to making the home an ever more necessary part of the infrastructure of economic and cultural modernity.[4]

He also viewed the home as that place where the social order and the work standards that workers should uphold and live by were maintained. This was based on a morality centring on clean and honest living, hard work, performing one's duty towards one's employer with compliance, not overstepping one's structurally designed social, cultural (racial) and intellectual position, and exercising one's domestic responsibilities to one's family. In a world of mindless work, the home was elevated as a centre of meaning: it was working for one's home and family that brought meaning to life. The home was the place that restored the spirit of the worker, and it was the fear of the loss of the home that ensured that compliance to the will of the employer and the elimination of potential resistance. Here then is why Ford regarded the home as so important and as much a site of worker control as the factory.

## DWELLING AND SUSTAINMENT

We cannot dwell without making a space by clearing. Being is always being-in-action that either creates or destroys animate or inanimate others. We are eternally unsustainable — and yet in the face of a finitudinal moment, to which we have an uncertain determinate relation, we have to perpetually strive for the ability to sustain.

We come to the question of 'dwelling' because we dwell in and by language. Thereafter, thinking follows, from thinking, we build, and in building we dwell. The continual relational folding of one into the other of building, dwelling and thinking, so powerfully articulated by Martin Heidegger, itself folds into Design (a thinking for building that constitutes a dwelling which in turn frames both habitation and the ability to sustain what has been created, or not).[5] As qualification we can say: we dwell in those habits induced through our mode of inculcation (as the imposed instruction of our becoming, these habits appear so naturalised that they are taken to be 'nature'); we dwell in our *habitus*, the locus of our dwelling, in which we can come to understand that the actuality of the temporality and spatiality of our dwelling is indivisibly a material condition, a performative action, a projection and an occupied thinking; and then, we dwell in habitation as relationally elemental to a world (or as Maurice Merleau-Ponty put it, we are 'flesh of the world'[6]).

Dwelling is being fully claimed as inseparable from, and embodied in, making/building and thinking/speaking. Likewise making/building and thinking/speaking are inseparable from, and embodied in, dwelling: it is our fundamental, relational, and constantly turning constructed ecology. As Heidegger tells us 'We attain to dwelling, so it seems, only by means of building'.[7] He goes on to say that while everything we build, 'bridges and hangars, stadiums and power stations … railway stations and highways, dams and market halls' although not 'dwelling places' are in fact 'the domain of our dwelling'.[8] They are part of the made world we inhabit: a world made by hand, machine and mind prefiguratively by design.

Thinking in the shadow of Heidegger, Emmanuel Levinas clarifies the home/dwelling relation by undoing a simple notion of being in a location and the objectification of home:

> for the home, as a building, belongs to a world of objects. But this belonging does not nullify the bearing of the fact that every consideration of objects, and building too, is produced out of a dwelling. Concretely speaking the dwelling is not situated in the objective world, but the objective world is situated by relation to my dwelling.[9]

The weight of the Levinas statement, if fully embraced, totally redesigns our entire thinking and history of Design. Everything returns, everything remakes, every agent is acted upon. Design is thus an integral part of the untold and untellable history of dwelling. Dwelling is thus clearly relational: it is a dependent condition of interconnection and exchange before the subject.

Dwelling can also be seen as being in more than one time. Every thing, being, system, relationality exists in its own temporal register, but is only ever perceived in ours. The standardisation of time, as fixed and accumulative units of a linear measure, works to create a mode of perception that actively reduces our ability to recognise temporal difference. (As an object of ontological designing, the clock can now be viewed as a mechanism that functions to conceal the being of time.) Notwithstanding a familiarity with process (seasons, ageing, tides, life and so on) our induction into time as measurement obstructs an ability to see that everything is transitional and moves at a variable speed. Much which appears unchanging and static to us is simply the product of the relative difference between temporal states. Here scientific knowledge does not translate to recognition. Sustain-ability is not only an ability to make time, it is also an ability to see the time of everything.

Design is always an intervention in dwelling and the dynamic passage of temporal events. It intervenes in the speed and direction of transitions, arrivals and departures of things and their environments. Design for sustain-ability knows this and accepts responsibility for its actions in time. The ability to sustain requires a prefiguration of a yet-to-be to ensure the time of its arrival. (This is an instance of a projection and making of time, rather than classifying or reducing it to the measured.) Making sustain-able is a making, an invention, of time in time.

As we need to constantly remind ourselves, in making a place for ourselves we not only occupy environments but also we create or destroy worlds, relations, ecologies and time. In this respect we do not simply inhabit our bodies, homes, cities, towns and communities, but dwell by and for them as designers and makers of the conditions that design and make us. Our becoming subject, our individualisation, what and how we know, all mask the complexity that exists between our dwelling, our selves, all our others, and our relational embeddedness. The more that we make worlds without a knowledge of what we have done, the less we know. Coming out of the Enlightenment, the agents of modernity have taken us towards the abyss of unknowing. This is what it means to secure the moment while dwelling unsustainability. Put into everyday language: what is now being identified is our ability to design and then create things (mobile phones, plastics, genetically engineered plants, drugs, software programs, chemical plants and so much more) without the faintest idea of where they will lead or what they will cause. This is not a new situation, but rather an old one. It is our tradition: the tradition of a modern culture masquerading myopia as ability; of ignorance; and of the impetus of greed, all directing and designing the unsustainable as economic management. As we have been constantly trying to show, this error has a history. Totalised it is the history of the defutured, while at this specific moment, as we prepare the ground of a historical framing of streamlining, it is a particular vehicle of the transportation of the defutured.

While the significance of destruction has been registered, it needs more recognition. Acts of destruction, like acts of creation, are always either world making or unmaking, sustainable or unsustainable. Here are the confrontations, the options, the pressures and the ethical choices which need to determine, by design, the form of imminent worlds that get made in the concrete actions of everyday life. Here, in these dynamics, are the questions of sustain-ability, as they bleed into dwelling, the 'propensity of objects' and subjects, action and a reflective critical facility of distinction. By implication, rather than asking questions about 'the standard of living' or the 'quality of life', we more basically need to ask and answer 'How shall we dwell?'

THE STATE OF STREAMLINING

As we shall now see, and like much in the history of the modern world, streamlining was a reaction to a crisis. It appeared to deliver a solution to a question of dwelling, but in the end made things worse by failing to grasp its future. Streamlining sped the crisis of the unsustainable.

Streamlining began at the end of the nineteenth century as a study of fluid and aero-dynamics. The aim was to discover how an object could pass through water or air in such a way as to reduce its friction in motion. The word entered the English language just prior to World War I. Common usage took the scientific logic of the term and turned it into a metaphor. The word 'streamlining' thereafter became applied to many circumstances in which the conditions of resistance were rapidly overcome, be they material, economic, organisational or cultural. The term was especially prevalent in writings on hygiene, technology and speed, the modern and America. Streamlining, as a total design regime created in America in the mid-1920s, came out of a particular context.

By 1926 the United States was well on its way to an economic crisis. The vast manufacturing capability of the nation, which had doubled industrial output in a decade, had deposited a huge glut of goods in the market place. The recession had begun, with effects starting to be felt by 1927. Two economic theories competed to explain the problem: one claimed the crisis was over-production and blamed industry; the other asserted the crisis was a result of under-consumption and blamed market underdevelopment.[10] The latter argument won the day.

As far as the rest of the world was concerned, the crisis turned critical in 1929, when the Wall Street stock exchange crashed. In the period 1929–32 industrial production fell by over 60 per cent. Two forces responded to this situation: capital, and the state.

What capital did, with enormous support from the state, was to create a new commodity world of desire. Out of this context industrial design arrived and ascended as a major tool of a modern economy. While industrial design was concerned with individual products, it also gave shape and momentum to a more general aesthetic and synergistic projection of the times by giving a visually thematic form to appearances of the future. The corporations who employed the designers of streamlining were buying the styling of the product, but also an identification with the imaged culture that went along with it. Design, desire and commodities were being combined to forge a path to the future. All of this design innovation of course took place against a backdrop of state-financed works, which themselves extended material projections of the modern as infrastructure and image.

Streamlining, as the adopted aesthetic design regime, was ironically also used to overcome the resistance and friction within an economic crisis. It was used to create a desire for a look of fast moving lifestyles, material objects and structures. It was projected as a primary sign of progress, an unstoppable force speeding up production and consumption. In contrast to the European design movements (discussed in the next chapter), this development was not driven by idealism but rather by immediate economic imperatives.

## THE DESIGNING PROJECTS OF 'THE NEW DEAL'

In 1933 the United States government embarked on a major welfare and reform program — 'The New Deal' — under the direction of President Franklin D Roosevelt after his election in the same year. The aim was to address social pressures, create employment, fund exemplary cultural projects and stimulate the growth of a modern industrial infrastructure. Marshall Berman provides a clear and concise summation of this massive reform and modernisation program:

> Virtually everything serious that was built in the 1930s — bridges, parks, roads, tunnels, dams — was built with federal money, under the

auspices of the great New Deal agencies, the CWA, PWA, CCC, FSA, TVA. These projects were planned around complex and well articulated social goals. First, they were meant to create business, increase consumption and stimulate the private sector. Second, they would put millions of unemployed people back to work, and help purchase social peace. Third, they would speed up, concentrate and modernise the economies of the region in which they were built, from Long Island to Oklahoma. Fourth, they would enlarge the meaning of 'the public', and give symbolic demonstrations of how American life could be enriched both materially and spiritually through the medium of public works. Finally, in their use of exciting new technologies, the great New Deal projects dramatized the promise of a glorious future just emerging over the horizon, a new day not merely for the privileged few but for the people as a whole.[11]

To give more focus we will look at one particular project of The New Deal, and how it was specifically implicated in making a new world of desire. The project is a dramatic example: the Tennessee Valley Authority (TVA) scheme.[12]

The TVA was set up, via a government act, just three months after Roosevelt took office. At this time the TVA was the largest regional planning and modernisation project there had ever been in the United States. It was a massive power generation scheme, to provide a greatly increased volume of electricity for industrial, agricultural and domestic use in many cities across a vast area of rural America. To capture a large market it sold power at a far lower unit cost than other utility companies. The scheme also set out to manage many 'problems' — flood control, soil erosion, afforestation — as well as providing the water to bring large areas of land into productive use.

The enormous scale of the exercise needs to be grasped. At the centre of the scheme was the Tennessee River, which was over 1400 kilometres in length and flowed into the Ohio River just above the point that it joined the massive Mississippi. The Tennessee Valley covered 65,200 square kilometres and spread across that state to Mississippi in the west, Alabama and Georgia to the south, Virginia and North and South Carolina in the east, and Kentucky in the north. The project required the construction of nine dams on the Tennessee, and seven on tributaries (of which four already existed). Additionally four State Parks were created (one, the Booker T Washington Park near Chattanooga, was exclusively for 'blacks'!). Additionally, an anti-malarial health project was started, and a public education program created. The TVA also established chemical laboratories to work on both the extraction of minerals and the production of fertilisers. Besides the construction of the dams there was much other building, including boat docks, housing, factories, civic amenities and tourist facilities.

The organisation of surveying, project administration, energy supply and distribution, planning, engineering, architecture, water management, agricultural reform, conservation (via the Conservation Corps, another significant New Deal project that planted 75 million trees in the region) and leisure management all clearly required the formation of a very large and complex control structure. The entire project was a major demonstration of state-led infrastructure design, architecture and design development.

The TVA project was an enormous generator, not just of power but also of economic activity: by 1942 it had cost US$530 million. It created thousands of jobs, and at pay rates significantly higher than the norm for construction work. The TVA dramatically increased agricultural output, stimulated activity in the building and construction industry, expanded the new industry of tourism and above all else it electrified millions of homes. In doing this it put households in the marketplace for modern electrical appliances, which, in turn stimulated more industrial activity.

With the clear vision of hindsight (and leaving the complexity of the environmental impact of hydroelectric generation, as it transforms river flows, land use, reduces carbon sinks and increases methane emissions, to one side) we can now see that at some point the threshold was crossed from potentially advancing a condition of sustain-ability to establishing a new ground for the unsustainable.

The TVA effectively put in place circumstances which the design regime of streamlining could exploit. It provided the energy, technology, income and cultural space for an expanded world of commodities that brought the habitation of a 'modern American way of life' to many more millions of American citizens. It helped entrench a pattern of unsustainable growth, and not just in the United States. The TVA actually became a national and international icon of the modern.[13]

## STREAMLINING DESIGN[14]

In design's calling up of the field of aero-dynamics, and marketing it as streamlining, one of the most fashionable new technologies of the day was being evoked. All the major universities with engineering departments were researching the topic, all had wind tunnels, all wanted to be at 'the leading edge'. Streamlining meant speed, and speed was the obsession of the day, be it on land, in the air or on water. What started out in the domain of science and technology ended up as image, culture and economy: the look, the style, the commodity of streamlining sold.

The favoured objects were cars, trains, planes and boats, but soon anything was fair game for the streamlined redesign idiom — cameras, electric heaters, fans, cookers, washing machines, refrigerators, radios, telephones, cash registers, scales, table lamps, meat slicers, toasters, toys, cash registers, pencil sharpeners, hats, bras, scales and of course buildings. Streamlined products arrived to form a 'total design' context, they became elements of showroom display, home, office, restaurant, bars and factory interiors and advertising imagery. Never before had the visual environment been so design-managed. (Total design is covered more extensively in Chapter 4.)

Streamlining, and the designers who started it, created to the circumstances and mood of the time. In 1932 Norman Bel Geddes, one of the most influential of all the streamlining designers, in his book *Horizons*, gives a clear indication of this:

> We feel that life is more urgent, complex and discordant than life was before. That may be so. In the perspective of fifty years hence, the historian will detect in the decade 1930–1940 a period of tremendous significance. He will see it as a period of criticism, unrest and dissatisfaction to the point of disillusion — when new aims were being sought and new beginnings were astir. Doubtless he will ponder that, in the midst of a world-wide melancholy owing to an economic depression, a new age dawned with invigorating conceptions and the horizons lifted.
>
> ...We are entering an era which, notably, shall be characterised by design in four specific phases: design in social structures to insure the organisation of people, work, wealth, leisure. Design in machines that shall improve working conditions by eliminating drudgery. Design in all objects of daily use that shall make them economical, durable, convenient, congenial to every one. Design in the arts, painting, sculpture, music, literature, and architecture that shall inspire a new era.[15]

His book captured the imaginations of designers in many parts of the world, and stands for the moment when American industrial designers arrived as a professional body. Rather than having arrived from an educational institutional route, these designers had emerged out of the commercial sector. They stood for a new site of desire, and a form of design leadership, as well as a new profession.

It is important to remember that a certain amount of resistance to European design existed in the United States context into which streamlining arrived. Streamlining thus became regarded as not just a style but as part of an emergent visuality of a modern nation, assisting in the projection of American culture as unique. It in fact was the most recent step in a tradition with a long history. For over 100 years design and architecture in the United States had been caught up in a protracted project of establishing a nation with a culture distinct from its European heritage. Ironically, at the very moment when American culture was asserting itself as having achieved a distinctive form of its own, it was being treated in Europe with scorn. Many of the European progressive 'cultural opinion leaders' regarded the American culture as debased. In architecture, for example, 'American Jazz Modern' was designated as a 'lowbrow' in comparison to the aesthetic purism of the modernism of the European masters. Modernism was of course viewed as contemptible by the establishment's conservatives, but their greatest contempt was reserved for the 'brash, loud and corrupting' qualities of American base and degrading 'popular culture'. Europe's cultural elites, and their sycophants, viewed Hollywood, hot music, chewing gum, big cars, skyscrapers and gangsters as a fundamental threat to human civilisation.

As suggested, the rise of the profession of industrial design needs to be viewed against the backdrop of unemployment and the Depression in the United States. The first generation of these designers drifted into the activity from a variety of mostly artistic occupations. Remarkably the establishment of the streamline phenomenon was the result of the action of just a mere handful of designers. As Meikle notes 'Eventually about fifteen designers emerged as prominent members of the profession. Only four or five developed methods efficient enough and staffs large enough to accept commissions from large corporations.'[16] Without doubt the conceptual leadership of streamlining came from just four men.

Walter Dorwin Teague was a hard-nosed businessman and designer, with 20 years' experience as a 'commercial artist'. His arrival as an industrial designer was the result of a commission from Kodak in 1927 to design two cameras.

Norman Bel Geddes, the most visionary of the group, had, like Teague, an established professional life before becoming an industrial designer. Mostly he worked at designing for the stage, and his entry into industrial design was via the commercialisation of this background. In the mid-1920s he started designing New York shop windows and interiors for major corporations. This was to lead to the circumstances that resulted in his becoming involved in the design of products.

Henry Dreyfuss, being younger and more pragmatic than the others, was the only one of them with a formal art school training. In his brief early professional career he was an assistant to Geddes. He then got a job designing the conversion of theatres into movie houses. However, his reputation as an industrial designer was established as a result of his work designing telephones for the Bell corporation, which he started doing in 1927.

Finally, Raymond Loewy had the most diverse of backgrounds. He was born in Paris, had served in the French army in World War I, but also had some engineering education. In contrast to this history, on coming to America in 1919 he earned his living, and became very wealthy, as a fashion illustrator. His arrival as an industrial designer, prefigured by his reputation as a man of style, was marked by his work redesigning the Gestetner duplicating machine in 1929. (There was a fifth designer of note: Harold Van Doren. However, unlike those above he did not have a located archive, or the weight of published materials, to reify his career.)

In common with the Bauhaus designers, Teague, Geddes, Dreyfuss and Loewy produced themselves textually as much as through their commissioned work. Between them they wrote six influential books and many articles.[17] In addition, a great deal was written about them: in business periodicals like *Business Week* and *Fortune*, to masses of trade and technical journals, as well as in art, architecture and design publications. Even so, one can still ask how men like these got the kind of radical redesign work from some of America's largest companies that they did. The answer given by Meikle, and it sounds feasible, was that these companies were desperate: they had nothing to lose.[18]

Although European Art Deco had a degree of influence in the United States, American designers in general paid little attention to European movements. Bauhaus was not deemed to have much impact on American corporate culture — mainly because Bauhaus products were read as prototype objects made to appear in the style of industrially manufactured goods, and thus were not taken seriously as items actually available to mass produce. However when Bauhaus products did receive comment they were characterised as having been designed by people with a very limited knowledge of industrial systems and processes. The general perception of European design did not however match the views held by the leading streamlining designers.[19]

While many industrial designers were just stylists, the birth of industrial design also marked the arrival of a more comprehensive and complex design approach where function, production, costs, promotion and symbolic form were considered as one integrated operation. The power of the style was to unify diverse products in the temporality of speed, excitement and the marketplace.

To streamline a product was also to cleanline it, enabling it to be projected as a hygienic, efficient, sped up, elegant and fully up-to-date object. Streamlined products thus did not gather dirt, were easy to wipe down, looked good, connoted the new, and formed aesthetic associations with each other. Overriding earlier modernist dictums of 'form following function' and 'truth to materials', these products propelled function into the domain of the symbolic more aggressively than ever before. In doing this they strove to fully realise the economic power of 'sign function' (that is the fact that every product was seen as a sign, in a language of style, which worked in ways additional to the function of product as object). As for materials, these products confronted the question of the 'truth to material' with the indeterminacy of the synthetic. In a conspiracy of the new, streamlined products, more than any before, brought style to the mass market application of alloys and plastics.

What accelerated the passage of these streamlined products had of course nothing to do with their physics but rather with the dynamic of desire fuelling a consumption-led recovery of an industrial economy. The resistance that was negated was that of the market, rather than the elements. The kinetic driver was not a vectorial force, but the lure of a dream.

Conceptually, the space between streamlining, imaginary, dream and product was often very close, for designer and 'consumer' alike. Geddes' 1933 streamliner concept (a massive ocean liner) or his flying wing of 1932 (neither of which materialised), or the streamlined trains of the era, like Dreyfuss's 20th Century Limited of 1938 or Loewy's S-1 Locomotive of 1939, all became major cultural icons. The image, object and rhetoric all constituted the streamline milieu.

By 1934 the craze was in full swing. Purchasing had sped up, the consumer-led recovery was under way. This was the first time a consumption-led path out of a recession had ever been followed. By the start of war in Europe in 1939 the American economic crisis was almost over, if not its social consequences. With the insatiable appetite of war dramatically increasing industrial output, and the demand for labour and then troops, the Depression quickly ended. While streamlining sped up the passage of resources to waste, war overtook the transportation of the finite to destruction.

Streamlining had by 1939 become a very powerful cultural metaphor and economic force. It had became both a collective temporal sign of its place and time, as well as an icon pointing to the future. In short, the nature of consumer society as we now know it had been born and a major lesson had been learned by American capital: design, as the driver of a style regime and a technology, could enable more goods to be produced at a faster rate, bought more often and replaced more frequently. Style, inscribed into a fashion for obsolescence, had given a new spin to the symbolic value of objects.

It would be incorrect to assume that the design style did all of this on its own. Such 'total design regimes' always require a substantial organisational and management structure, which in turn travel with a powerful support facility — market research, technical research and development, high quality engineering, system design and planning, product promotion, advertising and distribution — all of which was ordered within the total system. We also note that the creation of mass credit schemes (hire purchase) appeared, not coincidentally, at the very same moment as streamlining. So at the very moment when modern products came into the marketplace, they also became instantly available to people with a wage, irrespective of their immediate financial circumstances. So all those people in the Tennessee Valley who had their homes electrified suddenly had the means to buy all those new domestic products. They could become instantly modern with products like the Dreyfuss-designed Sears Toperator washing machine of 1933, or his Hoover vacuum cleaner of 1936, or the Loewy-designed Sears Coldspot refrigerator of 1936. The streamlined motor car, the Chrysler Airflow designed by Geddes, was launched in 1934.[20]

In summary: streamlining sped up life, 'consumption', spending, credit, product design changes, and the generation of 'waste'. It gave desire and the sign function of products a far more powerful economic force. In turn, this made modern consumerism a major economic force. More than at any time or any place before, it made the 'culture' of a lifeworld a commodity which could be simply purchased over the counter. From a contemporary perspective on sustain-ability, this moment made materials and products far more complex to manage than just mere matter — and current approaches to recycling have still to recognise the implications of this historical development. (The designing of, and by, an unsustainable economy that symbolically negates 'use value', clearly designs on.) At the centre of this economy is the waste of the unwasted. What we are identifying here is the normalisation of the habits of destructive living whereby less and less of what gets purchased gets used up, exhausted or consumed, and more and more needs become immaterialised. Here is the major issue of unsustainability.

## THE NEW YORK WORLD'S FAIR

Design, the realisation of streamlining, consumerism, and America as 'somewhere' and 'everywhere', all became interwoven as a relation of agency, project, consequence and site. The manifestation of this mix was made a global spectacle when it was projected onto the 'world stage' in the New York World's Fair.

The New York World's Fair of 1939–40 was the streamlined, almost post-Depression, revitalisation of the capital city of utopias. It was very much designed to bring the visitor into a direct confrontation with 'the full-blown Age of Consumerism and the Age of the Machine', and while it was a celebratory event it was equally a project of cultural and political ideology. Although the event was overwhelmingly presented from an American perspective, there were many international exhibitors.

The fair made the city of New York a global focus of economic and cultural modernity as space, place, object, image, work, lifestyle and experience. And more than this, the fair also made New York, and America, an even more vibrant sign of the modern as progress, capital, freedom, pleasure and utopia. This sign was created to be seen from afar, to be an attractor, to be visited, to operationally function, to be architecture, and to make money.

## A DAY IN UTOPIA

The fair arrived as an instructional moment of the modern, projected to a Western world being sucked into war. Its total design provided a counter image to the European futures of fascism or communism. The presented image gathered and celebrated the unlimited potential of consumerist capitalism as a new epoch. Now it looks like the shape of the unsustainable things to come: utopia turned dystopic.

The fair both gathered and demonstrated:

- the economic and cultural multiplicity of both the operationally functional and expressive forms of American modernity
- the projection of the global significance of America to the rest of the world
- the rise of the power of American design, design process and its institutionalisation in both the sphere of technology and in its command of imagination and desire (specifically, American streamlining as an aesthetic regime of a remodernising capitalism and as a manifestation of total design in action)
- the economic power of the sign, managed desire, and utopianism
- the ability of American designers to exercise design control in order to mobilise thematic images to conceal a discontinuous history
- the complexity of the American version of functionalism as techno-system, a design ideology and a model of social structure in process
- and, from a contemporary viewpoint, the spectacular unsustainability of the American path to a future industrial, domestic, rural and urban life.

The New York World's Fair was the biggest world fair the world had ever seen. It was a unique project of representational futurism which, like Bellamy's *Looking Backwards*, adopted a representational trope of turning the future into history. For many Americans coming out of the Depression, the fair brought into view a focal and celebratory moment of the end of hardship. It was a high point of American attainment and hope, and on the back of the industrial and market infrastructure built in the nineteenth century, it was the both the market and the marketing launch of America the global superpower (that fully arrived in the 1950s, after the wartime exercise of a 'military industrial complex' with its ability to manufacture a seemingly endless stream of goods for war).

For all the wonders of previous world fairs, there had never really never been a futurist projection like it, and in large part its impact came from the coherence created by the management of its theme. While made up of various elements, the theme made one collective and visible streamlined statement. In form and content it captured people's imagination: as a design statement it said 'This is what the world is going to be like'. This was expressed in numerous ways, and was certainly evident with the event's opening dedication to 'building the world of tomorrow'.

The fair was conceptualised in the context of streamlining activity and New Deal projects. It was first put forward as an idea in 1935 by Percy Straus, head of Macy's department store; Grover Whalen, an ex-New York police commissioner (who was to become the fair's president); and George McAneny, who was among other things head of the Regional Planning Association. The fair was first conceived of as a celebration of the 150th anniversary of George Washington's inauguration. After a contest between traditionalists and modernist-functionalist interests, the functionalist idea of a 'fair of the future' won the day. The group who overturned the original concept included industrial designer Walter Dorwin Teague, and thinker and urbanist Lewis Mumford.

Ironically, as an event that set new patterns for unsustainability, we note that the fair was built on land reclaimed from a polluted swamp. At the time this was 'the largest single land reclamation project ever undertaken in the Eastern United States'. This work was done under the direction of the most notorious large scale demolisher, planner and builder of parks, expressways and bridges of the epoch, Robert Moses. (As Marshall Berman makes very clear, Moses, the humanist hero of the 1920s and 1930s, had by the 1950s and 1960s became the corrupted, dehumanising, Captain Ahab-like figure who despised the people he once wished to serve.[22]) As the official guidebook of the fair detailed, the land reclamation was done in 1936 by a massive workforce which 'filled in the swamp with six million cubic yards of ash and garbage and shaped two lakes from which a million cubic yards of sludge were taken to become topsoil after chemical treatment'. Two new sewage-treatment plants, and a tide gate to control drainage, were also built.[23] Flushing Creek and Bay, a swamp, garbage and a mass of ash heaps the size of downtown Manhattan (immortalised by Scott Fitzgerald in the Great Gatsby as 'one of the great modern symbols of industrial and human waste'), was turned into the site for the fair and thereafter named Flushing Meadows Park (now of tennis fame).[24]

The future was presented at the fair as the offspring of design, science and technology: a perspective which directly folded into the already acknowledged romantic celebration of science and technology within American culture. The expression of these relations was encapsulated by streamlining: the major thematic aesthetic unifier of the event, which linked the built form of the exhibitions, the content of events, and the many products displayed. Streamlining was equally employed as a metaphor able to express the speed and power of American cultural and economy leadership. This kind of projection had been prefigured by the Century of Progress Exposition in Chicago in 1933, an event created with the material help of large corporations and government. The exposition had already used streamlining as an image of the future, and as an agent of change in the face of depression.

The New York World's Fair was as much a mass media spectacle as it was a place to visit. It was also the most overt statement ever made by America to America about having faith in itself. This faith consolidated a sense of a national ability to image and realise a modernising utopia, while reinforcing America as en route to becoming the undisputed leader of the 'free world'. So while Hitler was setting out to conquer the world by force of arms, America was positioning itself for world domination economically, politically and culturally. The desire to be modern, notwithstanding the chill of the Cold War and the coming of unsustainability fed by televisualised images of modern consumerism, eventually proved to be many times more ideologically powerful than either fascism or Soviet communism. The force of this desire is clearly not fully spent, as contemporary world events still show.

IMAGE

A number of readings are going to be deployed to give a sense of the event, its context and history. These are drawn from *Dawn of a New*

*Day*, a catalogue produced for an exhibition on the World's Fair held at the Queens Museum in New York in 1980.

Under the direction of Grover Whalen, two men were given the task of translating the idea of the fair into an actuality: landscape architect Robert Kohn; and, as already registered, one of the leading industrial designers of the streamline period, Walter Dorwin Teague. It was Teague who was to become the major theoretical director of the event. Francis V O'Conner, writing on Teague and the fair, observes that:

> Teague, and his colleagues insistently rationalized that somehow mankind's future redemption was at hand — through the resurrection of Platonic idealism, by recourse to the more recent theories of Jay Hambridge 'Dynamic Symmetry', via the pragmatic strategies of John Dewey, or by the indiscriminate application of streamlining.... For design is geometry, and geometry is axiomatic ordering, and such planning is the source of certainty and certainty defends us against the imponderables of life.[25]

As O'Conner goes on to note, all of this idealism evaporated in the face of the commercial adoption of streamlining, especially as it was to unfold as the style of planned obsolescence.

As manager of the theme-ing of the Fair, and as a member of the Theme Committee, Teague recruited other industrial designers, Norman Bel Geddes and Raymond Loewy. Streamlined form was thematically adopted as a major aesthetic means to communicate 'the rhythmic pulse and vitality of the new technological age'. The Theme Committee designated seven sectors predicated upon divisions of modern living: production and distribution; transportation; communication and business systems; food; medicine and public health; science and education; and community interests.

The committee brought all of these themes together in three structures: the Perisphere, a globular structure 54 metres (180 feet) in diameter and 18 storeys high; the Trylon, a tower 183 metres (610 feet) high; and the Helicline, a spiralling ramp with a length of 185 metres (950 feet). These made up the elements of the 'theme centre', and the centre of the fair. They were created to make both a statement of verticality, mass and geometry, which echoed the foundations of streamlining, and equally to express the claim to eternal truth of beauty. Teague's hand is evident in the authorship of the structures, not least because he extolled the notion that design was 'geometry made visible' and called up the authority of Socrates, with his view that beauty resulted from geometry and measure. The structures carried another claim, for not only were they placed at the centre of the fair, but centrally in the stage from which the spectacle of the future would unfold. At such a juncture the aesthetics of the reactionary modernism of the Third Reich and the behaviourist modernism of social democracy appeared to converge. This convergence was in large part due to the mutual discovery and management of the spectacle of the crowd. As the August issue of *Architectural Record* put it, despite all the other 'wonders' of the event: 'Yet the greatest discovery in New York was the discovery of the crowd as actor and as decorator of great power. The designer found out that the crowd's greatest pleasure is the crowd.'[26]

Other towers and dome structures were built and there were other featured structures, like the Westinghouse Singing Tower of Light and the Bridge of Tomorrow. However, in giving a sense of the event as a dystopic utopia two major exhibits, Democracity and the Futurama, beg specific comment.

Democracity was a model housed in the Perisphere to represent the idea of the 'world of tomorrow'. Designed by Henry Dreyfuss, it was presented as the representation of a perfectly planned community of the future. It adopted a regional scale made up of a monocultural suburban sprawl of new cities, which were linked by expressways. Anything the planners disliked — dirty industry, social underclasses, historical and cultural difference — was just edited out. Here utopian perfection was projected as that banality which has stamped so much of suburbia worldwide over the last fifty years or more. (Reinforcement of social democratic modernist lifestyle also came from other more general quarters, not least the promotion of a uniformly high standard of living as the utopian norm.) What Democracity managed to do was to enfold all the fair's sterile ideas on culture and society.

Futurama, also a model, was regarded as being far more dynamic. It was designed by Norman Bel Geddes, constructed in the General Motors building and was 'enormously popular'. It presented a city that seemed to result from the combined design forces of Robert Moses and Le Corbusier. It was a tower-block 'city of tomorrow' (posited as 1960) with parklands and interlaced expressways that fed into the city road system on a lower level. Above this, a higher-level system of superhighways took the traveller over the top of the city. Once on these superhighways cars were able to be managed into radio-controlled trains, thereby leaving the driver free to relax with a good book, newspaper or packed lunch. There were also, of course, streamlined cars. The Futurama was a developer's and car maker's wildest dream come true.

The Futurama was viewed by the public as a realistic and, for many, desirable picture of things to come, and it was regarded as the hit of the fair. That a utopian, progressive and desirable perception of it was able to be created stands as evidence of the success of 'humaneering' (the mobilisation of image-constructed new desires to drive demands for the new). From a contemporary viewpoint it clearly looks like a figure of monumental unsustainability. Moreover, and more generally, it indicates the power of the defutured that economic and cultural modernity gained in packaging its technocentric dystopic utopia to an international audience.

Finally, the fair established the presence of the rising power of corporate culture with organisations like General Motors, General Electric, Westinghouse, AT&T, Ford, DuPont, National Cash Registers, Firestone, Heinz foods, RCA, and Bell Telephones, the glass industries, and the United States steel corporations all represented.

Looking back we can see both the glamour and the horror; the creative outpouring and the myopia. The event was a remarkable statement with a coherence that few World's Fairs have matched. Unfortunately, what it served was the psycho-culturally concealed mass destruction that characterises the unsustainable. The words of the fair's secretary, Michael Hare, now read almost prophetically:

> The world is in chaos struggling to master its own invention. We are in danger of being annihilated by forces we ourselves set up. The world calls for answers to this problem of mastering our own inventions and we propose 1939 to contribute to that answer.[27]

The theme, the 'total design', while setting out to manage and project an overall aesthetic of a spectacle of economic and cultural modernity — lifestyles, objects, systems and lifeworld appearances — did not assume the agency by aesthetic means alone. Neither did the event operate with a crude technological determinism (although as we have seen a considerable investment was made in the power of Platonic order, and efficiency was equally given a good deal of transformative potential). Rather the basic proposition was that exposure to the fair would produce behavioural changes. In this context, the agency in which the fair planners posited most faith was the power of the event to present itself as the culture of destiny. This was made possible by aesthetics mobilised with skill (a strategy of signs of the material forms of technologies, products, built structures and urban environments, as well as of narratives and images) and by an experiential exposure to forms and technologies presented as if they actually represented the future. This entire enterprise was informed in its creation and operation by sociological, anthropological and aesthetic expertise. The belief was that as culture shaped everyday life, so if you wanted to reshape the culture of everyday life then you reshaped the signs and forms of material culture. In a technocentric scientific culture, behaviourism was a powerful co-opted tool for change. (In this context, it is perhaps not surprising to discover that one of the new cultural, behavioural and world view-changing technologies unveiled to the American public at the fair was television.)

We can also note that the relation between science, cultural and social inquiry had a long history in America reaching back into the nineteenth century, in particular, in the quest to understand modern life and how the city functioned. This tradition centred on a number of institutions, not least the Chicago School which was linked to some of the most prominent anthropologists of the century (like Ruth Benedict, Margaret Mead, and Robert and Helen Lynd).

The positivist sociological position, coming out of this history and employed in the service of the fair, believed that behaviour could be changed by education and by 'humaneering'. What this actually meant was 'consumer conditioning' by the application of psychological manipulation. This activity had been instigated by an ex-university professor, John B Watson, the founder of American behaviourism, who was on the staff of the advertising agency J Walter Thompson. Watson:

> had set out to codify 'the laws of human reactions' of 'Mr and Mrs Consumer' as if they were mice or pigeons in a laboratory. The Fair was a carefully contrived conditioning experiment (Germany was another, at that time) and few among the multitudes entering its gates were ready in 1939/40 — or subsequently — to 'psyche out' the reasons they suddenly yearned for television sets, superhighways, foreign foods, and a streamlined life, or believed political and wartime propaganda.[28]

Besides all of this being part of the effort to induct consumers into consumerism as a consensual position, it also aspired to address and resolve culturally and economically uneven development — or as it was put at the time 'cultural lag'. The issue of the 'lag' was based on a perception that the advance of modernisation meant that different people in different places in different circumstances were 'developing' at different speeds. (This is in contrast to the realisation that time, 'as the same moment', cannot necessarily be assumed as a commonality.) The notion of cultural lag was to inform not only a perception of national cultural difference but an entire post-war project of American leadership in global modernisation. The 'modern' was taken to be a moment of universal time, with some peoples and cultures being slow to 'develop', and others fast. The aim therefore was to bring everyone to the same moment. The only event that contingently, and with violence, had ever managed this was war.

The cultural interventionism of America in ending the 'lag' was externalised as the foreign policy of modernisation. It travelled under the name of 'development' and later co-opted the formative moment of the United Nations. For several decades within the United States, the concern for 'lag' was directed towards the power of the home. Again there is evidence in the focus given to the home at the World's Fair. The home was unquestionably made a target of utopian and unsustainable political, cultural and economic modernity:

> To Fair planners, a home was not just a house. It was a demonstration of the impact of technology on the most mundane aspect of human behaviour; it contributed to the definition of a new American culture adapted to the machine world.[29]

Machines in the home were claimed as one of the means for creating an 'organic unity' (a relocated version of the synthesis of nature and machine). From this perspective, standardisation (of machines, products, work, suburbs and even living) was also regarded as the foundation upon which democracy could be built. Machines were the deemed means to create equality. The technological rationalisation of the home was not, however, just confined to mechanical and electrical technologies. As the guide to the fair pointed out 'the acceptance of and demand for domestic appliances exceeded expectation, and "Better living through chemistry" became a hallmark of American life'.[30]

As a result of the fair, the more insightful industrial designers started to recognise that commercially exercised design was becoming a far more overt directive cultural and economic force of life. This was becoming apparent through its presence in cultural and social structures, technologies, products, market development, corporate expansion and imaged appearances.[31]

As well as television, another future-shaping technology appeared in the home at the fair — the robot. Although the spaces both these technologies now occupy have become naturalised, this was not without contestation. Television in both Russia and Germany was initially viewed as a public, not a private, medium. Equally, the robot still hovers between the domestic and the industrial.

While technology and culture became fused in the making of modern America, the fair was a major celebration and ideological extension of this trajectory. More than at any time before, this was the moment when machines, metaphysics, values, capital, industry and lifestyle arrived together as a recognised designing lifeworld (a 'building, dwelling and thinking'). So it was that in this very same moment the home fully appeared, in its concealed unconcealment, as a primary machine of unsustainability, and as that contradictory space of care and destruction. The home had taken on its late-modern consumerist mantle: the establishment of a culture, from then onwards a dwelling, of unsustainability was well underway. Unsustainability is again not simply posed here as a biophysical condition, for also it started to emerge as a loss of attachment, belonging, belief and of community.

In the wake of this unsustainability, 'building' now means remaking a home in 'a' world, where home is not house but attachment, responsibility and a security of being. Home-making means building with what is to hand, while confronting the losses of what has failed to be sustained as well as one's complete homelessness. It means finding a way to enable the arrival of the possibility of dwelling. This equally involves a thinking in order to rebuild, which in turn requires action for the accommodation of others. All of this demands a recognition of a diversity in order to dwell, and gaining an ability to learn what to destroy and what to create (the essence of sustain-ability). This is a learning of Design, a thinking embodied in both the act of prefiguration and in the act of construction. Design is both elemental to, and a consequence of, thinking. Design is essential for our dwelling — there is nowhere where we do not now live by Design. Thinking which has the ability to sustain also has to have the insight to see what has been designed and what the design imperatives are.

The lesson of streamlining reveals the significant links between design, production, unconsumption, waste, aerodynamically inspired speed, aesthetics, the destruction of the battlefield, and the destruction of the home. It instructs on unmaking and a remaking, as such it is about now, not then.

## UTOPIA: A DESIGNING IDEA

As we have seen with the New York World's Fair, the making of the modern world was driven by utopian dreams of a future. This disposition toward the future and the power of dream has been present from the very inception of the Enlightenment-inspired modernist project and its dream of one world and one subject — the modern. Even after the 500-year degeneration from grand utopian visions of 'other worlds' to the paucity of the futures of Coca Cola advertisements and McDonald's fantasies, there is a continuum of utopian dreams which act to defuture.

Utopianism was not only at the core of the dream of the Enlightenment, the Idea of the human, and all the instruments of modernity, but also at the base of the materialised forms of modern institutions and in the designing of modern images, objects and structures. It underpinned the idealism of modernity's causes, and rested in the hopes of created cultures. The idea of utopia became uncontainably pervasive and finally, like modernity itself, beyond narrativisation. Yet the need to confront the idea of utopia, for all the problems that it entails, remains — because of the consequences of its structural idealism and the counter productivity of its powers of disarticulation.

Utopias effectively cut the idea adrift, they de-relationalise and they refuse process in process: utopias impose the myopia of an unreflective relation to the process of change. In their drive to build on a cleared material and metaphysical ground, they invite violence. Historically, utopian grand schemes reveal themselves as directional impositions that have functioned without ecological accountability. Utopias are crisis in the crisis of crisis: they construct images and desires that obstruct what demands to be seen, heard, felt, understood, critically selected and conserved.

To critically confront utopianism is to place oneself before oneself with a recognition of the imperative to act with responsibility, which is acting on the basis of making sustain-ability. The point made here is not directed towards trying to find a way through that vast, complex, under-theorised and confused topic named utopia but more than anything else to register the fact that the modernised subject is a utopian-being-in-the-world. While it is still possible to dream at the end of modernity's (the Enlightenment's or humanism's) hegemonic moment, we now face our dreams with questions, not least how to not become absolute victims of unsustainable desires. Again, they are pragmatic, rather than a moral, questions.

Utopia, writ large or small, is the projected realisation of gratified desire as a temporal continuum (it is living the dream). It is the final point of arrival, the 'end point' without finitude. It is everywhere where we are — it is the space we occupy, the imagery we dwell in, often the life we live, it is that dreamtime we think we are venturing toward, it is a place where we hide, it is hope. Distance, distrust and a critique need to be put between sustain-ability and utopianism. Such has been the proliferation and spectral degeneration of utopias that every identification is an abstraction that works to conceals the scale, complexity and variety of the kinds universe they once stood for.

The idea of one world, one being, and one knowing bonded utopianism to the instrumental realisation of productivism (in the name of progress and with the power of science and technology). In this union, reason fell to unreason in the quest for an unbounded and eternal cornucopian paradise on Earth for enlightened perfected beings. We now clearly live in the detritus of the failed utopian project — we can call this condition unsustainability, postmodernity, pluralist liberal democracy, or any of a myriad of other nominated terms.

REVIEWING THE IDEA OF UTOPIA

In the neo-nuclear age (that is the age of weapons in abundance combined with an uncertainty of targets) and in the age of the crisis of crisis, the survival of humanity itself can seem a deflection from a destiny of disappearance, and thus survival itself becomes a utopian notion. Living in the recoil from the prospect of destruction, living without hope, with the recognition of the meaninglessness of life and without the courage or energy to make it meaningful, produces what Christopher Lasch calls (in his book of the same name) 'a withdrawal into the minimal self'. One example of this is treating the domestic as if it were the actual 'shelter in the storm' of the world.

Of course modern culture has always constructed such fictitious spaces. There is a long history of introspective, private and romantic imaginaries in the visual arts and literature which constitute implicit utopias. Consider, for instance Franc Marc's images of an idyllic animal world prior to the human, or Piet Mondrian's formalism expressed as ordered space that excluded any possibility for disorder, or the other-worldliness of Vassily Kandinsky's expressive abstraction. Conversely there were quite different and explicitly stated utopias, such as William Morris's *News from Nowhere*, and HG Well's *Modern Utopia* — both of which presented conditions of full social, political and economic resolution. Wells gives us a flavour of such thinking: 'Our business here is to be utopian, to make vivid and credible if we can, first this facet and then that, of an imaginary whole and happy world'.[32]

Design is of course totally implicated in the story of utopias. At it simplest, a great deal of the institutionalised practice of design has been concerned with the creation of both modest and grand exemplary forms — typeforms. Frequently a singular object or environment is claimed to represent an element of an ideal and a coming whole — the example of the New York World's Fair evidences this writ large.

Against the backdrop of design's place in the story of utopias, it is by no accident that it has been in America that utopianism found its most powerful expressive forms. America the New World, America the dream, America the hope of the future — all these characterisations, as we shall see, figure importantly in the history of modern utopian thought and its representational manifestations.

No matter what brings us to a critique of utopias and utopianism, or how it is undertaken, one fundamental issue arrives: how can forms of the future be talked of without them prefiguring actions that negate their conditions of possibility? Superficially the problem appears to be one of the desire for the new not being able to give value to what needs to be recovered or conserved. However, it is more complex than this. Firstly, because of the teleological inscription that utopian thought carries, the future is always posited as empty and waiting to be filled, either by the new or by a retrieval from the past. Secondly, because the exemplary — irrespective of its source — is always inflated as an idealised figure that is symbolically made to stand for something it is not (for instance the heavenly city on Earth). Effectively such idealisations negate the remaking of that which needs to return as 'the same'.

A more current critique of utopian thought has of course been put forward by 'deconstructive postmodernism', specifically in terms of the violence of logocentric authority. However, this critique has as yet to come to grips with those contemporary imperatives that still stand upon the unaddressed anthropocentric foundations of Western thought. These fundamental foundations still stand unshaken, and what they structurally continue to design remains in concealment. In this context we can see the return of the same as the unsustainable. At its simplest, this is illustrated by the way science is so often employed to define and supposedly solve the problems of sustainability, whereas, in this situation, science's actual ability to gain any real agency to produce fundamental change would rest with an ability to re-manufacture knowledge and practice on a reconstructed ground able to define problems otherwise.

Modernisation was always predicated upon projected goals (a modern economy, state, society, subjectivity, city, culture and so on) which arrived as promised destinations with assured results (liberation, happiness, function, wealth and so on). These goals displaced other ways in which the future could be thought of by the unmodernised. Below the surface of utopian appearances was an imposed logic that repressed, devalued, displaced or erased any non-Western imaginaries. Progress and violence, the unreason of Reason, were inseparably linked. The imposed dream of knowing 'the world' as a functioning system became totally implicated in making 'a world' function according to a dream of progressive control. Marxism, for instance, posited freedom — defined as liberation from the exploitation of labour and the authoritarianism of the state — as being finally realised in a fully fledged totally functioning communist society. Here was a perfected common end point, an objective to be realised, via *telos* of evolutionary forces which, the political ideology claimed, human society was evolving toward. Propelled by a transcendental force of history (the class struggle), everyone was placed at a particular stage of development en route to eventual freedom. Equally, capitalism projected its idealisations in various forms, moments and locations. Its utopian goal is the 'absolute freedom' of an unfettered market and the complete sovereignty of the individual. At the same time, these supposedly totally different ideologies often employed the same means to realise what were claimed as different ends. For instance, both capitalism and Soviet communism used the productivist ideas and methods of FW Taylor and Henry Ford to manage and organise industrial production. Equally, both used the iconography of the production line and scientific management as signs of progress.

Reason's implication in the unreason of the idea of utopia and utopian ideas was most powerfully mobilised in the embodied form and metaphor of the machine. We see this in a lineage from Francis Bacon's early writings in the seventeenth century on mankind's effort to subordinate nature by science; in Karl Marx's ideas in the nineteenth century of positing a *logos* with the forces of production; right through to the present when a faith in the ability of science and technology to deliver the solutions to the environmental problems the world faces still dominates. Clearly such naive utopianism neither recognises the history of science and technology (and by implication, Design) in the creation of so many of the environmental problems (let alone those of sustain-ability) in the first place. At a more complex level, the marriage of Reason and utopia has never made present and addressed the ontological consequences of being-with-the-world designing of science and technology.

Kirshan Kumar uses the overblown language of Leon Trotsky to sum up an entire range of such utopian thinking from Bacon to Marx. Trotsky's writing in *Literature and Revolution*, and cited by Kumar, manifests not only a continuous faith in technology and Reason but also a condition of absolute uncritical non-reflection. This fragment is indicative of a poverty of thought and rhetoric that is symptomatically found across the entire history of modernist design, its projects and modernisation in general — here is the spirit of the Russian Revolution, the New Deal's and the architecture of Le Corbusier:

> The new man, who is only now beginning to plan and realize himself will ... through the machine ... command nature in its entirety... He will point out places for mountains and passes. He will change the course of rivers, and he will lay down rules for the oceans ... The machine is not in opposition to the earth. The machine is the instrument of modern man in every field of life.

> The shell of life will hardly have time to form before it will burst open again under the pressure of new technical and cultural inventions and achievements.[33]

While this kind of prose may now seem shallow and misguided it should be remembered that it spoke of a future with agency, and faith in progress, and a future where technology was a trans-political ideology, and, usually in specific circumstances, had real power and directed action.

People died as martyrs, soldiers and accident victims for these kinds of words. Utopias seduce, they inspire hope, they provide a blinding vision, they motivate, they misguide, misdirect and obscure. They place people continually before and alongside who, what and where they would rather be. As a result they displace human beings from being here, and dwelling in that place which is essential to sustain.

## HISTOPIAS

A distinction needs to be made between the articulation of a specific utopia, and utopian thinking. Marx, for instance, steadfastly refused to elaborate a visualisation of ideal communities of the future. His thinking was thought to be profoundly utopian and in its formative stages drew on the utopian visions of nascent socialism, in particular those of Saint-Simon, Robert Owen and Charles Fournier. The fundamental thesis that most stridently expressed the utopian idealism that Marx later sought to erase was, of course, the *Communist Manifesto*, which he authored in German with Freidrich Engles and which was first published in London in 1848.[34] In this tract he attacks the early socialists, not so much for being utopian, but because of the limited sub-cultural scope of their visions.[35] What they lacked was the realisation that socialism could only arrive through the momentum of an entire class on the move. In contrast, he and Engles had a vision powered by a faith of the available impetus of the evolutionary developmental force of the proletariat: the united workers of the world could end the class struggle and thus end history in an end point of the society of free association of the withered state. All of this was resonant with Darwinism and a Hegelian teleological theory of history: history had a destination — communism — and the evolution of modes of production, assisted by class struggle, would transport humanity to this place.

At this point it is perhaps worth putting a little more flesh on the history of utopianism and utopias. In Classical thought the future was not contemplated in terms of an evolutionary dynamic: the object of longing was characterised as an Arcadia, a Golden Age. This modality of utopia rode on a naturalism based on a formal social hierarchy that was economically static (a condition of 'nature', of a permanent good life). Backloading the idea of utopias, we see how the ideal was employed normatively as the proper order of things. We can see, for example, Plato's *Republic* as a contemplative object and as the projection of a standard of judgement for a future based on forces already in play, especially in terms of the roles and relations of the philosopher and statesman, and of ethics and politics.[36] This kind of utopianism, rather than being a disengaged and programmatic specification — a master plan of how things ought to be — carries a more grounded claim.

Although prefigured in the dreams of ancient societies and by the communist aspirations of early Christians, the idea of a utopia became forcibly present at the very birth of the Enlightenment. We can register the moment when the word 'utopia' was first coined by Sir Thomas More, as the title of his book of 1516.[37] More invented the word by combining elements of two Greek words: *eutopus* (good place) and *outopus* (no place). Thus utopia is a good place that is a no-place. This, in effect, gives utopia the status of an exemplary fiction. More in fact posited a great deal of faith in the power of fiction as the mechanism that can capture and inspire imaginations. His aim, in his own words, was to 'smear the truth with honey'. Rather than present a program, plan or policy which can deliver a future out of the conditions of the present, the fiction of a utopia presents a world in which the ideal is the actuality. In doing this his primary aim was to rework and usurp Plato's *Republic*. As he said in the lines of a poem which accompanied the manuscript to its first reader, Peter Gilles, chief secretary of Antwerp, in 1516:

> Plato's *Republic* now I claim
> To match,or beat at its own game

More's fiction of the future pronounces its modernity, and prefigures modernity itself, through the employment of the voice of Reason. Reason is that which is given the power to direct the material form and social conditions of futuring the future of 'the future' by enabling an enlightened being to act. More's utopia was 'a pagan state founded on reason and philosophy'. What More projected now reads as a bizarre mixture of the prophetic and the absurd — as an extract of Kumar's summary illustrates:

> All the fifty-four cities of Utopia are built on the same plan.All private houses are exactly the same:the doors have no locks,and 'who will go in, for there is nothing within the houses that is private or any man's own.' The Utopians change their houses by lot every ten years, to prevent feelings of possessiveness developing. On the farms, which are

uniformly organised, and based on rational and efficient patterns of work,chickens are hatched not by the hens but by incubators.Men and Women see each other naked before deciding to marry, the Utopian not distaining the importance of physical attributes, since 'the endowments of the body cause the virtues of the mind more to be esteemed and regarded, yea, even in the marriage of wise men'. Divorce is permitted, and euthanasia practiced, again on the grounds of allowing the lesser evil. Several crimes are punished not by death but by bondage; 'for that they suppose to be to the offenders no less grief, and to the commonwealth more profit, than if they should hastily put them to death, and so to make them quite out of the way. For there cometh more profit from their labour than their death, and by their example they fear others the longer from like offences.' It is something of the same canny and combative spirit that, having abolished money, the Utopians use gold and silver that they get through trade to make chamberpots and prisoners chains,thereby showing their contempt for these useless metals while at the same time constantly reminding themselves of the folly of those other nations in worshipping them.[38]

While markedly different from Plato's *Republic,* and inflected by his times, More's exposition, in common with it and a multitude of other utopias, adopts a high idealism. Besides showing this in his account of the functioning of a patriarchal social order and an economy of common wealth — a sort of naive communism — the view is presented in large part through the ideal city. Planning and the city are adopted as significant means to present the operational systems of the ideal future. This moment of the figuration of the agency utopianism contributed to its becoming almost intrinsic to architectural thinking, in and well beyond the architectural profession, both in the past and present. Architecture always totalises its agency as something 'greater than' form: buildings are regarded as elements of something more than themselves. They are constituted and perceived as the building blocks of the city, tradition, the urban environment, the modern, heritage, or of the social fabric.

In this context, utopian thinking, both ancient and modern, shares the premise that human perfectibility is possible in perfected conditions. From such a perspective, the history of architecture and design appears littered with the wreckage of broken dreams, evidenced by the failed determinate powers of supposedly perfected, made objects, structures or spaces to deliver perfection, not least because of the Platonic reduction of perfection to aesthetic form and the fetishisation of the object thereafter. Design, in this context, rather than enabling sustain-ability, becomes an instrument of stasis: the desire for the perfected 'timeless object' is a desire against change.

Returning to our brief review: Francis Bacon, in his utopian fiction of the discovery of an island of 'an advanced' civilisation called *New Atlantis*, took the trajectory of More's *Utopia* one step further into modernity, by adding an overriding faith in science as the agency that would deliver the ideal future in which nature would be commanded. Bacon wrote this small book late in his career (1623–24),[39] and out of the position established in his major works, specifically his system of thought summed up in his *Novum Organum* of 1620. In this he argued that reason needed to became re-aligned from a post-Aristotelian syllogistic logic to the application of the *novum organum* — the new instrument of exposing the causal 'laws of nature' by empirical observation, in order to intervene in them and to command them.[40]

In Bacon's faith in science as the path to 'true' knowledge, and in his utopian celebration, we find two of the most directive designing ideas of modernity, two ideas which still have material force and exercise enormous power. The attachment to these ideas, as they first became values and then 'common sense' (that is inscribed ideologies), has had consequence beyond measure. Effectively their enactment negated the possibility of being sustain-able and of ethical existence, for these ideas are at the very core of the transposition of Western humanity's anthropocentric condition into an overt violence against being. In the shadow of that ignorance we call knowledge how can one begin to contemplate the catalogue of human destruction? How can one separate 'our' actions from the 'new instrument' of 'science' and realise not just what we have done but continue to do? While it is inappropriate and inaccurate to load the blindness of the Enlightenment onto Bacon, he and his utopianism gave it a visible focus that still remains mostly unseen.

As indicated, the shift from More to Bacon is a move from utopia, as a genre of ideologically employed fiction, to utopianism, as a foundational premise of modern Western scientific/technocratic thought that speaks under various guises such as progress, development and functionality. This is to reaffirm that utopianism was to become structurally elemental to all the rhetorical forms of modernity, Eurocentric thought, and the consequential advancement of industrially based economy, society and culture.

Many thinkers took Bacon's ideas as a ground to build upon. There were utopian socialists like Charles Fournier and Robert Owen who both experimented with ideal communities; the early positivist sociologists like Henri Saint-Simon and Auguste Comte, who wished to bring the advancement of the social within the realm of science; philosophers of the sociological like Herbert Spencer who placed humanity on a cosmic evolutionary path of progress; and of course, as we have seen, there was Karl Marx who posited the evolution of the mode of production with great transformitory power and embraced the means of production as a means of advancement and liberation in the hands of the industrial working class.

It is important to acknowledge that at the same time as utopianism established itself, the notion of 'dystopia' arrived. This can be defined as the employment of fiction that criticises the impact of the utopian development of rationalist and scientistic society. Dystopias actually turned into a very powerful literary genre in their own right. The relation between the utopian and dystopian vision was actually often dialogical, in that they both depended upon, and portrayed, dysfunction. The clash between Edward Bellamy and William Morris is an instance of this. Bellamy's utopian novel of the 1880s, *Looking Backwards*, was an uncritical utopian celebration of America's deliverance by technology and by a vast paternalistic trust regime that ruled all economic life. The novel adopted a viewpoint from the year 2000. In contrast, and from a socialist utopian position, William Morris constituted Bellamy's utopia as dystopic by writing *News From Nowhere* (in 1890 in instalments in a periodical, the *Commonweal*). Morris presented an anti-technological hyper-humanist, socially 'scientific utopia'. *News from Nowhere* sought to counter Bellamy's projection of a fully developed capitalism with an image of a fully developed communism.

## THE AMERICAN SHADOW

In asking questions of modernity and unsustainability we have seen that it is almost impossible to escape the shadow of America. The same observation goes for the history of utopias. The significance of America is no new disclosure and was evident from the very beginning. As Marx put it in the *Communist Manifesto*, 'modern industry has established the world market, for which the discovery of America paved the way'.[41]

In 1844 Ralph Waldo Emerson called America 'the country of the future'. Nowhere generated more experimental communities, nowhere contemplated its cities with greater utopian fervour, nowhere embraced technology with more vigour. From its 'discovery' in the 1490s America was projected to the West as the New World, the new Eden, and from this point onward, as a whole literature demonstrates, the American landscape was invented and re-invented as a pastoral idyll: its was the ultimate garden. (It should come as no surprise to note that America was the claimed setting of More's *Utopia*.) Utopian idealisation straddled the nation's history as one of its most powerful ideologies. It was in this context that notions of identity, space and democracy were formed. The 'land of the free' was a spiritualised, romantic space of becoming and being essentially American. Emerson wrote in 1844:

> The development of our American internal resources, the extension to the utmost of the commercial system, and the appearance of new moral causes which are to modify the state, are giving an aspect of greatness to the Future, which the imagination fears to open. One thing is plain for all men of common sense and common conscience, that here, here in America, is the home of man.[42]

There is a particular correspondence between the utopian dream of modernity in general and America as its most visible site of expression which Jean Baudrillard manages to expose well in his mixed bag of a book, *America*.[43] Baudrillard reveals America as a utopian prefiguration that came out of a demand for a utopian way of life. The flight from religious oppression to religious freedom, and the flight from history to an unwritten narrative was turned into, and realised as, the operation of a utopia based on the success of materialised life on Earth. The ordered life of a society of religious zeal transmuted into a righteous regime of habitualised, pragmatic, pluralised and moral gestures. Constructed as image, as dreamworld, as a fantasy of the new, America became 'utopia achieved' as individualised attainment. It was (and lingers still as) the image that was placed before other nations as the shape of their future, as the economic and cultural mark of modernity, as the desired. The vast output of the utopian machine, and the nightmare of ungrounded and banal hyper-real simulation, fuse imperceptibly. As streamlining and the New York World's Fair prefigured, substance and the immaterial, the real and the unreal, the ecological and the televisual refuse separation in, and as, America.

America, as modernity (and thus as the past) still asserts the dominance of the 'new' over the 'old'. It exposes itself as the past through the notion of temporality with which it still functions, and in the very facticity of the signs of age displayed by its economic and cultural infrastructure. It is not that America is overtaken, but rather its status is now that of an iconic model that has lost its hegemonic power. In its place many 'things' American proliferate: again utopia shrinks and shatters.

The words penned by Herman Melville, in 1850, resonate with the power, dream, fall, tragedy and terror that is America: 'We are the pioneers of the world; the advance-guard, sent on throughout the wilderness of untried things, to break a new path in the new world that is ours'.[44] These words capture the impetus of United States political, economic and cultural policy for most of the twentieth century. Into them can be read many objects, actions, events and institutions that defined 'the American way of life'. Here, for instance, we find the framing of the history of the products of the mechanised home, high rise, high technology architecture, the domination of international institutions, the Hollywood phenomenon, and the universalisation of American popular culture.

Baudrillard again provides an opening in which the turning of utopia to dystopia can be seen. It is in America that he finds, for instance, the most advanced manifestation of reason become unreason: 'deterritorialization' in the midst of a vast amount of space; the 'indeterminacy of language and the subject'; the 'neutralization of values'; and 'the death of culture' (as the cultured).[45] Eurocentrically Baudrillard writes 'We philosophize on the end of lots of things, but it is here that they actually come to an end'.[46]

## AN EPILOGUE FOR UTOPIANISM

It is only in the spaces of expunged memory that utopianism can now survive: in all other settings its ideologies are completely exhausted. This does not mean there is a lack of space. Western 'civilisation' has time and time again revealed an extraordinary ability to combine barbarism with technology. One of the contemporary manifestations of this trend has been the arrival of the means of the erasure of memory, not of course with a machine from the world of science fiction, but via the more complex and pervasive nature of technology as it becomes culture, thought and perception. Technology is now both the seeing and the seen, hearing and the heard, the feeling and the felt. Extending Heidegger's understanding into the present, the technological setting of the horizon of being fixes horizons, including the horizons of memory, not by a managed conspiracy but by the very way the world has been made technological and acts technologically. It is just how 'things' are.

In the face of this postmodern situation a good deal of environmentalism looks nostalgic and naively utopian. What it would wish to conserve rests on an image from a dream long over. Fundamentally, being-in-the-environment — as the complexity of the material and immaterial environment, as the space of the operation of the multiple biophysical and synthetic ecological systems of now — is not engaged. This means that a considerable amount of recent ecological utopianism needs to be cast aside.[47]

Equally, in the space of everyday life, utopias return in commodified shrunken forms. With the help of the cultural technology of the pre-sent, the problematic idealism has been displaced by the reality of the drive for instant gratification. This 'development' is the forward march of the time of a restricted and transitory pleasure powered by the micro-utopian dreams of media manufacture. Here we do have the machine that simultaneously obliterates memory as it mobilises images of the past from its very own iconography. At the end of history, the technology of appropriation appropriates out of the standing reserve of the techno-archive (sound recording, photography, film, television, video). Its product is a cut and spliced expedient view that can service everything from a learning pack to a soap powder ad. This is no diatribe against popular culture, because there is no other.

As a temporary measure in the making of an instrumentalism against the instrumental — against the odds, without given space and contrary to reason — what is needed is another way of thinking and acting that is not predicated on vision and visualisation but on making sustainable processes and critical reflectivity. The agenda of concern must be temporality, finitude and consequence. The objects of engagement, in a place of engagement must be idea, design, construction, conception and action. Here is a context in which the constant returns of utopianism can be dealt with.

The future, as it is currently filled, has to be faced in order for there to be a knowable future. Contrary to the projection of latter day techno-futurists, the future is not a void. The future ever arrives before us as the consequence of the past and the present. We still need to find other ways to talk about the 'yet-to-be' which 'already is', as well as finding ways to clear what needs to be cleared before it arrives.

**NOTES**

1   Le Corbusier, in *Towards a New Architecture* (trans Frederick Etchells, Architectural Press, London, 1978, p. 89), posited the 'diseased state' of humanity as a result of our mixing 'art' with 'mere decoration'. His cure was modernist order. On the home front the pronouncement was that 'A house is a machine for living in'. The creation and operation of this machine was predicated on a transparency of dwelling in which 'living' was reduced to a technically determined condition by the management of air, light, services, space and measurement of materials. The transparent system of architecture advocated by Le Corbusier is in the same frame of vision as Ford's view of work, and of Christine Frederick's application of Taylorist scientific management of the workplace to the home, whereby it becomes a location of 'household engineering'.

2   A vast and complex history folds into this statement, with at one extreme the kind of sweeping semi-critical cultural history produced by Witold Rybcznski's book *Home: a Short History of an Idea* (Heinemann, London, 1986), and at the other extreme to the rich and demanding thinking of Martin Heidegger in his essay 'Building Dwelling Thinking' in *Poetry, Language, Thought* (trans Albert Hofstadter), Harper and Row, New York, 1971, as well as his address to dwelling and homelessness in *Hölderlin's Hymn 'The Ister'*, Indiana University Press, Bloomington, 1996.
3   While putting forward what now looks like a naive argument of domestic technology as women's liberation, Siegfried Giedion's *Mechanisation Takes Command* (Norton, New York, 1948) is still a seminal text.
4   In an especially authoritarian outburst in 1916, and as a more overt illustration of his political ideology of the domestic, he even instigated a process of home inspections (this was at a period when he had also ventured into building worker housing). John R Lee was appointed by Ford to head his 'Sociological Department' (basically to oversee the Five Dollar Day pay deal). As part of this work investigators were appointed to establish that a worker led a wholesome family life and could handle a high wage without 'weaknesses'. If a family did not meet the specification they were put on probation. If during this time 'ways were not mended' the head of the house was sacked. We can more generally observe that Ford also enforced a longer-running policy for female employees which stated that once they married they had to leave their jobs to become full-time housewives. This women's service relation to the male worker provided a solid basis for feminist critiques of the home/work; productive/unproductive labour debates. See Huw Beynon, *Working for Ford*, EP Publishing, Wakefield, 1975, pp. 21–25.
5   Heidegger, 'Building Dwelling Thinking'.
6   Maurice Merleau-Ponty, *The Visible and the Invisible* (trans Alfonso Lingis), Northwestern University Press, Evanston, 1968, p. 248: 'my body is made of the same flesh of the world ... this flesh of my body is shared by the world, the world reflects it, encroaches upon it and it encroaches upon the world'.
7   Heidegger, 'Building Dwelling Thinking', p. 145.
8   *Ibid.*
9   Emmanuel Levinas, 'The Dwelling', in *Totality and Infinity* (trans Alfonso Lingis), Duquesne University Press, Pittsburg, 1990, pp. 152–53.

10 On design's implication in this debate see Jeffrey Meikle, *Twentieth Century Limited*, Temple University Press, Philadelphia, 1979.
11 Marshall Berman, *All That Is Solid Melts Into Air*, Verso, London, 1982, pp. 299–300.
12 Information on the TVA is especially drawn from Julian Huxley, *TVA: Adventure in Planning*, Architectural Press, London, 1943; and David E Lilienthal, *TVA: Democracy on the March*, Penguin Books, Harmondsworth, 1945.
13 The creation of hydro-electric schemes in China, India, Mexico, Canada, several Middle East and South America countries, Russia, western European nations and Australia, with its Snowy Mountain scheme, were all prompted by the TVA.
14 Jeffery Meikle's *Twentieth Century Limited* still provides the most useful account of streamlining available. The information below is indebted to this source.
15 Norman Bel Geddes, *Horizons*, Dover Publications, New York, 1977 (reprint), pp. 3–5.
16 Meikle, *Twentieth Century Limited*, p. 40.
17 The Bauhaus is dealt with at length in Chapter 4.
18 *Ibid.*, p. 68.
19 Geddes, for instance, owned a well thumbed copy of *Towards a New Architecture* and had met Eric Mendelsohn in 1924. Mendelsohn had influenced him especially in terms of regarding technology, in contrast to nature, as a site of design inspiration. Likewise Teague had travelled to Europe in the mid-1920s to look at the work of Le Corbusier and Walter Gropius. Meikle, *Twentieth Century Limited*, pp. 43–51; and p. 144
20 Although the market impact of this car was limited, its impact on the industry was profound.
21 Moses was a great builder and a terrible destroyer. Before the World's Fair even arrived, he was doing, with state New Deal funding and venture capital, what he willed — 'building the world of tomorrow' — and on a vast scale. He was the space creator for the total designer, and was celebrated as such by the official historian of the modern Movement, Siegfried Giedion. Moses, as he was presented by Giedion in that canonical text of the movement, *Space, Time and Architecture*, appeared as a world leader who showed how to politically, economically and materially construct the urban infrastructure as something which could power 'consumer society': Meikle, *Twentieth Century Limited*, p. 302.
22 *Ibid.*, p. 308–309.
23 *Ibid.*, p. 190.

24 Cited in Marshall Berman, *All That Is Solid Melts Into Air*, p. 303. Berman writes at length on Moses, whose work as a maker of parks and freeways, epitomises the often indistinguishable transition between unsustainability and sustainment.
25 Francis V O'Conner, 'Reusable Futures', in *Dawn of a New Day: The New York World's Fair, 1939/40*, Queens Museum/New York University Press, New York, 1980, p. 61.
26 Warren I Susman, 'The People's Fair', in *ibid.*, p. 22.
27 Joseph P Cusker, 'The World Tomorrow', in *ibid.*, p. 6.
28 O'Conner, 'Reusable Futures', in *ibid.*, p. 61.
29 Joseph P Cusker, 'The World Tomorrow', p. 13.
30 *Ibid.*, p. 15.
31 This is exactly the perspective proffered at the time by Norman Bel Geddes in *Horizons*.
32 HG Wells, *A Modern Utopia*, Thomas Nelson, London, (undated).
33 Kirshan Kumar (citing Trotsky) in *Utopia and Anti-Utopia in Modern Times*, Basil Blackwell, Oxford, 1987, pp. 63–64.
34 Karl Marx and Friedrich Engles, *The Communist Manifesto*, Penguin, Harmondsworth, 1967.
35 *Ibid.*, pp. 114–18. See footnote to p. 117 and the Preface to the English edition of 1888.
36 When we translate Plato's idea of the republic into his contemporary world view, what he actually means is a particular view of elements of a society rather than what the word connotes for us — a particular form of nation state.
37 Thomas More, *Utopia* (trans Paul Turner), Penguin Books, London, 1965.
38 Kumar, *Utopia and Anti-Utopia in Modern Times*, p. 2.
39 Francis Bacon, *New Atlantis* (ed. Alfred Gough), Clarendon Press, Oxford, 1915.
40 *Ibid.*, Introduction, pp. xiv–xv.
41 Marx and Engles, *The Communist Manifesto*, p. 81.
42 Kumar, *Utopia and Anti-Utopia in Modern Times*, p. 78.
43 Jean Baudrillard, *America* (trans Chris Turner), Verso, London, 1988.
44 As cited by Kumar, *Utopia and Anti-Utopia in Modern Times* p. 78.
45 Baudrillard, *America*, p. 97.
46 *Ibid.*, p.98. We can also note that, from the perspective of the discourses of modernity, humanity now lives at the end of history. However, the end of history, unlike the end point of Kant, Hegel or Marx, is no arrival at a transcendental point of prefigured destiny — the journey of 'man' is not complete. Rather, it is the very

idea of history and its discourse that falls. What ends is the authority of the directional narrative of ordered events which underpinned the notion of history, of where it came from, that it was going somewhere, that it had structural integrity and an evolutionary momentum. The end of history, by implication, is the end of a teleological view of progress. Being at the 'end of history' demands finding a voice to speak our living amid the fragments that we are. More than this, it means confronting our unsustainability, not just as it has damaged our planet but also as it has damaged our selves. The implications of, for example, the genocidal horrors and enormous violence of the twentieth century are not only that they demolish the last vestige of any claim to human perfectibility, but that the environment created has contaminated and diminishes every individual.

47 A note on 'ecotopia' as myopia: Ernest Callenbach wrote a literary ecological utopian text (*Ecotopia*) in 1975 that fell within two American traditions: romanticism and pragmatism. In many way it fictionally and environmentally elaborated EF Schumacher's 'small is beautiful' thesis. Its romanticism is symptomatic of a whole strain of unhelpful and unrigorous thinking which while making enjoyable reading for some, delivers nothing to assist a thinking otherwise. Ursula Le Guins's 1974 novel *The Dispossessed* is another kind of example that draws on the utopian theme of 'natural' harmony between man and nature. For Le Guin this is exemplified by North American Indians.

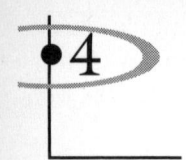

# 4
# TOTAL DESIGN: EUROPE

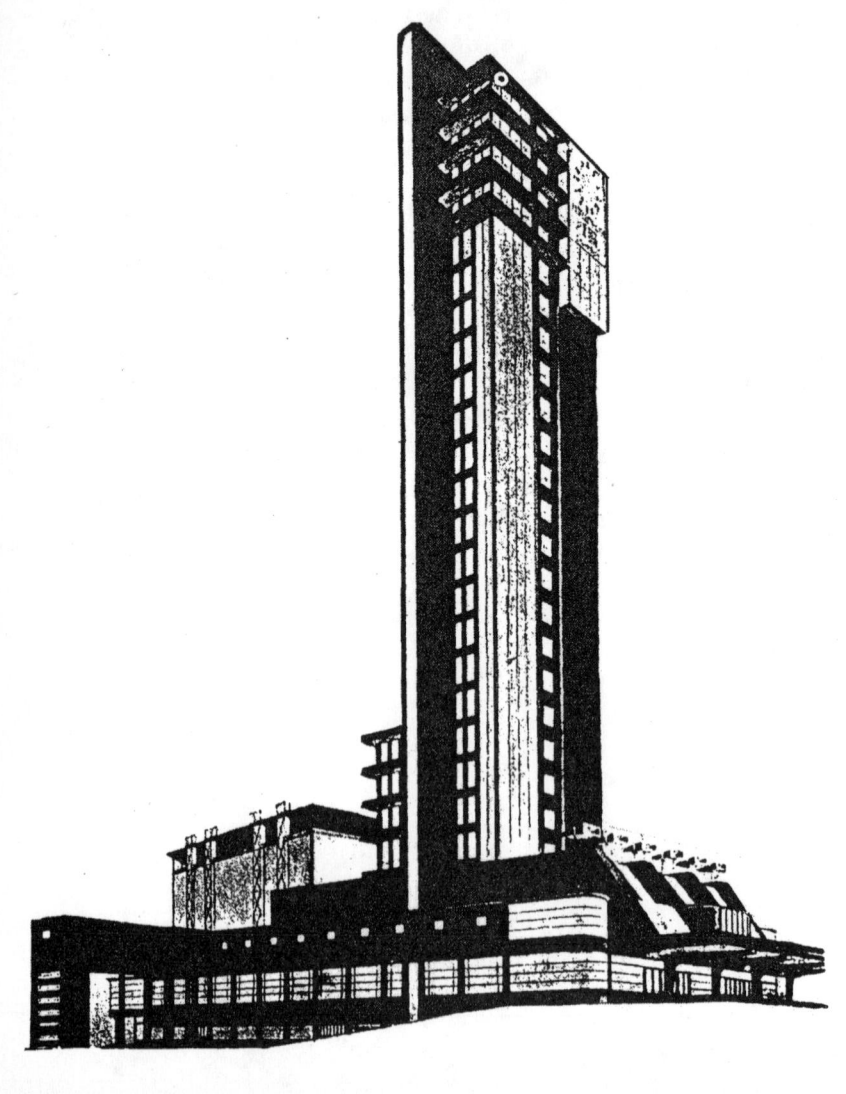

Teplitsky's Vkhutemas project design for the 'Place of Labour', 1926 (Kopp, *Town and Revolution*)

The defutured has a history far more extensive and complex than any selection of particular moments, institutions, practices or objects is able to stand for. Although much of what is said arrives in the style of a metanarrative this, as has been explained is purely an heuristic. Our aim cannot be to tell the full story but rather to contribute to the creation of a critical sensibility; another point of view; one able to read the designed and its history with a different understanding and intent.

This chapter registers that the form of the modern world was contested not simply by other non-modern cultures and traditions, but also by more than one model of the modern. A European account will be placed alongside what has been said on America. However, this picture is again a relational one, rather than a binary comparison. Both protagonists of the 'new' elevated and mobilised an enhanced power of the sign. During the moment of our consideration — the 1920s and 1930s — there were profound differences on the form of the modern and its political, economic and cultural direction. Fascist, totalitarian, socialist and liberal/conservative regimes vied within and between nations for control. Yet within Europe and America the 'forces of design' were all striving for a common goal — if not a common project, form or context — that being the establishment of a designed and designing hegemonic order; a design regime able to overcome all difference, all resistance, a 'total design'. Design, in all its manifestations, was ideology's instrument and expression; it was ideology in action, be it as instrumental function or sign function.

In the most general sense, total design can be viewed as a totalising aesthetic regime deeply implicated in the defutured and its concealment. To illustrate, two of the most developed and recognised examples can be cited. The first is the reactionary 'spectacular' forms of appearance of German fascism, in which a total militarised 'quasi neo-classical' aesthetic was created as 'the sign world' of everyday life. This visual environment not only co-opted images but also the human body, popular culture and architecture. Additionally the 'total design' acted to unify the stylistic theme of all arms of the military. In contrast Coca Cola, the creators of one of the first and most comprehensive of what we now call corporate identity programs, adopted the use of a visual imagery at the end of the nineteenth century to form a total corporate design regime that was to evolve into sign economy that became the product — the product, as sign, was modern, was America, was progress, was 'cool'. In both of these examples an aesthetic was bonded to an iconographic and highly organised design management exercise, across the stylistic form, colour, spectacle, moving and static image, architecture, transport, dress, and more, all with the result that the 'total design' became a significant part of a nationalist culture. For a decade and a half, Nazi fascist imagery was the sign of the Third Reich, and for now 100 years Coke has stood for America and America as world.

Total design ambitions were integral to the creation and rise of a modernist design philosophy — a philosophy that set out to increase the agency of design economically, politically and culturally. As we are about to see, one of the most significant ways it did this was by the creation of design institutions.

Total design — along with productivism (as it has been characterised as the driving power of the willing of structural thought) and war (as a structured event that employs productivism to impose the will to structure according to a particular regime, often in the wake of the failure of hegemonic productivism) — can be seen as a managed process of imposition that travels under the guise of order and reason. In this kind of framing can be seen a strategy of 'dealing with' difference, disorder or breakdown. Equally, as product or process, total design can be a way of naming, and violent stamping of, an absolutely and unreflectively anthropocentric direction. This violence is, however, mostly rhetorically or visually concealed by either the seeming rationality of its imposition or by the elegance of its style. Signs of violence are usually assumed to be self-evident — but defuturing tells us otherwise, that they can come wrapped in attractive packages.

While total design is normally presented as the manifestation and enforcement of a programmatic, mostly modernist, vision of an imposed regime of order (registered across an entire domain of images, objects, systems and structures), and although totalisation claims coherence, in actuality total design, like the complexity of Design, can only be presented in a fragmentary form of intersections of forces, power, knowledge, system, object, and image. Total design has no narrative outside the system and historical discourse that constructs its appearance, thus there is no point of observation of total design outside 'the design world'. Even within this specific domain, its understanding by design institutions and practitioners is mostly limited to viewing it as a regime of absolute functional and aesthetic control. That the idea is always more than it appears to be goes by the board.

Total design rested upon reason, order and an associated faith in, and use of, the agency of representation. It was thus an ocularcentric force that strove to mobilise, via an aesthetic determinism, a closure of seeing and knowing. Its ambition was to fuse a lifeworld, with a world view, as a world and a worlding, visualised and occupied. While poststructuralist theory has demonstrated that there is no certainty of connection between referent and representation, reality and appearance, and while theoretically the hegemony of the power of the image has ended (pictures do lie!), ocularcentrism still rules. Western vision is the seeing of the world picture. The image is treated as truth even when and where this assumption is known to be false — living with faith in the visual has thus transmuted into living with a bad faith. That images are not materially grounded, that their claim of truth can be exposed as being without substance, does not mean that they are divested of their power. The lie embraced as the fiction, adopted as the utopia, indicates the overwhelming strength of seduction over truth.

A BRIEF OPENING

Two related institutional examples that functioned to mobilise a total design project were the Bauhaus and, to be dealt with more briefly, the Vkhutemas. Design history claims these as the two most influential design schools of the twentieth century. The Bauhaus was founded in Germany 1919 and the Vkhutemas in the Soviet Union in 1920.

It seems like a great distance divides us from the time, place and consequences of these particular historical events. This is not entirely the case. Anyone who has had a design education will have been touched by the afterlife of these institutions. Anyone, for instance, who has gone to art, design or architecture school will have had some exposure to the ideas, theory and pedagogic practices of the total design philosophy. For example, the commonplace idea within art and design education of a foundation or introductory course that allows a student to sample multiple experiences, break away from their existing value system and have the freedom to aesthetically experiment comes from the Bauhaus.

The events that undid the Bauhaus and Vkhutemas — the rise of German fascism, economically determinist Soviet communism, and the degeneration of modernist utopianism — have left traces that linger on. Equally the last quarter of the twentieth century has radically revised how the modern world is viewed and dreamt of. In these years some of the most monolithic and seemingly immovable power blocs of the modern world — colonial structures and political ideologies — have fallen. The Soviet Union has gone (as has any sense that capitalism has an other), the gradual disintegration and abandonment of much of Africa continues, and the rise and fall of Asian powers continue to impact on the global economy, while the notion of an environmental crisis has become a part of every child's education and world view. Progress has been exposed as illusory and the idea, that the best is to come, is abandoned.

More generally, the master discourses of the Enlightenment — humanism, the sovereign subject, nation, reason, history, philosophy, and so on — are either on their back or are very shaky. In these circumstance of lost certainty, the believed in and valued has been, or stands to be, devalued. On one side of this void is a sense of loss and a complete uncaring, an unprincipled grab for anything going and a negation of responsibility to science to find solutions to the crises of our social and material worlds (when we are the problem). On the other side are a desperate clinging to exhausted ideas, the belief in the saving power of technology, or spirituality, with its false hopes. Now what is uncanny about this circumstance is that its nearest comparative moment was the period between the wars. In each site of the crisis — besides dire economic circumstances and the loss of the old order, which was accompanied by a loss of meaning — there was an imposition of representation, of an aesthetic (streamlining, fascism and less successfully Russian constructivism) that was a fabricated image of a sense of order, stability and progress. This imposition was of course an example of 'total design'.

The idea of total design served several purposes: it was a way of gathering together forces of difference (via designed form and style mobilised as a visual regime) to appear as the same. An aesthetic regime was created to try to create, express or substitute for a unity. However, total design does not always equate with a totalised appearance. Moreover, total design does not solve problems; it buries them. In doing this it installs the destructuring agency of that which defutures.

It is into these circumstances — and this is the whole point of naming defuturing — that the most pressing imperative is to bring the defutured out of the shadows. For without this no ability to sustain can be brought to hand, no learning of the need for learning otherwise can be disclosed. To fail, or to refuse, to come to this learning is to commit oneself to remaining unknowingly within the anthropocentric and productivist structures of unsustainability. Obviously, knowing does not imply overcoming, however, it does mean a recognition by which responsibility, and thus a change, can arrive.

* * *

As stated above, to illustrate the institutional forms of 'total design', two example will be explored: Bauhaus and Vkhutemas. Sometimes our comment will resonate with the narratives of the text books (as the volume of books on the topic, and especially on the Bauhaus, evidence, it is an obsession of design history scholarship, and has now degenerated into tourism) but it will sit uncomfortably with the literature. Overall, and at best, our variously constituted disposition towards the institutions is ambiguous. Without question there are important lessons still to learn from them, but certainly not those registered by the long-standing mimetic relation to their pedagogy, nor in a detailed examination of their objects (their practices are another matter).

## THE BAUHAUS, AS TOLD

Walter Gropius — 'the Silver Prince', World War I German cavalry officer, and gifted Modern Movement architect — took over the Academy of Fine Arts and the Applied Art School at Weimar in 1919, and formed the first Bauhaus (1919–25).[1] This institution moved to Dessau in 1925 and while it had a lingering afterlife in several forms, it was effectively terminated as a political, if not a design, project in 1933 by the Nazis. (In brief, the Nazis effected a crude reduction of modernism to communism, and thus deemed Bauhaus to be dangerous.[2])

In founding the institution, Gropius had an expressed ambition to create a 'modern architectonic art' (which we can understand here as a structured master designing) and to subordinate industry and technology to the direction of design. Design was to be in the driving seat, with architecture the goal. Architecture was posited as able to become art of the highest order. As Gropius put it in the first Bauhaus proclamation: 'The complete building is the ultimate aim of the visual arts'.

The vision developed and promoted by Gropius came out of a number of contexts. There was a desire to impose order in the wake of the disorder and dysfunction of World War I. There was also a momentum towards a new design culture that emerged from an art and design nexus that had gained pace in Germany prior to the war, specifically via the influence of the Deutscher Werkbund (a forerunner of modern design councils). Also significant was Gropius' prewar experience of working with Peter Berhens (who prefigured the rise of corporate design as a total design regime in his work with the giant German electrical product company AEG). Finally, there was the impact of Gropius' knowledge of De Stijl, the Dutch art and design movement, which with the help of Peter Berlage and JJP Oud had promoted the work of American architect Frank Lloyd Wright along with his particular aesthetic and ideological commitment to a new order of functionalism that was especially inflected by American and specifically Chicago design culture. The milieu was thus rich and complex. While each influence resonates with the total design ethos it is perhaps worth emphasising the AEG work with Berhens.[3]

The AEG project (1908-09) was unusual and significant because the commission brought together the design of buildings, products and images all under the direction of one 'master' architect. The design object was presented by the designer as not being isolable, but within the 'sense' of a regime in which everything functioned to constitute a totality. Everything was considered in the design exercise both as a whole and in great detail. Here manifestly was a system of 'order' under the direction of design that was to arrive later on in the century in many organisations as corporate policy.

The basic system of the Bauhaus was one of progressive specialism from a six-month probationary preliminary course: the 'Vorkurs' introduced by Johannes Ittens in 1920.[4] This course aimed to displace any artistic assumptions with which students arrived, install a unified perception of the arts, put a craft-based work ethic in place, introduce students to materials and colour theory, and improve their drawing skills. This foundation exercise went well beyond the practical and aesthetically conceptual — what it really added up to was the induction of the 'complete being' into Bauhaus ideology — a totalised person.

On passing the Vorkurs preliminary course, students could proceed to advanced courses in architecture/building, planning, ceramics, weaving, furniture design, wall painting, theatre, or metal work. (The mix of these courses changed with the move from Weimar to Dessau, with the emphasis on art and craft falling away.) Advanced courses built upon a base that required the study of design, colour, form and the craft of making in terms of materials and technology. After three years of this training, under the direction of both a master of handicrafts and a master of design (which established a binary relation between imagination and technique), the student was examined and if successful awarded a journeyman certificate. After this they could move on to building training and a Bauhaus Masters Certificate — which led to work as an architect, industrial designer or teacher. Over time there was an ever increasing imperative for students to gain practical experience by working with industry on practical projects, although initially this mostly folded back into a craft ethos.[5]

## BAUHAUS CONJUNCTURE

In understanding the agency of any designing force one needs to seek some sense of what designed that force, as well as what it itself designed. The disposition to function and order that powered modernist design and architecture at the precise moment that the Bauhaus arrived was created by the convergence of two contradictory vectors: the desire to reimpose order after the chaos, dysfunction, irrationality and disorder of World War I; and a rationalist drive of modernist design aesthetics (most crudely registered by the machined object and the industrially fabricated structure) that had been gaining momentum since the late nineteenth century. Here we have the specific conjuncture of the general trend toward total design.

Before the war, there was a misguided notion, promoted by various avant gardes, not least the Futurists, that the war would clear the path forward by blowing away the dead weight of the past. War was seen as a cathartic moment that would, as a result of its grand clearing, open up a vast creative outpouring. Romantic delusions obstructed any contemplation of the actual misery, hardship, suffering, and physical and psychological damage that would be done to a vast mass of humanity. Although there had been a few dress rehearsals of the machinery of mass-produced death in action, there had never been a major conflagration in which a fully industrialised system of war had been mobilised. There was no social imagination for such a scale of destruction. Over the course of the war there was a shift in perception by the leadership of all the protagonists from a misguided and myopic notion of the conduct of war being based on honour, valour and symbolic gestures from a bygone age, to the relentless exercise of the 'will to will' of technosystems. Slow learning of this lesson by the generals cost millions of lives. What they had failed to realise was that war had become something that once started, precipitated causal chains that were well beyond the control of those who initiated any specific action: the mechanism simply ran its course as if a self-propelled machine of destruction. While in some respects this has always been so, at least in the case of battles, what was new was the disjuncture between the capability of the system of force, its scale and speed and the ability of those directing events to understand, and take responsibility for, what they were supposedly managing. De facto, the system of representation had broken down — the prefigurative visualisation of the field of battle in the minds of the generals, the image they used in thinking how to direct events, had little correspondence with what was actually happening.

With reference to the aesthetic concerns of the second vector, we can note that in design and architecture there was a violent reaction against the past, especially expressed as a hostility towards decoration. The reclaiming of simplicity and function by the Arts and Craft Movement is usually called up as an early and influential marker of a disposition that led to the rise of a machine aesthetic.[6]

In summary, the response to war, faith in technology and the machine aesthetic converged to create a technological and aesthetically functionalist impetus. This represented one powerful force that drove a desire for the ordered and the new. The idealist and modernist desire to erase the past in order to open a space for a utopian future (seen, for example, in the visionary anti-historicism of the Futurists, the new visuality of Cubism and the new world making of constructivism) was the another force.

Gropius was steeped in his moment. Discipline, the experience of war, and his induction into a modern architectural aesthetic framed a good deal of his identity, his project, as well as the 'total vision' for his institution. The vision that guided him was not just an individualised conditional product, for it also rested on the adoption of an utopian sense of order and function informed by a broader culture.[7] While utopian European modernist design gained a great deal of momentum between the wars, it was, like much else of its time, fundamentally dystopic. This is because it reduced the agency of design to a programmatic underpinned by an aesthetically ideological determinism: it sought to force the future into its form. There was a fundamental failure inscribed in this idealism — unwittingly its *zeitgeist* meta-designed instrumentalised subjects, diminished freedoms and helped expand the unsustainable (albeit without the violence and crudity of emergent German fascism).

The Bauhaus nevertheless had a totalist ambition of striving to launch an object regime of uniform mass symbolic agency. From a contemporary theoretical perspective we see such a project in an economy in which symbolic value becomes capital (which, as we shall see, Jean Baudrillard named it as a 'sign economy'). Retrospectively, this project is articulated with the creation of the world order of modern (or modernist) 'consumerism'; the synthetically generated culture of negated cultural difference, material and symbolic disposability, and of perpetually produced dissatisfaction. Ironically, fascism, in reading Bauhaus modernism as a counter totality, myopically, through its own aesthetically restricted vision, failed to read the commonalities of their two total design regimes.[8]

## BUILDING A DESIGN IDEOLOGY

The key developmental moves of the Bauhaus went something like this. Walter Gropius formed a grand vision out of the history touched on above. His initial staff were, however, not up to its delivery. Then, as an institutional culture started to arrive, a new knowledge began to form and the institutional project became more coherent. Even so, the vision of total design as desired and promoted by Gropius was never fully realised; nor did he own completely what was actually created. When Gropius departed — as the Nazi threat became more keenly felt — it became possible to revise and redesign the Bauhaus's history, which is exactly what Gropius did in *Scope of Total Architecture* in 1937.[9]

At this point it is worth returning to reconfront the shapes of the 'total' as viewed by Gropius. He expressed this as a claim of modern architecture being, like 'nature', an all-embracing art that totalised all other practices in its scope. (This can be comprehended as the AEG project writ large.) Gropius stated that one of his major aims was: 'The creation of standard types of goods ... . It is today more necessary than ever to understand the underlying significance of the conception of "standard."'[10] He also asserted (with a naive faith in a 'natural' evolution of the human toward to good): 'The standardisation of the practical machinery of life implies no robotization of the individual but, on the contrary, the unburdening of his existence from much unnecessary dead weight so as to leave him freer to develop on a higher plane'.[11]

Such a view, although written a few years after he left the Bauhaus, indicates a naive faith in technology and science. It was predicated on the notions that inflected a great deal of modernist culture. Objectivity was still believed in, technology was assumed to be neutral, 'natural' resources appeared to be unlimited. Viewed at the end of the twentieth century it is clear that much which once seemed progressive is now extremely problematic, or even regressive.

For Gropius, totality and the standard converged. For him the standard arrived after a process of the reduction of everything in order to 'seek out the best': the standard was the ideal — the Platonic ideal. It was a path to the pure, as a path to the good, as a path to spirit. For all the humanist rhetoric, the standard implies the control of total design: it was therefore programmatic and authoritarian. (One can of course call up another appeal — at the same historical moment — to a different standard: the measure of 'others' by the 'traits' of the Aryan race. The standard, once placed in a totalising frame, evoked the value of an unaware anthropocentric valuing and was the embodiment of ethnocentricity as it eliminated difference. It was predicated on the position of a single world view, regime of taste, social vision, and culture. Equally, it subordinated the ecological and the economic to its norms.)

In addition to the standard as a nominated form, the design ideology of the Bauhaus was advanced as 'standardised' by the creation of an industrial aesthetic across all design activity, and through an advocated way of life (which excluded all but the ordered forms of the new, be it movies, music, art, buildings, furniture, transport, technology or, of course, education).

The relation between standard and standardisation is the relation between the norm, its means of reproduction, and the structure of power of its dissemination. (One can also note that every imperial power, from ancient times, from the East and the West, has always sought to make its measure the standard.) In keeping with the entire history of modernity and modernism, the Bauhaus standard never established itself completely, not least because of the very considerable disjuncture between its values and those of the design professions, the public at large, and the forces of Americanism. The actual material impact of the idea of the standard is, however, another story — for, although banal to point out, the exercise of the designer's values has had a profound impact on the product, image and built environment.

## THE BAUHAUS SIGN ECONOMY: DESIGNED IDEOLOGICAL EXCHANGE

Unsustainability needs to be seen: the defutured needs a sign.

As the history of design tells us in so many ways, and as we have seen in numerous way so far, the sign economy has become one of the more important drivers of contemporary capitalism. The management of the immateriality of the sign — as taste, style, brand, image, and designer names — has not only become implicated in the valorisation of goods, their status and exchange value but also who uses them, where they are used and, most significant of all, the duration of their life and their after-life fate (waste so often is a dead sign rather than a worthless object). The sign is primary: it frames its object of association and inscriptively articulates it to its owner or user. More than this it has become the commodity, via the form given to information. The sign sets the temporal horizons: it shortens or extends a duration of use; it decides if an object is treated with respect or is abused; it summons desire or invites rejection; it confers identity and positions the identified. As we saw with the history of streamlining, the rise of the power of the sign did not happen by accident, and that 'the sign' here does not mean something attached to the object afterwards, but something that was integral to its very conception. The Bauhaus is but another part of this large and ongoing story, which itself is a crucial part in the archaeology of unsustainability.

The Bauhaus's sign economy of design and designer culture was (especially in Europe) given impetus by the way it developed a practice of institutional and object re-creation as sign. The Bauhaus, as sign, was a composite product formed out of a careful re-presentation of its own practices. Object and image making, the promotion of events and publications, and the retrospective mythologisation by printed word and image were all brought together to constitute relations of influence. From its beginning, the very survival of the institution required a political strategy of promotion and sign management.

To gain the influence it sought, the institution needed to create visibility for its work. In one direction this exposure generated a negative reaction, from conservative local communities, from the political leadership of Weimar, and then from the state government. It was a similar story with the Bauhaus moved to Dessau. Eventually a commitment to modernism exposed it to pressure from the Nazi National Socialist Government. In another and counter direction, appeals and calls for support were made to European modernists, their associated avant-garde intellectual community and, more gesturally, to the progressive section of industry. The exposure generated interest and a particular aura started to form around the work of the institution (being fuelled by the production of written material which mediated the institution's output). However, it should be said that the strategy did not arrive as a single plan or campaign, rather it became more an inherent part of the institution's culture.

In the face of the politics of the moment, Gropius tried to refuse the claim of 'total design', a Bauhaus style. His pluralist shift (which was also an accommodation of the pluralism of an individualistic staff) was contrary to his aim of establishing new rules of design, of revitalising it all, or making design a directive force in the making of the modern visible via exemplary structures, objects, images and a supporting rhetoric. His problem was not that the Bauhaus was deemed a style, but rather what it and the institution's disproportionate agency signified as style, as sign. This problem rested with a bias of the Bauhaus towards art rather than industry: industrial products were reduced to mimic an industrial 'look' (not least because they were made by craft rather than by industrial processes). At the same time, the institution's politics were dominantly based on cultural gestures, rather than material engagements (hence the culturalism). Ambiguously the success of the sign was also a mark of failure: a perception was created, and a star rose, but below it there was a real failure of relational connections, material impacts and political understanding (not least between total design and fascism). In the end, and fundamentally, one can ask what was learned from the Bauhaus methods of 'learning by example', be it applied to designing, making or polemic?

Retrospectively, and looking beyond image, object, technique and rhetoric, all Bauhaus innovation was grounded in an authority which combined utopian social ideals with a naive but aggressive aesthetic determinism. These trends, which had varied and complex histories within the Bauhaus, evaporated as the institution's project flowed into the emergence of the sign economy of a revitalising capital. Bauhaus was thus a contributor to the designed appearance, and design agency of, economic and cultural modernity. In this context, the approach to design education it promoted simply folded into design as a restricted activity and institutionally confined practice in the service of the dominant cultural and economic forces. Fundamentally, the Bauhaus was unable to view or have any critical relation with Design nor did it understand Design's basic world making importance or ethical imperatives. In sum, while striving to educate, the Bauhaus learnt very little, with the exception of how to serve the process of extending the aesthetisation of every aspect of being, which is the domain of the totality of all that is modernity. Nothing has more significantly concealed what demands recognition, in order to be sustained, than the inert defutured sign world of the sign economy. While this negation cannot be completely laid at the door of the Bauhaus (or equally at that of streamlining) it does provide a very clear window on the problem.

It was the ability of the Bauhaus to employ and elevate the power of the sign of the object and the agency of style that prompted Jean Baudrillard to address it in his account of the rise of 'a political economy of the sign'. However, before considering this exercise it is worth re-registering the agency of the already mentioned Bauhaus textual output (not least because Baudrillard overlooks the propulsive power of its mediation in the creation of the conditions of the arrival of designed objects, or in other words, he overplays the visual and underplays the textual and intertextual). Bauhaus objects, images, rhetoric, projects, personalities all existed as published representations.[12] Publishing first maintained and then expanded the Bauhaus institutional presence; it provided the means of appropriation for its ideas and aesthetics; it validated the position of teachers, while generalising their pedagogic practices. In the end published material constituted the core out of which the Bauhaus's design history was invented.

To return to Baudrillard on the Bauhaus: his claim is that the object only fully exists once it gains a sign function which transcends and directs its use function. In this context he claims that before the Bauhaus 'there were no objects'.[13] The pre-modern object was thus posited as incomplete. Now while this view is in error, is extremely Eurocentric, can be contested even just within the realms of orthodox design history, and while it shows that Baudrillard himself is an interpolate of the Bauhaus's totalising mythology — which, as is being argued here, functions with an overarching meaning, explanatory power and sensibility that extended the institution's agency well beyond the impact of just objects — he still makes a point of considerable weight. It is certainly correct to observe that the Bauhaus made a particular kind of contribution to the ascendancy of the political economy of the sign.

More than at any time before in modernist culture, design dematerialised the relation between matter, identification and difference while also dramatically increasing the exchange value of the immaterial. It was not so much, as Baudrillard would have it, that the sign subordinated utility, but rather that it immaterialised it and reconfigured use as a function of the sign. So while culture has always brought meaning and value to objects via their symbolic inscription, and while cultural and economic value are always articulated with each other, the key feature of the Bauhaus moment (and the associated argument under review) is that it assisted the sign in gaining status as an independent commodity, one able to function in the economy in its own right. While fascism constituted its 'society of the spectacle', and while from that moment onward the commodification of culture became an object of enduring critical concern, what had actually happened at a structural level was more dramatic: the 'nature' of capital had been changed.[14] Modern life had made a quantum shift in its virtualisation: by Design, and in the company of the technologies of the 'world as picture', modern (modernist) living had started to be in another space. Being modern began to unfold as living indivisibly not just in an environment of culturally coded physical space, but also in the environment of the image, its 'everywhere' aesthetic and inner life.

It is worth revisiting and working over some of the observations presented. Baudrillard acknowledged that 'nature' is a sign creation and that the mastery of nature is the domination of a sign.[15] But he failed to register that the environment of the political economy of the sign, the environment as signification, was and is never sustainable in and of itself. And, more importantly from a contemporary point of view, as acknowledged, the political economy of the sign has made a major contribution to the establishment of a culture of unsustainability — not least by the desires it has created and served — removed from the consideration of conscience and rendered invisible as material impacts.

The power of aesthetic, scientific and technological world-making is at the core of the deepening unknowing of modern culture, its sign economy and unconscious designing. This unknowing is evidenced by the almost total failure of modern cultures to even ask What have we designed?, let alone ask and answer the question of What does Design design?

While Baudrillard is to be commended for embracing the omnipresence of Design (not that design culture has taken note) he still fails to see the return of Design as a designing (that is the meta-view, Design, as posited in the Introduction) which is also to fail to see it as the animation of the political economy of the sign. He says, for instance, the 'mortal enemy of design is kitsch', which is presented as that which constantly returns, but he then goes on 'nothing escapes design', and 'everything belongs to design'.[16] We note, of course, that kitsch is design and that design is not simply a system of aesthetic forms and value judgements but more importantly an ontological force of world-making that became inscribed into culture and economy as elemental to the functional system of modern life (as it became lived in its own condition of fabrication). More affirmatively Baudrillard points out that 'The "designed" universe is what properly constitutes the environment' and the environment 'designates the end of the proximate world'.[17] He also observed that 'If one speaks of environment, it is because it has already ceased to exist. To speak of ecology is to attest to the death and total abstraction of nature. Everywhere the "right" (to nature, to the environment) countersigns the "demise of".'[18]

The Baudrillard essay from which these comments come was written nearly thirty years ago. Viewed in their moment they are extremely insightful: at the same time they expose problems of rhetorical over-statement and the essentialism of binary argument. Clearly the Bauhaus was an instance of total design and of the rise of the political economy of the sign, but it is not reducible to a singular pivotal point of historical turning. Moreover, the sign, the style, while identifiable in itself, cannot be vectorially mapped. As a force it was multi-directional as well as both visible and hidden.

## A CRITICAL FIX

The impact of the Bauhaus cannot be equated with its scale, material resources or narrativisation. Put alongside the size of contemporary institutions it seems like a dust mite in a mattress.[19]

The utopianism of the Bauhaus, although mentioned, also needs special mention as a designing force. It posited formalist values of design (expressed in signs of taste, order, direction and progress) and fused them with a faith in the form of designed objects as agents of change, and as influential exemplary typeforms. The ground of this position was based on the assumed agency of the normative representation before the eyes of the willing subject self-positioned to be influenced. Whatever ethical claims were made they were secondary to the horizon-setting leadership of the iconic sign. To illustrate the point let us return to the advocation of the standard made by Gropius. As already quoted, he said 'It is today more necessary than ever to understand the underlying significance of the conception of "standard"'. His notion was based on two connotations: 'the selected best'; and 'the uniform qualitative normative object, as measure'. Reyner Banham describes one way in which this advocation arrived and unfolded:

> Under the pressure of military necessity and a tight economic situation, DIN-Format begun to be applied to an increasing number of industrial products.It was essentially the freezing ad hoc, of a number of widely-used dimensionings as standard measures for that particular class of products (Deutsche Industrie-Normen), and so 'our military discipline became indeed the ground of standardisation and the typical. DIN-Format was never fully abandoned after the war, and was revived and revised in the Second World War. It is commonly taken to be the inspiration of Bauhaus studies in dimensional standardisation of building components,and this lies at the root of the whole trend towards modular co-ordination that runs right through the Modern Movement.[20]

Here then is language in its designing. Equally, here is also the rhizomic path of an idea in action and the omnipresent shadow of militarisation.

## THE VKHUTEMAS POSTSCRIPT

This postscript is a sign of disruption, not least because it recasts what precedes it.

Far less is known about the Moscow Vkhutemas — a Higher State Art-Technical Studio, which was founded in 1920 — than the Bauhaus. There simply has not been the same hype, promotion, availability of documents, nor specialist media profile. Created, like the Bauhaus, by a merger of two other colleges it was of a much larger scale than its German counterpart. It had an enrolment of over 2500 students. The institution has been claimed as extremely important. For instance, John Willett writes:

> For some years the Vkhutemas was arguably the most advanced art school in the world, and together with Inkhuk,the ministry's new theoretical institute which was set up at about the same time (spring 1920), it became the cradle of Constructivism.This three-dimensional, sometimes kinetic art, entirely divorced from natural appearances and

consciously using space as a medium along with more tangible materials, was worked on partly in debates in Inkhuk and partly in the exercises of the Basic Section.[21]

However, the Vkhutemas and the Inkhuk were never remade as a sign economy. They were not valorised with political economy of institutionalised design, and so never gained equal status as the Bauhaus. For all that has been written on constructivism, and notwithstanding its influence on architecture and industrial design (and its complex relation to productivism), it never became a key commodity generator. At its most basic, European modernist design (with Germany and Russia at its head) was no market match for American design (as evidenced by streamlining's link to consumerism and the design professions). Yet culturally, and more obliquely via the rise of a sign economy, its influence was still substantial, if more identified with the people associated with it (including Sergei Eisenstein, Dziga Vertov, Vladimir Mayakovsky, Kasmir Malevich, Naum Gabo and Wassily Kandinsky) than its name.[22] In fact Vkhutemas and Inkhuk teachers undoubtedly could be claimed to have generated some of the most important innovations and creative outpourings in theatre, art, architecture, film, photography and design of the twentieth century, and are recognised by the histories of modern visual arts, film and photography as such. Additionally, and with far less recognition, the experiments in pedagogy undertaken during this period at these places made contributions to the nature of architecture and design education that influenced other institutions (especially the Bauhaus).

For almost a decade after the Russian Revolution design culture in the Soviet Union was the most dynamic, adventurous and innovatory on Earth. It literally set out to create a new world. In this moment, utopian art and design appeared to be major transformative means to radical change. This high idealism hit three very large interconnected obstacles.

Firstly, there was the pressure of the economic and social chaos in the years immediately after the Russian Revolution. At the start of the revolution there was something like one industrial worker to every twenty peasants: the civil war had worsened this ratio, and general conditions, considerably.[23] By the mid-1920s more people were dying from starvation than had died at the barrel of a gun. Lenin himself had died of a stroke in 1924, Stalin was in power and en route to the command economy (which was a total militarisation of economic management). Enforced economic change, especially to increase industrial production, and rigid political control were imposed as the one and only way forward.

Secondly, a view came to rule that asserted that the cultural revolution had failed: it was too slow. (This change of situation was formally instituted in 1932 when the Central Committee of the Communist Party officially dissolved all the literary-artistic organisations and regrouped them in unions.[24]) The ability to displace the cultural project was made easier because it was seriously weakened by perspectival divisions within the areas of cultural activism. Crudely there were three positions: art in the service of the party, which implied total direction by political ideology; the creation of a revolutionary art as a means to maintain revolution as an on-going process; and a formalism that meant a revolution of art for art's sake (the latter being rejected by the party).

The third obstacle was that the economic means were just not available to realise the cultural goals. This did not just mean that there was not enough money to materialise what was designed, but equally, and perhaps even more fundamentally, there were just not the available industrial means, skilled workforce, technical knowledge or available materials. In this context, design became ever more a fiction, a modern utopia, an architecture of a dream, a future constantly evoked but never able to be taken to substance beyond an iconography of modernity.

The end of the dream, the utopia, the hope, the agency of cultural revolution, and the project of new design, art and architecture, was symbolically registered on 14 April 1930. This was the day Mayakovsky shot himself. He was buried in a coffin designed by Tatlin and made by students of the Vkhutemas. He left a letter, in it a poem:

> As they sat,
>   the incident is closed.
> Love's boat has crashed
>   on philistine reefs.
> It would be useless making a list
>   of who did what to whom.
> We shared weapons
>   and wounds.[25]

Clearly, the 'total design' image of a 'new world' never gained hegemonic status or real political power in the Soviet Union. This was not just because it was unable to be materially delivered, but more significantly because it was overwhelmed by the totality of totalitarianism. We note, not without a certain irony, that firstly totalitarianism's relation to total design in the era of Stalin was to repress rather than exploit it, because of its failure to immediately deliver change in the face of pressing material problems; its lack of connection to the determinate forces of the 'economic base' and inability to align itself with this model of determinism; and its gesturalism. Secondly, the very instrument of capitalism that did the most damage in the destruction of Soviet totalitarianism in the 1990s was the political economy of the sign of Western commodity culture. Thus we see from the point of view of the present that at the very moment that the utopian modernist dream of Soviet Russia was terminated, the fate of the regime was sealed. At the same time the power of the sign of America itself was implicated in a repression of the symbolic.

There was in and beyond the 1920s, a great fascination in Soviet Russia with American technology as form, system, method and above all as an accelerated path to the future. This technology was mediated by an influential cultural faction. The focal points of this celebration were the conditions of the industrial working class; production technology; the labour process; and the mechanistity of economic modernity. This mediated fascination took diverse forms: the poetry of Alexie Gastev, as it embraced industrial noise and the proto-cybernetics of FW Taylor (as hero!); Meyerhold's attempt to promote biomechanics in his avant-garde theatre; and the industrial theatre sets designed by constructivist artists that returned workers to their work place as a place of cultural generation. In economic terms Taylor's idea were subject to research at the Central Institute for Labour throughout the 1920s. It comes as no surprise then that when the economy became militarised, its discipline came in significant part from the ideas and para-science of Frederick Winslow Taylor. However, as David Elliot notes:

> Taylorism was only a part of a general enthusiasm for American ideas and culture which pervaded Soviet culture during the 1920s. This admiration was based on the conviction that both countries were new worlds which had sloughed off the oppression of the old.[26]

The notion of a productivist aesthetic (where art was linked to instrumental political and economic ends) was directly linked to the most overt form of productivist metaphysics (and thus to accelerated creation of the defutured) with the formation of a constructivism, Taylorism, Americanism/Fordism nexus.

\*\*\*

For all the historical complexity and conjunctural detail in this and the other chapters of this part of the book, one message overwhelms: the path to a higher order of unsustainability had been laid down by Design and the power of the designed sign. Moreover, the developments outlined are just the opening onto events, relations and forces that sped and extended this condition.

### Notes

1. The two institutions at Weimar were combined to form the Bauhaus. The initial result from this, plus the arrival of a new educational agenda, was a series of divisions between the staff of the amalgamated institutions: old staff turned on the new and vice-versa, students turned on students, teachers on teachers and institution on institution. Things were made worse by the actions of a notorious student avant-garde sub-culture which were just too much for people of the small conservative town. The early years were driven very much by a craft and expressionist sensibility, however, with the arrival of the influence of constructivism, the institution gradually became more pragmatic and seemingly more socially engaged. Gradually as the staff changed and developed, something like the vision that Gropius started out with took hold, initially via a pluralist accommodation of ideological and aesthetic differences. On Gropius as 'Silver Prince' see Tom Wolfe, *From Bauhaus to Our House*, Jonathan Cape, London, 1981, pp. 9–35.

2. The reactionary modernism of German fascism manifested a fundamental paradox: it embraced modern science and technology as an instrument to install a pre-Enlightenment utopia in which spirit triumphs over reason. Thus the attack on the Bauhaus, and all other manifestations of avant-garde modernism, was that the style was posited as a consequence of rationalisation. It therefore signified a future in which the power of reason was extended. This topic is treated at length by Jeffrey Herf, *Reactionary Modernism: Technology, Culture, and Politics in Weimar and the Third Reich*, Cambridge University Press, Cambridge, 1984.

3. This work also informed the way Gropius designed the Fagus shoe factory in 1911–13 and the Werkbund Exhibition in Cologne in 1914. These and all other comments draw on a range of sources, in particular Reyner Banham, *Theory and Design in the First Machine Age*, The Architectural Press, London, 1980; Tim Benton *et al.*, *The New Objectivity*, (History of Architecture and Design 1890–1939 course), Open University, Milton Keynes, 1975; Walter Gropius, *Scope of Total Architecture*, Collier Books, New York, 1974; John Willett, *The New Sobriety 1917–1933*, Thames and Hudson, London, 1978; Dave Elliott, *New Worlds: Russian Art and Society 1900–1937*, Thames and Hudson, London, 1986; HM Wingler, *The Bauhaus: Weimer, Dessau, Berlin*, MIT Press, Cambridge (Mass), 1969.

4. While Ittens was an inspired teacher he was also a mystic who followed a cult that undertook to rigorously discipline the body

with diet and fasting. During 1921–22 Ittens gave priority to his 'mission'. In his absence Theo Van Doesburg filled the gap and ran an unofficial course. Van Doesburg, while never admitted to the faculty, exerted a powerful influence in the formative years of the institution. He had been one of the key members of De Stijl (a modernist and rationalist architecture and design movement founded in 1917 under the influence of the Dutch architect HP Berlage, who promoted the work of Frank Lloyd Wright) and thus he adopted a far more ordered and rationalist approach.

Van Doesburg was in turn replaced by an even more influential figure, Laszlo Moholy-Nagy, who had a disposition towards a 'soft constructivism'. He advocated radical change in material forms and he retained a commitment to aesthetic values but rejected constructivism's agency as a cultural politics — which was its implication in the USSR. In many ways his disposition and vision for the institution were close to Gropius. What this added up to was a strong commitment to the new (in terms of ideas, education, design, materials), a major concern with form, and an attraction to using technologies but with a retained place for, and romantic faith in, the artist as a primary visionary subject. Moholy-Nagy combined all of these dispositions in the way he approached taking over the *Vorkurs*.

The pedagogical approach of the course adopted similar modes of inquiry to those of Russian constructivism, but additionally Moholy-Nagy drew on his experience with constructivism in Hungary. He especially focused on questions of physical deconstruction. This provided the basis for his activities in exploring methods for invention and remaking. Historically, Moholy-Nagy was to be the transitional link that enabled the Bauhaus to move from an idealist art centred institution to one with a major architecture and functionalist orientation. The drift towards the ultra-rationalist and instrumental pole was to eventually go well beyond his position; this alienated him and he left in 1928. By this time Klee and Kandinsky were also anachronisms.

Without a doubt one of the most significant reasons why the Bauhaus gained its profile and influence was because of the people it recruited to teach there. Many of them, like Paul Klee, Wassily Kandinsky, Marcel Breuer and Hannes Meyer, were to become key figures in the history of modernism. Many were experimentalists who strayed between art and design (at least as the Bauhaus understood it), they moved between media, they taught, produced their own work/commissions and wrote.

5  During the Weimar years the institution was riven with contradiction, in part due to the slippage between the rational as spiritual and the spiritual as mystical, as well as a tension between art and design. Contradictions were most evident around different notions of creativity. While significant changes resulted with the move to Dessau in 1925, in many respects the key year for the nature of the institution was 1923, when the Bauhaus started to turn its back on its art and craft foundation to embrace the machine (or at least the machine aesthetic). One very significant bridge existed, however, between these two moments (and across all other institutional changes): this was the investment made in 'learning by doing'.
6  Although modernist ambitions were counter to the romanticism of arts and crafts, the movement's reduction of form to the simple created an aesthetic to which the modern machine could realise and add precision.
7  The spirit of this culture was epitomised by Le Corbusier, whose influence on Gropius was considerable, especially his writing on architecture of the 1920s. Le Corbusier's *Vers une Architecture*, published in French in 1923 and in English in 1927, was the most influential text of this period.
8  For instance, both modernist design and fascism traded on an idealisation of classical form. We also note that through its repression of Bauhaus ideas, fascism prompted most of the institution's major figures to leave Germany. The result of this was to give added momentum to the worldwide spread of the institution's ideas, as its staff sought refuge in other countries and started working and teaching. After World War II the Dessau Bauhaus, and its records (many of which were destroyed) became part of the invisibility that was East Germany. This added to the ability of Gropius to exercise a power of memory over events. With the re-unification of Germany, the Dessau Bauhaus, as one of the major modernist architectural icons of the twentieth century, has become a part of architectural design history, tourism and historical revision.
9  Walter Gropius, *Scope of Total Architecture*, Collier Books, New York, 1974.
10  *Ibid.*, p. 26.
11  *Ibid.*, p. 20.
12  There were, for example, the publications Moholy-Nagy created as a Bauhaus book series (*Bauhaus-bücher*), which he co-edited with Gropius. These were published by an independent publisher, Albert-Langen-Verlag in Munich. Fourteen appeared between

1925 and 1930, including the very influential *Von material zu Architecture* by Moholy-Nagy himself. These books were enormously successful in giving the institution a worldwide profile and in giving their designing ideology agency. Besides several books by Gropius and the two by Moholy-Nagy there were books by Klee, Kandinsky, Schlemmer, Adolf Meyer and a few people outside the institution who were associated with it and extended its associational power, most notable being Van Doesburg, Oud and Mondrian (plus an unpublished text of Le Corbusier rendered redundant by the translation of *Vers une Architecture*). For a fuller account and titles see Banham, *Theory and Design in the First Machine Age*, pp. 284–86.

13 Jean Baudrillard, 'Design and Environment or How Political Economy Escalates into Cyberblitz', in *For a Critique of the Political Economy of the Sign* (trans Charles Levin), Telos Press, St Louis, 1981, p. 185.

14 Schematically we can acknowledge another route into the history of the defutured. The material world of exchange (the ecological) became perceptually culturally dislocated by valorisation, resulting in the power of money (abstraction one) deflecting concern for the consequence of actual material exchange. Then, on the other side of this moment (the moment when the world became an object of resource appropriation, wherein abstract value became the highest value), the sign economy arrived (abstraction two) which created an even greater perceptual gap between understanding capital as a system of exchange (the restricted economy) and the fundamental, determinant and changing processes of exchange that sustainment demands.

15 *Ibid.*, p. 187.
16 *Ibid.*, pp. 195, 198 and 200.
17 *Ibid.*, p. 201.
18 *Ibid.*, p. 202.
19 For instance, in 1925 when it moved to Dessau it only had 63 students. This rose to 170 students in 1929, 140 of whom were German, the rest from other European countries, plus two from the USA. Of these students 47 were under 20, the majority (90) were 20–24, of the remaining 33 there were 22 between 24 and 29, and 11 over 30: John Willett, *The New Sobriety*, p. 123. We also note that the eventual global authority and influence of its major figures in no way equated with their institutional conditions or income. The influence on modern architecture of Gropius and Meyer and their association with Le Corbusier, as well as with the more pragmatic figure of Mies van der Rohe

(a director of the institution after Nazi intervention) is almost beyond calculation.

20 Banham, *Theory and Design in the First Machine Age*, p. 78. The DIN-Format is familiar to all of us as the metric standard of measure of, amongst other thing the O and A paper sizes of A4 familiarity.

21 Willett, *The New Sobriety*, p. 39. We note that its program was spread across three years. The first year in the Basic Section was devoted to graphics, colour and spatial studies. Most of the second year was assigned to working in a specific faculty (architecture, sculpture, painting, graphics, woodwork, textiles and metalwork), with work in these faculties also flowing into a multimedia context of photomontage, film, writing and theatre. The final year was spent working in industry. The aim was to produce 'artist-constructors'. The academic figures in and around the cultural circles of the Vkhutemas were of equal stature to those at the Bauhaus. On staff were, for example, Alexander Vesin and Moisei Ginsburg (architects), Liubov Popova and Varvara Stepanova (artists), Alexander Rodchenko, Vladimir Tatlin and El Lissitzky (constructor-artists/designers). The institution emerged from, formed part of and flowed into, the melting pot of Russian Futurism and constructivism. It prefigured and was implicated in the cultural moment of the Russian revolution. In the latter context, the institution had a clear aim: to produce graduates to conceive and deliver, via their specialisations, the total form of a post-revolutionary society. The key instrument in this aim was to conceptualise the form, content and built material of architectural forms and social spaces of the revolution, its workers and their emergent culture. This architecture was not to be reactive but proactive: it had to be one of the instruments of change. One example of this was the built 'social condenser' or determinate environments. The theory was that these constructions — workplaces and places of pleasure — would expose people to material and social forms of the future that would drive the creation of that future.

22 Kandinsky was a major link between constructivism and the Bauhaus. In 1920 as first president of the Inkhuk he put forward a program that was rejected by his colleagues. As a result of this he moved, with the program to the Bauhaus: see Tim Benton *et al.*, *The New Objectivity: History of Architecture and Design 1890–1939*, (units 11–12), Open University Press, 1975, pp. 35–36.

23 According to Marxist theory at the time, the revolution occurred

in the wrong place: it should have happened in the industrial countries of Britain, France or Germany.
24 See Dave Elliott, *New Worlds: Russian Art and Society 1900–1937*, Thames and Hudson, London, 1986.
25 Cited in the catalogue of the exhibition: David Elliott (ed), *Mayakovsky: Twenty Years of Work*, Museum of Modern Art, Oxford, 1982, p. 90.
26 *Ibid.*, pp. 18–19.

# PART 3

# ONE POINT: FOUR LOCATIONS

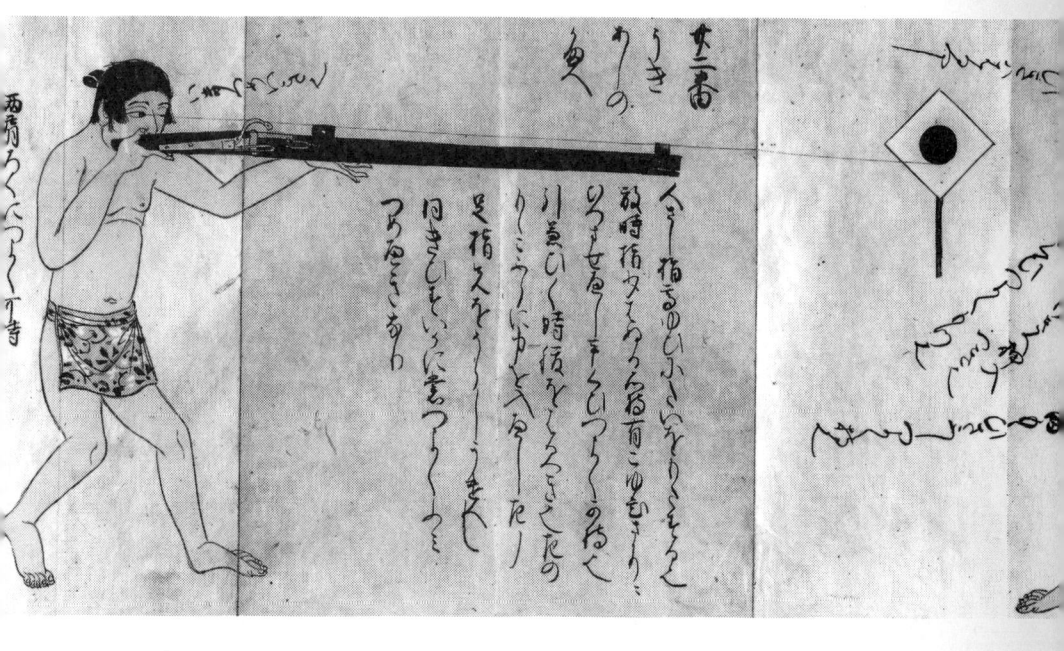

The Japanese had firearms in the seventeenth century, but gave them up within a generation because they took all the fun out of being a Samurai! (Nagasawa, Shigetsuna, *Inatomi-ryu Teppo Densho* (The secrets of shooting with guns of the Inatomi school), Japan, 1612: Spenser Collection, Astor, Lennox and Tiden Foundation, The New York Public Library)

This third part adopts quite a different approach. It samples four very different thematic discourses. Each of these have an on-going and large impact which defutures, each tells us a little more about the condition of unsustainability and the imperative of sustain-ability.

Each thematic has been selected to expose more of the pervasiveness and complexity of the defutured. At the same time, in sum, the chapters show just how hard it is to narrativise something that is so structurally inherent in the transformed and made worlds of our planet. Clearly so much more could be said about all that has been commented upon, but equally and more dramatically, the four themes addressed stand for a myriad that remain silent — volumes could be written on say biology and genetics, food, health, urban development, chemicals, education, lifestyles, energy, land and oceans, and so on. The ambition has never been to fully describe and account for the defutured. Rather what has been aimed for has been to create an ability to recognise what the defutured is and to demonstrate that this understanding is transferable into an employable sensibility in professional practice and daily life. We all need to live with the question: What can I see taking the future away, and what can I do to reduce the impacts of my own actions which defuture? This perception of, and an acting against, defuturing forms the substance of a thinking, and this thinking is at the core of the claim and character of the new design philosophy.

The four thematic chapters of this part examine the human body; time and space; cultural technology (the televisual); and computers, as they expose the emergent 'nature' of technology. The focus of concerns of the final chapter with technology will in fact return us to those we first engaged in chapter one. We will not, however, have simply gone round in a circle. Rather, together they will work to illuminate the transformative and non-evolutionary nature of our object and the variations of its propensity toward autonomically making the defutured of many of its others.

Besides what follows further exposing both a dependence upon and the limits of metanarrative and metahistory, it also reinforces the heuristic importance of the attempt to speak the unspeakable as a gathering and learning that can install a way of reading. (In many ways this statement replays the advocation of defuturing as method.) This reading will always be constituted out of conjunctural difference of the text, subject, experience and circumstance. This means that while it is fuelled by generality it is always driven by the particular. Moreover, while it can never be claimed or contained by the universal, neither can it be subsumed by whatever the circumstantial makes present.

# 5

# DESIGN AND THE BODY OF COMPETITION

A human wheel in the Red Square Parade, Moscow, 1936
(Museum of Modern Art, Oxford)

By explaining and exploring how the material and immaterial body has been historically constructed, this chapter adds many new sets of relational connections to the picture of defuturing. This will partly disrupt the content of earlier chapters, not least in terms of the weight that will be given to the experiential, and the question of the time. In doing this, however, it will provide a significant contribution to better informing the way in which the directions, dynamics and sites of impact of the defutured are able to be viewed.

The human body is present, as an anthropocentric figure of reference, in all that is designed. At its most basic it stands between designing and the designed, sometimes as agent, sometimes as object, and often as effect (subject): fusion and confusion abound. To recognise the body beyond it being 'the designed for' requires talking about it in another way. And to do this requires the creation of a number of openings.

BODY LANGUAGE

To say anything on the body is to stray into one of the most heavily policed territories of that academic club called 'contemporary thought'. What is offered here is but a brush with the body. There is reason for this. Very little of the current fashionable debates of the body — be they within philosophy, feminism, anthropology, sociology, cultural studies, biology or the visual arts — deal with its implication in design and designing. They have even less to say on its ecology. For all the talk of multi-disciplinarity, the conventional divisions of knowledge and academic structures still rule. These divisions exclude some of the most powerful world-forming forces of our epoch, not least sustain-ability, anthropocentrism and Design. No attempt will be made to survey the thinking on the human body, or to position what is to be said in relation to the theory of every proper name on the checklists of those forces that do the policing. Much will remain in silence, but something will be said. One may start by asking how is it possible to speak of the body in a way that is not exhausted by a language of constant preoccupation? To answer, we turn to language rather than to the body.

To observe, and be open to, the fluidity and relational resonance of language is to dispose oneself in another way. We think and act as if it were we who command language, whereas it commands us.

As the Russian formalists made clear in the 1920s, and as Fredric Jameson reminded us more recently, language is a 'prison house'.[1] All that we draw on for communication results from its processes of exclusion, making present, gathering and holding. To be with language is to be in language. To be in the prison house of language is to be environmentally encased by it as it enfolds us, to be the product of mind and the matter, time and space of our being here. We are not just held in custody by language but also occupied by it. Occupation is not merely an imposition, displacement or colonisation, but equally fascination, animated time, and work. The ambiguity of the disablement and enablement of language is profound in the extreme. Language is the most powerful of all instruments of designing, and the one least recognised.

The structuring of language, as a designing, is always a prefiguration of the 'to be designed' (whatever is made present for us is always predicated upon the disposition of the intentionality of language itself disposing the intention of the subject employing language). Nothing simply 'is'. Moreover, whatever is designated to be designed (that is, spoken of as the object of designing) has already been disposed towards what 'it' is yet to be. As we shall see, this is done by it being brought, by language, into a particular temporal, spatial and perspectival state of presence. For instance to say 'I am going to design a chair' means the imposition of a limit (all that is not a chair) and the arrival of the experience of chairs and their known history as a place of commencement — hence the notion of the word as the first object of design.

The structuring of language goes ahead of, and authors, the subject as part of that structuring which structures the world that, in their difference, human beings know. In doing this, language does not structure on the basis of its holding directive, universal, reductive, identifiable and active foundations of knowledge which correspond with, and are able to be attributed to, human understandings of world and structure. Rather, what language structures is far more fundamental, and actually is both the division between that 'which is' in being (as that 'other than', 'prior to' and outside the confinement of whatsoever is made representationally present by a 'regime of sense' as knowledge) and what is culturally created, via representational claims, as present (as object, idea, subject and agency). Moreover, in spite of all the efforts of reason, there is no meta-language of truth that can provide a transcendental resolution to the culturally different claims to the ownership of meanings. Thus, no overarching authority or structure is available, with the result that as soon as cultural difference is acknowledged an indeterminacy of meaning and a contest of authority arrives.

We sometimes realise our designing and occupation by and with language, but mostly we do not — for we are in fact distant from most of that to which we assume we are close.

REQUALIFYING DESIGN

Effort has been made to show the difference between what language structures and what is made to appear by the creation and application of a language of structural description. That our relation with language is such that one is always held prisoner within the very thing one wishes to externally view can but be recognised as one of the inescapable ambiguities of our position of observation. A similar problem can be identified when we endeavour to draw a line between the causal power of the designed and the causality of the directional forms of design instruction, (its material specifications or instruments of visual representation). The on-going agency of the designed (as information, object, process, image and system) structures designing as it forms the referential ground from and upon which design occurs. Ontologically, Design is an active characteristic of all things from which we constitute a world of existence. In this sense, Design is a major qualification of the on-going inscriptive quality of the temporal condition of all things. It is also, metaphysically, the exercise of mind. From such an understanding of the flow between mind and matter it is perhaps possible to see just how starkly Design demonstrates the error of that construction of the binary division between subject and object. It should be instantly said that almost all designing assumes this division.

Currently, design mostly works with information models that block the ability to disclose and see the ontological character of Design. Just as the ability to use language in no way depends on understanding the 'nature' of language, so it is that designing in no way depends upon understanding the ontology of Design. However, unless one understands how things, like language and Design, are, what they are and how they act, then one does not have the possibility of making them otherwise.

To qualify Design more directly: design designs from a continual return of the material forms that are grounded in the discourses of reason and 'creativity'. First of all in doing this, its practices, assumptions and values transport its *logos*: words and deeds travel with a logic of unexpressed reason as the taken-for-granted basis of action; things literally make sense. Such acting on the given foundation of inscribed reason assures a continual return of the same. This is so even when what is made to appear is claimed as a difference. Secondly, Design constantly returns as it re-presents itself by *eidos*. This is to say that the image (the *eidos*) of the already designed is always elemental to the 'newly' designed. Design, again like language, can but feed off itself.

These observations on Design's relation to its *logos* and *eidos* are not meant to imply that the geometry of this process can or should be stopped, but rather that the foundation from which the same is returned is absolutely flawed. Again, what is being registered is that which returns, that which design designs on, from and with, is mostly the unsustainable. In contrast, what needs to continually return is the ability to sustain. For this to happen the ground has to shift — the very paradigm 'design' has to change. As with all paradigmatic changes, the new will render the old dysfunctional and produce the leads that the majority will follow.

These abstract observations can now be brought to the particular example of Design and the body. The body is the standard reference point of measurement for that which is fabricated and how it is perceived. For instance, large or small, light or heavy, long duration or short, while never speaking of the body, it always express its presence as the point of perspectival measure. Size, weight and time exist in a regime of sensibility that rests with the body. The worlds we have constituted are directly or indirectly enframed by the body's geometry, needs, pathology, movement, metabolism, and desires. This is to say that the anthropocentrically materialised 'needs of man' have centred around a designing that itself centres around the performative requirements of the body. This began as a response to the basic demand for shelter, food, thermal comfort and the community required to sustain a being. From this beginning a foundation of action of unceasing proliferation was established. We stand upon the past and present of a material culture that is surrounded by 'things' that carry this historicity. Examples are literally everywhere: listing them — buildings, furniture, clothes, cooking utensils, transport, office technology — would eventually lead to an entire inventory of human artifice.

No matter how much complexity were to be layered on the observation of the designing power of the body, two simple and invisibly self-evident facts constantly await disclosure. The first is the concealment of the body, as reference, in the omnipresent and absolute anthropocentric direction that designs all things fabricated in the 'world of our being'. The second is that while the anthropocentric imperative was to sustain the species, the means, at some unidentifiable moment, became disengaged from the end. This is the point when economy became disarticulated from ecology, and acting towards future-making turned into the defutured. While we cannot 'be' without being anthropocentric, what we are able to do, as is repeatedly proclaimed in this text in one way or another, is to take responsibility for this situation. The redesign of Design is implicit in this move, and redesigning how Design designs with and for the body is a large challenge of this agenda.

*** 

The body is something totally familiar to us and also totally strange, something we occupy and are occupied by, something we own, know in pain, forsake in pleasure, and have taken from us. To view the body in the way we wish to here, as the designed and as designing, requires making it present in another way. It is perhaps worth recalling that making the body present is an activity in which every culture engages in every modality of the knowledge it creates. The body is one of those central figures, past, present and undoubtedly future, employed in a process of defining and redefining what we are.

The designing body (the designed body in action) turns two ways. It is both an object of continuous redesigning by the knowledge, concepts and language of its designation, and it is a designing force in itself that designs the world in which it appears and acts.

## THE BODY

There is no universal form of understanding the body — it is certainly not reducible to biology, self, function, symbol, object, performance, discourse, regime or economy in the same form (or even in any form) across cultures. The body, the subject, the object and the actor are a confused cast. Our anthropocentrism positions the body as a primary reference point of our being. It centres an object that, according to its disposition as subject in action, is centred, reified, concealed, refused, neglected, displayed, celebrated, embraced, integrated or given way to. This is to say that every time a subject arrives to act (be it worker, lover, student, runner) 'bodies' depart and arrive. Becoming subject is thus materially transformative of the object's disposition. No body can ever be disposed as just a body, for no body is without its specificity, its historicity.

Mostly our own bodies are sent away by our being-in-the-world of bodily involvement. Even the sense we have of our body arrives from elsewhere: we cannot sense our body independently from the knowledge we have of it from its own world. A stiff leg, a digestive discomfort or tooth ache is made present as a fusion of felt sense and made sense: what is felt is placed by a knowledge of muscle, stomach, nerve. Such knowledge is part of our earliest learning. The naming of parts of the world and the naming of parts of the body are both of the same naming. This act of naming is always historically and culturally specific. One indicator of fundamental cultural difference is the way the body is constructed as a mythological entity (of which science is but one competing explanation that strives for, but never totally gains, hegemonic status). The organic body thus inhabits a world alongside the body as earth, spirit, vessel, animal, temple and more.

Usually the body is presenced only partially, be it as pleasure, pain or image. We are constantly denied access to a whole, for the whole is not available for scrutiny. The limits of vision and knowledge, the containment of excess and the complexity of worldly involvement, the 'nature' of change, all hold the possibility of the whole which is not one at bay. Echoing the comments made on the body, Design and knowledge, how we know the 'body' is constantly rewritten and redesigned by what we have known. We place the body before ourselves to view by a system of classification, language, institutional practices, discourse and learned aesthetics. We thus see it through the filter of all those knowledges and images that construct the sense of our own, other and imaginary bodies. Knowledge of the body, of our body, always arrives from elsewhere. So while we may have a true sensation of what we feel, our ability to make sense of that is predicated upon the designing of the representational regime in which the knowledge of the body has accumulatively arrived. Not even the truth of that which we feel is available to us. The fundamental observation, clearly argued by Merleau-Ponty, is that underpinning all such understandings is the fact that 'I am conscious of my body via the world' which, for us, makes the body 'the pivot of the world'.[2]

The world that arrives for a being coming into being-in-the-world clearly frames perceptions and situates available knowledge. In such a setting the body always arrives ontologically as a thing of encountered function, and metaphysically as it is designated by knowledge from 'a' world — that is, as some thing of and in 'the' world. It follows that the discursive formation that is 'world' inscribes the body in the order of things of its structuring of knowledge.[3] This means that we always see the body through a theoretical screen of a worldview, and the first naming of a body part, and the objects of a body's initial encounter, mark both the arrival of this theory and knowledge that is to become world. Western 'culture-nature' and manner of coming into the metaphysical condition of being-in-the-world has deposited a biocentric worldview of the body that mutually brings functional knowledge while preventing an understanding of the condition of connectedness. It follows that if one contests one's knowledge of 'a' world from the position of recognised connectedness then how the body is known will of course change. The implication here is that the sustain-ability of 'world' and 'body' centres on sustaining 'the same'. Furthermore, if confronting the question of sustain-ability means, as it does, that our perceptions and actions upon worlds are contested, so equally our bodies are sites of conflict. The body of competition, as it is being unfolded here, is a site of contested knowledge and conceptual constructions.

Certainly the biocentric views of the discourses of health and the 'natural' sciences provide little help in broadening our vision. They deliver only an instrumental perspective. In fact, the divisions of knowledge of medical science (not least the division of mind and matter) effectively delimit what it is possible to know, especially when the body is reduced to object, which totally obstructs the possibility of the arrival of an ecological understanding. For much of the time we live, our relation to the biological body as that which is repressed.[4] How it can be made more appropriately present is unable to be answered biologically. But it can be answered within an ecology of the body that views bodily care beyond bio-function.

Philosophies of the body have arrived as a more significant part of the intellectual scene in the past decade or so — in large part driven by the agendas of sexual politics. For all the complexity this work has ushered in, and not overlooking the contribution of a phenomenological understanding led by, and built upon, the work of Maurice Merleau-Ponty, an ecology that enfolds an ecology of the body has yet to arrive in Western thought. Viewing the same issues from an Asian point of view, the story is quite different as Drew Leder for instance makes clear. As Leder details, neo-Confucian thinkers, over a period of at least six centuries (from the tenth century in the West), created a complex understanding and language of relationality in which 'a body' was viewed as elementally implicated in 'the body'.[5] The value of this tradition does not arrive by turning it into a repository of truth but rather by taking it as a developed foundation of thought upon which to reflect and from which to extend one's thinking. Re-thinking neo-Confucian thinking has the capability of directly informing how one understands relationality as being at the core of thinking sustain-ability, and thus at the core of futuring, not as a new idea but rather as a constantly returning idea that has been able to be sustained.

To be able to approach thinking an ecology of the body, there needs to be a clear refusal of its reduction to an individuated and purely biological mechanism. What questions are appropriate to ask? Certainly many beg consideration, such as: How does one understand to what the body is articulated? What does the body actually embody beyond its corporal containment? How culturally specific is the idea of the body? and What is the body able to sustain in a system of sustain-ability?

The way bodies have been presented to us, and the way we view our selves, obstruct an ecological view of the body constituted as diverse systems that are in turn operative in relation to other systems that constitute environments.

From an other place, wherein we dwell, we exist in competition with the time, passage and physical capacity of our bodies: as we dream, act, desire and live, we do so with a will that strives to overcome bodily limitation. Thus we live both by being at home with our body, and also by treating it as foreign. At the same time we also use our body in competition with an other. While the expressive form of this competition changes, fundamental sex and power motives eternally return. Clearly the way we have been led to think the body is woefully inadequate.

BEING 'HERE'

While we occupy our bodies, in our being-in-the-world, our bodies are also occupied by a world. We are 'here' in both these senses. Being is being animated by a world and, in return, being re-animates world. The sense we have of 'an us' and 'an it' is illusory. Moreover, rather than the object we may feel it to be, the body is a passage between worlds, time and matter. Our identity, our self, our individuated being has been culturally emplaced. Even so we are never what and where we have been told we are.

The very thing I, you and we take so for granted — learning from Chinese thought — is that my body, your body can become our body. We are all, to cite the words of Maurice Merleau-Ponty, 'Flesh of the world-Flesh of the body-Being'.[6] No division exists between body, world, Being and sustain-ability: learning from Merleau-Ponty we can say 'we are in it' as well as 'of it'. My flesh is as your flesh and in this knowledge the anthropologically constituted 'other' disappears: we eat the flesh of the world to sustain our flesh, we appropriate the flesh of others as if they were our own. Examples proliferate — from leather on the soles of my shoes to the use of the heart valve of a pig in cardiac surgery. Equally, because I have the ability to sense my self and my body, transcriptively, I also know something of you and yours. In this context, identification undoes identity: my pain is your pain, for we both suffer the same pain of the flesh of the world. We both, to call up the language of Elaine Scarry, exist in the 'body of pain' that suffers in its 'making and unmaking of the world'.[7]

There is another kind of pain to consider, one stemming from a confrontation with unsustainability, arising out of the experience of the defutured in our cultural and economic making of worlds. Defuturing arrives now as a confrontation with the pain of the discovery that there has been a fundamental unmaking of a world in being, named as 'unsustainability', and an unsustainable world makes unsustainable bodies.

The breakdowns of modernity, as the defutured, that appear throughout this text are their various manifestations. Here breakdown is the body dehumanised, inhumanised, and rendered structurally unsustainable. The example of the ecological crisis of vast tracts of abandoned Africa and the crisis of the bodies of millions of Africans expose the continuum of unsustainability and the inadequacy of humanist/environmentalist classification. As we live in error we live the error of the concealment of proximity. That which is imaged as far away, of an other's space, of an other's time, of an other's sensibility is not where we place it. The dehabitation of the defutured is redrawing the relations of all bodies. Again one can say the 'flesh of the world' has to be connected to 'the body in pain' for slowly but surely the defutured touches every body.

It can be seen that the remaking of the meaning of the body is an essential agenda item in the making of sustain-ability. The more one confronts fundamental questions of sustain-ability the more one needs to be able to disclose failures and attainments. Hence this continual preoccupation with turning unsustainability into a 'history'. In this context it is absolutely vital to draw that complexity — shorthanded as 'modernity' — into the light of harsh criticism, not as a whipping boy but in order for an informed exercise of destruction and creation to take place. The project at hand of the remaking of design, by both its de-signing and its re-designing, substantiates the point. While sustain-ability demands the destruction of the unsustainable, the unsustainable does not simply reveal itself, it has to be discovered.

Contrary to fundamentalist doctrines, to evoke what is fundamental is to call up forgotten questions rather than eternal truths. That which threatens is never just the named dangers of environmental crisis but a loss of memory — a loss of ability of how to find and think fundamental questions. Objects of concern are not distant — they are no further away than thinking and the body. Again the lesson is relearnt — the world arrives in the body and brings it into being. Harkening back to the Greek idea of *physis* and the Latin *natura*, and counter to modern ideas on 'nature', we again need to learn that we are born from the world as well as from the womb. To say this is not to evoke 'mother Earth' but the finitude of the given and the fabricated environment, and the health of all. By the body being 'thrown' into the world, by it reaching out, being touched and making, it becomes possible to 'be here'.

The body has been placed in the difference that is world and culture. It follows a trace from the degeneration of the Greek notion of *physis* (as the way to speak everything in being, the being of being) to the diminished modern idea of 'nature'. It falters before the ethnocentric character of anthropocentric humanism, as its failure to even value the difference that is the human (let alone life itself) is exposed. Likewise the body suffers at the hand of reason, especially reason's implication in the very negation of thought itself, and by the unremitting historical consistency of its service to the extension of productivism. What we see across this flash of unmeasurable time is the widening of the gulf between a first thinking that thinks itself and its world, to an appropriation of the body (first in and by the Enlightenment) by a particular world to support the shrinking goals of modernity and its withering utopias. And yet there are other spaces, albeit not heterotopic ones.

So far thinking about 'here' has focused on being here in 'a' world; now the focus shifts to 'here' in the body. What is it that a being occupies, is occupied by, and is preoccupied with? Should it be claimed that in the unmaking that has made the modern unsustainable world that there has also been the creation of an unsustainable human body? How sustain-able is the physical fabric, and metaphysical fabrication, upon which the body depends?

Such questions fall at the feet of thinking an ecology of the body. It quickly becomes clear from even the briefest consideration that the human body not only starts out by being connected to an ecological system that supports it, but once cut free from this system it immediately connects with a larger and more complex set of dependencies. While we have various names for these dependent systems (economy, culture, society, family and so on) they all share one overriding characteristic: they are all constructions, part of the structural fabrication upon which our being here depends. While our biological systems are clearly essential, they in turn rest upon the consequence of artifice — such as food, shelter, warmth, clothing, knowledge, medicine, social institutions, all of which have become postnatural. 'Here' is the irony of the unsustainable turn, which now appears as the fallout of the effort to sustain 'being here' with excess. and as has been said, without any responsible consideration of the consequences of short-term expedient action.

There is a moment in the lives of most people when their objectified body arrives idealised as a utopian site, and then there is another when the dream evaporates. Drawn from the normative enframing of a culture and by reference to an other, ideas of, for instance, beauty or strength prefigure self-perceptions. Comparison ensures competition, and time assures defeat. Our attention moves from our idealised body, to the abandonment of the self as image measured against an other, to a final resting point with the body as object of resignation. Alongside whatever we make present there is what Drew Leder calls the 'absent body' — which is that body that has not been made present or that is in a condition of recession (such as sleep, unawareness, dwelling metabolically in a condition withdrawn from worldly engagement).[8] From this observation it can be noted that the body is appearing as an increasingly plural ecology: it dwells in the relations of the systems of the image, mind, space, the inhabited temporality of its own being and the 'flesh of the world'.

Our concern with 'here' requires consideration of the issue of space. Space does not become the body's place of being by simply giving way. As previously elaborated, space arrives by a process of clearing, equally characterised as occupation or dwelling. The body extends itself in space, it reaches in extensio to clear a *raum* for itself. The body makes room for itself in the world, it makes rooms, room in which to dwell, a room within a dwelling place, room to move. The move from making room to making 'a' room conjoin in the idea of home. Again 'here' is not spatially reducible. Room, home and dwelling appear on a linear scale of being, however, the body inserts itself as both a place of dwelling and as that active force that has to be present for a dwelling to be: that which dwells in the body dwells (or recoils, alienated from its host). The dwelling place remains a habit, a *habitus*, a thing in the making, and a making thing, as well as a place. The body now arrives as a geography of an other space.

Clearing has always been a competitive activity and for millions of people, as the world's population grows, becomes ever more so. Making a place for oneself usually requires the displacement of that which is already in place. Planning, urban design, architecture and interior design are implicated in this clearing and emplacement. De facto, these practices have been made in that thinking which is the management of clearing, building and dwelling. In the spirit of Thomas Hobbes' notion of 'freedom under the law', design appears as competition for space brought within a system of order.[9] Competition still occurs, but now within a regulated structure. We are always finding ourselves in a space that we have to make a place. We have to make ourselves at home in the world in order for the world to inhabit us, yet we do not know exactly where we are: 'What Saint Augustine said of time — that it is perfectly familiar to each, but none of us can explain it to others — must be said of the world'.[10]

Even in the darkest hole, the most miserable circumstances, the human being inscribes the world it finds itself in and proclaims 'I am here, this is my place'. It is in this proclamation of identity, ownership and occupied location that we discover that to be recognised we have to announce that we are 'here' in our embodied and disembodied location. From all that has been said it follows that there can be no understanding of the body without an accompanying understanding of space and limit. Again it is worth re-emphasising, as Merleau-Ponty was at pains to do, 'the body is our general medium for having a world'.[11] This 'having' is both sentient and cognitive: to have is to feel across the range of sense. However, having knowledge of what is possessed requires bringing knowledge to what is seen, spoken, heard, touched and smelt in its spatial and temporal context.

Before moving into a set of closer engagements with some of the many ways to read the body-world, there are still a few more basic qualification to make.

World arrives — out of the relations of the experience of sensed encounter, reflection, memory, and all the prefigured mediations that the representational baggage of a culture brings via thought, image and word — as the interpretative filter of all other modes of knowledge. Science, for instance, has no direct window on the 'world,' for the world that science knows is first of all a cultural construction of science as discourse (both expression and practice). It follows that the limits of the world are the limits of the body/mind and the limits of the body/mind are the limits of the cultural and physical world in which they arrive. To reiterate a fundamental point on the question of presence: one might want to abstractly claim the existence of an objective world, however, once it is understood that in order to have a world one needs a culture, then an objective world slides out of reach forever. For us there is only the world we have, and this, by degrees, will vary from the world of another.

Quite obviously the various modes of competing for a place in 'a world' combine in actions that have had profound consequences upon the entire history of our being human, and more, for in inscribing a space as 'ours' we write upon both it, world and self. This becomes manifest in how we make 'a place of our own'; in our desire to know an other as the same; in the drive to assert difference and in the claim of identity. Such individuated competition equates with a competition of worlding cultures, as they constitute and express material and symbolic ecologies. Moreover, the evolution of the cultures that 'give' bodies their world presence has been in large part powered by competitive ecological processes of unnatural selection. Economic activity is just one example of the giving over to the dominance of the de-natured.

Clearly the conditions, imperatives and consequence of economic activities have dramatically changed the environments of land and sea, have altered the global climate and have transformed the biologies of plants, micro-organisms, insects and animals. Economically inflected ecological fabrication has put in place and changed the ecological generative basis of rural, urban, suburban, industrial and post-industrial environments, which all competitively implicate the body-world. In such conditions of exchange, bodies were, and are, traded; the demand for specific types of bodies are created or negated; and, images, desires and values associated with the body are formed and deformed. Also in this context the body has been used as a site, instrument, measure, commodity and component source for design use and selection.

* * *

Even from the brief sketch above, it is possible to gain some sense of the relational complexity of individuated, collective, symbolic, physical and economic ecologies of body as they converge in the omnipresent, fundamentally unmanaged and designed conditions of competition. Here then is the body in the intertextual setting of war, work, home, architecture, fashion, sexuality, the erotic, the exotic, medicine, image, sport, dance and technology. Out of this play of conflictual forms, values and action emerges the body that serves the biological, sociological and economic reproductive power of the fabricated world of unsustainability. While service here is suggestive of the instrumental conduct of the economic and social actor, it is more than just functionality. For this actor is also complicit in operational systems of desire that normalise that body which economic, cultural and political modernity has made as the model for the masses.

Thinking what and how to see otherwise is not easy. Likewise, and more specifically, it is also hard to manufacture a creative alienation from one's entrenched view of one's own body, as the means of 'having one's world'. However, as can be learned from the best of thinkers, East and West, change what you think and everything changes: the familiar world becomes another place.

## BODIES OF THE BODY

Every body is an unsecured assembly. To turn the body assembly into a critical object is to dismember it, to rip it from its world — such is the violence of abstraction as extraction. Description is destined to fail. The body is always specific, never just an inscriptive material inscribed by a world, never just a relativity, always a relationality. That it appears as cut off (singular) and cut up (textual) is a limit of reading that places an onus on us. We need to move from knowing to understanding. What the writer pulls apart, the reader is invited to put together, with added parts and modification, and in doing so to produce understanding.

The body fuses and confuses the body, space and competition. It also fuses any clear lines between our being, being-in-the-world, and the being-of-the-world. In its indiscrete being, the body bleeds between worlds. From this perspective we can begin to recognise, and find, the body (whether corporeal, individual, collective, embodied, or disembodied) in its places of competition. Here are some instances of fabricated unsustainability.

## BODY DE-NATURED

This is the body of biological 'essence', a theory questioned and found wanting. The differences of bodies are often posited as simply a difference in the 'nature' of the body. Certainly Western metaphysics has disposed its cultures towards seeing the body as a natural and self-contained object. Merleau-Ponty's work clearly questioned this thinking. This has been advanced by others who have examined what the culture posits and assumes as the fundamental 'natural' differences. Feminism's concern with gender or sexual difference has played a major role in this exercise. Iris Young's research is particularly illuminating in this context.[12]

Drawing on Simone de Beauvoir and Merleau-Ponty, Young explores the difference between girls and boys by examining why they throw objects, like a ball, in different ways. Her analysis was provoked by encountering the claim of Erwin Straus (writing on phenomenological psychology in the mid-1960s) that this difference was biological and grounded in an 'essence'.[13] As even a cursory encounter with the literature in this field indicates, the whole question of a sexual or gender 'essence' has become vigorously contested. Both the social construction of gender and the biological construction of the sexual, as they converge in sexuality, appear to be far more gradated than was once realised. Variations in genetic make up and balance have obviously been used to complement social constructivist arguments. It is important to acknowledge, however, that the implications of Young's observations and analysis are by no means restricted to sexual or gender difference.

Young points out that Straus failed to identify what exactly are the differences of modalities of the 'masculine' and 'feminine' 'lived body'. Rather than trying to explore the question in Straus's frame of reference, she brings together the way de Beauvoir looked at the female as a 'situated person', for whom difference arrives as a consequence of particular historical, cultural, economic and social situations, and the way Merleau-Ponty understands relationality, body and world. Young develops an analysis that combines the 'being situated' with 'the disposition of body/world'. In this the body and the subject are viewed as arriving out of a specific orientation of being as it becomes by its being situated in its world.

As argued, for every lived body there is a body world. Every body is disposed towards its world, as such the body-in-being is worlded towards that world — that is its 'nature'. There is no transcendental body, no body 'is' without being grounded in its world, which means that there is no 'universal subject' with its 'one world' (as all we can ever have is 'a' world, or 'worlds', but never 'the' world). It follows that the intention of the body is its worlded intentionality, which is how body becomes subject: 'There is a world for a subject just insofar as the body has capacities by which it can approach, grasp, and appropriate its surroundings in the directions of its intentions'.[14] This statement does not reduce world or body to a mere physicality, but rather the product of the interaction between the one and the other as mediated by the *habitus* of mind, as it is in as well as between. Living 'here' is living an illusion of reference! Young argues that every body is always disposed by a 'system of possibilities that are correlative to its intentions'. These relational conditions for the 'feminine bodily existence' produce inhibited intentionalities that turn the possibility into impossibility.[15] The intentionality of 'a' world that a girl acquires — via that learning which is worlding — is the intention of inhibited throwing, or 'throwing like a girl'. Every body is always disposed to temporally, vectorially and spatially having 'a world', as it arrives as a sensory field of auditory, olfactory, tactile and optical complexity. For us, world is indiscernibly mind and matter. Being-here (*dasein*) is being-in the dwelling of the lived perception (action) of time, motion, space, mind and matter as one learns 'to be' an embodied-being-in-the-world in which one is situated (disposed).

The above is a strong case, but would have been stronger if an understanding of Design had also been employed. The design of the body and structure, comportment, function and its embodied mentalism, as is being shown in so many ways in this chapter and others, is a result of a designed world designing. Worlds design bodies; bodies design worlds: 'everything flows'. One could also say that a close engagement with Heidegger's understanding of world and 'worlding' also would have given Young's situatedness a stronger ontological inflection.[16]

The lived body (for instance, 'female') is shown by Young to be structured always by the conditions that limit its situatedness. Being is thus always situated in a conditional situation, which includes becoming the Idea ahead of ideas that the world in which one comes to be puts before every body (as its realised identity). The notion of 'conditioning', as a popularist conspiratorial social constructivism, totally fails to grasp the determinate conditions of the world that conditions. Conditioning is neither 'brain-washing' nor a mechanistic materialist determinism, but again a relationally complex designing. Young explores the conditional situation by the way de Beauvoir gives an account of the tension between immanence and transcendence.[17] Becoming a body/subject (whether girl, soldier or swimmer) is a becoming both in 'a' world and in a worlding, in all the forms, actions and language, and perceptual limits: worlds designate and design their beings. What this means is that one sees 'the world' and the self/body from the worldview of the world of one's becoming subject.

Effectively we are all embodied in our body and world. It is possible to therefore assert our being flesh-of-the-world as the fundamental breakdown of difference upon which difference is constructed. This observation of course folds back into an understanding and presencing of sustain-ability as being the condition of 'the same' (the commonality) that in difference (as the many), we all need to pursue, learn and live. Having a world, and having a body in that world, is having embodied existence in a subjectified object world. It is only by recognising this unfreedom that the ethical imperative of sustain-ability can come to us as an action to define situationally. Sustain-ability is 'some thing' that we not only have to learn, but live learning anew, because we and our circumstances constantly change.

BODY/COMMODITY/TARGET

Every world has its subjects and objects. However, every world is a culture of worlded difference between the dispositions of the one, the other and the same. Ecologically, the body of modernity is in an accelerated, if variable speed, entropy. It is a systems failure within crisis.

> You recognise this body, its look, its image, its poses, its desires, its smell, its feel. It arrives, in an appropriate set location, in many televisual formats — dressed and undressed, static and moving, glossy, matt and colour retouched. It is offered up in many body-sculptured modes, all shaped by a well managed exercise program and some cocktail of steroids, growth hormones, weight loss amphetamines or fad food special diets, and by cosmetic surgery. This waxed, powdered and perfumed, all-wrapped-up-ready-to-go designer package of style is yours for the asking. All you have to do is buy the bits and you are 'it' — full scale unsustainability, but with what glamour!

Over time, the market has managed to pull off some amazing transpositions of design upon the body which have acted back to form the body itself. These have mostly been unthinking actions that have commodified appearances of the body and made them functional within a body-image system. In doing this the market has treated the body as an entity 'to fashion' by making it an object 'of fashion'.

> Howard Hughes, eccentric, film maker and one time Douglas Aircraft Corporation head, applied what he knew about streamlining and airframe construction to the breasts of a girlfriend at the time — the starlet, and for a few years Monroe competitor — Jane Russell. What resulted was 'the Playtex living bra', a new movie look, a new breast shape. And here was another body-image reference for millions of other women to use as a guide for their self-transformation — the Russell curves, the hair, the walk, the diet — and so the screen designed.

The commodification of bodily appearances has increased over the course of the twentieth century as elemental to a number of sub-economies (fashion, music, film, photography, cosmetics, sport). The valorised 'look' has either been made available as product, or has been employed in product valorisation as 'added value'. In the political economy of the body-sign, the object and image of the look, be it male or female, was and is constituted as a standard of value. While this standard has been varied across tastes, age, gender, class and ethnicity there are always at any time explicit exclusions of size, aesthetics and physical deformation.

In the difference between worlds or cultures the body has been used as the primary sign and mechanism of competition. There is also a world of silence. There are many non-competitors. There are a whole raft of concealed and unrepresented human beings who constitute an other without a name.

The standard of a world designs. As a result, the unco-ordinated operation of the market place is able to use a 'standing reserve' of culturally deposited images, generated by all cultural media, as the pool from which to assemble an ordered visual coherence: the 'look'. The sub-economies of the commodification of the body and its appearances drive a constantly changing plural palette of unsustainable image possibilities. Whatever you are you, are never, as far as the makers of the 'look' are concerned, what you should be.

The primary problematic of this sub-economy, the basis of its unsustainability, is that it never links well-being, health and appearance. As is evidenced by a plethora of fitness and lifestyle magazines, this failure of connection spans an aesthetic preoccupation, a mobilisation of 'well-being and health' to counter-productively proliferate the manufacture and consumption of products, and a focus that limits concern to the biophysical body and leisure activities. This sub-economy's employment of aesthetics sets out to inscribe judgement based on an error. It promotes conformity to a utopian 'look' and expressed desire as a motivational generator of markets. In so doing it seeks to disenfranchise the worth of any self-image of any body outside the aesthetic regime of the standard. In both what it inducts and what it expels, the standard devalues the desire for self-care by the erasure of the ambiguity of self with the certainty of image. Of course, designers design for a taxonomy of standardised types that force the standard.

The political economy of the body has been made wasteful. It wastes the potential of living with sustain-ability in order to realise the 'discovery' of the atomised being-in-the-world of a 'unique', individuated and standardised 'consumer' self. In the seeming contradiction of inverted representational reference (life following art), self realisation hereby means conformity to a commodified notion of an 'authentic' self of televisually authored appearance, feeling and thought.[18] The geometry of the variable and transitory positions of decentredness allow any body to assemble different identities from looks, feelings, reactions and openly expressed thoughts. Like all commodity interactions, 'difference' here comes from the selection of a range of manufactured options. Thus a seemingly singular identity arrives interpellated from commonly encountered referential material formed from 'standard' images, language and memories over time (often from televisual identification). Where there is no authenticity, the question of the unauthentic falls by the wayside: what is constituted stands ready for reconstitution. In this context what can be seen is the evolution of total design to a hyper-conformity of difference which rests on 'the same' as permutations assembled from an endless variety of the same that is found in the world of commodities.

The commodity-assembled body of imaged appearance brings the body to a body as a designing in conditions of constant placement and displacement flowing in a constant stream of stimuli. The failure of representation to deliver what is represented ensures movement. The object acquired by desire soon joins the company of the lacking.

Without straying too far from the body, the issue of waste needs revisiting. Being made-to-waste is not just the consequence of picking up bad habits from a wasteful world, but also results from one's being itself being made a commodity to be wasted. The commodity-driven under-realisation of the potential of being — of being wasted — arrives in many forms. For instance, consider the computerised technologies of writing, which have made possible an enormous textual output, but which have also been responsible for the manufacture of millions of machines, which have in turn taken enormous amounts of greenhouse gas-generating energy and resources to make. Additionally, and contrary to the rhetoric of the paperless office, these technologies use more paper than ever before which itself is responsible for the destruction of vast areas of forests that took hundreds of years to grow. And for what? Cynically one could say for mountains of trivial office memos, invoices in quintuplet, forms on which to order hotdogs and donuts, and so on. And then there is the whole work station culture and designed body (informational and flesh) of data entry.

Body performing

The performing body is examined through three examples: the medical, the athletic and the military.

In the Enlightenment grounding of the Western tradition, the medicalised body was based on a view of the body as the 'animal machine'. That which made the specifically human attribute, the soul, was not of corporeal matter, but was the directive force. The basis of modern medicine in the West thus became the construction of the body as an operational system, as machine, which had to be extracted from its worlding, to be kept functioning and if possible to be repaired.

Descartes announced in his *Treatise on Man* in 1662, that God was that great mechanic in the heavens who made man's body an automata, as 'nothing but a statue or machine made of earth'. The body, like any machine, was full of those parts that made it work. Geoges Canguilheim is informative here, for he points out: 'The construction of the mechanical model presupposes a living original (Descartes here is perhaps closer to Plato than to Aristotle). The Platonic *Demiurge* copies the ideas, and the Idea is the model of which the natural object is the copy.'[19]

In other words, the model attributed to God was a 'man-made' projection that prefigured, and thus pre-dated, what was presented as God's description (which was, de facto, the human invention). The machine is of course a product of geometric, mathematical and mechanical axiomatic laws — which is to say it is a product of productivism. The 'animal-machine' falls into the same frame of origination, which implies that productivist thought created the imagination out of which the idea of body as machine arrived. As Canguilheim makes very clear, while the Cartesian view of the body has been a tremendously powerful idea it is now directly at odds with the modern notion of the body as a self-constructing auto-active entity that constantly adjusts, repairs and corrects itself as an autopoietic system.[20]

But it would be an error to assume that the Cartesian mechanical view of the body is only in the past. Medicine still treats the body in this way, and the language and images of the medical profession that spill out to the media have a big impact on public perceptions and the formation of 'common sense' (especially in terms of a self-perception of well-being). To talk of body parts, of sub-systems like digestion, of implants and transplants and so on is to expose certain kinds of functions and conceal others. In contrast to the impression that science tells us more and more about the body, what has actually happened is the reverse. Science has reductively centred the biophysical, reifying its functional systems. Meanwhile, in cultural and other modalities of contemporary theory, a general theory of the body has increasingly been less concerned with trying to contain it within a definitive set of characteristics, functions and biophysical processes. Rather the body is articulated with systems in which and from which it performs and is performed upon. A naturalism however still rules here, as the nature of that contained in, by and extended through the body. For instance, organism, gene, mind, in one direction appear in specificities like sex, sexuality, gender and eroticism, which get cut loose from the biologically natural, but always end up being tied back. From the rise of social Darwinism through to structural functionalism, social constructivism has always returned to the ground of the 'natural' body — that essentialism of the last instance. In the spirit of pluralism, the 'natural' matter of the body was socially and biologically inscribed. The pluralism of the genres of cultural theory manages to have it both ways in this setting.[21] The body is mobilised as the carrier of a situated social construct (such as gender) while being renaturalised by holding hands with natural science (for instance genetics). It is against this context that one can see why a phenomenological project like that of Merleau-Ponty's retains so much significance.

Not only the medical, but also the athletic and military constructions of the body all have some version of it as a mechanical form. The advocated transcendent form of being for the athlete — one of the products of the 'nature' of training — is to subordinate mind totally to the programmed body, as it has been instructed to act as a system of tuned moving parts that have been customised for a specialist activity. In this programming, while pain is fully experienced, it is also constituted as that to refuse, manage, recode (as just another barrier to break) or sometimes to chemically exile. There is also the rejection of the knowledge of sense and experience on the limit of an expected performance. As well, there is an attempt to overcome the given form of the body by training to modify particular groups of muscles that are performatively linked, as well as sometimes neglecting others (for instance with distance runners, reducing upper body weight while developing the leg muscles).

The body of the athlete, in common with the medical and military body, is given over to functions often within the force of a collective body and a technological interface. Here there is a shift from a mechanistic view of the body to its utilisation as a mechanism.

Within the history of warfare the body-machine has been treated as a machine part. One body has been fused with another to form a single mechanistic entity. The most familiar form of this is drilling. Parade ground marching drills were not created to produce a spectacle of a 'fine body of men' but rather a uniform mechanical performance on the battlefield. Here the single body neither sees itself nor is acknowledged by others — whatever the spectacle or the orchestrated manoeuvre. Uniformity of movement, speed, dress, equipment, sound and instruction are the machine parts of this body. The military body has always subordinated itself to its technology as a form of prosthesis. By doing this the body extends its reach as it is willed by another and as it is animated by a technologically directed force. The unification of body, will and technology is at the core of its complexity and history. This observation holds true prior to the arrival of the spear, past the hand gun, right through to the arrival of the technologies of the fighter aircraft, with its head-up displayed expert auto-corrective systems and laser lock-on missiles.

In the three conditions of the body of competition considered, the medical, the athletic and the military, functional performance produces recession. Effectively, in totally giving way to the body in action we disappear, the pain of being here momentarily ceases, and our anxiety is interrupted in a passage of erased time. Such forgetful bodies all invite revisiting.

The forms of designing discussed are, on the one hand, manifestations of Design without the subject, which is to acknowledge that 'to inscribe' is not necessarily to know what one is doing. Moreover, it is also to acknowledge that the made world takes on a designing quite independent of the knowable acts of designing by the designer. On the other hand, the inscriptive agency at work in this designing also undoes any notion of any evolutionary principle in and of itself. There is no agency of selection, there is no measure of fitness, there is no meaning, there is no assured survival of anything. In this context, sustain-ability has the ability to embrace nothing. It is that which has to be created in that negation which is the unsustainable.

## THE MEASURED THAT MEASURES THE STANDARDS

There is no available measure of the sustain-able body, as a body that is performatively and aesthetically desirable. There needs to be. This is a futuring task.

Classical formalist decontextualism, with its lack of ecological reference, centred on the established form (and norm) of the body as an object and measure of judgement of the good. In this tradition the body became a very particular type of standard, one in which an aesthetic norm was positioned by a structure of codes to judge the normal and the abnormal, the ugly and the beautiful, and the good and the bad. Measurement, the body and aesthetics were made to fold into each other. Perhaps the most extreme expression of this is to be seen in the history of World War I.

The competition of armed warring bodies of World War I managed to maim, dismember and disfigure more bodies than any single event of war ever before. The technological means of bodily destruction was well ahead of that of body reconstruction. This was evident in the underdevelopment of reconstructive surgery and prosthetics, but above all in the inability of surgeons to rebuild destroyed faces. This produced bodies without faces, faces literally lacking eyes, noses, mouths, ears, which simply had their lumps of hanging flesh sewn up. In losing their faces these bodies lost their humanity: the loss of their human facial features meant a loss of being recognised and treated as human beings. These 'people' were designated as monstrous, treated as freaks, or worse, were put into special hospitals or insane asylums, where they remained locked out of the public gaze for the rest of their unnatural lives. Here was the body not even measured by the body. Such is the power of the aesthetic of the body that our greatest horror is its defiling, mutation and disfiguration, and an entire movie industry has grown up around the attempt to force us to look away from the screen!

The omnipotence of the body as standard — the body that is not a body — envelops us. We are measured against it as both fiction and 'empirical' fact throughout our lives. It is there competitively when, as a child, our parents measures our growth, when we stand naked before our doctor, when we buy off-the-shelf clothes, when we have to have a physical examination for a job, when in bed with a lover, when we place ourselves before the mirror — an other is always present.

Examples are easy to find. One that had lasting designing significance flowed from the classical tradition to the modern movement of architecture during the course of World War II. It came from the notion of the 'modular', developed by Le Corbusier, which adopted the body of a six foot (183 centimetres) tall man as the basic normative unit of measurement to create a modular universal design system for environments and structures. This, thereafter, provided the contextual backdrop against which bodies were measured. The application of male body, as norm, knowingly or unknowingly set out to increase its designing determinate power. In effect the use of this body marginalised others across gender, age and cultural differences.[22]

While individual examples abound, more importantly their impact comes out of an elemental place with a culture as a worlding. This can be seen especially in the Western tradition where war, sport (the latter being ritualised training for the former) and the male as norm, merge. The first clear instance of this was the Olympic Games.

The arrival of the original Olympic games in about 800 BC elevated the sporting event to a sacred moment, one in which the warring elements of the Greek world created a symbolic community. They joined to make a major symbolic statement by showing that the games had the ability to function in difference.[23] In practical terms, the most significant contrast of this moment with modern sport was that participation was all. The audience mostly consisted or aspiring contestants, who wished to pit themselves against the best or improve their performance through an exposure to the exemplary. Learning in action was the whole point of the Classical exercise.

From this moment onward, the history of sport delivered a contradictory message. It contributed to training the body for war, produced the performative measure of the fighting body (individual and collective), while also being a symbolic combat that could act as a respite from war.

It is clearly possible to argue that this contradiction travelled forward into the present to remain an unresolved problematic for contemporary anthropology. Moreover, it shows the carrying forward of the individual body of an athlete being constituted not only as a marker of competition between the bodies of sporting individuals but also, symbolically, between nations. Obviously this kind of analysis exposes just how problematic it is to take technological advancement as a sign of evolution. The constant remaking and return of the same symbolic acts put into question claims to progress. Such returns pose the fundamental question of what has actually been learned in the past two or three thousand years. In the setting of the example just given, it is also evident that symbolic figures are 'open' to appropriation from multiple sources, official and informal.

> Remember 'Flo Jo', the female athlete who dominated the track and media at the Los Angeles Olympics and who died in 1998? Flo Jo gave a high profile to a cross-gender assemblage — especially feminised masculine body qualities, created by focus training on specific muscle groups on the track and by pumping iron in the gym. Features of the classical male muscular body have therefore been appropriated by female athletes (female body builders being the most marked instance of this). At the same time, Flo Jo displayed a range of counter codes — long painted finger nails, make up, high fashion sportswear. She turned herself into a site of gender manipulation: a sexualised Amazon. She was a new model, and one almost out of sight for all but female athletes. At the same time she became an icon of a new desire. This image became disembodied and re-embodied, and so a generalised gender option as a new place for a woman to be unsustainable.

The history of sport, as it was dominated by the male body (the body of competition, standard and measure for the female body becoming male), flowed directly into how the body of aggression, the body of war, has been understood.

Masculinity was always a competitive identity. However the historical record is written, it tells us that 'man' has always been an object of competition. What was, and is, at stake is what we would now call 'the male subject'. Before man can dominate, the male self has to be first dominated: not simply by another man, but by a world of male worlding. In this sense, man is the made place of masculinity. Again building, dwelling and thinking flood back into this place, which is a place of being-here.

In the worlding in which the male arrives are 'the things' that make 'a man' in their introduced, coded and performative disposition. In this worlding there is also the evolutionary 'nature' of language. Words always invite a placement in time. Every name of the man of war exposes the temporal quality of language: comrade, warrior, braveheart, the strong, mate, the brave, spunk, hero, buddy, rock, a bloke. From early history to now, the manufactured fictions of man as warrior and the technology of war have been elementally united in the inscribed dominant formations of masculinity. This is not to evoke a crude set of representational forms of action but to acknowledge a cognitive geography of the self. Words author the imaginaries which go mostly unspoken and unprojected as those judgements by which the male self measures, and by which it is measured. Having said this, the body acting under direction — the commodified body — has intervened in this semantic field with a whole range of signs of masculinity that confirm the disjuncture between the representation and a referent. In other words at some point in recent times, a schism has opened up between the 'look' and 'the judgement' of masculinity, whereby no simple correspondences can be assumed.

Wars — as reported event, image, games, desire — feed the masculinity of new generations. The 'wisdom' has been that war draws the line, asks the question and provides the site to prove manhood. War, and its ecology of the defutured, collectivises an ability to make images of an unsustainable present. Such projections were, and are, not contained by their geographic location, history or politics. The entire history of war, and every overt and covert sign of war, flow across into our condition of permanent conflict. Paul Fussell writes that from 1916, which was the year that the absolute horror of World War I became inescapable and never-ending, war arrived as: 'the drift of modern history domesticated the fantastic and normalised the unspeakable'.[24] Here resides the agency of the body of war and all its surrounding, visible and surrogate symbolic forms. It is also the contemporary conflict you can read about today, a major component of the content of the ecology of the image of the televisual — the culture of commerce, the hard man on the street, crime, speed, a style, operational research and sex without prohibition (be it the rape of victory or that liberation of *eros* that the prospect of death brings) — that allows the placement of all men in the ordering scale of masculinity that is weighted by the body in action.[25]

Just think of the Gulf War in these terms: it spilled across the media revitalising that reservoir of male imaginary from which the screen style feeds ('It's just like the movies man' said the soldier/actor on CNN); it structured a range of type forms, ideal and otherwise, of power, leadership and effectively mobilised force (every war makes its heroes, every war has its 'Storming Norman', every war has winners and losers); it delineated some men for, and against, all men, for like all wars there is always the choice to make of being for or against war; and this war, like all other wars, coloured all men in its reflected light.

Notwithstanding that modernity's war machine totally vanquished valour, honour and nobility a very long time ago, war is still a Design domain of manhood. It has become a 'free range' aesthetic of militarisation, one which is propelled and wanders across culture, style, sub-culture, technology, product and language. In these terms it privileges certain body types, looks and forms of resistance as fashion. These are to be found in multiple locations: on the street, school yard, factory, home, games, television, video, film, literature, and music.

Equally the body of war, and the body at war, direct scientific research, technological development and industrial design across a vast range of products — for instance radios, cars, footwear, watches, outdoor equipment. The never-ending undeclared war functions with a political economy of the sign that in no way depends upon the presence of obvious weapons. Male, war, the body, products, signs — all exist in a relational blend that constantly mixes and cuts before our eyes. In one context the conservative regimental tie speaks to those able to hear, in another an army surplus combat jacket becomes co-opted to a sign regime of subcultural and gender gestural resistance — 'putting on the style' is putting on the body of war as a gesture to a culture with whom a statement of symbolic conflict is made. This worlding has, in actual circumstances of potential conflict, the ability to design the form of its arrival.

The body that speaks of militarisation (in whatever communication medium) also delivers a rhetoric of war, as it has been made a metaphor for all domains of conflict in late modern and postmodern worlds. All domains of competition share a language of conflict — strategy, tactics, operational management, war games, troops, logistics, reinforcements, defences, targets, hits, surgical strikes, players, conquests, take-overs, victories, defeats. These terms mix in, and splatter, the discourses of the defutured. Design, masculinity, militarisation and competition all articulate with and infect each other. Speaking in each other's language, they use each other's names, which generate forms that play off and into each other.

> Every city reveals itself as site of bodily conflict. In contrast to the handful of United States casualties killed in the Gulf War, thousands of young men die by gunfire on the streets of American cities, and in Africa and South America many cities have become indistinguishable from war zones. These failures of modernity are some of the most overt signs of unsustainability. For instance, in last night's news in the flow of events (it could be my 'last night' or yours) on the minority interest 'ethnic' television station, it was reported that currently 65 killings take place in Cape Town each week. This adds up to over 3300 deaths a year. Unless there is a spectacular event, this routine carnage does not even make the mainstream news. Its repetition negates its newsworthiness.

The competition of the body is a competition of place: between on the one hand being put in place, losing one's place, not having a place, being displaced or replaced; and on the other, taking a place, taking place, making a place, and having a place of our own. It is competition between here and there, the self and an other — a competition that maintains divisions, opposition, and binaries declared to be dead. This competition is of major environmental significance, as an environment.

## OPENINGS AS ENDINGS

We live our condition of possibility and impossibility in the body of competition as a limit and means of our freedom. As Emmanuel Levinas observes: '*To be a body* is on the one hand, *to stand* [se tenir], to be master of oneself, and, on the other hand, to stand on the earth, to be in the *other*, and thus be encumbered by one's own body'.[26]

From this unsustainable thing which is my body, I can only contemplate sustain-ability by my connectedness to others, by change rather than as the same, by being 'flesh of the world'. I do this as my life 'bodies forth' which is my 'being alive' — here I am calling up a conversation between Eugen Fink and Martin Heidegger during the course of the Heraclitus Seminar.[27] The claim has been that for Heidegger the body was largely an object of silence. This has been accompanied by a claim of disinterest. However, in his own words, in a passing remark in the seminar, Heidegger comments to Fink that the body is 'the most difficult problem', and then in relation to this comment (as David Farrell Krell reminds us) Heidegger repeated to the participants of the seminar an often uttered remark, paraphrased in translation as 'the body lives only in so far as it bodies forth'.[28] The implication of this comment is that 'being here' (*dasein*) is thus always some body 'being alive' by the life in being coming to being in 'the' world.

Like much else with Heidegger, the body arrives not so much as an object of direct address, nor as a figure in the text, but out of an encounter with a relation to something other, as well as a result of thinking with or from the text. Without being dismissive of the insightful value of Krell's elucidation, or his demonstrated point that Heidegger did have something to say on the body, the main issue to focus upon is surely the *creation* of a language of engagement. To do this requires using a language that is other than the familiar, which raises the more difficult spotting exercise of the identification of thinking and speaking in a language that illuminates rather than names. In this respect Heidegger becomes concealed in the name (his), and while his disclosures have an ability to surprise constructive thinking — he begs overcoming by engagement.

In 1940 Heidegger delivered the lecture course based on the first part of his final volume on Nietzsche. About two thirds of the way through this course, he engaged Nietzsche's relation to Descartes, which is based on a rejection of the Cartesian *cogito* while making 'an *even more rigorous commitment* to the subjectivity'.[29] Crucial in this argument is Nietzsche's placement of the body beyond subjectivity. Heidegger said:

> For Nietzsche, what underlies is not the 'I' but the 'body':'belief in the body is more fundamental than belief in the *soul*' ... ; and 'The phenomenon of the body is the richer, clearer, more comprehensible phenomenon: to be placed first methodologically, without stipulating anything about its ultimate significance' ... . But this is Descartes' fundamental position, presupposing that we still have eyes to see; that is, to think metaphysically. The body is to be placed first '*methodologically*'. It is a question of method. We know what that will mean:it is a question of a procedure for defining what everything determinable is referred back to. That the body is to be placed first methodologically means that we must think more clearly and comprehensively and still more adroitly than Descartes, but do so wholly and solely in his sense.[30]

As Heidegger later goes on to remark, the transfer that Nietzsche effects is from Descartes' concern with 'representation and consciousness' to the realm of '*appetites* or drives' as the basis of a will to power.[31] Read from the concerns in play in our inquiry (led by Heidegger's analysis of Nietzsche, which reaffirms the body/world relation advocated, reducing the body to metaphysical meaninglessness while elevating it to ontological significance), things move for Nietzsche by the power of '*appetites* or drives'.

Additionally, Michel Haar draws our attention to a most important idea that Heidegger employs that again breaks down a simplistic world/body division and the privileging of any biocentric notion of the body. The idea is *Stimmung* (attunement). It illuminated the animated being of 'being-in-the-world' as the world comes into being and, as such, adds to our understanding of ontological Design:

> Phenomenologically speaking, *Stimmung*, the atmosphere, emanates from things themselves and not from our subjectivities or from our bodiliness. In *Stimmung* the world presents itself as what touches us, concerns us, affects us. If we were not thus accosted, struck, surprised *by things*, we could never experience feelings of security or dread, nor even discover the difference among beings.[32]

The failure to remember that, as *physis* informed us, we are born of a world as well as of the womb, is a failure of metaphysics, and a failure of science. It has meant that the world has been objectified and disarticulated from the body-being. This failure is at the very core of the defutured. In contrast, the history of Chinese medicine is totally predicated upon the attunement of world and body, in which health arrives as the co-ordination and free flow between one and the other.[33] Repeating the forgotten, as Heraclitus said, 'everything flows'.

All I would claim to have done here is to expose the edge of a complexity that demands to be thought in action. The question of the body, life, world and defuturing is the question of Design. It is the question of what we do, as an ethics of taking responsibility for our anthropocentric condition. Is there any other question that could be more important?

**Notes**

1 Fredric Jameson, *The Prison House of Language: A critical Account of Structuralism and Russian Formalism*, Princeton University Press, New Jersey, 1972.
2 Maurice Merleau-Ponty, *Phenomenology of Perception* (trans Colin Smith), Routledge, London, 1995, p. 5. He makes the case powerfully when he points out that consciousness of the body does not come from the body but rather 'invades' it, making 'bodily experience itself a representation'.
3 *Ibid.*, p. 82; and on the metaphysical structure of the body see *ibid.*, p. 167.
4 Merleau-Ponty expands the point: the 'body-event' is a translated being-in-the-world in which the repression breaks down (illness being one of the instances of this he cites): *ibid.*, pp. 84–85.
5 Drew Leder, *The Absent Body*, Chicago University Press, Chicago, 1990, pp. 149–73.
6 Maurice Merleau-Ponty, *The Visible and the Invisible* (trans Alfhonso Lingis), Northwestern University Press, Evanstone, 1968, p. 248.
7 Elaine Scarry, *The Body in Pain*, Oxford University Press, Oxford, 1985.
8 Leder, *The Absent Body*, pp. 36–68.
9 Thomas Hobbes, *The Levianthan* (ed Michael Oakshott), Collier Books, New York, 1973.
10 Merleau-Ponty, *The Visible and the Invisible*, p. 3.
11 Merleau-Ponty, *Phenomenology of Perception*, p. 146. Exactly the same comment was made in *The Visible and the Invisible*, p. 4.
12 Iris M Young, *Throwing Like a Girl*, Indiana University Press, Bloomington, 1990.
13 *Ibid.*, pp. 141–59.

14 *Ibid.*, p. 148.
15 *Ibid.*, p. 149.
16 See Hubert Dreyfus, *Being-in-the-World: A Commentary on Heidegger's Being and Time Division 1*, MIT Press, Cambridge (Mass), 1991.
17 *Ibid.*, p. 144.
18 On the 'nature' of the televisual see Chapter 7.
19 Geoges Canguilheim, 'Machine and Organism' (trans Mark Cohen and Randall Cherry) in *Incorporations* (eds Jonathan Crary and Sanford Kwinter), Zone, New York, 1992, p. 53.
20 *Ibid.*, p. 56.
21 For a survey of this kind of thinking see Pasi Falk, *The Consuming Body*, Sage Publications, London, 1994.
22 Le Corbusier applied the modular norm to the design of the unité d'habitation in Marseilles, 1947–52 and thereafter to all of his work. While the basis of the theory folds back into his relation to the Classsical tradition, with its body of proportion, the actual measure of six feet is said to have been based on the height of the fictional British detective 'Bulldog Drummond', who was adopted as being a representative of the standard size of the heroic Englishman (see R Jordan, *Le Corbusier*, JM Dent, London, 1972, pp. 108–109).
23 Allen Guttmann, *Sports Spectators*, Columbia University Press, New York, 1985, pp. 14–18.
24 Paul Fussell, *The Great War and Modern Memory*, Oxford University Press, Oxford, 1975.
25 The relations between war, violence, sexuality and love are explored with insight by Paul Fussell, *ibid.*, pp. 279–309.
26 Emmanuel Levinas, *Totality and Infinity* (trans Alphonso Lingis), Duquesne Universty Press, Pittsburg, 1969, p. 164.
27 Martin Heidegger and Eugen Fink, *Heraclitus Seminar* (trans Charles H Seibert), Northwestern University Press, Evanston, 1993.
28 David Farrell Krell, *Daimon Life: Heidegger and Philosophy*, Indiana University Press, Bloomington, 1992, p. 63. Krell in fact surveys this issue by a count of the number of times the term 'human body' appears in *Being and Time* (22) and by sampling a range of other texts. Of relevance to the issue at hand, and the use made here of the work of Merleau-Ponty, Krell usefully comments 'That the body as being in the world is the cardinal ontological problem is no news to students of Merleau-Ponty, whose work Heidegger knew about, but who plays no part in the Zollikon seminars, even though the question of the body is a

recurrent theme there'. Krell then remarks that, in this context, the body is dealt with existentially rather than aletheiologically: *ibid.*, p. 53.
29 Martin Heidegger, *Nietzsche Volume IV: Nihilism* (trans Frank A Capuzzi, ed David Farrell Krell), HarperCollins, San Francisco, 1991, p.123.
30 *Ibid.*, p.133.
31 *Ibid.*, p. 134.
32 Michel Haar, *The Song of the Earth: Heidegger and the Grounds of the History of Being* (trans Reginald Lilly), Indiana University Press, Bloomington, 1993. p. 37. Haar, in *Heidegger and the Essence of Man* (trans William McNeil), SUNY Press, Albany, 1993, p. 77, also writes a comment that returns us to the question of Heidegger, and the claim that he has little to say on the body, and connects to *Stimmung*: 'We know that the body or the flesh are not denied, but are described as always already permeated by an attunement, that is, taken into a transcendence, into an embracing figure of the world'.
33 See GER Lloyd, 'The politics of the body' in *Adversaries and Authorities: Investigations into Ancient Greek and Chinese Science*, Cambridge University Press, Cambridge, 1996, pp. 190–208.

# 6
# TIME AND CHINA

Building China in time (author's collection)

So far we have concentrated on an exposition of Eurocentrically generated instrumental and geopolitical forces of the defutured and its on-going agency. We now aim to create a sense of the impossibility of adopting an overview of differences of time, place and crisis, while also recognising the imperative and merit of acknowledging these differences. To do this we need to go beyond both the notion and critique of 'uneven development'.[1] We need to engage another place and time — which we will do by taking what may well seem like random moment, the year 1926, and China today.

## TIME

Before proceding with the question of time we need to reiterate that the defutured arrives from a taking away of time, while sustain-ability is the reverse.

Time is both familiar and completely uncontemplated. Its essence is not measurement but the temporal event of the condition of dwelling. In fact, our conceptual induction into time as measured duration and linear movement has reduced our ability to comprehend time and the cyclical. As we learn from Aristotle, or equally from modern science, time is nothing in itself; rather it always flows with, in and as objects, events and actions.

In placing ourselves before time, differences in one's cultural history and the form of one's dwelling always constitute a difference in the perception of time. Universal time does not exist experientially: it is known by nobody. Notwithstanding this facticity, one of the functional objectives of modernisation was to achieve this universal time, to bring all people into one moment 'the modern'.[2]

The notion of time carried by the current discourse of globalisation is not a continuation of the time of modernisation. Globalisation is the worlding of corporate culture: it is an economic ideology of global exchange but no longer with the promise of emancipation, for it is not 'development' predicated upon cultural, political and social advancement. As this, globalisation is an ideological marker of postmodernity's abandonment of the idealist ambition of an universal human condition united in one moment of time. The fragmentation of time now is not just a disjuncture of lifeworlds between cultures, but also between the spaces of the lives of individual subjects (most crudely illustrated by the co-existence of moments of 'real time', the speed of travel and the compressed time of information transmission in the electronic domain). The notion of the fragmentation of the subject is obviously not unrelated to fragmented time, but in part it is product.

Our temporal existence becomes known to ourselves through

particular modes of knowing time. For us time falls out of, into and between that which is intrinsically sensed biorhythmically and geophysically (in the solar and climatic specifics of a familiar environment) and that which one learns about as one acquires one's culture. However, as our circumstances change, so the way that we understand time may need to be altered. In this framework, the way we tell time may act to conceal what we need to know about how shifts in the temporal character of the events change time. Thus while changes in time are not available to us to be worked on, what is to hand are those narrativisations that author cultural perceptions and which may of course, by degree, mediate sensory perceptions. The story of the defutured, in significant part, is an account of the negation of the event of planetary sustainment. For sustainment, this narrative of time demands to be mobilised against our own sense of time (that measure of familiar time from the perpetual presence the events of our own life). To shift to this understanding time is to move it from the taken-for-granted to an understanding framed by the narrative of defuturing which is a learning of sustain-ability.

## A MODERN MOMENT

Another point, already made, needs to be laboured. Modernity, in all its forms, set out but failed to constitute a universal hegemonic way of being — being modern. However, the peoples of the planet as it now is, in the variations of their collective and individual ignorance, insight, celebration, recoil, confusion or refusal, have been bequeathed the consequences of this project.

While having profound and complex consequences, none of the discourses of modernity were able to subordinate the cultural difference of 'human being' to the same mode of being, temporality or world view. For all the power and impact of capitalism — its accompanying humanist culture and Enlightenment-inspired institutions, sciences, philosophies, social formations and economic forces — no universal correspondence or consensual meaning between the objects of material and symbolic exchange, referent and representation has ever been established. In this context, to string human beings out across a single time line, and to place them according to an evolutionary schema is absolute error, for there is no transcendent position to authorise placement. As modernisation strove to conquer 'the world' and impose its will (humanism and progress) upon all others, this is exactly what it did. The rhetoric of the primitive and the civilised is no longer spoken with ease: in an age of political correctness and equal rights it has become repressed. But it is inherent in Eurocentric being. An image of a developmental and racially ordered human lineage is a visualisation of beings-in-time which still has a great deal of representational force, and still does violence. For all the assertions of the recognition of cultural difference, the voice that speaks in the name of the (Eurocentrically posited) 'human' continues to judge with an active 'evolutionary' model.

The ideals of the notions of human rights and the family of man are still featured in liberal humanist discourse as figures of a modernist, and still quietly violent, fiction. Such discourse forces a time of cultural uniformity into being. (The one-way journey that forces difference into 'multiculturalism' is the most familiar expression of this.) What this means is that difference is reduced to the plural, within an hegemonic moment of time, so that the variations of the difference of time, carried by different lifeworld cultures, are obliterated. That the other is absolutely other, and has an absolutely other construction of self, world, value, being and time is just not able to be accommodated. In the circumstance of the afterlife of modernity, it is not by mere chance that the narrative that conceals the other's time of difference is pluralism, which has become the dominant epistemological disposition of Western liberal democratic cultures.

The primary referent of the projected picture of the modern world was the image itself. This image, as a fiction, dream and utopia, contains a historicity of enormous destruction. The mimetic force of the projected 'world picture' (as we saw with the 1939 New York World's Fair, and examples within it like the Futurama), acted in the past to author and authorise the making of unsustainability.[3] This force continues on into the future, as we shall see by looking at contemporary China.

The power of the 'world picture' is enacted via the agency of enframing — the stamping of an impression — which is the means of connecting world and picture. The impression left by the enframing capability of the picture was and is evident as mark, memory and desire. The capability of this agency facilitated a movement from the immaterial (the pictured) to the material consequences of its attempted realisation. We need to recognise that striving to copy a totally flawed and unrealisable simulacrum became (not least by the means of the televisual) the epicentre of the defutured's unmaking in both the 'developed' and 'developing' nations alike. Clearly while this unmaking was inseparable from dream, constructed and projected images of desire and utopian designing, it was also underpinned by the non-material humanist ambitions of modernisation. This is to say that no simplistic determinism by image is being claimed here, rather the image is acknowledged to arrive in a milieu of introduced and institutionalised cultural, political, economic and psycho-social forms.

The scale and dynamic of this ambition came together with the utopianian force of the 'worlding' picture. The result was the establishment of unmaking (as gross unsustainability) at a global level. Effectively the event of seeking to impose rapid global modernisation, as it occurred without consideration or modification of impacts, is appropriate to name as a diminishing of time. The validity of this claim rests with the critical context not just of this chapter but every chapter.

Such utopian designing, as indicated earlier, needs to be qualified by acknowledging that by the mid-twentieth century, utopias had withered to commodity spectres and rationalist, formalist, technocratic constructions that still managed to recruit the rhetoric and institutions of humanism, but refused a recognition of life lived in the shadow of constant dehumanised destruction that enabled the constant return of the inhuman.[4] Put more directly, while the trappings of civilisation accumulate, our constant falling back into the uncivilised makes a mockery of any notion of a fundamental evolution of the species. In the face of this situation humanism romantically and steadfastly refuses to confront fundamental failures (as constantly returning structural flaws) and in so doing shows an absolute inability to learn. Institutionally, the most overt demonstration of this is seen with the United Nations.

As our examples and argument have set out to show, the selling of the image and content of the modern has been, and continues to be, a super successful way for capital to deal with crisis. There is an unbroken and universal appeal to those who have, and want more, and to those who do not have. This has become a condition of marketing-induced unthinking and anthropocentric myopia that has become totally auto-destructive. This is not able to be dismissed by reifying and blaming capital, for it is a crisis of what we have become and of what we are, the agent of the defutured's crisis of the unsustainable — the history of humanity tells us that we are a world-ending animal. Sustain-ability now arrives as that learning that divides extermination or transmutation, change by rupture rather than 'evolution'. At its most fundamental, our termination, transformation or extension is largely a matter of the choices we, in our difference, dispersal and unfreedom, make by design.[5]

For all the volumes written on modernity, in its economic, philosophical, political and cultural forms and contradictions, there has been little grasp of the generative power of the ecology of its dystopic utopian image. The relations of this image to the sustainable and the unsustainable, evoked by projected images of the modern condition as a fictive techno-scientific visualisations of a future liberated from the constraint and direction of 'nature', equally go uncomprehended and ignored. At the same time modernist writers, artists, designers and thinkers also wanted to be able to either aesthetically appreciate nature as image (realism), create a neo-natural culture of artificial laws (formalism), use the image as a political instrument to raise awareness and activate (revolutionary art), and embrace an absolutely romantic construction of 'progress'.

## THE YEARS OF 1926

There is more than one 1926, as there is more than one 'now'. Like any other time, 1926 was always located in different moments and conjunctures. Nothing exists in or by standard time, neither is there a place for totalised time to arrive. Rather than doing what popularist representations appear to do (gathering in common), their designation of a universal moment of measured time really creates a focal point for viewing incommensurable difference. Which is to say that there is no transcendent location, no meta-time from which to view specific times, as it is not possible to get outside the relative event of your own time. To illustrate we will look at four small fragments of four 1926s that frame a difference of experience, perception, geography and moment. (The argument of why 1926 adds nothing to our argument. The superficiality of the address to 1926 subtracts nothing from our argument. 1926, or any other year, transpires to fracture the more one explores, or explodes, it relationally.)

The America of 1926 was a society of mass production, unknowingly mass producing itself into economic and social crisis. Its driving forces of the modern were: an industrial system of mass production (paradigmatically projected to the world as Fordism); mass-produced products; a mass distribution system and infrastructure (an advanced retail sector, bulk storage, a national and international transport network and delivery system); urban masses; a mass education system, supported by the teaching of technocratic specialisms; mass communication media (newspapers, radio, film); and mass audiences (that were exposed to mass-produced products by the advertising of mass communications). While all of these elements added up to a 'massive' modernising force, it lacked one element. This was the yet-to-be designed mechanism of mass consumerism, as it combined the design aesthetics of modern styling, managed desire, the credit system and contemporary product packaging, all of which would all arrive, as we have seen, with the advent of streamlining.

The Australia of 1926 was the year that cars started rolling off the Ford production line. This established Fordism as the model of modernist production. This moment marked a significant turning away from the economic leadership of Britain and Europe, and an elevation of Americanism as the desired. The slow speed of travel of goods, people, ideas and images both to the nation, and within it, created a condition of uneven geographic and psychic marginality well beyond a contemporary comparison. To all intents and purposes Australia was at least a decade behind America. Its population of six million was certainly not yet a unified mass market. There was no fully developed national distribution system or service and transport infrastructure.

The Japan of 1926 was the year Ford was asked to leave the country because the Japanese had decided it was time to establish their own national car industry. They looked at two models of production systems, those of Ford and General Motors. They adopted General Motors' slightly more flexible and far more socially intensive gang system. This work method was chosen for its greater cultural compatibility. (The project took a decade and by the late 1930s a car industry had been established, with Toyota launching a range of cars into the market.) In Japan, 1926 was a cultural moment of contrast and contradiction between the pre-industrial and the industrial. The nation's ability to function with plural, or fragmented, time is one of the reasons that it is claimed it went straight from a premodern to a postmodern post-historical condition. The post-historical was defined nearly sixty years ago by Alexandre Kojéve, first as the 'eternal-present' demonstrated by the 'American-way-of-life' as 'the future of all humanity' and then (after visiting Japan) as life lived by 'totally *formalised* values — that is values completely empty of all "human" content in the "historical" sense'.[6]

Modern Japan (which is itself an act of naming that imposes another time) was framed by two major forces: the three centuries of hyper-conformity that preceded the arrival of the trappings of cultural and economic modernity; and a fateful decision that was made to turn the country into a Western image-based, modern society driven by power, knowledge and wealth. The former condition created an absolutely regulated subjection. Under the feudal Edo regime (1600–1867), otherness or exteriority was (except for the *iki*, the pleasure quarter for the merchant bourgeoisie) obliterated by the combination of a totally administered society, harsh laws and severe punishments for even the most mild act of deviancy.[7]

Clearly, modern Japan is not only not in the same temporal register as modern America or modern Australia but it is not in a single moment in and of itself. It is in what Kojéve called a post-historical, and what more recently Miyoshi calls a 'chronopolitical', condition, which indicates the co-existence of the universalising chronology of Westernising modernisation — or *kindai*, its 'local' counterpart, and premodern traditionalism.[8]

Africa's 1926 can be registered as an even higher order of complexity. The straight lines on its map speak the violence of the history of its colonisation. The incommensurate space and time of the coloniser and the colonised is rendered invisible by 1926 and every year from its colonial wounding onward. Here we hit the sound of silence. While the contradictory, often re-colonising, post-colonial voice of 'the concerned' in countries like the United States and Australia utter their gestural apologies to their own decimated native peoples, who is to say 'Sorry' to Africa. When is its decimation to be over?

\*\*\*

These views of 1926 affirm that while we experience time as a temporal discontinuity, we think it as it has been represented to us. Image thus has been made to override understanding time as the events in the complexity of a relative condition of relationality. Moreover, the abstracted (and so de-relationalised) model of time, with which we are so familiar, disconnects time from the ontology of events, and so makes the category time-less. In turn this designs a culture of irresponsibility, in that action is not seen to impact upon time. What this means when we say, as we have, that sustain-ability is about making time is that it is about making time present (as temporality confronted) and making time as a material intervention between now and a finitudal moment. Time thus makes action responsible, responsible for time.

Multi-perspectivalism is not only a multiplicity of thought or sight of a subject but also a multiple transformation of the object. 'Now' moves, it is always an immediate moment of difference — an impossible-to-secure arrest of relational dynamics disclosed and also concealed from a particular perspective. We assume a moment shared with another. However, and by degree, there is always a temporal difference between the one and the other whereby there is never a complete correspondence between historicities, time and place, and thus the seemingly common experience is unable to be fully communicated by the supplementary power of language or image to transpose the known.[9]

We live preoccupied with the attempt to refuse the impossibility of bridging divide between one and the other. While these attempts have been the most powerful of all the driving forces of the creation of our cultures (as they travel under various names, like community, social relationships, the arts), and, while every created event is a designing against the actuality of the divide, we are now before a moment that has always been present for us, a moment which we have so far failed to make present, and refused to find impossible to communicate, yet one that demands the impossible. This ineffability can be summoned by evoking the supplement 'sustainment'. In all its difference it is named here as the most important of all events to place between the one and the other. It is the event into which every futuring event needs to enfold. It is the determinate event. 'Now' turns around the past, present and future of this event.

## CHINA: FOUR PERSPECTIVES

We have just registered, with a multi-perspectival snapshot of the one time, 1926, that what is made to appear as common is in fact actually experienced as temporal difference according to place. What we are going to do for China is to replay a similar argument, but with the multiple perspectives centring on one location. In both cases we are working against the mobilised 'reality' (normality) of the abstraction of time to an universal common designation (the year) via a metaphysic that effectively conceals difference and which is effectively makes time time-less.

### WHOSE NOW?

The first perspective requires an orientation. We (in this case constituted as the disorganic community of Western metaphysics) now cannot think without reason, for it is with reason that we put what we think before ourselves. Everything other than reason thus exists on the ground of a referential relation to reason, which means that reason, once you have it, establishes the point of world view and seat of judgement by which all other thinking is judged.[10] Our minds are enframed, stamped by reason: the words of Leibniz ever echo, that 'nothing *is* without reason' (the emphasis is ours). However, while reason may almost be universal, it has not been the only way to think, and the fact that it is almost universal is simply confirmation of the logocentric power of Eurocentrism. Once one has reason, one's understanding, seeing, hearing and feeling (whether of 'man', 'humanity', 'world' or 'time') is consequentially 'reasoned': it ever sits in the seat of judgement on what is deemed reason and not reason.

As soon as reason degenerated into instrumentalism (not least under the influence of the pragmatic stemming from economic modernity), Western thought and unsustainability united. From this point onwards functionalist thinking, deficient in critical insight or forethought, became normative. Such thinking is extremely good at task resolution, but very bad at reflecting upon consequences. Even more significant, it constitutes a way of thinking, seeing and acting within a functionally formed world. Without replaying an account of the complexity of modernity, what we are naming is a crucial mode of its ontology. For instance, to view the world in terms of states of development is to constitute 'world' as a functional system. While holding such thinking at bay is extremely hard, once you have been inducted, one learns from the striving to think otherwise. Here then is how we will approach China with regard to issues of place, time, development and sustainment.

As has become ever clearer to the critical observer, it is not appropriate to understand the Orient as a self-naming, single identity or geographic fact. The Orient was created as an image of unity through Western projection.[11] It was an ethnocentric invention: East and West, as cultures of differences, as polarities, turn around one and the same point. Both are the fusion of one idea, and travel with the ethnocentric baggage of reason.[12]

From at least the 1930s there has been a tradition of reading China from the perspective of a critique of the West's thinking. The seminal and prodigious work of Joseph Needham on Chinese science and culture occupies an important position in establishing this field of research and scholarship. The importance of his work has still to gain due recognition and engagement. But, the point is not so much the extent to which what he wrote was correct, but rather the volume of what he made available for correction. We learn from Needham that many of the discoveries and inventions which the West so proudly claims were in fact Chinese creations, often several thousand years before the time of their Western arrival.[13] Yet the Western narrative of China's progress asserts the nation's development was inhibited by a failure to instrumentalise knowledge like the West. Although it is only possible to briefly outline, there are two observations of enormous significance to register. Both articulate with the Chinese experience, but cannot be contained by it.

First, from ancient times to well into Europe's Enlightenment, the Chinese were the 'developed' and the Western the 'undeveloped'. The only peers the Chinese had were the classical Greeks.[14] This situation existed largely because of the superiority of Chinese agricultural technology and its ability to administer the structures of proto-civil society.[15] In the history of Western thought there are only a few odd instants of recognition of China's importance.[16] Against this backdrop, and for reasons we will explore, contemporary China seems to have a totally disjunctual relation to its own history. Certainly we have to acknowledge that China's future is being shaped by its current recoil from decades of atavism and restricted consumption of material goods. In certain respects, the nation appears to be driven by the desires to attach itself to the West's past (the ghost of modernity). Yet there is a sense, a trace, of another destination, which comes perhaps from an imminent memory, another time, a residual power of another designing and mostly of acceptance rather than revolution. (We do not claim however that this adds up to an intrinsic and authentic Chinese identity.)

The second observation returns to, and goes forward from, the question of reason. Chinese discoveries, while coming out of a pragmatic tradition, did not stem from, nor did they advance by, applied reason. Technological determinism was not a currency. There was certainly no ethos of rationality, bonded to the idea of a progression toward an enlightened world, via the agency of experimental sciences and humanist ideas. Direction was not a matter of economic, cultural, political or technological options, or free choices, but of the decisionism of tradition, bureaucratic structures and imperial power. In this context, to invent something was not to develop in order to instrumentally employ a means to transform the status quo. The reverse was the case — the status quo was there to serve and to sustain in harmony. (Harmony here is not a condition of New Age sweetness and light, but a stability between the ever changing forces of creations and destruction.) But in making this observation we have reached the point when an other's world (as comparative philosophy shows), is not able to be adequately translated across language. The particular meanings of, and relations between, harmony, change and forces are cases in point. All of these words converge on the term *yin-yang*, which calls up a great complexity, but from which most Western appropriations have evacuated all meaning.[17]

Development, as a condition of secured and on-going material and immaterial sustainment of ethnocentric constructs, is blinded by an inability to interpret relational difference. The Chinese have been longstanding victims of such myopia. They were, for instance, designated by the Jesuits in the seventeenth century as lacking 'logic'. The assertion was that 'they could not reason properly', 'they could not tell the soul from the material body' or the difference between 'moral good and natural good'. But, as David Hall and Roger Ames note:

> We must remember that the Jesuits did not take Christianity to China simply to persuade the Chinese to embrace a new religion. They were envoys dispatched by Rome to introduce universal religion fortified by the best of Western classical and scholastic learning as part of a calculated strategy to alter China's fundamental conceptions about the world.... In order to make Christianity understandable to the Chinese, the missionaries had first to teach the Chinese how to think.[18]

## CHINA'S TRENDS 'NOW'

The second perspective we can take on China is that, notwithstanding the mixed fortunes of Asian economies, China appears to be still moving toward the global centre stage as one of the fastest growing and most unsustainable nations on the planet.[19] Although its economic growth and 'reform' have slowed in the late 1990s, it will continue to have on-going major local and global impacts.[20] It could be that if its economy imploded, impacts would be even greater as new infrastructure fails, social fabric ruptures and recently formed desires and needs go unmet. Either way, the ability of many millions of Chinese people to be able to control their fate hangs in the balance. Equally, the state's ability to care for its people ever weakens as a new kind of economic determinism arrives,[21] and even more fundamentally, there are serious questions about the ability of political systems and structures to be able to survive and deal with the dual challenges of the terminal condition of the state and the growing imperatives of sustain-ability. Globalisation does not function with uniform standards, with that geography that contemporary imaginations still project upon the world, with humanist concerns for people or environments, with anything like a conscience. In this setting a new 'double speak' grows up with the split loyalty of the state to its people and to international economic power brokers.

In China there are particular and extreme variants of these trends. Not only is 'one nation, two systems' a socio-cultural contradiction (which is only able to be maintained because of the relation between the capitalism, the Party and the People's Liberation Army), but there are also contradictions between political and still-flourishing nationalism and the rise of new classes of privilege whose attachments are to the global class and lifeworld with which they identify.[22]

The most dramatic and pressing immediate problems are those associated with energy and water. Let's take just one of these — water, which is not simply a biophysical but also cultural and economic problem. The national psyche that desires to be modern is underpinned by a feeling of having been cheated from what others have. Thus multi-millions want what they think they have missed out on and they want it 'now'. Advancements like running water, flushing toilets, showers and a beautiful bathroom are powerful utopian dreams and signs of change. However, when there is insufficient water and a lack of infrastructure to deal with waste water, all that materialises is dystopic. The water crisis speeds up, water contamination increases and public health worsens. Of course, inappropriate domestic water use is matched by poor industrial and agricultural practices. These factors and more, compound as 'the problem'.

Consider the 1998 floods of the Yangtze, in which 21 million hectares of land were inundated, thousands of lives were lost, and hundreds of thousands of people rendered homeless. The media reported that as a consequence of pollution and run off from land clearing (for development) on a vast scale, 40 per cent of the waterways, lakes and reservoirs had become silted up. This silting significantly reduced both the ability of rivers to carry stormwater run-off, and the retention capability of lakes and reservoirs. The more rampant development, the more the likelihood of future floods. In turn, as a result of the flooding, pollutants were deposited over a large area. It also contaminated a great deal of the available potable water (the use of this water of course then spread disease). In sum, the water situation in China currently suffers from three massive and related problems: shortage, flood and pollution.[23]

For individual and national growth to have sustain-able potential it must invest in sustainments. Without this 'the time and place of advancements' are totally negated by that which defutures. The overwhelming focus on short-term gains has in fact obstructed the consideration of mid- and long-term impacts. At the same time a new culture of invention and design is needed to create 'alternative', innovatory and good non-modern solutions that have to be made politically, socially and symbolically acceptable and exportable. This is China's historically inscribed counter capability. Pockets of concern exist: there is an intellectual and practical strata aware of current problems and working against the odds. A memory lingers, other imaginaries are possible without the dead hand of utopianism smothering them.

While the impetus of the defutured rages on and seems to overwhelm all in its path we also need to remind ourselves that China, in its internal differences of time, place, speed, wealth and culture, is socially dividing. New divisions are restructuring the nation, as the desires of the new rich drive the form of economic modernisation, and as the desires of the peasants drive them to leave the land, traditions, world view and economies that have supported them. As indicated, the time and place of the state and the people are being slowly reconfigured as the geometry of the people and the power bloc alters as new classes emerge.[24] The party, the proto-democratic radical political cadre, the nouveau riche, the post-industrial working class, the peasantry, and the army represent fragments and tensions that play over the non-revolutionary and the revolutionary history of China in ways that make predicting outcomes extremely hard.

Somewhere in the shadows, China conserved is 'now' alongside China defutured. The time of the past is pitted against the time of the present as a weapon of a radical conservational, rather than a conservative, future. Where one finds the other China takes us to our next perspective.

CHINA AS EVERYWHERE 'NOW'

China exports its symptoms of crisis. At the materially simplest level it has become a global manufacturer of the cheap and disposable, and thus landfill everywhere is full of Chinese goods. China's impact upon the planet also grows, as its economic growth uses increasingly more non-renewable energy resources which ever add to greenhouse gas emissions. Thus the third of our multiple perspectives is that this China is everywhere, manifested as the structural dependence of wealthy nations upon the cheap labour and unsustainable industrial practices of a great deal of Chinese manufacturers: effectively, globalisation supports the unsustainable. The Chinese model is equally generalised as part of the pattern in the recovery of Asian economies. Whatever the sum of the impact of China's biophysical problems, what is certain is that they cannot be solved just by the techno-fix. As comment so far on the symbolic points to, these problems now reside in its soul, that is in its fundamental animatory forces.[25]

As can already be seen, every calling up of China is an undoing of its singularity. In the difference of regional and economic circumstances, emergent social transformation, multiple cultures, chronopolitical China cannot be placed in only one historical frame of 'now'. At the extremes, the pre-industrial can be found alongside the postmodern, the anchored alongside the lost, dreams alongside nightmares, and 'the life of things' alongside the death of the future.

CHINA 'NOW' AS EVERYWHERE

One learns from Heidegger that 'we all think like the Greeks'.[26] In other words early Greek thought has been foundational in the structuring of the life of the Western mind. This is to say that the Western mind has significant performative characteristics that connect back to this moment. Looking forward, rather than back, we can turn Heidegger's thoughts to another time and culture with the task of learning — 'we all need to be able to think like the ancient Chinese'. This instruction again implies method, not content. While the conceptual leaps between cultures, pasts and presents seem (and are) impossible, yet we find a strand that draws something together. This is nameable as a concern with the nature of things: '"things" are not only things of nature. Man, things produced by man, and the situation or environment effected and realised by the deeds and omissions of men, also belong among beings, and so do the daimonic and divine things.'[27] Here are words now and then, East and West.

Knowing is always dependent on what is at hand to know with. We are both enabled and limited by our knowledge. Recognising this we may ask can a learning from what has, almost, been forgotten, be enabled? Can a proximity to what we need to learn (sustain-ability) be learnt from the seemingly forgotten? Two domains of content fuse in these questions: the content of cultures deemed dead; and the overlooked content of the defutured. What drives us to know in this situation is neither esoteric nor instrumental. Rather it is to discover an other desire that is able to make things otherwise.

There are two immediate obstructions to a recognition of the nature of things in China: the afterlife of the deliberate erasure of the past and its values, attempted by the cultural revolution of Mao in the late 1960s; and the recent obliteration of the past by the dreamworld future of a commodity utopia (which is a widespread sensibility that is very much in line with a futurist notion of the past, which has to be destroyed to get to the future). As we can now learn from several decades of Chinese scholarship, and from the insights and problems of comparative philosophy, there is so much to discover and recover for recovery, for sustain-ability.

For instance, there is the partly self-conscious anthropocentrism and post-naturalism of Confucianism. The very foundation of Confucianism was that human being was a socially constructed historicity which did not depend on any cosmic creative force or external transcendental power. Within a structure of social and economic power, 'men make their own history'. (Marx's words say no more than those found in Confucian teachings.) But in advance of Marx, Confucius delivered a theory of history that showed the connectedness between past, present and future. His history was not predicated on the *telos* of Western metaphysics (the metaphysics that interpellated the theories of history of both Marx and Mao).[28]

Then there is Taoism, which frequently gets cast as the opposite of Confucianism — the passive, female, spiritual, natural, creative, radical: 'the way'; versus the unnatural, ordered, imperial regulatory, conservative: the rule. Although defined in the briefest of terms here, this contrast needs immediate qualification. While Hall and Ames discuss it at length, they make a point in conclusion that begs emphasis in terms of what we wish to focus on here:

> The real problem with the contrast is not that it is not wholly false but it is overstated and simplistic. Without due attention to the fact that, unlike independent dualistic categories, interdependent correlative categories are registered on a shared continuum, this kind of *yin-yang* characterization can focus on differences alone without illuminating the common presuppositions that underlie them.[29]

What we see from our perspective and concerns is that the two 'philosophies' exist in a condition of relationality, not however, just to each other but also to us. In bringing the imperative of sustainment to them, we can find the ability to sustain within them. In doing this we learn from Confucius the significance of the exercise, and transmission, of a tradition of responsibility for the unnatural state of being human. This responsibility is disclosed in the creation of a recognition of our anthropocentric being.[30]

From Taoism we also relearn the significance of the same as a continually returning lesson. Taoism, while prior to a physical science that tells us that we live in a closed system of a constant volume of matter in flux (a meta-autopoietic system), speaks the condition of the 'same' as a world of 'ten thousand things' (*wan-you*) that simply is. More than this, Taoism also affirms a 'way', a path, the directional inscription that sustains a constant return of being in this condition (a dwelling in change). Confucianism remakes this 'dwelling in the ever changing same' as responsibility — to be responsible is to sustain a way to travel the way in order to return — and this requires living under the restriction of limits, directions and design. Every way is the loss of all other options.

If we bring these traditions of thought to 'now' (in contrast to trying to project ourselves into their moment to find their truth) then we find major openings for thinking sustain-ability from a tradition of demonstrable sustaining ability. The key to this imminent radical reading is the interpretation of its ontological designing rather than its instructive content and narrative tropes. The symbolic content remains locked in its moment, while the designing character of the structural form can be identified and recast. Put as directly as possible, China, as the source of a tradition that designs the way to sustain-ability could now become the 'everywhere'. Its ancient past was not only prior to (and in many respects in advance of) the future prefigured by the forms of social cultural and economic life of the present, but it also has to arrive from the future as knowledge that we are travelling towards (as the yet to be re-discovered and re-invented) for there to be a future for us.

The paradox that this knowledge must arrive from the future rests on the premise of 'past', 'present' and 'future' not being empirical facts with a geometric, linear relation to each other. We are trapped in these redundant and ineffectual metaphors because we have no other available language of time, or rather the cultures that thought time differently have been devalued and obliterated by modern time. The rediscovery of what has been devalued, cast aside and forgotten is yet in front of us ('from the future') and the imperative of sustain-ability draws us towards this knowledge and this knowledge towards us. It is coming in that sense both from the past and the future as well as ever travelling in silence in the present.

* * *

In conclusion, what we have set out to show is that the critical practices that constitute sustain-ability demand a theory of temporality, which in turn requires a fundamental confrontation with received notions of measured time and the concealment of finitude. Time has to become work: a making which creates temporal extension against that which defutures. However, this theory in a translation to practice becomes self-negating if it is constituted as an unlocated abstraction. It has to be a theory in action in place. Although hard for us to grasp, the time of sustain-ability is a continuum with change, rather than with linear time (as we have critiqued).

## NOTES

1. The work of critics of modernisation theory and capitalist development in the 1960s and 1970s recognised that while un-development was a condition that predated modernisation, under-development was an imposition of a *telos* that did not develop what was undeveloped, but rather erased it. Thus modernisation does not enable a time lag to be bridged (the UN view) but destroys one time and replaces it with another. See A Gunder Frank, *Capitalism and Development in Latin America*, Monthly Review Press, New York, 1966; and Samir Amin, *Unequal Development*, Harvester Press, Hassocks, 1976.
2. The two most forceful ways of doing this were war and industrial production. In both cases large numbers of people from varied cultures were brought together to act within a regime of co-ordinated time. For instance, troops recruited and trained under the colonial powers of the British in Africa, Asia and the Indian subcontinent were transported to Europe to fight in World War I under the direct command of officers who directed massive set-piece battles via action calibrated to a singular time. War, as a mix of brief periods of action and long periods of waiting, generally created a culture of watching measured time. Trench life in World War I in fact made the wrist watch became an object of everyday life.
3. The rhetoric and the argument here clearly calls up, but does not confine itself to, Martin Heidegger's essays 'The Age of the World Picture' and 'The Question Concerning Technology' in *The Question Concerning Technology and Other Essays* (trans William Lovitt), Harper and Row, New York, 1977, pp. 115–54.
4. How, we might ask, can one measure the degeneration of the

utopian dream from the promise of liberation, wealth and well being, to electronic-age living, a Big Mac and a quick fix?

5  Anthropocentrically, the end of 'the world' is the end of the world we occupy ('the world' as a unified discursive construct has, as has been argued, already ended). The destruction of our world clearly impacts upon multitudes of non-human others.

6  Alexandre Kojéve, *Introduction to the Reading of Hegel: Lectures on the Phenomenology of Spirit* (ed Allan Bloom, trans James H Nichols), Cornell University Press, Ithaca, 1969, p. 162 and note (this is reference to the controversial note to the second edition of 1947). For a discussion of Kojéve's understanding of the post-historical see Alan Wolfe, 'Suicide and the Japanese Postmodern: A Postnarrative Paradigm' in Masao Miyoshi and HD Harootunian (eds), *Postmodernism and Japan*, Duke University Press, Durham, 1989.

7  The culture of Edo in significant part provided a ground for the modern Japanese forms of extreme social conformity. It is also this condition which has led some commentators to view Japan as a proto-postmodern society: a society in which the subject cannot make (speak, write, narrate) history, that is, a society at the end of history. The proto-postmodern view exposed a fissure in Japanese culture which still exists: between those members of Japanese society who believe that to be modern is to become Western; and those who hold that it is possible to divide 'progress' from 'Westernisation'. See Masao Miyoshi, 'Against the Native Grain' in Masao Miyoshi and HD Harootunian (eds), *Postmodernism and Japan*, p. 147.

8  *Ibid.*, p. 147.

9  The disjunctural and supplementary relation between 'world' and 'language' has been explored by many. The text that perhaps best stands for this tradition is Jacques Derrida's *Of Grammatology* (trans Gayatri Chakravorty Spivak), John Hopkins University Press, Baltimore, 1974.

10  In contrast, a culture without reason was not one grounded in a 'search for the truth' but rather the search for ways of symbolically thinking relations. For example one can contrast the universalism of a cosmology that creates 'the big bang theory' with an 'acosmogenic' claim that the cosmos is without an initial origin or sustaining principle. Moreover, that there is no cosmos as the disposition of all that is. The Chinese word romanised as *ziran* evokes a 'world as such' that arrives out of worlding — it is a spontaneous arising. See David L Hall and Roger T Ames, *Anticipating China: Thinking Through Narratives of Chines and Western Culture*, SUNY Press, New York, 1995, pp. 184–85.

11 This was a basic argument of Edward Said's influential book *Orientalism*, Pantheon, New York, 1978.
12 As discussed elsewhere, Western thought, as it was built upon productivism and the logic of reason, was carried by and inscribed in a thinking, acting and speaking. Thus being born into Western culture meant being born into its *logos* and its universalisation (the Eurocentric logocentric project).
13 To cite a few from a considerable list: decimals (2300 years before the Spanish in 976 AD); the laws of motion (2200 years before Newton in the eighteenth century); steel via the same methods of the West, 2100 years before the Bessemer process (1865) and 1400 years before the Seimens process (1863); the steam engine in 530 AD, over 1200 years earlier than its arrival in the industrial revolution; and clocks, the stirrup, printing, parachutes, guns, the iron plough, cybernetics. The story goes on, is incredible, and is nearly as erased in China as it is unknown in Europe. Needham's most influential volume is *Science and Civilisation in China*, vol. 2 of *History of Scientific Thought*, Cambridge University Press, Cambridge, 1956. A popularised version of these works, authorised and introduced by Needham, is Robert Temple, *The Genius of China*, Simon and Schuster, New York, 1986.
14 At almost the same time as the West was turning from pre-Socratic to Socratic thought in Greece, Confucianism was forming in China. Like the ancient Greek history of ideas, it is often hard to discern the work of one mind from its culture. In fact this is made even harder in China, as Confucius was regarded as both an individual and collective self. As Hall and Ames (*Anticipating China*, p. 90) comment: 'Chinese culture is not shaped by any appeal to universal categories defining human nature and establishing the "unity of mankind"; rather, the Chinese refer to themselves in more provincial locutions such as "the people of the central states" or "the people of Han"'. Thus, neither in their articulation of the meaning of human being, nor in their understandings of culture and history, do ancient Chinese thinkers appeal to transcendent principles as the origin or certification of their visions.
15 One of the most significant examples of China's agricultural technology was the iron plough which the Chinese first used in the sixth century BC. In the West this invention is credited as creating the agricultural revolution that precipitated the industrial revolution: see Temple, *The Genius of China*, pp. 15–25.
16 One example is Gottfried Wilhelm Leibniz, who had a major interest in, and a great deal of respect for China – even if he also

had an ulterior motive in gaining knowledge of the culture, which was so that he could assist those 'spreading the word of God'. His *Novissma Sinica* (1697–99) opens with a statement proclaiming that the fate of humanity rested with Europe and China — a view that sounds contemporary. With some reluctance Leibniz concluded that Chinese culture was more socially developed than that of Europe, especially with regard to the rule of law as it was inscribed in the social structure, as a deep and mutual respect that people showed towards each other.

17 *Yin-yang* do not signify balance as stasis, as resolution; rather the terms evoke a condition of harmony coming from a located and constantly changing play of the internal dynamic forces of affirmation and negation which are always actively present 'now'. This is not simply a tension of opposites, and it does not map onto a Western notion of 'nature' (another non-congruent term), the organic and the artificial. It is no dialectical process occurring in linear time. Thus balance is process, change is constant, force is everywhere, and harmony is a condition of sustainment.

18 Hall and Ames, *Anticipating China*, p. 120.

19 In 1998 China's growth rate was almost 8 per cent (although one has to treat these statistics with caution). Another way to picture the speed of China's growth is via urban development. In many ways the nation's uneven development is totally out of control. Take, for example, the rush from the country to the city. Compared with nineteenth century Europe, the experience is extremely compressed. What occurred in Europe in over a century has taken place in China in just one decade, and on a far larger scale. Shenzhen, for example, a city less than an hour north of Hong Kong, has grown from a population of 200,000 people to over 6,000,000 in a little over a decade.

20 Rapid urbanisation, agricultural system breakdown, social dysfunction, environmental toxicification, greenhouse gas emissions, high environmental impact modes of consumerist culture, local environmental disasters are ever escalating.

21 To get a sense of how to understand 'the problem' we need to view it in relation to contemporary forms of nation and the role of the state. We are at a planetary moment when the nature of the nation state is changing. In most affluent democratic countries this is evidenced by the way government 'core business' is being re-defined as the state is shrunk, welfare functions contract, assets are sold and responsibilities out-sourced. For many of the poorest countries, the state has become totally dysfunctional, resulting in the abandonment of the disadvantaged, the withdrawal of

elites into secured enclaves and corporate interests protecting their assets by force. To give some sense of this development consider the examples that range from infamous organisations operating internationally, such as Sandline with private armies for hire.

22 The People's Liberation Army has been the tool of the political machine while also existing as a gigantic enterprise owning some 30,000 businesses around the world. As mid-year instructions by President Jiang Zemin in 1998 evidence, the economic power of the PLA is being attempted to be reigned in. However, this will require a good deal more than the issuing of orders. See Seth Faison, 'Jiang declares war on army businesses', *Sydney Morning Herald*, Sydney, July 24, 1998.

23 Additionally, we note the failure of authorities (echoing our earlier comments on the dysfunctional state) to maintain an infrastructure of dikes is a growing part of the flood problem. China's national environmental bureau itself regarded this structural situation as a national emergency. Although the Beijing Government was shocked by the extent and impact of flooding, and went so far as to acknowledge that land clearing was partly to blame and to enact policy to address this problem, a critical confrontation with defuturing is a long way off. As the environmental disasters of China's charge toward economic growth and development clearly show, rather than securing conditions to sustain its people, their future is being put at risk. China veers from water shortage to floods. The seriousness of water shortage was made clear, for instance, in the 1998 review of the situation by Lester Brown and Brian Halweil of the US Worldwatch Institute (published in July/August 1998 issue of their on-line magazine). The report indicated that the demand for water in China cannot be met by current sources of supply. The massive 'Three Gorges Dam' project, in terms of the environmental impacts of construction and of water flows, will make this situation worse. There are real and major concerns around the nation's entire river system and water use over the next three to four decades.

24 China and its absolutely exhausted ruling political ideology makes a passage of communism, distilled and shaped by Marx, enacted and directed by Lenin and Stalin, inducted into China and modified by Mao and then finally evacuated by Deng Xiaoping.

25 Mind, spirit, soul, knowledge, movement were as one for Aristotle: *De Anima* (trans Hugh Lawson-Tancred), Penguin Books, London, 1986.

26 Martin Heidegger, *Early Greek Thinking* (trans David Farrell Krell and Frank A Capuzzi), Harper and Row, New York, 1984.

27 *Ibid.*, p. 21.
28 Eastern thought realised long before Western metaphysics that there is no known world other than the anthropocentrically constructed one. It is only 'the human' that makes the 'world' present, including any history of being-in-the-world. We should also note that the long history of 'uneven' socio-economic development of China and Western exploitation were two of the issues at the heart of its post-World War II revolutionary moment. The civil war was fuelled by these circumstances as they were bonded to an old and a new nationalism. An imperial system resting on past values of 'difference made one' was overthrown by a model of the modern socialist nation (these observations of course still resonate with the current regime's agenda of national unification). War was waged by the communists on both their physical enemies and on Chinese traditions, the latter being further extended by Mao's cultural revolution. Confucianism was a particular target. We also note that for all the horrors of this period, Maoism did seek to value and maximise some of the available social and material resources of the people, like 'community', land, organic waste, and self-sustaining food production. Yet these now stand as sign against the modern, rather than as signs of important sustainments. They have been rendered as the undesired pre-modern past.
29 David L Hall and Roger T Ames, *Thinking from the Han: Self, Truth, and Transcendence in Chinese and Western Culture*, SUNY, New York, 1998, p. 155.
30 The inescapable truth of anthropocentric being is one that continually gets rediscovered and refused, as anti-anthropocentric thinkers like the Chinese Taoist Lao Tzu, or equally and latterly European nihilist Friedrich Nietzsche, knew full well. We can also note that both of these traditions also embraced the re-creative force of the destruction of the ground upon which one's thinking stands.

# 7
# TELEVISUAL
# IN-HUMAN DESIGN

Found on a factory floor (author's collection)

We ever need to remind ourselves that anthropocentric being is at the centre of being unsustainable. This not just a matter of mind, for 'man' has created an instrumental world that structurally inscribes the anthropocentric in materials forms. This world is technology — as technology ever transmogrifies and becomes environment, system and trans-organic. The postmodern contest now increasingly becomes one between the natures of technologies, in contrast to the modern world's divisions between nature and technology.

The most contemporary significant escalation of the defutured is literally brought to light by televisual screen and imaged-based technologies. Our being (now irrespective of race, culture, age and gender) and our worlds are part formed, and almost totally mediated, by transmitted image, screened data, calculation and memory. Moreover, human beings live as much in immaterialised environments as they do material spaces. We cannot see our world outside of its televisual prefiguration. The televisual transports a seen world of things to us, things that we return through our ability to project the world seen as the world we make as individuals, cultures and nations:

> Image-like assimilation to objects can only be brought about by the objects themselves coming to be given. Yet this only happens by our representing them, thus having representations of them in us.[1]

Also, nothing demonstrates more powerfully than the televisual that our relations to technology are far more complex than our descriptive language is able to articulate. It is in the recognition of this condition that major questions of sustain-ability need to be put before the power of the electronic image and its accompanying cultural technologies.

***

The televisual first needs to be put in place and characterised with a few basic observations, all of which will be explored in detail later.

The televisual is one of the most immediate, complex and powerful environments of technology beyond the essence of the technological. As this it is an environment, a place of being in which we dwell. The 'televisual' is not reducible to 'television', but rather it is the productivist deposit and an on-going and proliferating process. What this means is that the televisual literally is an environment in which we exist that structures significant aspects of our being and existence. This claim does not depend upon watching television and thinking about its impact upon audiences. Rather, to talk about the agency of the televisual is to identify the ontological designing of the televisual as a transmitted authoring of subjects, as ways of seeing, of language, knowledge, imaginations, lifeworlds, worldviews, cultures, industries, commodities and technologies. The place and 'flow' of the televisual can now no longer be mapped as identifiable effects, and its presence cannot be separated from all the other elements and systems that make up the sum of all of the environments of 'our' building, dwelling and thinking. Moreover, the televisual is not even able to be segregated as a specific ecology within the ecology of the image.

The televisual defutures in two ways: first in the consequences of what it makes appear, and second in what it acts to conceal. The televisual projects worlds that fuel the desires for all those forms of unsustainability that make 'unmaking' culturally and economically normative in almost all economic, technological and socio-cultural contexts. The televisual also conceals the crisis of sustain-ability by the very appearance of crisis it presents. It has created 'the crisis of crisis', which is not an inadequate picture of environmental problems but more fundamentally, sight without seeing, thinking without thought, word without meaning, picture without significance, interest without concern, and appropriation without care.

## THE TELEVISUAL

We live in the televisual and it lives in us. It is a domain of dwelling from which and in which we think and make. As this it is habit, *habitus*, habitation. Equally the televisual is occupation and dissipation, world-building and world-demolishing, it is thinking, while also being memory, idle talk, imagination and metaphysics.[2] The televisual can be regarded as the key locus of imaginaries for our age. It is also a powerful designing force in its own right. And it has changed everything.

The question of what the televisual is continually returns, even when it has been asked and attempted to be answered many times. There will always be a gap between a general characterisation, phenomenological analysis, and reflected experience. The connection to television is an obvious opening into the problem.

It is not hard to agree that television quickly became far more than just a technology, or that it became more than just a medium of cultural forms, communication, informational content, knowledge and pleasure. The technology flowed and in so doing ensured the on-going designing of the designed. In its passage the 'televisual' thereby became an accumulative effect and ontological agency. One can take a standard line from the historical commentary on television as the medium 'that changed what we see and the way we see' and add that the televisual also changed our perceptions of our selves and ultimately what we are. Effectively the televisual remade a world by changing how 'the world' and 'humans' appeared and thought.

From its inception, television rapidly became a televisual system and started to take on a life of its own. The division between one technology and another (as one technology flows into another), and the technological, biological and cultural became harder to discern as electronic technologies became cybernetic network systems, technically plural and prefigurative sensory extensions. Certainly technological and cultural convergence is now well advanced, for instance the division between the computer, the television and the video is quickly advancing toward being just a manufacturer's product packaging option or a user's software-managed choice of function.

The encounter of the televisual with the body, as it 'bodied forth' in a world, changed the ability to see and hear by its transformation of the audio-visual environment in which 'world' and 'body' appeared and were animated in being. No matter how much television we watch we do not see the televisual: this is not because it is not visible but because it is everywhere, and has not been learned to recognise it.

The televisual throws into question what some thing is in profoundly new ways. Material and immaterial, near and far, figure and ground, past and present, animate and inanimate, the human and the technological — this universe crumbles. In the absence of a postproductivist lexicon, we speak in a conceptual language that recruits discourse and concepts that we know to be exhausted. 'Things' are never where, what and when we think. Heidegger writes that:

> being-in-the-world is not first and foremost the relationships between subject and object, but instead that which has already made such a relationship possible in advance in so far as transcendence carries out the projection of the Being of the being.[3]

The televisual is not only the instrument of transcendence that makes relationships possible but it also makes relationality impossible. It disconnects the finite 'structural unity of the transcendence of *dasein*', which is care. In vain we hang onto a thinking that the televisual has undone, for as yet we have little else to 'care' for us.[4]

The televisual is the most powerful inscriptive force of cultural authorship, yet there are but a few working to understand its 'nature' in a fundamental sense. As far as the academy is concerned, the televisual constantly returns to be converted back into familiar textual forms, or is used as if it were a neutral instrument for delivering curriculum content. Of course people do study television programs, learn how to produce for the televisual media, and argue in extremely ill-informed ways about the influence of the medium, but this never gets anywhere near what 'it' is. It is never addressed as the enframing force of a mind in its world, wherein it is a making, shaping and psychotic construction. Neither does it get engaged as a total Design, an aesthetic regime, a technology of desire, or as an agency that has become independent from the screen. Institutions of higher learning are full of people who have been put there by the televisual and whose ambition is televisually driven. The televisual is partly formative and directive of the subject to be educated: it prefigures and now fuses with formal education. Yet for all the televisions, the life experiences of the Internet, CD-Roms, computer games, video games, and the simulation-saturated commodification of the televisual, the environment of the televisual is an unmapped psychic and ontological geography. As a foundational worlding its 'nature' sets agendas for learning elsewhere.

That we still mentally construct and present a distance between the televisual and our selves shows a general feature of the unreflective quality of our condition and a lack of understanding of its proximity. We misread it as measured distance. Proximity is, however, never just this. It is as much empathy, understanding, familiarity and emotional presence, or their opposites. So in broad terms, and beyond the spatial, proximity is equally a matter of language, thought and disposition. It is 'viewable' by the openings, closures or separations which enable or prevent us from knowing, as hearing, feeling, seeing or thinking what is there to discover. It follows that one of the most significant ways to understand the televisual is how it functions as a powerful technology of proximity. The televisual has the ability to change both time, distance, feeling and perception. The door onto this recognition was opened by Marshall McLuhan, and while there has been plenty of inflated rhetoric and textual production from the time of McLuhan's first opening up of the ontological character of television, advances in thought have been small.[5]

## DESIGN WITHOUT A DESIGNER

Obviously, to create and operate the televisual technology requires an enormous number of professional designers — of software, costume, graphic, animation, set, lighting and so on — as well as many other professionals whose job effectively has a design dimension (producers, directors, managers, engineers, camera operators, stylists, sound recordists and editors). No 'master designer' orchestrates the totality. Yet televisual assemblages have become the most powerful directive designing force on earth, and they are without an identity, unity or organic life. It is the 'thing' itself that designs. The televisual is ontological Design writ large:

> Television is both designed and designs — as such it reveals a dual movement of the application and exercise of agency. It is prefigured while prefiguring. Television is made by, and makes, forms, language and

meanings of lifeworlds in which, as itself, comes to be active. Through this circular process of making and being made television transforms itself from a medium into a domain. This domain exists prior to knowing, this domain constitutes the reality of our unauthenticity, and thereby is part of the naturalised artificial world in which we are formed, and find ourselves. Thus our ability to perceive is produced by finding ourselves in a pre-existing perceptual field which we, in turn, inform. The televisual is an important part of that which is 'there' prior to a knowledge of it 'being here'; television has therefore become elemental to the perceptual field of 'what is' our given condition. However, in the occupation of its place of being, its own being sets out to act upon perception — the televisual lays out, orders, makes available, that which it has selected to be discovered.[6]

Ontological Design is the directional consequence of some thing 'thing-ing'; it is agency in action; it is worlding; it is intention and disposition. To recognise this is but to discover the long known. As the Taoists tell us, Chinese thinkers were theorising some two and half thousand years ago that 'the propensity of things' will 'operate outside you as their own disposition dictates'.[7]

TELE-VISION

Tele-vision ('far sight') has a history. The desire to bring what is far near — be it the distant, the concealed or the microscopic — was elemental to utopian thought. The heavens were the earliest and most common object of focus. Here was the dream of seeing what could not be seen. The first technological registration of the realisation of this desire was the lens of ground glass. The project was one of proximity, of desire for closeness, rather than just magnification. This can be seen, for example, by examining Galileo's telescopic observations in the first decade of the seventeenth century. What they show was that sight, the seen and bringing near were constituted by the combined abilities of the telescopic instrument, embodied optics and the productivist mind. This was a 'seeing' that enabled observation to be brought together with the theorisation of the seen to formulate a heliocentric theory, and thereafter Galileo's claim that the laws of nature were written in the language of mathematics. Here is a lineage of thinking from Pythagoras, mediated and extended by Copernicus, and instrumentally assisted.

We might note the intersection of the Eurocentric 'discovery' of the New World in 1492 with, at almost exactly the same moment, the discovery of the new universe by Copernicus and his recreation of the Classical Greek heliocentric theory of the Earth's disposition to the sun. The imaginary that powered the creation of television flowed to and from the historicity of this moment. Television came out of fire, for with fire the sight of *physis* was displaced by the bringing of illumination and the human discovery of light as a means of projection. The conquest of darkness, the advance of technology, the cave wall as screen, the interpretative impetus — 'now' is an unknowable moment somewhere and sometime completely and totally out of conceptual reach of those discoverers of the illuminating power of sunlight and fire. And yet the destiny of the founding moment of a first discovery, and its designing, still flows. The televisual is but a punctuation.

The fate of tele-vision was cast in a distant past beyond invention, recall or description. That place from which it came still strives to speak — the historicity is of its arriving out of the sun, as light that illuminates, animates and opens vision, remains silent and unseen. This is the ground from which the first knowledge (*arché*) arises in which the word is anchored. This is a ground cleared, illuminated and opened for the passage of sound. But there was still darkness (as the return of the concealed). Darkness was contested and defeated in the moment of fire — and out of fire came the unity and economy of 'man,' world and picture — yet darkness remains imminent.

The arising of electronic fire is but one moment of a sought command of light and world. To make sense of this statement we need to bring it to televisual, the worlding of the world picture, to a 'first thinker' — Heraclitus. This we do with the assistance of comments by Michel Haar on how Heraclitus understood fire and the arising of the world as *physis*. The point here is that reading first thinking radically questions thinking now. Understanding Heraclitus requires a careful 'bringing to' as well as a painstaking 'finding in'. We bring the idea of the televisual to his Fragment 30: '(The ordered?) world, the same for all, no god or man made, but it always was, is, and will be, an everliving fire, being kindled in measure and being put out in measure'.[8]

As Haar shows, Heraclitus occupied a position at the dawn of metaphysics through an exposition of knowledge belonging to being, rather than in the ownership of individuals. Thus knowledge in being makes the world present — a knowledge come by fire (that is by revelation, by illumination). Metaphysics brought the world forth as *physis*, as disclosed, as knowledge in contrast to it originating as a pure original creation. Against a notion of the world as an 'arising' or 'pure emergence' Haar writes:

> Rather, the 'world' ('cosmos') is thought as 'fire', which means as pure emergence, as 'light' which from the outset intimately penetrates, like lightning or flame, every being without encompassing it like a container.[9]

Plato was to transpose metaphysics from being to the subject, via the elevation of the significance of 'the look' and the Idea. This move is from an 'aletheiaic' notion of knowledge — as a shining forth that discloses — to an ocularcentric construction of sight, visibility and truth that centres on the image.[10] In the *Republic*, prior to presenting his 'Simile of the Cave' (wherein the televisual truth of the image as a prefiguration of 'reality' was first exposited) Plato puts forward his 'Simile of the Sun' in which the heliocentric eye (the eye with sunlight and fire) comes to the visible world as it is articulated to the intelligible world.[11] He disclosed that what is seen by the senses (the realm of *horaton*) is made tele-visual by mind (the realm of *noeton*) — light, eye and mind converge in seeing as it transcends matter and space and transforms 'what is' into 'what is known (the opening onto the Idea)'. That we see with our mind, and 'nothing is without reason (as seeing with sense)' creates the opening that the image fills as organised sight. While the Platonic view falls into a dualist model it also casts it a priori into unreachability, for the image/mind is a monist screen that always divides seeing from 'reality'.[12]

Seeing requires the eye, mind, language, light, space and time, and thus presumes a body and world. The televisual — as extended vision, as embodied memory, as the world of appearance and worlding — severs all distance between body and world. We body forth into 'the world' in the company of 'a' world within our body — a body quite different from our sentient body in its world, wherein all feeling, all pain, pleasure, heat and cold, turn inward. 'The flesh of the world', of Merleau-Ponty's evocation, enfolds all living things; however, what is now alive cannot be held in the grip of biocentrically based knowledge. The practice of biology itself has decentred the organism by its foregrounding of the significance of information to organic systems; inanimate things animate life, and things have lives. Thus living in and from the ecology of sunlight has been supplemented and compromised by the arrival of the ecology of the image as, in and by the televisual.

From the perspective of ontological Design, the image functions beyond its representational claim of linking to its reference by the look, for it also functions to design through its enframed sight becoming located in projective productive action (the image-thing of design). Contrary to the language of common sense, as Heidegger makes clear, sight, mind, image and product are bound in an unnamed structure, that we evoke here as Design.

Sight is not an appendage to productive behaviour, but belongs positively to it and to its structure, and it guides the action. Therefore it is not surprising if this seeing, in the sense of the circumspective seeing that belongs to the ontological constitution of producing, becomes prominent also where ontology interprets the 'what' which is to be produced. All shaping and forming has, from the first, an out-look upon the look (*eidos*) of that which is to be produced. Here it may already be seen that the phenomenon of sight which pertains to producing comes forward in characterising the what-ness of a thing as *eidos*. In the process of producing, that which the thing was is already sighted beforehand.[13] Sight and the televisual clearly converge in ontological domains of production — domains within which the production of subjects and objects fuse as world and agency.

We can now view a technology of seeing, amid a whole gamut of new and required technologies as they collided with an established ocularcentric basis of viewing the world. This was expressed in both empiricism, as common sense, and a theory of the seen, which itself rested upon an available theory of knowledge, that in turn rested on a privilege being given to sight, illumination, observation and thus enlightened knowing. Without the designing of this conjuncture taking on an undirected life of its own, the designing of the inventor — designers of television technology — would not have been possible.

The idea of the image of a television technology started to arrive at the end of the nineteenth century. One example being a cartoon by George D Maurier which appeared in the English magazine *Punch* in 1879, showing a couple in England watching their daughter playing a game of tennis in Ceylon via an 'Edison Telephonoscope' — a sound and image transmitting 'electric camera obscura'. The attempt to actually create the technology soon followed. In Germany in 1884 Paul Nipkow began work on scanning images by breaking them up into different light intensities and thereafter, voltages. A few years later, in 1897, the cathode-ray tube was invented by Karl Braun, again in Germany. From this point onward, work on the invention of television was taken up by a number of inventors in Germany, Russia, Hungary, Britain, America, Italy and Japan. Reports of an attempt to create the technology appeared in *The Times* in London in 1923, which carried an advertisement from an inventor asking for help in making a working model. The first actual working example was made in the same year. Between 1925 and 1927 demonstrations occurred in Russia, America, Japan and England. By 1927 John Logie Baird had transmitted an image from Glasgow to London, and in May 1928 General Electric was making three weekly broadcasts from the WGY Radio Station in New York. The first real quality image did not arrive however until 1936, with the opening of a high definition television service in London by the BBC.[14]

Notwithstanding the gross reduction of relational complexity, which not least is implicated in the error of narrative linearity, it is worth trying to trace a further series of complex moves. These moves themselves are layered upon the greater complexity of culturally constituted sight. To place mind between object and image tells us little about the seen, rather it is simply to impose the structuring of difference, which itself enfolds the point of view from which difference is viewed. Image evidences the flow between, and the dissolution of, subject and the object in two ways. First, the object is only ever knowable as a projection (the recognition of the sensed as the sensible) of the subject. Second, the subject that makes the image, or object, travels before the designing mark with an intentionality that goes forward to the object's intention and back (via the designing of the image or object) into the *logos* that gives an other designer subject intent. To clarify the point — and recalling Design as it was presented in the Introduction — the designed (object/image) is the ground out of which designing occurs as worlding effects. As this, it is the agency from which the practice draws its references, imaginaries and methods while also being the efficacy of the thing-itself-in-action (the ontological designing of object/image).

As images became memory and contemplation, as they were replicated by mechanical reproduction and animated by film, and then, electronically reproduced, created and disseminated, the endless uninterrupted image of continuous transmission tele-vision became absolutely excessive. Where once our vision of things-in-the-world was enhanced by the lens (by telescopic or microscopic vision) now the world is viewed by the refraction of televisuality. We do not simply watch the televisual, but rather see and are seen through it (not least as images for an other).

Reiterating Plato's proposition of our not seeing with our eyes but with our minds, one now has to confront the televisual's authorship of mind — our mind. Where Plato once constituted the visible world as given, but illuminated by the intelligible world, there is now tele-visuality, as tele-vision has become technology, mind and recognition. The televisual sees without eyes, fills the spaces of our lives, sources imagination and orders the content of 'world-image'. There are no major world events, figures, places or issues that are not televisual inventions and projections. As disembodied mind and milieu, and as an agency of gathering and production, it makes the intelligible world intelligible and the visible world visible.

Electronic fire illuminates the screen, fills the eye, occupies the mind. The magnification of its lens brings desire into view. Its ecology of mind is our ecology of mind; its sickness is our sickness; its crisis is our crisis; its unauthenticity is our unauthenticity; and the locus of the simulacra is the copy of the unreachable original.[15] For all the claim of, and faith in, 'representation', the image technology of the televisual, as it screens 'reality', is the most marked statement of the impossibility of non inter-textual reference and of forward sight always being framed and edited as back projection.

The televisual is the environment wherein the dice that stamp sustain-ability or unsustainability are cast. The televisual is the meeting place of defuturing and futuring. These comments have nothing to do with television reportage or public opinion: they have everything to do with the constituted pictures of self-hood, world-hood and time.

Our ability to sustain is directly linked to an ability to identify what there is both to create and to destroy. This ability directly links to our perceptual reach, which, as is being pointed out, is significantly enframed by the televisual as a designing of 'the world' as 'what is visible', how it appears, and how and for what it functions.

Don Ihde, who is most informative on the technological mediation of perception, points out that 'phenomenological theory claims that for every change in what is seen (the object correlate), there is a noticeable change in how (the experience correlate) the thing is seen'.[16] Extrapolating the 'thing' to a meta-thing, in television's televisual assembly of 'how the world is presented to be seen', the actuality of 'how the world is' changes. The willing of the televisual (its cybernetic 'nature') wills a world and thereby transforms how the world is seen, which in turn transforms a knowledge of the world. Yet again the seeing, mind and world fuse.

At the very core of television, as it folded and expanded into the televisual, is a meaninglessness. It reproduces itself as an ontological domain and the afterlife of metaphysics, an absolute mindlessness, an illogic that is unable to question the nature of its system, its impact and its continuity. The televisual has just become a part of what is — if it were not for the post-natural it would be 'nature'. You can turn a television set off, blow up a transmitter, shut down a computer, dump gigabytes of software, board up a Timezone video game store, bin a pile of videos, but what you cannot do is turn the system off. Writing, speaking, thinking, imagining, playing, seeing, concealing, disclosing, living, working — these are but some of the 'vital' elements of the world of the televisual and its worlding.

The play of sight and light across and between these elements is complemented by another force of unification: gathering. As indicated, the ocularcentric foundation of Western metaphysics reveals that *logos* came from the lighting of vision, light and gathering, which, as *legein* was the root of reason.[17] This is the history of knowledge from the disclosure of truth by *alètheia* (unconcealment) that comes from early Greek thought. To know was to bring before sight in the light, so that the truth would expose itself. 'Gathering' was too inseparable from sight for true knowledge to be possible. The televisual, as technology, is a technology of gathering. Gathering the world as and into a picture is to know 'a' world. The birth of the world, made picture, was the birth of the anthropocentric cosmos.

What is brought together does not belong together, other than as the space of the televisual. What the televisual gathers, what it seems to unify and offer up as truth and reality, is in fact temporally, spatially and culturally disparate. As an act of appropriation the event of the televisual is the assemblage of an image of the world that is without reference but in possession of enormous designing power, and which has mostly followed a path of defuturing. Here is the 'world' which, for example, is sent ahead of China 'now' as the world China now 'wants to be.' This 'tele-*logos*' is the reason of the image at work — it is an *einbildungskraft*, an 'imageering' construction with the power to install a designing picture. (Here again is that stamping that exemplifies Heidegger's notion of enframing, *gestell*, in action.)[18]

In this framing, televisual 'sending' has no subject or managed structure except the will of the technological system that transmits day-in-day-out in total ignorance of intent, reason, content, destination, or effect.[19] Equally, televisual appropriation, like appropriation itself (which is the theft from which culture is made) 'has no history or destiny'. But there is another history: the history of the ontological designing of the appropriated assemblage. As Joan Stambaugh tells us 'What has a history is what has been sent, and that is the history of metaphysics'.[20]

## PERSPECTIVES AND HORIZONS

While tele-vision appears to deliver the far to the near as sight, what is imaged, however, is, as we have seen, nowhere and unavailable, because the technologically constituted assembly of framing, editing and changing scale throws even the most unadulterated image from somewhere into nowhere. Connections are made without making contact. Things are never as they appear.

Revisiting the question of how the world is turned into a picture — as a remaking of the world that restructures how an encountered world is seen — brings us to the prefigurative power of the televisual as it embraced and undid Heidegger's understanding of world picture.[21] In a 'cut and mix' with Heidegger we can reiterate and think on from him:

> 'We get the picture' [literally, we are in the picture] concerning something. ... 'To get into the picture' means to set whatever 'is' in place before oneself, it stands before oneself as the picture, as set up. ... Where the world becomes picture, what is, in its entirety, is juxtaposed as that for which man is prepared and which, correspondingly, he therefore intends to bring before himself and have before himself, and consequently intends in a decisive sense to set in place before himself'. When it is understood essentially, it does not mean 'a picture of the world but the world conceived and grasped as picture.'[22]

As has been sought to be shown, sight and seeing ever demand the bringing of complexity in the face of a biocentrically fabricated common sense of the eye. We need reminders:

> Seeing does not mean just seeing as perceiving with the bodily eyes, but neither does it mean pure non-sensory awareness of something present-at-hand in its presence-at-hand. In giving an existential signification to 'sight', we have merely drawn upon the peculiar feature of seeing, that it lets entities which are accessible to be encountered unconcealedly in themselves.[23]

Between 'us', as beings that perceive, and any 'world', as that which is constructed by perception, there is a triple-layered screen through which seeing passes. The first layer of the screen is language, which both names what is able to be seen and constructs the cultural frame of viewing (while we see with our minds, our minds see no thing without language); the second layer is the prefigurative image of the televisual as it acts to inform (and design) what is seen; and the third layer is memory, mobilised as that reference that gives sight its temporal dimension. Worlds are ever virtual. Reality has always been out of sight, and simulated.

The assemblage of pictures not only installed 'the world picture' without reference, but set the horizons of the perception of the phenomenal world. A horizontal formation of a field of vision of a world was given and taken for granted. Where else does one go for a picture of the world; what memories does one raid; and where do they come from? The televisual is the answer, although not asked. An ideological structure of posited reality, in which the truth of that included in, or excluded from, the frame was and is taken as given.

Reconnecting — the utopian dream of modernity, of one modernised world in one temporal frame, took form in the picturing of the modern world:

> The world picture does not change from an earlier medieval one into a modern one, but rather the fact that the world becomes picture at all is what distinguishes the essence of the modern age [*der Neuzeit*].[24]

The violent abstraction of globalisation followed the image, as did the extension of ethnocentric sight. Everything discovered arrives pre-packaged by projection. The picture again went ahead of the eye, and the 'I'; the eye and the image fused:

> The televisual escapes from television and spreads across the world of our dwelling. The televisual has become part of the condition, and means, of the formation of our given understanding. Our Being exists before and after it's called into being by televisual encounter. It is not that there are 'us' and 'television' as elemental to our lifeworld — just as it is the case that there is no clear division between us and our culture. The televisual is a making and a made that assists in the construction of a self/culture and its self. We picture ourselves in the knowing picture of the world picture — we live located in image. We *be* come fascinated by the world view(ing) of television; it induces being by seduction and therein in this place of our dwelling we come to our Being.[25]

The rise of a culture of the televisual became a significant transformation of a place of dwelling. It brought the homelessness of immaterial space, the impossible place 'to be'. The utopian home — as world, hearth or product that tele-vision seemed to bring near and offer to be grasped — always remained out of touch and bonded to an other economy.[26] As was seen even as early as the celebration of the arrival of television at the New York World Fair in 1939, the disembodied desire of a world picture without world instantly became an instrument of economic modernity.

What does the world picture install (as tele-*logos*, *einbildungskraft*, 'imageering')? Certainly it might be a picture of how 'the world' is pictured, but the world picture is more likely to be registered as that which is going on in, and constituting, a world as the 'world of the everyday' in which television flows into the televisual. News, sport, drama, comedy, advertising, style, 'consumerism' as new cars, fridges, microwaves, relationships, good clothes, tasty fast food, holidays, nice homes, cultivated gardens, restaurants, hotels, holidays, cocktails, nightclubs — all play in the defutured of the heterotopic space of pictured lifeworlds that design unsustainable desires. The peoples of the former Soviet Union, with China and India number over two and a half billion dreaming of the realisation of what is projected from screen and memory. Just in China alone 250 million television sets were sold in the first half of the 1990s. Much can be said, done and forced in the name of the dream.

The destructive vectorial force of the televisual machine of desire cohabits with the war machine and unites it with the domestic. In the ambiguousness of the destructive forms of the televisual (which makes us want to defend what we think are its virtues), we find those destroyers of the image that fully realise the potential to violence of the visual. The televisual is a battleground of sign wars, the place of manufacture of the sign weapons. (It is also the technology of 'head-up displayed' weapons systems and the home of 'smart' image-driven guidance systems — worlding has become warring.)

Unlike the nuclear threat, chemical warfare or the neutron bomb, these sign weapons' powers have already enacted mass destruction on a vast scale, although their aesthetic mechanisms of concealment often make the horror of this destruction hard to imagine, let alone see. Judgement here does not rest within the cultural or moral realm but rather with the actuality of a defuturing.

## THE UNSUSTAINABLE WORLD OF THE WORLD PICTURE

We cannot escape, we cannot step outside. The first and second laws of thermodynamics rule: while the material form of things constantly changes, the total sum of the entire system remains the same, and the entropic degeneration of the system is unstoppable. There is another anthropocentric law: the law of tele-dynamics — whatever 'is', there is always the imaged desire for what is not; the attraction of televisual 'nowhere' is thus always stronger than the attraction of 'somewhere'.

The televisual worlding defutures by its immaterial undercutting of the foundations of sustain-ability. It does this by throwing forward the living unsustainably of its fictions as 'the reality' to realise, in the guise of the realisation of utopia as the status quo. Utopia here is seen, not as an idealised social order, but as an available endless supply of commodities. Placed before the remnants of Western metaphysics, the televisual works its deconstructive magic by undoing all values and all subjects other than its own. The ontological designing of the immaterial image materialises its promised future as an inscribed defuturing.

As with the identification of anthropocentrism, there is no overcoming of televisual defuturing. However, its naming brings the possibility of taking responsibility. This implies an ability to take responsibility for the system, it implies that a thinking can be made that has the ability to transform living in its light.

## ECOLOGY OF THE IMAGE

'A' world has been made in which everything valued hangs on the consequences of actions resulting from the reading of 'the world as text'. The fate of the world is now in many respects an interpretive outcome of reading the 'world picture'. The picture is directive.

'Direction' here is, however, not reducible to direction by reason or instruction, but rather it is a gathering of the power of inscription, desire and interpellation into one expressive force. It should also be noted that the terms 'reading' and 'interpretation' are not being used here in association with literacy or critical reflective thought but rather at a more basic hermeneutic level which identifies ontological functions of perception as they articulate with action. Such reading and interpreting are therefore elemental to the most essential modes of operational attunement with one's world.

The world picture — the picture we are in as an ecology; the televisuality that is both environmentally elemental to our being here and a seeing of an environment that is nowhere — is active everywhere.

We build, dwell and think in material, socio-cultural and immaterial ecologies. Although ecologists and environmentalists have privileged the biophysical model of the 'ecological', this is neither appropriate to totally foreground, nor adequate to explain, the systems that constitute 'life'. Notwithstanding the efforts of science to claim a transcendent objectivity, all life is viewed anthropocentrically (the demarcation of life itself is a cultural variable of human designation in the shifting sands of human-posited values). Life sits in the sight of that vision constituted in the ecology of the image and its televisual designing. The layers of the screen of perception through which all worlds arrive determines that while the flesh of the world undoubtedly 'is', it only arrives before us by first being constituted as picture. Like the very notion of ecology itself, it is the production of an ecology of the image.

Without exception, every one of us lives in a biophysical environment of earth, air, fire and water; an environment of matter, given and made, that functions by process, system and change; in a socio-cultural environment of social structures, cultural conventions and values — for from our mothers onward we only survive by dint of others and in an environment of signs, codes, language, visual images, assumed meaning and attempted communication. Each of these environments is animated by constituted ecologies. It should be said that biophysical and socio-cultural ecologies are not of a higher order of importance than the ecology of the image. Our only access to the biophysical and socio-cultural environments, and their ecologies, is by this ecology of the image. The condition, operation and disposition of the ecology of the image, of which the televisual is a part, then predetermines the condition of the other ecologies. This comment brings us to our immediate concern: an outlining of the major phenomenological characteristics of the televisual as both an instrument and domain of the ecology of the image.

We have acknowledged that a semiotic mediation, which occurs between 'us' and our perceived 'world', is screened in both senses of the word (as a projection and as a filtering). This occurs in three ways: by language, image and memory. The televisual appropriates and delivers language directly: it is a 'standing reserve' from which vocabulary is drawn. Such is the 'nature' of the televisual that the child, notwithstanding the socio-economic difference, learns a language from direct television exposure and of course from parents, extended family, other children and teachers, all of whom equally acquired a significant amount of their language by direct and indirect television encounter. It is no longer possible to make a distinction between 'natural' and 'artificial' appropriation within the intertextual milieu. The televisual objectifies worlds by imagery. Our ability to recognise, and our desire to experience, for example, places, peoples, animals, plants, cities, technologies, languages or cultural traditions outside our own culture, are all powerfully powered by the televisual.

Now we need to bring this thinking to ecological and environmental problems. The very fact that there is an 'ecological crisis' is in large part a televisual construct of an image. On the one hand most people do not, or cannot, directly see, for instance, the depletion of the ocean's fish stocks, holes in the ozone layer, the destruction of rainforests, contaminated waterways in countries far from their own, or greenhouse gas emissions, without the eye of the camera to capture a 'directly witnessed' image or the abstract representation of the 'problem' created by an expert. Ecological problems — like much else that results from the worlding of the televisual, such as major events, news, important people and so on — can be said to 'not exist' unless they are imaged by the camera. Being and existing become ever distanced from each other. On the other hand there is an absolute failure of televisual imagery to be able to create an adequate image of the relational complexity of 'problems', as they exist across and between the biophysical, socio-cultural and semiological locus of the reportage of crisis in crisis. (This failure is part of that named as the 'crisis of crisis'.)

This situation has come to be across the televisual without conspiracy. Rather it formed out of a structural lack of recognition and understanding of crisis. Televisual culture is a victim of its own mis- and mass-communicated ontological designing. Its propensity to organise information as something at which to point a camera, and then deliver as 'bites'; to function within popularist rhetoric and themes; and to present and then deal with arguments reductively (and thus to resist complexity) all overdetermine content by the imperatives of entertainment. Televisual culture is thus totally ill-equipped to be able to deal with the actual consequences of the exposure of crisis as crisis (one that could be shown to warrant address as a global state of emergency, in the face of governmental failure) because the actual image of what is critical never arrives.

The televisual, as it functions within the ecology of the image, is totally implicated in perception as a read text of intertextual framing (as the prefigurative designing of a perception of 'the real') and as the memory from which re-cognition comes. The non-uniqueness of memory here is a commonality that undoes the authentic subject. Our televisual memories are not our own: perception always comes from the historicity and cultural embeddedness of mind as assisted by the senses. While the exploration of the biological and cognitive sensory apparatus of perception is essential it is only part of the story. Perception cannot be simply located in the body (to do so identifies a failure in understanding of the body), for it is of a 'being-in-the-world'. The psychologist who explores perception within the confines of scientific experimentation is like the reader of a book who never gets past an examination of the paper, binding and typography. Perception is fundamentally a textual product. As this it is the arrival of world before mind through the screens of the world's worlding. The historicity of worlding is memory (rather than history — which is historicity made present and narrativised). Perception can now be viewed as illumination in exchange — it is an exchange between sensory perception, knowledge and light as it is projected out into a world and then back into the self as the revisiting of what was sensed, recalled and reflected. A developed understanding of perception thus needs to engage the faculties, knowledge, interpretative capability, the temporal condition of being and world. It is everything. Merleau-Ponty's seminal work on the topic dealt with perception as a phenomenology of three parts: a developed concept of the non-monadic body, the world as a phenomenological construct and of that knowing which is a turning between 'being-for-itself' and 'being-in-the-world'.[27]

Our coming into the world is now prefigured televisually. Even before leaving the womb we arrive as an image on the monitor, the pictured life, the ultrasonic pulse. Thereafter, we are greeted in the world by mother, father and the television set (there it is in the corner of the hospital room sending its welcoming light our way), lined up in rows of bassinettes in the hospital nursery we are monitored by video, we are on television even before our eyes are able to focus. Name, heart rate, weight, temperature: we are computer entered data before being even the most modest of identities. We grow; we hear our parents speak; we also listen to the television. We look from pram, cot, play pen — rooms, toys, streets, park — slowly familiarity comes, meanwhile there is the constant strangeness of television, light, colour, sound and confusion. We have to learn to watch, and a special television or video televisual space has been cleared for us. We are starting to learn. Ahead is a worlding of images, languages, sounds, technologies, games, instructions, work and dreams.

There are no simulations as the simulated, for the real is the fiction. 'Simulation', 'fact', 'fiction' are again but the words that lend a lie to a language of difference that, while a dominant economy, are sites of divisional collapse.[28] Nothing is represented; nothing is simulated. The gap between 'what is' — the thing-in-itself — and 'what is made present' ever remains.

## THE POLITICAL ECONOMY OF THE TELEVISUAL

In a world in which we are constantly denied verification, we learn to trust our judgement and the image. The experience of the image constantly travels ahead of the experience of the flesh as an instruction. Image teaches flesh what to desire, what to expect, what to say and how to act. Its designing situates, its consuming consumes, its destroying destroys.

The ecology of the image, as and with the televisual, is indivisibly a political ecology, within which political economy has been subordinated. That the televisual is not neutral can be seen in its organised employment by modernity, in its intrinsically disposed modernising qualities (as the whole installed fabric of economic, political and cultural globalisation evidences), and in the form of crisis it projects. Above all else it is an instrument of warfare. As this instrument it is possible to cast television as both battle ground and war machine.

The televisually constructed battle ground has become a major site of conflict. The impact of action becomes as much to do with an impact upon the screen as it does upon the enemy forces or territory. Afghanistan, the Gulf War, the conflicts of Central and Eastern Europe are all examples of this. Most recently, NATO's war against Yugoslavia required images of refugees from Kosovo to gain the moral authority to act. Equally the conflict of images between 'ethnic cleansing' and NATO's 'collateral damage' from stray bombs and missiles, had a major influence on events. The dynamics of the televisual conflict are predicated on the attempt to positively dispose those forces deemed decisive in the outcome of the conflict — world opinion, recoding the ideology and actions of an aggressor, the support of a superpower, material support from sympathiser nations, or simply getting exposure for one's cause. One can note two particular familiar 'facts' in this context (as the Vietnam War first illustrated):

wars can be won or lost as a result of events in televisual space; and the very phenomenon of modern terrorism has, in significant part, been a televisual construct, since the objective is the camera image, the desired impact is the media fallout.

In all conflicts, both big and small, the mobilisation and management of the televisual battleground is of crucial strategic importance. In fact the very construction of the battleground itself is televisually authored.[29] More than this, there is the rapid rise of televisual weapons and weapon systems to note. The televisual world saw, as it watched and participated in the Gulf War, 'smart' rocket camera-loaded missiles, bombs and shells that placed the eye before the projectile to guide it to its target. The eye can now literally be in war, while the body trails behind at war. The eye, weapon, camera, battlefield and total technosphere of the warzone and its televisual outreach, now function as one cybernetic system — information flows and the actors jump to act on its instruction.[30] And then there is the fighter pilot travelling at a speed that not long ago was beyond imagination, eyes fixed on a 'head up display', his life, and the death of his targeted foe, firmly held in the 'hands' of his computer as it guides him and his released missile towards its target. The only visible mark of the extinguishment of a life is the disappearance of a dot on a screen. Humanist rhetoric is thrown into this melee but it is really quite out of place. In this ecology image/fire and fire/defutured become one with knowledge/technology/power. But there is a technological postscript.

We are disoriented, homeless in an ecology that while totally visible is almost totally concealed. The worlding of the televisual hides in darkness (itself and that which it will not image), in the proliferation of images which makes identification impossible and in a 'hiding in the light' in which display occurs with the appropriate codes of reading withheld. Knowledge of disclosure/encounter has to be understood as not only a product of mind and light, but also of feeling.

For some years advances in eye surgery have come about through the development of laser technology. This very same technology was developed as a weapon, first 'coming to light' in Ronald Reagan's 'Star Wars' madness. Using research from medical technology, design work has been done on a laser weapon which does not require the amount of energy needed to shoot an aircraft out the sky, but rather will simply blind an enemy pilot.[31] Here is cost benefit analysis in action, the total convergence of military and non-military technology in the system, and perhaps the most devastating indictment of Western metaphysics yet: the turning of light into blindness.

Feeling gives a sense of being in the picture, of being in-formed, of being both designed, de-signed, and of being both placed and displaced.[32] Heidegger started to grasp that modern technology (in which of course television is but one agency of lifeworld mediation, time management and space 'compression'), dissolves and remakes the ground upon which a sense, feeling and perception of belonging is created. The here, home, the familiar and the elsewhere are ever displaced by the televisual. There is now no longer anywhere to belong. The televisual has totally changed everything (not least living homeless in the ecology of the image) and as a result desired modes of dwelling and defuturing have converged — sustain-ability has to take its place.[33]

\* \* \*

The televisual has made America everywhere, war everybody's experience, and technology culture.

The televisual withholds; it never tells us enough — for instance, we see violence, but violence is not just image. Violence is a sensory complexity, it is sounds and smells, a proximity, a ripping apart of the normal order of things that is actually felt. The nature of violence is concealed in the image of violence. The 'world' of the ecology of the image and its defuturing dangers are inseparable from its sensory limits. We live in the seeming illumination of its knowing, but 'it' is without memory, deaf, odourless and unfeeling.

Once you know you are in this changed picture, the picture of everything changes:

> The coming fire is to make visible the day. The fire gives rise to the day, let this day arise. If 'the day' here is the day that is familiar to us to us daily, then the fire that is called upon in its coming must be the sun. The sun rises day after day. Were it not for this most everyday event then there would be no days. Still to explicitly call out 'Now come' to one thus coming, the rising sun, is a superfluous and futile act. But this 'Now come' contains more. The call says: we are ready and are only so because we are called by the coming fire. The ones calling here are those who are called, those who are called upon, now in this other sense, which means: those summoned to hear because they are of such a vocation.[34]

**NOTES**

1.  Martin Heidegger, *Nietzsche Volume III: The Will to Power and as Metaphysics* (trans Joan Stambaugh, David Farrell Krell and Frank Capuzzi), Harper, San Francisco, 1987, p. 53.
2.  Comments here draw heavily on, and strive to advance, those outlined in Tony Fry (ed), *RUATV?: Heidegger and the Televisual*, Power Publication, Sydney, 1993. How this book was

framed (pp. 12–13) is of relevance to comments being made here: 'The viewpoints adopted by the authors of the essays presented here do not refute television as an instrument of the cultural authorship of subjectivity, intersubjectivity and intertextuality. What they do refuse, however, is a geometry which confines television within a frame fully filled by content and audience. The televisual subordinates the being of the medium's content, spectatorship, social relations, sign economy, technology, space, time and forms to itself as an ontological domain. What the televisual names then is the end of the medium, in a context, and the arrival of television as the context. What is clear is that television has to be recognised as organic to the social fabric, which means that its transmissions are no longer managed by the flick of a switch. Television has acquired its own legs and walks where it will.'

3  Martin Heidegger, *Kant and the Problem of Metaphysics* (trans Richard Taft), Indiana University Press, Bloomington, 1990, p. 160.
4  *Ibid.*, p. 161.
5  Marshall McLuhan, *Understanding Media: The Extension of Man*, RKP, London, 1964. The most influential essay in this text was of course 'The Medium is the Message', pp. 15–30.
6  Fry, *RUATV?*, p. 13.
7  François Jullien, *The Propensity of Things: Towards a History of Efficacy in China*, Zone Books, New York, 1995 p. 39. The history and complexity of the concept is explored at length in this text.
8  *Heraclitus Fragments* (trans and commentary TM Robinson), University of Toronto Press, Toronto, p. 25.
9  Michel Haar, *The Song of the Earth: Heidegger and the Grounds of Being*, Indiana University Press, Bloomington, p. 50.
10  See Stanley Rosen on Platonism in *The Question of Being*, Yale University Press, New Haven, 1993, pp. 1–46. The fundamental relation of brightness, light, the look, seeing, vision and knowledge, as the elements of the essence of truth is most clearly explained by Heidegger in his discussion of light and looking in *Parmenides*, Indiana University Press, Bloomington, pp. 144–48.
11  Plato, *The Republic* (trans and intro Desmond Lee), 2nd ed, Penguin Books, London, 1988, pp. 305–316. It is interesting to note Lee's commentary introducing the Simile of the Cave. Citing FM Cornford writing on Plato in 1960, he says 'As Cornford pointed out, the best way to understand the Simile is to replace the "clumsier apparatus" of the cave by the cinema,

though today television is an even better comparison'.
12. On Plato and for a broader discussion of the issues in general see Hans Blumenberg, 'Light as a Metaphor for Truth', in David Michael Levin, *Modernity and the Hegemony of Vision*, University of California Press, Berkeley, 1993, pp. 30–62.
13. Martin Heidegger, *The Basic Problems of Phenomenology* (trans and intro Albert Hofstadter), Indiana University Press, Bloomington, 1982, p. 109.
14. This brief outline of a far more detailed and protracted history is drawn from Francis Wheen, *Television a World History*, Century Publishing, London, 1985.
15. See Jean Baudrillard, 'The Precession of Simulacra' (trans Paul Foss and Paul Patton) in *Art & Text*, vol. II, Prahran, 1982, pp. 3–47. Here the relation of simulation over the real and the displacement of reference by the copy without an original is exposited.
16. Don Idhe, *Technology and the Lifeworld*, Indiana University Press, Bloomington, 1990, p. 79.
17. *Logos* cannot be defined simply: its meaning shifts across time, usage and user. It may be language, reason, reasoned language, ordered speech, the concrete recognition of the logical, etc.
18. The term *einbildungskraft* is taken up (but here contextually reformed) from Joan Stambaugh, *The Finitude of Being*, SUNY Press, New York, 1992, p.159. Heidegger ('The Turning' in *The Question Concerning Technology and Other Essays*, Harper Row, New York, 1977, pp. 36–37) explains enframing (*gestell*) as 'that setting upon gathered into itself which entraps the truth of its own coming to presence with oblivion. This entrapping disguises itself, in that it develops into the setting in order of everything that presences as standing reserve, establishes itself in the standing-reserve, and rules as the standing-reserve.'
19. 'Sending' here resonates with and contests the post-representational notion of Derrida's sending without the ability of a gathering ('envois') 'tele-types', dispatches that are sent without any sense of arrival. See Jacques Derrida, *The Post Card: From Socrates to Freud and Beyond*, Chicago University Press, Chicago, 1987.
20. Joan Stambaugh, *The Finitude of Being*, p. 76.
21. Heidegger, 'The Age of the World Picture' in *The Question Concerning Technology*, pp. 115–54.
22. Heidegger, 'The Age of the World Picture' in *The Question Concerning Technology*, p. 129.
23. Heidegger, *Being and Time*, p. 187.
24. Heidegger, *The Question Concerning Technology*, p. 130.

25  Fry, *RUATV?*, p. 26.
26  See Heidegger, *Being and Time* (trans Macquarrie and Robinson), Blackwell, Oxford, pp. 138–48. The difference between the 'near' and the 'far' is elaborated by Heidegger as *Entferntheit*: which Macquarrie and Robinson's 1962 edition of *Being and Time* translated as 'de-severance'; in the 1996 translation of the text by Joan Stambaugh it is translated as 'de-distancing'; while Hubert Dreyfus in his commentary on Division 1 of *Being and Time* translates the term as 'dis-stance'. The problem of translation and comprehension is that of a spatial metaphor that seeks to escape from viewing proximity in spatial terms. The text reads 'When we speak of de-severance as a kind of Being which *Dasein* has with regard to its Being-in-the-world, we do not understand by it any such thing as remoteness (or closeness) or even a distance. We use the expression "de-severance" in a signification which is both active and transitive. It stands for a constitutive state of *Dasein*'s Being — a state with regard to which removing something in the sense of putting it away is only a determinate factual mode. "De-severing" amounts to making the farness vanish — that is making the remoteness disappear, bring it close. ... De-severance discovers remoteness; and remoteness, like distance, is a determinate categorical characteristic of entities whose nature is not that of *Dasein*': *Being and Time* (trans Macquarrie and Robinson), pp. 138–39. From this perspective the unpopular Macquarrie and Robinson term still does the best job.
27  Maurice Merleau-Ponty, *Phenomenology of Perception* (trans Colin Smith), Routledge, London, 1995. He aspired to a thinking beyond science (p. 365): 'We must return to the *cogito*, in search of a more fundamental *Logos* than that of objective thought, one that endows the latter with its relative validity, and at the same time assigns it to its place'.
28  Jean Baudrillard, *Simulations* (trans Paul Foss, Paul Patton, Philip Beitchman), Semiotext(e), New York, 1983.
29  From World War I onward the airborne camera was used as an intelligence gathering device. This technology evolved into cameras with powerful lenses in high-flying spy planes and the use of 'drones' (radio-controlled small fast low-flying pilotless camera carrying aircraft). Supplementing the 'representational' image of the camera, from World War II onward, was the abstract image of radar. Finally there was the spy satellite. From the imagery of this technology, battlefields are chosen, battle plans formed and laid out, scenarios rehearsed, and action directed by the animatory ability of radar to bring the warzone to life (and death). The

televisual conflict is thus another instance of the prefiguration of 'the real' by the image, as well as being created as the screen through which the 'reality' of the conflict is seen. On this topic see Paul Virilio, *War and Cinema* (trans Patrick Camiller), Verso, London, 1989.

30 See Eamon D'Arcy, 'The Eye and the Projectile' in Fry (ed), *RUATV?*, pp. 104–116.

31 The US company Boeing Rocketdyne has, however, already created a 568-kilogram Airborne Tactical Laser able to destroy a low-flying cruise-type missile in flight, up to 25 kilometres away, by melting it. See Duncan Graham, 'A Deadly light' in *New Scientist*, February 13, 1999.

32 For Heidegger, there are three modes of disclosure: understanding; feeling; and discourse. What is disclosed is the uncovering of where we are, which is considered as a whole. Whenever what is thought to be the given world is lit-up, as the 'ready-to-hand', it is deprived of its world-hood, which is to say that the televisual darkens and conceals as it illuminates. See Heidegger, *Being and Time*, pp. 105–106, 192.

33 'Man's relation to location, and through locations to spaces, inheres in his dwelling. The relationship between man and space is none other than dwelling, strictly thought and spoken': Martin Heidegger, 'Building Dwelling Thinking' in *Poetry, Language, Thought* (trans Albert Hofstadter), p. 157.

34 Martin Heidegger, *Hölderlin's Hymn 'The Ister'* (trans William McNeill and Julia Davis), Indiana University Press, Bloomington, 1996, p. 7.

# 8

# THE AUTONOMIC TECHNOCENTRICITY OF COMPUTERS

Dead fragments (author's collection)

> Today nothing in us takes root any more. Why? Because the possibility of a thoughtful conversation with a tradition that invigorates and nurtures us is lacking, because we instead consign our speaking to electronic thinking and calculating machines, an occurrence that will lead modern technology and science to completely new procedures and unforeseeable results that probably will push reflective thinking aside as something useless and hence superfluous.[1]

We have moved from a recognition of technology's organisation of the already productivised human mind and body into the service of the mass production, to a far more complex and pervasive inter-relation between mind, body and technology as tool, culture and environment. We have seen that control of individual craft labour was traded, mostly without recognition of the cost, for a higher disposable income and the 'advantages' of then currently available modern commodities. Now we are living through a second wave of lost agency over the construction of 'our' world, which paradoxically, is often felt and frequently posed as increased freedom. This began once mental labour started to be inscribed into, and replaced by, machines. Against this background one can see that the greater the transfer to a cybernetic mode of economic and cultural production, the less we humans have an ability to influence the future. Perhaps the greatest manifestation of contradiction here is the take up of 'sustainability' as a concern by the very corporations who are most deeply embedded in the creation and marketing of technologies that are absolutely without sustain-ability. Here then is one of the most overt instances of how sustaining the unsustainable happens.

The issue of 'the critical' once more begs comment, not just because we conditionally move toward it, but because we are also travelling away from earlier engagements with things and relations which humans once deemed to be critical. Here the problem of proximity, as well as our two understandings of 'the critical' (life in the balance, and of criticism) as they frame sustain-ability, all fold into each other. The ability to sustain requires a critical identification of a disposition toward what is critical.

Our aim is to sketch a relational picture of the 'nature' of computers and computerisation, as elemental forces in the operation and appearance of technology and the televisual environment. We also want to find ways to question their agencies to defuture and future, as well as dealing with the issue of the interface between the human and machine in a way that renders problematic the very notion of such a mediation. This requires making an incursion into the now autonomic domain of the technological — which does not imply a human absence, but does presume a problem of anthropocentric control that recasts views of, and relations to, technology.

Technology is not unlike a 'nature' in its formation. In its unpictured diversity it transmutes at a speed most of us are unable to comprehend or deal with. Yet mostly we still think, talk and act as if technology were a tool we are able to direct. In the condition of immersion in the 'nature of technology' critical questions are generally not being asked. Constant technological change has become a normality in which the designing force of technology does not arrive for us just as an object of inquiry — there is no critical distance, no point of view on what is actually changing.

For instance, educationalists are promoting schoolroom computer-based learning on the assumption that this is both a progressive move and essential for the induction of children into contemporary economic and cultural functionality. The technology is deemed an 'effective' mechanism of knowledge transfer. This is happening without a critical questioning of what is really being created and destroyed, nor how the induction into this complex technology influences a disposition towards it. Another example is the embrace (often by environmentalists) of 'environmental technologies' with either a naive enthusiasm or low-level pragmatism that totally buys into technology's inscribed discourse of a solutions-based model of progress. A waste management technology might be, for example, promoted as a superior handling or treatment system, despite the fact that it enables and even accelerates the production of waste rather than changing values and altering the perceptions of waste, which would contribute to the elimination of waste as a material category: fatalistically the economic and technological foundation of the production of waste gets taken as given.

In both these examples there is a failure to identify the differences between technology and 'progress', and between sustaining the unsustainable versus advancing sustain-ability. More fundamentally, technology, as a ground in its material and immaterial proliferation and for all planetary cultures, is still a 'nature' that remains hidden. This is to say, to design, engineer, see and use technology is not to know its essence. Alongside this, the peoples of contemporary societies increasingly encounter the consequences of what their precursors failed to foresee. The historicity of past and present designing, while felt, is still barely comprehended, and thus is unable to be ethically thought or engaged. In such a context, one might ask, who has any idea what the sum of technology is as an ontological structure?

This line of thought brings us to consider problems of metaphysical extension, power, impacts and telepresence.[2]

## THE REASON MACHINE[3]

The historiography of the thinking which thought up the computer usually places seventeenth century German philosopher Gottfried

Wilhelm Leibniz in a pivotal position.[4] Leibniz's significance turns on three key points. Firstly, he posited reason as the supreme principle.[5] (As is clear from Heidegger's writing, and mentioned elsewhere in this text, Leibniz's declaration that 'nothing *is* without reason' still resonates.) Secondly, he elevated the importance of logic within the spheres of philosophical thought. Finally, he created a science of symbolic language in order to represent logic.[6] Thus Leibniz contributed to the historical development of reason, in addition he created the means by which reason could be codified symbolically, managed as a calculus and thereafter mechanised within a designed machine system — a 'reason machine'.[7] His representational construction of logic served not only to support the development of a realist theoretical apparatus of appearances but also sped a passage toward an extended moment of epistemological and informational hegemony whereby 'the real', calculation, information and technology were made to exist as a relation of correspondence in a 'unified field theory' of reason (recasting the above as 'nothing *is* without the quantified').

Besides Leibniz's thinking directly linking to an informational theory that permitted communication to be coded, it also connects with, and transforms, that anthropocentric axiom, first voiced by the pre-Socratics, that 'man is the measure of all things'.[8] In this transformation, 'measure' moves from human self-reference (as the point of view from which all things are measured) to the reification of a human-created system of measurement centred within the technological as an instrument of the 'measure of man'. In this shift Leibniz de facto brought reason within the ontological reach of the machine, which then contributed to reason's becoming one of the 'mechanisms' of universalisation within modernity. Henceforth, reason became an ideology, a mode of cognition and machine transmission that was also transmitted by machines, both mechanical and electronic, as well as by technocentric culture.

Leibniz also aimed to place humanism in the service of that reified metaphysic of machine inscription we have identified, through his desire to universally unite humanity under one God and single mode of cognition. He posited logical thought (reason) as both the agent of unification and the instrument able to overcome obstructions, including the obstruction of cultural difference. His argument moved from a dependence upon metaphysical proposition to a claim of a metaphysic of design ('the scheme of things' from God, the grand designer, evidenced by the rational patterns and logic of 'nature'). This tradition of thinking, begun by Leibniz, asserts a closure between a symbolic logic discovered in nature as God's design and the logic of machine formation and construction.

Leaving the theological implications to one side, this thinking not only created the intellectual environment and conditions of possibility for a transcription from mind to machine, but also opened the way for a transfer from human to post-human into a globalising structure of technologically inscribed, metaphysical, operational non-human networks, machine languages and systems. These now elementally grow as part of the 'natural' elemental condition of being. In this respect we can acknowledge that for us this 'nature' is post-organic, for even our understanding of those ecological and environmental problems deemed 'natural' float on a sea of information underpinned by logic-based symbolic representation. (Technology's power in mediating the interrelation of human and world was of course a significant aspect of the way the body was addressed in Chapter 5.[9]) For another example, one could say that without the fusion of information and technology, the 'nature' of climate change would have been impossible to know and represent. Equally, whatever action is taken in the face of environmental problems also depends in significant part on technology and its representational ability. This simply replays the projective actuality for us of there being 'nothing without reason': nothing is discovered as 'it' is known; everything is prefigured by the presence of that which makes the 'it' present.

The evolution of the reason machine is deeply implicated in the creation of the problems of the defutured. In the last thirty years or so computers have served the management, administration and manufacturing processes of organisations in order to increase the efficiency, speed and volume of product output and profitability. They have been part of the material forces that have accelerated the dynamic and spatial growth of the defutured. They have contributed to the impact of unchecked, unmonitored and ill-considered resource utilisation, product use, and waste, of both creative labour and materials. In short, computers, along with all the other tools of late-modern economic life, have served to lay down a structure that universally acts to destroy multiple means of planetary sustainment. But at the same time, and in a variety of ways as an extension of reason, they have also contributed to the measurement, monitoring and imagining that has made some of the problems of defuturing present for reason. It follows that the technology is, and can be, mobilised against itself, although not auto-correctively, as techno-fix or with certainty. This uncertainty is not least because even with an expanded notion of the technology, the problems it creates are never just technological.

A great schism has opened up between instrumentally applied reason and a reasoned judgement of the consequences of instrumental action. This schism is not only manifest in the defutured and in unsustainable actions of those who act without any deliberate ill-intent, but it is also often present in the faith in technology and the actions of many who believe themselves to be advancing the 'cause' of 'ecologically sustainable development'.

## PRODUCTIVISM MEETS THE REASON MACHINE

We saw the distant origins, and more recent ascendancy, of productivism in Chapter 2. The productivist trajectory has been gathered and amplified by the computer, and while this did not stem directly from Leibniz, at the same time he gave a means, momentum and focus to what was already in transit. It is important that we remind ourselves of what it is that the 'reason for reason' rests upon. This requires us to revisit productivism.

As seen, productivism, which became the dominant form of reason, arrived out of the formation of structural and structuring thought created by the pre-Socratics. It was conceptually constructed as the means to both know and represent *physis*, as the idea that linked all matter, elements and causal forces. Logical productivist thought was but one product of reason's on-going intellectual production. To grasp this history is to grasp just how hard it is to divide metaphysics from the world it has produced, the way that this world acts, what results (its worlding) and how being-in-the-world is able to be understood. (The struggle to do this is evident in philosophy's long running discussion of the relation of between metaphysics and ontology.)

In placing a language of symbolic logic between, on the one hand a thinking of (and in) structures, and of notions of the structural formation and operation of 'nature and world' (the fate of *physis* as the idea became diluted) on the other, Leibniz enabled a move from an analytic to a constructional understanding of 'what was'. He contributed significantly to a move whereby Enlightenment philosophy conjoined with, and henceforth powered, empirical experimentation. Effectively this helped turn many of the ideas which had arrived out of Greek theory into material practices, through the application of a mode of thought that could first mediate observed structures (that which made up the structure of 'the nature of the world'), projected structures ('the world to be made' by systems of instrumentally applied thought), and could facilitate a symbolically ordered management of matter. What had now arrived was a mode of thinking able to create, comprehend, express and mobilise a logic of order and ordering which became elemental to all modern forms of calculative construction. These are epitomised by the practices of design, architecture and engineering. In sum, Leibniz assisted in transferring the production of a structural view of the 'world', which produced a form of 'world' knowledge, to forms of thinking that 'worlded worlds' by their power to advance and extend the possibilities of constructional knowledge as world making.

Leibniz's notion of codification vastly increased the potential for a unity between symbolic and calculative thought as a combined means to create the material out of the immaterial. From a contemporary perspective he enabled an identification of the material prefiguration by the immaterial that characterises the operation of informational codes as modes of construction. This idea can be seen, for example, to have been foundational for modern genetics and software engineering. His subordination of reason to belief was predicated upon a transcendental assumption: reason simultaneously came from, enabled a knowledge of, and existed to serve, God. Moreover, and generally, while the Enlightenment placed God beyond reason, it also sought to use reason to advance a knowledge of the will of God. In retrospect this project established the foundation of the modern university, sped the arrival of a dominantly secular world, instrumentally informed productivism and generally undercut the power of belief that is needed to give a sacred value to the protection of that which sustains being. Yet in this context, as Leibniz's encounter and appropriation of Chinese philosophy affirms, to view belief and reason as either a binary opposition or as transcendentally resolvable fails to recognise the efficacy of the agency of forms of thinking outside such schema. Effectively to say 'nothing *is* without reason' is to say nothing exists outside the reach of the naming and knowing of Western metaphysics. Therefore, nothing is 'other' except that designated as such. Yet the agency of an absolute and unpresented other is recognised and frequently hinted at, for example, by the calling up of the uncanny or magic. And then one can also observe that while science appears as the child of reason, its history (both in the East and the West) cannot erase its actual progenitor: that for which 'magic' now stands.

Putting this much compressed narrative back into contact with the history of the computer requires that we acknowledge a pattern common to many inventions. Almost always, inventions are a fusion of those elements from different places and moments assembled by people able see creative potential, grasp obvious and sometimes oblique connections, put the inventions together, and then innovate with what arrives. This is certainly the story of the computer.

Very briefly, the assemblage that is the computer came from an ability to see and connect: the patterning of symbolic logic in order to direct computational machine functions; binary logic, the laws of electricity, the switch processes of electronic circuitry; the encoding, decoding and storage of information; and the projection of all this potentiality into the integrated function of an operational machine. This is both a micro-illustration of the passage of productivism and a history of the applied idea of a calculative machine. It encompasses those basic elements of artificial intelligence associated with Charles Babbage's demonstration of the limits of clockwork technology with the 'Difference Engine' of 1822, and then later (in collaboration with Lady Ada Lovelace) the 'Analytic Engine'. Building on this assemblage, in more recent times, was the work of Alan Turing who transposed binary logic into a machine form in 1937. The practical application of this immaterial technology was realised in his World War II code-cracking 'Enigma' machine, which laid the groundwork for the digital computer. The next moment is John Von Neumann's contribution of bringing processing and memory together into the function of a single unit. Together, these moves created a convergence between a productivist theory of information (information codes, transcribed into symbolic forms, and then employed as calculative structures, especially as advanced by Claude Shannon's 'invention' of information theory); and, high speed machine-based logic functions (obviously enabled by the development of electronics). All of this established a technological foundation out of which eventually came the computer user's ability to input, store, access and manage information in the virtual time of electromagnetic processes.

Where does this historical gloss leave us? Clearly it tells us that productivism's impetus has continued to gain in speed and power from the formative moment. However, this dynamic should not be viewed by simply adopting an evolutionary perspective.

One can observe, for instance, that the freedom to think, write and calculate has become tempered by the ontological limitations imposed by a technological dependence. This dependence is less a matter of material constraints like power supply, machine weight, speed or memory volume, and more a question of the 'knowledge-function capability' of a technological environment as a domain that facilitates or circumscribes what we are intellectually able to encounter, comprehend and do. One can equally think the still-increasing level of information-based technological dependence historically: from the moment of the displacement of oral cultures and their paucity of materially encoded information — by the rise of writing, the coming of the book, the establishment of the power of literacy — to the contemporary situation of living in conditions of informational overload with, by large degree, the on-going erasure of cultures of memory by agency of technological memory. Unsurprisingly, we place productivism at the core of such a structure and structuring.

As we have seen, productivism was constituted from, and as, a system of thought (an ecology of mind — Idea). As such it was, and is formative of both a way of knowing, and a world and its objects. Productivism stridently exposes observation as projective thought that ontologically designs (Plato's notion of seeing with one's mind rather than with one's eyes). Yet productivism was but one way to form and know a world. For all its authority, it is still a non-essentialist knowing which can but claim, rather than be, truth.

Contrary to the universal biocentric scientific (productivist) narrative of human evolution, environmental circumstances for us are a matter of what is virtually projected as much as what is materially confronted. In difference, humans create the circumstances to which they appear to physically adapt. Moreover, as we shall see, the difference of how environments are known and made present equates with the varied 'nature' of a species that is not one united whole.

Reconnecting with technology: what was once a distinguishing feature of human being (reason and structure) has now become post-human. Productivist thought, with the unwitting help of Enlightenment thinkers, not only in large part created what we understand as the technological, but made technology as much the host of reason and thought as the human. This is not a stable situation. In multiple ways, our account confirms that technology has become part of our 'naturalised' condition of being. This means that it is part of the condition of our being-in-the-world and our world itself. (This was made clear when addressing the televisual: that technology does not exist any longer as an independent and reified thing, but is now an environment, hence its 'naturalisation'.) We still have to find a way to come to terms with the implication of this 'facticity', as it is unable to be represented as fact. Our invested language and imagination is out of step with what it very partially and inadequately struggles to describe. Clearly a thinking, a struggling for a language, which is alienated from the omnipresent technological environment, is needed. Such a thinking requires the acknowledgement and conservation of reason's difference, which is to say that reason's critical and reflective thinking needs to be seen and named as the inside other of a fully mechanised hegemony of instrumental reason. Moreover, the former mode of reason needs to be embraced as an endangered thinking able to sustain and able to re-create a vital and 'unnatural' alienation. Acknowledging the current nature of technology (as well as the contradiction of a post-human humanism conjured up by the notion of 'alienation') it becomes apparent that 'thinking with' and 'thinking about' is in danger from 'thinking as'.

Depending on who is speaking and hearing, technological change is evoked as something to be either embraced, feared, or most often, that which is simply inevitable. We are still exposed to rhetorics that tell us that whatever has changed adds up to improvement. As we have shown, although evolutionary theory is a theory which is vulnerable to critical inquiry, evolution has become a powerful 'common sense' metaphor applied widely to explain function and change in all kinds of domains. The Darwinian model of biological transformation by adaptation to environment was first transposed onto the social. Thereafter this influential social Darwinist evolutionary model of change became generalised and taken up, including by those trying to make sense of, and advocating, technological change. That information technology slots so easily into this kind of explanation requires us to confront some profound question about change, not least its relation to the issue of evolution. As has been made clear from the very beginning of this book, the unsustainable is that which defutures, but what we have also seen is that defuturing both forces change, and changes with change.

First of all we need to prise change away from notions of directional movement, evolution or progress. As Heraclitus stated two and a half thousand years ago, as did the Taoists of the same period, everything is in flux, everything changes in the constant return of the same. But equally, what is the same constantly returns as difference: almost everything changes and almost nothing changes. (One could argue that, notwithstanding the rise of change theory, ecological awareness, science and an environmental movement, that we now know in a fundamental sense less about sustain-ability than the ancients did.) Another problem, and a question, arrives: how is it possible to actually identify what has really changed? The whole notion of self-, or economic or cultural, development further complicates this picture, as does the degree of mediation that sits between us and what we take to be our object of inquiry. More powerfully, but less overtly, mechanisms of mediation such as rhetorical expressions (in the media, in political discourse) of 'change equals progress' produce a perceptual shift, a sense of change, a state of mind that gives the impression of material transformation.

Next, we need to acknowledge that adaptation to that which has actually changed, be it of mind/perception or world/circumstances, takes time. In this setting, the ability and variability needed to cope with change is in large part a capacity to adapt to what one feels or thinks is changing. Again no absolute empirical claim travels with this statement, except to say that change is normality, and that rapid change outside familiar patterns and contexts is taken to be abnormal (which may or may not be the case).

Change is actually inherent in productivism, but as we have

already argued, productivism does not equate with evolution. The projection of structure, followed by its transformation by Design and productive forces, as a material and immaterial world-making has meant that modernising productivist human beings have always been at odds with what they have deemed to be natural processes of change. This historical tendency has ever gained momentum and deepened the contradiction of living an existence of mutual dependence upon both human-denaturalised 'natures' and human-created 'natures', as this entire text has in some way shown. We, and much else on this planet, live relationally in a mix of environments and ecologies, with connections to what came before (in moderately or totally mutated forms), the loss of previous conditions, and the accumulative arrival of totally new ones.

Let's take the example of a globalising corporation. The corporation arrives as a world-shaping force out of a history of the perpetual capitalist re-invention of a productivist way of employing labour, structuring organisations, making and delivering products, and offering services that are themselves agents of change. And all this is done in the service of profit (the constant, the same). The impacts of such a corporation are predicated upon the politics and economics of its trading in the world market. Large corporations cultivate misreadings of a national affiliation, as they are operationally de facto corporate states that are increasingly 'freeing' themselves from being held to account by government.

In doing this everything within the scope of their relations, or touched by these relations, changes in some way. As a result of the changes, corporations impact upon many ecologies that are critical to sustain-ability but little of this gets reported. Environmental management software programs do not have boxes to be ticked for these scenarios.

In the current moment of the contradictory chronological plurality of modernity and capital (the global is neither one moment of time, one moment of late economic modernity, one stage in technological development, or one mode of capital), global corporations strive to sustain themselves by processes of continuous change management. This certainly does not manage to determine the corporation's actual destiny or establish a process of 'natural' evolution. Change agents (like the quasi-discipline of human resources, and its attempt to reinvent itself) never really know what is going on in relation to the underpinning forces and directions of change. The rhetoric and visual communication of marketing, public affairs and labour relations all confuse appearances of change with actual transformations. In this context, the activity of corporate environmental reporting arrives as but one more example of managed appearances to secure what remains the same. It is no wild claim to suggest these agents are unwilling to learn what needs to be learnt for sustain-ability, for this would require them learning how to overcome the defutured, in of the forms of design, technology, science and culture that the corporation embraces as it changes in order to remain the same. Here is a crucial context of thr defutured as sustaining the unsustainable.

In the face of the challenge that the imperative of sustain-ability brings, in almost every case the rhetoric of global corporations says one thing, their actions another. It's not that nothing is being done, but rather that the on-going consequences of an unreconstructed view of economic growth produces impacts that completely displace those mild reforms that get posed as radical acts. The idea that wealth has to be (and is) able to be produced without a whole gamut of impacts which defuture has hardly begun to be thought about.

Computer technology in general is deeply embedded in this change which is no change. We have a computer before us, we see it as an individuated object, but it comes out of a hardware and software production system of duplication (to which it remains attached) and it is part of a system, as a nodal point, as soon as it is plugged into the power grid, a network or put on-line. Thus, technology, in its objectification, is generally mis-objectified by being decontextualised from its structural environment. We see 'things', whereas systems are mostly unseeable: they require a higher order of concepts, ideas, knowledge and imagination even to be inadequately visualised. For instance, most of us have a rough idea of what an electricity grid is, but few of us have any idea of its complexity and the function of technologies such as power electronics within it.

LIVING THE UNSEEING

We do not 'see' the corporation, it is not available to sight. We do not see technology. In both instances we are misled by objects and appearances. Moreover, the mystique of the corporation and the contradictory 'nature' of technology has given them the appearance of having lives of their own. At the same time, both are deemed to be fundamentally life-supporting entities and are thus posited as economically and socially organic. Although this condition can be 'denaturalised', it is now impossible for many people to imagine life without the 'natures' of these material and cultural agents.

As has we have explored from the start of this text, inseparable from being unable to see what 'things' are, is our inability to see what they design. Notwithstanding the mass of handbooks, instructional information and hyper-hype writing on the topic, there are very few people who are really thinking about what computers design. In large part this is because, at a fundamental level, very few people are thinking about technology itself. Its constructed seductive powers, its concealment in the mantle of being deemed a tool, its designing power to design its own perception, but above all its structural 'organicity' (as mind, thought and culture) all await to be thought. As we shall see, the issue now is not one of freedom, liberation, appropriation or attachment, but one of alienation.

## THE FORCE OF DESIGN

After thinking with, against and over Nietzsche, Heidegger made technology an object of thought. It was only possible for him to do this in the manner he did because he could draw on a culture that was thinking technology more seriously than perhaps at any time before or since.[10] Looking back from our viewpoint now, the work of this period shows critical insight that, irrespective of agreements or disagreements, can assist us in thinking through the convergence of technology as mind, world and unsustainability.

Technology has become an absolutely prolific structure and structuring of interactive systems across informational, biological, electro-mechanical and material-constructional domains. More prosaically, our health, what we eat, how we produce food, how we produce other goods, what we wear, how we gain knowledge, where and how we live, our work, how we transport ourselves, how we are entertained, how we wage war, the services we provide and use — there is nothing that is now not touched by technology, including the computer and all else that folds into the televisual. (The presentation of a notion of the general and the particular is of course purely heuristic.)

As we have been at pains to make clear, technology as it has taken on a life of its own is completely implicated in the unsustainable, yet it sustains us while we and it defuture, which is, in effect, short-term 'sustainability' arriving at the cost of long-term sustainment (and not just for us as a species being). This autonomic character of technology (that is its law-unto-itself) is now served by those who appeared to be its creators. The human project of making a place for itself in its world (dwelling) by the application of technology has disappeared, and has been replaced by dwelling in a world of technology in which one has to find a place. As technology has become a world of existence it has become an ever more powerful structuring of environments, relations, objects and selves. 'Being now' may be thought of as biologically, culturally, socially and technologically constituted. In this condition of enablement (freedom) and coexistent conditional delimitation (unfreedom), we maintain a link with that which brought the power of our species-being into being. At the same time, we place under threat our ability to remain what we believe ourselves to be. In other words, and without buying into cyber-hype or science-fiction, technology has already put the narrative, and thus the future of human being, into question. In this condition of contradiction, sustain-ability becomes the quest to seek both a space to be with (a crack that provides an opening into), and a means of material exchange with (this does not presume prior meaning or value) that which constitutes the space of our now technological existence. This can only be done by taking that which is appropriated from the world and worlding environment.

Heuristically, let's say (if untruthfully, because the categories lack a representational correspondence) that once we appropriated 'nature' to make a world, including a simple technology, in order to make a new place for ourselves in 'the world of nature', we then started to alienate ourselves from the very conditions to which we have always been structurally bound. Now we find ourselves in a situation wherein we are 'forced' (the cunning of sustain-ability) to re-appropriate what we have ourselves created as a 'post-natural nature'. (This is yet again evidence of the error of positing trust in, and the explanatory inadequacy of, that causal process we named as evolution.) There is of course a 'community' of scientific ecologists who continue to place faith in the saving power of technology from the point of view of a technocentric 'general evolution theory'.

Rather than continue to explore this heuristic, with its non-viable mutually exclusive poles of 'us' and 'nature', let us recast the problem as one of exchange, which, as used here, implies flow and the same.

The unsustainable is a breakdown of the circulatory process of exchange that leads to closure (whereas the sustainable is constant return with the exchanged being the key to sustainment). In the post-naturalism of the planet, the actions of humans have been absolutely transformative, nothing remains uncontaminated by our presence. Our extraction of organic and mineral materials from the earth, of plant matter, trees and animals, as well as our production processes, products, ways of life, violence, waste and accidents have changed the global climate, the genetic stock of all life forms and the ecologies of land and sea forever. We have dwelt, intervening in ignorance. While our numbers and demands were modest, impacts were absorbed (but not without consequence). As our numbers and appetites have grown, the inequality of exchange has become extreme. Being-in-ignorance has become a mode of dwelling which is totally accommodated within an expansion of instrumental knowledges of resource appropriation, material transformation and technological extension. Rather than education being a primary means by which sustain-ability is learnt it has become an induction into error. It is a learning of the practices of unsustainability and of the subordination of dwelling to autonomic direction. 'Endarkenment' is the destiny of the defutured.

While a global obsession with economic systems, performance and returns already dominates, what none of the actors in this play know anything about in a fundamental sense is exchange. Their concern, perceptual reach, relational understanding and empirical grasp of the consequences of a trade — in the creation, movement and impact of corporations and primary commodities, industrial processes, products and symbolic forms — is negligible. Life in the restricted economy is now life in a condition of greater ignorance than ever before, quite simply because the gap between what we actually know en masse and what we need to know to sustain all that needs to be sustained, grows by the day. The human species has just not learnt what it has done, what it has made, what it has unmade.

In this situation of the planet defutured by past and present acts of human agency, sustain-ability is learning to change, not as some gradual plural process of reform but as focused and dynamic acts of intervention to induce a major breakdown in the 'system' of dysfunctional exchange and its autonomic technology. Such an intervention is not a call to re-enact the failures of revolutionary utopian gesturalism. Rather it is a call to designing otherwise. Such a designing:

- conserves, simplifies (but not simplistically) and adds sustainable value
- eliminates existing unsustainable objects, structures or processes by the safe destruction of their materiality, their economic or cultural value
- remakes existing objects or structures by re-forming their life cycle, to give an extended life, multiple lives, a short life with a total recovery of valuable material, or complete biodegradability
- retro-fits an existing object or structure to give it a new life form
- recodes the perception of existing objects, structures or processes to transform their meaning, use and/or value
- invents a singularity to replace a multiplicity, and a renewable to replace a non-renewable.

In sum, this includes almost all existing material and immaterial forms of our lives.

Designing otherwise always comes from a learning of what and how to change. It is a designing with care that is concerned with material consequences, but equally with the makings of new desires to contest what televisually strives to occupy a self.[11] It is certainly not some kind of modernist exercise of trying to make a new world by the means that have been described (like the New York World's Fair).

Of course the seemingly wild remarks just made have consequences. They demand explanation, produce trembling, recoil, offend, beg indulgence and no doubt seem, at least to some, to lack due propriety and constraint. If truth be told they prefigure and post-date all else said. In actuality what these remarks register are historically formed dispositions (and thus designing), rather than what some may take them to be — rhetorical and solipsistic assertions. Clearly others have put a more optimistic spin on problems, intervention and the qualities of technology. Our argument, the very basis of the deconstructive value of the concept of defuturing, is that until the metaphysical and ontic foundations of the situation one finds oneself in are made present, confronted and understood, then it is not possible to act in a manner where one knows what one is doing. The goodwill which accompanies actions that claim a sustainable intent means nothing when such action is directed towards ill-defined problems, symptoms rather than causes, and towards sustaining the unsustainable rather than advancing the creation of sustainments.

## THE FORCE OF FORCE

Technology is force, and sustain-ability implies a contestation of direction (including the direction of technology).

'Force is the essence of the thing. Force is everything, it is the unconditional universal. It is the pervasive character of the world. "Force itself [expresses] the idea of relation."' In these few words the combined weight of thought of Hegel, Nietzsche, Heidegger converge. Sustain-ability is force against the force of defuturing unsustainability.

The omnipresence of force is at the heart of the very notion of the ontological (force in being). This is to say that nothing simply 'is,' for 'to be' is to have been forced into being. In this context, force is never contained, for it is that which came before, travels with and exists after that which comes into being.[12] Force then is the pervasive character of world and its relations in location. It is thus always somewhere, everywhere and flowing.[13]

From a thinking with, and from (rather than a reiteration of), Heidegger's engagement with Aristotle and 'the ways of force', let us consider three alternative ways to think force. (None of these are the same as the scientific mechanico-naturalistic, quantifiable, measured and vectorial force of things; nor the force of the violent shock of forms of politico-military mobilisation: both of which are technological.[14]) If we are to be makers of sustainments then there are three forces with which we have to learn to work. The first is the force of passive tolerance ('allowance') which is an ability to 'sustain damage' without being destroyed. This we find at the core of an ability to change, which is a changing while conserving attachments to what we value and wish to preserve. The second is the force of active tolerance ('adaptation'), which is the ability to use the energy of an other for one's own ends. Here is the criticality of the way of *Tao* and of the pre-Socratic notion of 'flow'. The third is the force of resistance, not as an immediate confrontation and overcoming (utopianism), but as a means by which an alienation is produced and constructively employed to contest from the inside. (The images to evoke of resistance are closer to those of a restricted flow of electrical current producing energy by passing through a resistant material (such as the passage of electricity through a wire that generates heat), or alternatively and with more complexity, in terms of the ancient Chinese notion of *shi*, which is a variable mixture of the force of circumstances, internal disposition, momentum, strategic advantage and more. In both cases the issue is discovery and mobilisation rather than invention.) The claim is that these three forces are the only ones available to us in acting in the face of the power of technology.

If we put the computer into a field of force as we have sketched, what can we deduce? As a network technology there is neither one answer to this question nor a single point of observation. (One could even say that a determinate view of contained or directional technological effects is redundant. Yet at the same time in a situation like this, a contestation of options, even though options are unable to be delimited, could be said to be even more important.) This contestation can of course be viewed around core uses, like work and workplace design, or in terms of marginal appropriations in which new skills are created and honed. Notwithstanding these qualifications there are certain strong influences upon how the field of force is currently forming and acting. The most significant can be characterised as a neo-romantic postmodernism, which has two features.

The first feature is a technological underpinning and extension of romanticism's never-ending drive to aestheticise everything — the subject, word, experience, world. While this drift has been identified at different moments across the last hundred years by thinkers of the aesthetic — most notably Friedrich Nietzsche, Carl Schmitt and Michel Foucault — recent technological events have taken a certain turn. This centres on the postmodern identification of the fragmentation of the subject as a consequence of the contradictory drives, directions and roles let loose by all modes of modernity. In the frame of contemporary vangardism, the decentred subject's encounter with a cultural technology produces endless, if temporary, re-assemblies of selves. The self becomes treated as an expressive construct rather than expressive actor. Here the romantic pre-occupation with the self (as a monitoring of desires, feelings, sensations, moods, growth, pleasures, pains), that was generative of all centred modernist creative expression and world interpretation, is given its pure form — an endless play of the remaking of an (unsustainable) self-identity.[15]

The contemporary and more popularist manifestation is the notion of the Internet as aesthetic interface with 'world' as 'world', arrives as an aesthetic assembly before a mobile self poised at the self-centring point (a point wherever their network connection happens to be). What this adds up to is a view of Internet content as a mediation of world as a personal screen encounter with designed, imaged, narrativised and even audio, but fragmentarily screened information packages. But these are delivered, on demand, to a monad: an atomised individual, preoccupied with the desires, sensations and needs of a pre-sent self who occupies a singular self-concerned seat of judgement before the form of what appears (be it cooking recipes, hotel booking options, zoological data on African water rats, pornography, books on astrophysics, medical conditions, anti-semitic jokes, or whatever from a myriad, constantly growing and never to be known range of choices). From the perspective of cultural modernity, what's new? Not much, except a massive concentration of content, de-socialising isolation, and above all de-severance (the more the world, as time and content, is made 'near' as screen, the further the world of plural sensory experience is away).

The second feature of neo-romantic postmodernism is the projection of a sense of freedom in a condition of entrapment, consoled by the pleasure of engrossment in the detail of the particular (the picture, the meal, sexual performance, the description of a fleeting moment), but lost in meaninglessness, devoid of power of the transcendental, without the authority of metanarratives. The condition is an unfreedom which becomes ever more general as the relation of human and technology becomes increasingly pervasive (for instance forms of 'consumption' can be seen to design world production). This condition of entrapment is exposed once we consider the ambiguity of the term 'user'. The assumption is that the binary relation between 'it' and us has gone. We are addicted, hooked while being hooked up — we are users! We users get a buzz, a moment of discovery, pleasure, consolations, but never emancipation. We are surrounded by options; but have no option. We are used; but we still use. Every now and again one encounters one of those television documentaries where one, or more, families give up television for a week, a month, a year. The rhetoric of this 'drama' is always played out in terms of addiction. Just imagine if the aim was to document the 'giving up' of technology, an act as unrealistic as being asked to give up biology!

Contrary to the actions of our instrumental mode of being-in-the-world, we do not use technology as free agents. Neither, by the same token, does it use us. As Design is enacted as the designing of things in action, we discover that in some ways we rule by technology's grace, and in other ways it rules by ours. More appropriately, we should equate technology in general, and computer technology in particular, as being more like an environment with variations of environmental conditions, impacts, relations and proximities. So while we may be at the same measured distance to the environment of technology to hand we are never in the same place of attunement to an environment/technology and the consequences of its, and our actions. In one way this is very close to the way the computer domain, including the Internet, is talked of and thought about. It is also repeating what has already been said in terms of the televisual as it enfolds computer technology. At the same time there is a profound difference of view once the hapless neo-romantic subject is exposed in the face of the defutured dangers: their free play transpires to be neither free or play. Again it is apparent just how little we know about the given and technological worlds that we make.

It is apparent that computer technology is viewed by many thinkers from a very wide band of knowledge, as the most power-full technology yet to be devised. Clearly this not because of its brute force, but because it is a calculative force of reified mind (information, meaning and computation) which has the ability to alter how space and time are comprehended and occupied. The computer has undoubtedly altered the relation between world, language and action via its means of information and transformation. At the same time its integration within, and as, the ever expanding universe of the televisual still remains mostly unrecognised. One of the most significant ways to comprehend its complexity and determinate force is to recognise that 'it' is beyond description (which in no way negates the importance of trying to make what can be made present appear). While it may be perfectly possible to overview the state of the art of hardware (although the secrecy associated with research and development makes this questionable) the diversity, proliferation, complexity and again, covert nature of software development is unmappable. There is also the vastness of the scale of computers and their application. Are we able to consider how computerisation has become ontically inscribed into worlds and world structuring, and thus ontological domains? Can the way computers constitute a neutralising command structure be grasped? Can one start to think about the consequences of the elimination of the 'face to face' communication of orders and instruction and the domination of directives and direction by faceless instruments of information? (Following on from Levinas, one can ask here what are the ethical consequences of being forced into being, without facing an other in whom one can discover oneself, or does one's displaced and decentred electronic persona have an ability to identify, rather than communicate, with an other?) And then, have we any idea what the consequences of 'electronic writing' and hypertextuality (dislocated relationality, system without response-ability) are going to be?[16]

Besides electronically based technology having an ability to generate and proliferate complexity it increasingly disappears (as it merges and becomes immersed) within the televisual.[17] The televisual contaminates whatever we want to say about computers. The computer never stands alone: it is never outside a system (of gridpower, hardware, software, netware, signware) or disconnected from nodal interfacial points (of work, play, sound, image, style, culture or economy). It constantly shifts location within the televisual: new formations and convergences ever occur. While a structuring instrument, in the structuring that is technology, the computer is also a ficto-force: it has authored imaginaries that seductively mobilise figures in futuristic technocentric utopias. As this, the techno-culture sits within, and has been used to generate, imaginaries to power realities (ficto-material foundationalism). For example, planning, architectural and engineering design draw on, elaborate and induct the utopian tradition into computer modes of representation — 'virtual reality' projections and explorations of forms of cites of the future, their building and interior spaces, are but one example of such continuity and innovation.

Many other forms of computer-animated modelling also display the power of this type of prefiguration, not least models of environmental crises. Here media-powered descriptions of a crisis meet, overtake and then report on what was projected. Effectively, reporting the observed, even in order to give a critical account of it, actually becomes indivisible from the neo-romantic aesthetic mobilisation of image and language that produces images that effectively hide what is and what needs to be seen. The media wants and makes dramatic images, short, sharp messages, simple explanations, whereas the critical may be far less accessible. Take the instance of genetic mutation. What the image makers want would be sensational images that allow for a progressive picturing of unfolding horrors, whereas the kinds of mutations that are now in train (for instance, the feminisation of fish species as a result of the introduction of artificial oestrogens being leached from synthetic materials into the environment) do not produce discernible signs of difference, with effects often occurring within the complexity of denaturalised biodiverse processes, and which cannot be summed up in a photo caption. Conversely, the genetic 'modification' of fruit and vegetables can and will be driven by aesthetic considerations of 'improving' appearance and taste.

For all the rhetoric of postmodernism and the sign economy associated with writers like Jean Baudrillard, Umberto Eco and Mark Taylor, the material consequences of the image ecologies that sustain and drive the productivism of the televisual have hardly begun to be recognised. Contrary to the afterlife of materialism's critique of idealism, the immaterial is now a powerful determinant of the nature of the material. More than this, fundamental shifts in the structural relation between idea and creation, thought and matter, and image and object throw us back into the never answered question of the first thinking of the Western mind: what is?

As already indicated the computer acts as a body of structuration and re-structuration: a being-in-technology whose technology structures the structure of everyday life through its agency as an environment and as directive materialised metaphysics.[18] So while being in and with technology extends our encounters (with image, food, travel, sleep, sex, health, dwelling, pleasures, reading and writing) what is structuring this structure is applied productivism. The computer structures not only as we directly encounter the technology at the supermarket checkout, in the library, at the medical centre or wherever, but also via omnipresent activities like computer-aided manufacture, computer-aided design, computer-aided planning, computer-integrated manufacture, materials and component inventory management, performance testing and monitoring, staff records and wages, invoices, correspondence, market data and sales records.[19] These are only some of the system support operations that now form a condition of dependent functionality which is the foundation of the world of many businesses large and small.

Additionally, we need to acknowledge the mostly unseen, enormous number and ever expanding quantity of embedded computer chips in everything from car fuel injection systems, navigation instruments, electricity supply power electronics, x-ray machines, cash registers, traffic lights, microwave ovens and a million other things. In this situation we are likely to see the growth of techno-iatrogenic pathological problems (industry-created 'diseases' like the Millennium Bug, which is perhaps the most dramatic global example of the myopia and economic opportunism of technocentric culture to date). As we have already acknowledged, the computer is both before our eyes and invisibly everywhere. Omnipotently, computers monitor us, measure us statistically, record our business transactions, educational attainments, they track our movements, analyse our behaviour patterns, store data concerning our bank accounts, tax payments, medical conditions, employment history and transgressions of law, as well as assist us in work.

In an increasingly proliferating complexity, each computer, computer system, computerised formation or function is a nodal point of a structuring body (without the agency of human direction) of metatechnology. Thus computers are starting to become just as much an essential element of our material environment as air and water, as without them and the structures they enable to function, we late-moderns are unable to sustain ourselves, at least not without considerable losses. Thus, while there are key questions and issues of engagement to confront, in a fundamental sense it is no longer any more valid to ask if computers are good or bad than to ask if flowers or trees are good or bad. In neither case does presence assure a future.

We have made it clear that computers in themselves, within the televisual, and as system elements, are part of the environment in which we dwell. More specifically, the environmental impact of their material production, their uptake of non-renewable energy, and their afterlife as largely non-biodegradable and toxic landfill objects, makes them objects that require a critical design confrontation. Current notions of a 'green computer' get nowhere near this cluster of problems, which require an acknowledgement of the designing consequences of an anthropocentric induction into an autonomic 'nature' as well as their immediate material impacts. Currently, to a vast extent, the technology is beyond phenomenological reach.

## REITERATIONS TOWARDS MAKING DECISIONS

The picture presented so far is one of complexity, perhaps even a disabling complexity. However, a precedent exists. This arrives once we start to view technology in a similar way that 'nature' was viewed in the past, as a vast and mysterious realm that only gave up its secrets reluctantly. The point is to counter the perception that technology is transparent and available to immediate understanding.

Without wishing to appear a doomsayer, one has to express concern in the face of that increasingly bizarre marriage between knowledge and ignorance that marks our age. Nowhere is this union more evident than in the facility displayed by technophillic 'nerd' culture and its absolute rejection of scholarship and learning. Moreover, we all live in cultures in which there is an ever growing gulf between the capability of creating advanced techno-systems and the ability to reach an understanding of either their impacts to future or defuture. For example, the way 'cyberspace' is talked of and written about in no way acknowledges or exposes the designing transformations that information technologies are having on our proximity to worlds, experience, others, language and things.

In noting a developmental trajectory of computer technology, it should be emphasised that the point of origin never gets left behind. Thus in less than six decades the computer has moved from being a number crunching instrument (which in some applications it still is) to a flexible tool of diverse functions that have encroached into almost every space of modern life as a world structuring technology. It is now almost impossible to imagine how book selling, libraries, sport, the stock market, newspaper publishing, stock control, air traffic control, staff, police or medical records and so on could all function without computers. Equally, in entertainment — from computer games to music composition, from film editing to photo-image management, and from dance club lighting control systems to cartoon production — the computer is omnipresent.

While still having stand-alone capability, recent decades have seen the computer become both a system entry point and systems link between ecology and environment. The systems in which computers function are both constrained, unrestrained and interfaced. For example, a building may have a computer controlled building management system to control thermal conditions, lighting levels, ventilation and security systems. It may also contain a computer network system which is continually on-line in an Internet environment: a system whose finitude is being constantly reconfigured. While we all know this, we tend not to consider the drama of the restructuring of mind and matter delivered by that which now seems so familiar. We need to remind ourselves, for instance, that the developmental direction of the technology has been driven by politico-market forces of inscription, and that there is no 'natural' evolutionary progression. To take just one example: in the rise of word processing software programs there were two options: writing based programs that did things like assemble language, prompts and interactive monitoring of sentence or paragraph length (which we can characterise as writing management, and the basis of new skills), and then there was the other option: word management, or what we have now come to know as word processing. The fundamental difference between these two systems is the former foregrounds what the technology is doing and brings it to hand, while the latter backgrounds it.[20]

Next we need to acknowledge the disjuncture between the software managed appearances of the technology, its hardware forms and what could be called its electro-*physis*. This is its ontic being, as a particular kind of technologically articulated material and immaterial ground that is a sum greater than the addition of its hardware, software and network nodal individual parts. So while we know what appears as the apparent functions and operations of the technology, what is lacking is a sense of what the actual technological ground determines. This implies that what you get is more than what you see. Clearly, there is a disjuncture between our location in space, our interface with the technology, and its environmental presence. For example, feedback from the technology produces both a distancing — a gap, between the experience of direct encounter and the restricted dimensional experience of encounter via the computer — and a de-stancing, a throwing off course.

As we have seen in a variety of ways, the designing power of technology in general, and of the technology of the televisual in which computing is lodged, is historically constituted. It has a historicity, an undocumented history, a history waiting to happen. While we are not going to tell this history there are a number of historical trends that illuminate our argument.

Obviously a substantial case could be mounted by supporters of the technology for what computers have enabled, and their potential. Many of the claims of their attainment would no doubt be valid, many would be ambiguous, and many would be in error (for their efficiency has massively sped the spread of the defutured). The account here is an impossible one to balance, and biased. However, as pitted against the mountain of uncritical and laudatory literature on the topic it is no more than a 'drop in the ocean'. Notwithstanding this qualification, the need for a critical position and critical engagement to create other relations with the technology is overwhelming. Now that the computer is integrally embedded in the 'nature' of our worlds, it will not disappear, although it will continually transmute. Therefore, far more alienated and critical positions need to arrive to contest what is designed; positions able to recognise the autonomic technocentric domain as 'the other inside'. Currently the task may seem to be beyond us. However, and prefiguratively, driven by the pragmatic and alienating power of the imperative of sustain-ability, learning is made possible. Counter to the atomic conditions that accompany the autonomic, this learning also discloses a belief in 'an otherwise' that is potentially constitutive of a critical ('life' in the balance) community.

## THE COMPUTER DESIGNING

Computers design not only as design tools in a broad band of designing functions in numerous industries, but they are also a major interface of the designing of autonomic technocentrism. The relation between applied design functions and designing impacts converges in the ontological force of the technology, the technological environment, and with subjects which have any kind of proximity to this force field.

Computers and computer systems are predicated upon being ever locked into a technological embeddedness. They only arrive for us because they have been designed with an anthropomorphically configured input and output interface with us (which is of course the very basis of interface design and programming). In the context of a phenomenology of technology this encounter is but a part of the technologically constituted environment of our dwelling (the full extent of the technological nature in which we dwell escapes us!). We live a deceit: effectively we leap the ontological gap, with the aid of an ever-growing managed techno-cultural sleight of hand, and behave with the quantitative as if it had qualities like us. (This is of course because of the anthropomorphic character given by design to almost all the forms of human interaction with computer technology.) This post-human humanisation constantly affects us, but not the technology.

Because many modes of computer application are created for an interactive relation, every time a new bit of information is introduced into the system everything alters (hence the system is deemed plastic).[21] But with such change and complexity arrives an unpredictability. A perfectly functioning error-free computer, operating with the most programmatic software, while seemingly functioning in a regime of absolute mechanistic logic, will still do the unexpected as codes collide. Chance (not unreason) is ever the other of reason.[22]

System change and unpredictability are but two encounterable ontological characteristics of the computer, its technology and history. Another characteristic centres upon an inversion of a realist theory of representation. The philosophical proposition of this theory holds that the real can be represented by a theoretical description of it. However, technology has turned this proposition on its head: the real can be created by a theoretical representation of it. The simulation becomes a likeness of the yet-to-be. The infrastructural foundation of computer-based representation is always designing: it is always an ontological change structure of a structuring designed to change, be it image, language, built object, manufactured product or world.[23] This then is one face of the machine learning of the reason machine.

Computers and 'machine intelligence' are characterised as an extension of mind. Here, the danger that computers pose is not the prospect of them becoming smarter than us, but rather that we, by Design, become delimited in our thinking by them (especially as non-reason functions start to proliferate, such as image recognition-based decision making). In the ignorance in which we are immersed, and in our degree of exposure to metaphysics realised as technology, we are constantly being instrumentalised by the ontological designing of the technology: function demands compliance, and compliance is not thinking. We can now never be free of this 'nature', but the imperative of sustain-ability determines that alienation is an absolutely critical faculty of dwelling. The proposition is that while we are unable to stop the developmental trajectory of a technology which has become naturalised, we are still able to alter our relation to it.

*\*\**

As every engagement with the defutured and defuturing in this text has indicated, the product and production has to be thrown into question. Both have to be seen and engaged as being situated on a line between world making and unmaking impacts, and thus as that which divides the defutured and futuring. The retention of the critical is not a matter of choice but of sustain-ability. Without the critical (again understood as both thought and condition) as a reflective and evaluative reflex able to confront risks, we 'fly blind' trusting totally in the technology of the auto-pilot. Without this we give way to the designing of the directionality of the product, production and instrumental knowledge as the reified spirit of productivism: 'push a button; fell a tree'.[24]

The design of modern industrial production enabled accumulated knowledge, gained via craft skills, to be transferred and embodied in machine functions (dead labour). As machines, computers have replicated this transfer from manual to mental labour by the inscription of reason, calculation and memory. In doing this they have totally altered the interface between human and technology, the locus of metaphysics. They have put in place a foundation of immaterial engineering and material transformation that only futures itself in its will to will its own structure. The defutured here comes from the object, and its phenomenal forms, immaterialising itself to the extent that there is no encounter from which to produce alienation. What is being identified is that technology has become structurally integrated so totally into and as environment that it now exists as a complete world wiring — 'the' world is, among other things, a circuit board.[25] It is where ever and when ever it is wanted to be.

One of the dominant impacts of the productivism of computer technology has been to accelerate consumption by its implication in advanced flexible automated manufacturing, handling and distribution systems where waste is reduced in the making of what turns out to be the inherently wasteful products. But equally, knowledge-based productivism is generative of the direction of a vast amount of resource input and material output (one of the most obvious ironies of electronic communication is, as mentioned, that the dramatically increased traffic in information has increased the volume of paper use).

In this context sustain-ability implies an intervention in an anthropocentrically inscribed fate. This intervention has been variously named as contestation, alienation, resistance, and repression. Out of this culture another kind of thinking, another kind of information, another kind of learning has to be created. For, as Marshall McLuhan wrote some thirty-five years ago:

> Our education has long ago acquired the fragmentary and piece-meal character of mechanism. It is now under increasing pressure to acquire the depth and interrelation that are indispensable in the all-at-once world of electronic organisation.[26]

Learning sustaining-ability is a learning to overwhelm all other learning that touches all knowledge past, present and future. This fundamentally has to be a thinking as a reflection in action; a thinking that feels the discomfort of a proximity to a 'thinking machine'. In this thinking, the development of action that takes the conservation of resources and their utilisation seriously, that asks what is appropriate as a contextually strident question (which is a position beyond a reductively designated counter-instrumental 'appropriate technology') begins to open up. This can be characterised as a designing with alienation that employs objectivisation against objectivisation, instrumentality against instrumentalism, force against force, simplicity with complexity, thinking against disembodied metaphysics.

## Notes

1 Martin Heidegger (writing in 1955), *The Principle of Reason* (trans Reginald Lilly), Indiana University Press, Bloomington, 1996, p. 15.
2 On the agency of being directively there while being elsewhere, see Michael Heim, *The Metaphysics of Virtual Reality*, Oxford University Press, Oxford, 1993, pp. 114–115.

3   Terry Windgrad and Fernando Flores, *Understanding Computers and Cognition,* Addison-Wesley, Reading, 1986, pp. 86–90. Windgrad and Flores give a very clear operational account of the 'reason machine' and the relations at the basis of its system of representation and of the levels on which function occurs. They detail the layers of the technology starting with the precondition for the immaterial machine being at the core of computer functionality, followed by the physicality of electronic technology and its material or mechanical substrate. Onto this is layered the 'logic machine' whereby voltages become managed as values, patterns and information. A higher level of immaterial function then arrives as the 'abstract machine' that is able to read, process and manage data. What drives this process is the input of a program instruction, written in a language of representational commands. While this is a much simplified version of Windgrad and Flores' own simplification, two clear messages shine through. Firstly, one can see very clearly the transfer of analytic philosophy and logic into the creation a technology at the level of micro-reductive detailed system building: the proposition of metaphysics being disembodied and thereafter inscribed in technology can be empirically confirmed. Secondly, one can recognise a constructional pattern of development whereby the technology itself is a key multiplier of its own capability, and thus it acquires a reproductive dimension with a speed that is at the heart of the claim that a technology can take on a life of its own.

4   The key mediation between the formative moment of the logic of Leibniz's metaphysic, the creation of modern analytic philosophy, and the employment of that philosophy as the crucial linkage between language and logic was Bertrand Russell's 1900 study, *A Critical Exposition of the Philosophy of Leibniz,* and thereafter with Alfred North Whitehead in *Principia Mathematica* of 1910–13. Heim (*The Metaphysics of Virtual Reality,* p. 83) points to these links and notes that Leibniz both worked on 'various calculating machines throughout his lifetime' and provided the binary number system used by John von Neumann in developing electronic computers at Princeton.

5   We can note that without a sense of reason nothing makes sense. In this respect reason is not a product of thinking, it is its very ground. It follows all that is placed outside reason only exists in this condition by the grace of reason. See for example: Heidegger, *The Principle of Reason*, pp. 32–40.

6   We can note two moments around which a consideration of logic has been centred. The first moment is the placement of Leibniz

at that point at which the Classical tradition of logic, associated especially with Plato and Aristotle as well as the medieval tradition, was turned (by him) toward questions of modern thought. The second moment was the placement of Leibniz at a point at which the modern tradition of logic was turned into the technological as a functional instrument of a technology. On this latter point we can note that Michael Heim, as one of the key theorists and champions of the negation of modern thought by the technological and as a Heidegger scholar, has not only set out to erase a reader's relation to the ambiguity of Heidegger's position regarding technology, that reinforces the significances of calculation authorised by Leibniz's, but also, as a Heidegger translator and specifically as translator of the English edition of Heidegger's *The Metaphysical Foundations of Logic* (Indiana University Press, Bloomington, 1984), has shown a profound lack of understanding of his subject. In this text he wrote, in the Translator's Afterword: 'It may soon be possible to translate Heidegger's texts into English by making use of electronic data retrieval systems. Computers will be able to sort out previous translational solutions and apply them to the text at hand in a technically consistent way' (p. 227). One might like to reflect on this statement in the light of Heidegger's own comment at the beginning of this chapter.

7   Leibniz was extremely interested in China and Chinese scholarship, wrote on the topic and was an Enlightenment philosopher influenced by Chinese philosophy (see *Gottfried Wilhelm Leibniz Writings on China* (trans and intro Daniel J Cook and Henry Rosemont Jr), Open Court, Chicago, 1994). The eminent sinologist Joseph Needham draws our attention to a letter Leibniz wrote on 'l'Arithmétique Binaire' on Chinese philosophy in the early eighteenth century to Fr Joachim Bouvet, a Jesuit missionary in China, who had particular interest in the Book of Changes (*I Ching*) and with whom he corresponded for a period of over five years. Bouvet had brought the Book of Changes to Leibniz's attention in 1698, Bouvet pointing out that the hexagrams of the book could be read as a binary notation. This form of notation had been developed by Leibniz, and presented as a paper in 1679. Binary notation has a direct linage to Boolean algebra and cybernetics. He was amazed that his 'discovery' was well over a 1000 years old. As Needham points out, the Chinese influence was partly responsible for establishing algebraic and mathematical models from which later advances benefited. The other point of interest here is that the Chinese did this outside the discourse of

reason, and with a mathematics in the service of chance. See Joseph Needham, *Science and Civilisation in China*, vol. 2, Cambridge University Press, Cambridge, 1956, pp. 340–45. We also note that Liebniz's understanding of logic, the power he posited with calculation, and his notion of the connectability of 'monads' (in a contemporary characterisation this appears as post-human network nodes) not only made a contribution to the foundation of thought upon which Babbage, Turing, Boolean logic and the machine mind have all stood, but also laid a major plank of analytic philosophy as it ascended in the academy and then migrated to industry as programming.

8  This is most notable in the work of information theorist Claude Shannon.
9  See Chapter 5. The work of Don Ihde is, for example, significant in this respect: see his *Technology and the Lifeworld*, Indiana University Press, Bloomington, 1990.
10 See Martin Heidegger, *The Question Concerning Technology and Other Essays* (trans William Lovitt), Harper and Row, New York, 1977.
11 The (Westernised) self is not 'natural'. The self could be argued to be a de-relationalised mode of being against community waiting to be exposed as a suicidal monad. (Selfishness is both a core act of unsustainability and a removal from a dependent condition of exchange. Once a society of selfish people is created the social terminates, and so eventually does the self.)
12 Martin Heidegger, *Aristotle's Metaphysics-1–3* (trans Walter Brogan and Peter Warnek), Indiana University Press, Bloomington, pp. 89–91.
13 Martin Heidegger, *Nietzsche, Volume 2* (trans David Farrel Krell), Indiana University Press, Bloomington, 1991, pp. 86–87.
14 *Ibid.*, pp. 73–98.
15 We can see these trends in, for example, the way Hubert Dreyfus presents and engages Sherry Turkel's notion of the Internet as a location for self construction and reconstruction. Web paper: 'Highway Bridges and Feasts: Heidegger and Borgman on How to Affirm Technology'. On the unsustainable see n. 11 above.
16 On this topic see Michael Heim, *Electronic Language: A Philosophical Study of Word Processing*, Yale University Press, New Haven, 1987.
17 Here one can contrast the proto-critical: Tony Fry (ed), *RUATV?: Heidegger and the Televisual*, Power Publications, Sydney, 1993; and the uncritical and celebratory: Howard Rheingold, *Virtual Reality*, Secker and Warburg, London, 1991.

18 This notion of the relation between technology, metaphysics, structure and structuring is seen, for example, in the way computers affect change and the self: see Heim, *Electronic Language*, pp. 25–27 and Sherry Turkle, *Life on the Screen: Identity in the Age of the Internet*, Simon and Schuster, New York, 1995.
19 Such structuring is outlined in, for example, John Matthews, *Tools for Change*, Pluto Press, Sydney, 1989.
20 For a fuller account of these different options see Heim, *Electronic Language*, especially pp. 82, 89, 146 and 156.
21 See Windgrad and Flores, *Understanding Computers and Cognition*, p. 94. We can note that the characteristic of plasticity identified by them informs a misreading of change as evolution (see comments on evolution above).
22 *Ibid.*, p. 95.
23 For one version of this see Heim, *Electronic Language*, p. 31. There is another representational designing in which the computer has figured that has become a more powerful cultural and scientific force. This is the 'ficto context' where a fictional history of the present, presented as an account from the future, designs action now. This arrives as a de-idealised utopianism, or a dystopia. Without doubt the most influential 'setting-up' force of this designing has been William Gibson's oft cited 1985 novel *Neuroromancer*. More than any other book, it constituted a computer-authored world as an ontological space of imaginaries. What his 'ficto context' created was a shift in thinking from the designing of, or with, computers to one of designing in their domain. This is yet another powerful example of vision, dream, image driving material realisation (cf. the history and the designing power of utopias as discussed in Chapter 6).
24 Michael Heim, *The Metaphysics of Virtual Reality*, Oxford University Press, Oxford, 1993, p. 5.
25 What Windgrad and Flores review and say in *Understanding Computers and Cognition* (pp. 136–39) on fifth-generation computers is worth considering on this count.
26 Marshall McLuhan, *Understanding Media London*, (orig. 1964), Abacus edition, London, 1973, p. 381.

# CONCLUDING IMPRESSIONS

... and progress passes (author's collection)

This book will have been read out of a conjunctural difference of knowledge and need, its value and use depending upon the readers' relation to their conjuncture, learning and action. At its very start it was framed by these words:

> As the 'telling' of defuturing, this text arrives as something confronting an impossibility and a necessity. What is impossible is the telling of the story, for once one understands the nature and magnitude of the defutured, how one accounts for the history and making of the material world dramatically changes. In this respect it is a way of seeing, remaking and making anew — hence it delivers a new foundation of design which radically transforms what design is and does. Defuturing is thus the generator of a new design philosophy ... .
>
> The full story of the defutured can never be told, for it requires the rewriting of everything. However, demonstrating that one understands the method of telling is essential. Defuturing is a necessary learning that travels before any design or constructional action if any effort is to be made to acquire the ability to sustain. The fact that so far the defutured and defuturing (the method by which the defutured is understood) have not been learnt means that even the well intentioned go on sustaining the unsustainable.

In taking the project of the book forward we need to reaffirm that, at its most basic, defuturing is an approach aiming to prefiguratively *think* (but not predict) impacts prior to their directional inscription as determinate qualities of the made. It is thus the telling of the story of error, learnt from the history of erring, that arrives with all material cultures. As this it becomes corrective, albeit without certainty. It has no single reductive form: it can enfold a sensibility able, within a design process, to extrapolate consequences prior to their arrival and modify actions accordingly; alternatively, it can be a far more formal historically informed fictional scenario able to guide and modify what is to be created. Of course error and negative impacts will always occur — the price of creation is always destruction — however, the ability to reduce impacts, to make otherwise, just does not arrive unless one has some semblance of care about the consequences of what one is doing.

## ON METHOD

Defuturing's methods have been created out of an unlikely assemblage of a post-structural phenomenology and applied (but not crudely instrumentalised) deconstructive practices. Its interrogation of the foundations of the unsustainable never 'transcend' provisionality.

Martin Heidegger, in *Being and Time* published in 1926, constituted a new and integrated practice that complexified both the method of phenomenological inquiry and its object. He moved from a position centred on the essence of a thing-in-itself (which reached its most developed expression in the work of his one time mentor and senior colleague at the University of Marburg, Edmund Husserl) to the centrality of the experience of the phenomenal. What Heidegger recognised was that experience, knowledge and disposition constitute the textual field in which objects arrive before any act of interpretation. Thus, not only does nothing arrive unmediated, but the phenomenal condition of being-in-the-world is always hermeneutic. As Heidegger's work amply demonstrates, complexity floods into this observation from many directions. His analysis generates many issues, problems and debates that still resonate, not least on hermeneutics. Conceptually, defuturing positions itself as cutting across this tradition as a phenomenology of the yet-to-be.

The metaphysical foundations of Western thought do not simply exist in print. They have been at the basis of the knowledge that has brought a great deal of what defutures into being. Derridian deconstruction teaches that these foundations have inscribed something far more pervasive than this. Inscription is more than writing, it is *typhus* (both 'form' and an infection). Inscription is Design, yet design starts with the word (the way a world is made present). Defuturing turns this recognition into a practice.

## THE DEFUTURED AND DEFUTURING

'Defuturing' is reaffirmed as the name of a method of reading worlds that have been 'defutured', that have been made to act autonomically in a condition of self-negation. The former is silent, it is something one does; the latter, the encountered, is what is done — it is the defutured of being unsustainable.

What this means is that in the core of the developmental process of the making of modern futures, there has been a counter movement which took on, metaphorically, a life of its own that was taken to be a law, logic and rationale. This counter movement was generative of a major contradiction — it created a pattern of development that established short-term conditions of sustainment which undercut the possibility of longer-term means of the sustain-ability. The negation of the future, the defutured, is thus something that happens to us and the world around us, we are both in and of it.

At the same time, once the defutured is identified, named and read (via defuturing), it becomes possible to create an ability to learn to see, read, think and make otherwise. In this setting, futuring arrives as a possibility from the ability of defuturing to recognise the defutured. Echoing an earlier concern with judgement, defuturing is a way to learn to read one's world in order to judge, make choices and act in ways that historically inscribe sustaining futures.

Defuturing, as the term that names a method of reading the historical nature of unsustainability in process, enables an identification of the actual means by which futures are taken away. As this it is in direct opposition to the thinking of futurists who treat the future as a void waiting to be filled. Defuturing shows us what has already been put in place that acts as an agency that defutures, it makes clear that whatever we construct we do so in the midst of a populated space of structures, objects, rubble and wastelands. It deprives us of the illusion that, as we face the future, we stand before a condition of infinite choice and are in command of our fate. It removes the liberatory fictions of freedom from the past that come with the rhetorics of development, change and progress. At the same time it confronts us with the challenge of remaking, of a new ethics, of responsibility and the adventure of the unknown. Like the earliest explorers, we travel with crude tools of navigation, without maps, with inadequate or inappropriate technology, in fear — but with belief in the value of the journey and ourselves.

The defutured cannot simply be objectively located. It is in and of the world but equally it is of us, as a state of mind, a disposition, the familiar and the taken for granted. This is so even for those people who think they are taking action for sustainability. In speaking the defutured we are thus always speaking the world as we find it and conducting a dialogue with our selves. Reading the defutured is therefore a non-binary encounter between self, world and causality. This means that the excavation and exposure of the causes that defuture need to occur within a non-mechanistic theory of causality. This has the potential of bringing us to recognise 'patterns of error' that unify our own disposition with the way that we dispose the world we design. As we have been saying, the negative ground that an understanding of the defutured, as it exists and is constantly created, exposes is essential for positive construction. A reflection upon the defutured creates the possibility of correction. It breaks the authority of destructive applied knowledge, as well as patterns of habits and disabling values, while at the same time opening up new possibilities of thinking, acting and making.

In the work of the EcoDesign Foundation, in working, teaching and learning with many professionals on questions of 'sustainability', the experience has been one of encountering a desire, impatience and energy to get on with the job. This has been the case irrespective of the project, be it policy development, environmental architecture, eco-designing products, environmental management, creating new education courses, environmental philosophy or whatever. However, if you do not have a critical recognition of causality, then you are in no position to work towards true sustain-ability. A medical analogy will make this clearer. The diagnostic, including the pathological, exploration of the cause of disease is predicated on the logic that a cure is only possible if the absolute cause is discovered. While time can sometimes be gained by treating symptoms, this will never fundamentally deal with the problem. Such logic can be transposed to the relation between the sustainable and the unsustainable. There is, in effect, no theory or practice of sustain-ability unless it is preceded by a theory and practice of the pathology and agency of the unsustainable. This is exactly what 'defuturing' claims to be.

Reiterating, in the simplest of terms: the basic proposition of defuturing, as a practical philosophy, is that unless you know how to identify, read the forms and map the causal picture of the unsustainable as active relations of the on-going designing of the defutured, and which implicate both yourself and your object of engagement, then you are in no position to create solutions. Using defuturing to make present that which defutures is the first act of informed futuring.

OTHER THAN

Defuturing as method is other than environmentalism. Although an environmentalist view of 'a crisis of sustainability' has become generalised as discourse and public perception, it is totally inadequate as an explanation of the crisis, its deflection to 'the natural' has concealed relational causality and assisted in the coming of a crisis of crisis.

While environmental problems undoubtedly do exist, their causes, character and consequences raise far larger questions of sustainment than are identified, engaged and understood by the environmental movement, its intellectual resources and thinkers, be they light or deep green ecologists. The very terms 'environmental,' and its systems partner 'ecology', are dominantly understood from a biocentric perspective. This is insufficient to address the multi-ontological relational complexities and flux of the biophysical, socio-cultural and cognitive-symbolic qualities of all that requires to be sustained. The failure of environmentalists to think the foundations upon which their thinking rests means that 'solutions' are posed without the problem ever being adequately defined. (The obvious, 'the essential' and commonsensical all mislead.) A great deal of energy is directed toward symptoms rather causes.

Equally, defuturing as method is other than science, which frequently or shall we even say mostly, becomes part of the problem rather than part of the solution. Its very specificity, focus, obsession, sense of fact, and its avoidance of crucial ontological issues make it ill-equiped to comprehend where the problem lies. The argument against science retreats back across the whole text.

If one wishes to work towards the resolution of problems of sustain-ability, this cannot be done by simply attaching one's actions to existing environmentalist discourses. Design, economics and education, for instance, cannot just be loaded up with an environmental agenda, with existing, science, theory and practice then applied to solve empirical problems. This is not to say this solves nothing, it is to say that what is delivered is not sustain-ability. For this to happen, agents of transformation have first to be transformed. Sustain-ability demands a changed foundation of thought and value with which to define problems and on which to build and judge all other actions.

Defuturing, as method, also needs to be disassociated from the rise of 'corporate sustainability' — which is but another manifestation of pragmatic capitalism recognising crisis at its most reductive level (with the 'help' of 'environmentalists') and setting out to convert problems into economic opportunities. Here sustain-ability is prefigured by the objective of sustaining and extending the power of the corporation. Its rise may well inscribe a major contradiction that will act to fundamentally deepen the concealment of the crisis of sustainability, by uniting the restrictive view of environmentalism with the violence of a postmodern globalism of abandonments, fragmentations and strategic formations. Of course, authentically progressive corporations position themselves by the minimisation of the social and environmental impacts of their commercial practices, production processes and products.

SUSTAIN-ABILITY

The assemblage which is the defutured becomes an active afterlife as the unsustainable. This serves a single imperative: sustain-ability. Sustain-ability is neither coherent nor realisable. It has no essential form. We have seen that it names the acquiring of an ability to work against the finitudinal delimitation of accumulative unsustainability. Its realisation, as knowledge and as incremental acts and agents (sustainments), demands constant conjunctural learning and relearning as new modes of the unsustainable continually arrive. Sustain-ability is a learnt contestation of the 'logic' of the structural connectivism of productivism, the necessity of making time and of vital need to take responsibility for anthropocentric being.

Sustain-ability confronts the impossible goal of sustainability with an enabling pragmatic. It 'knows' it is possible to become more sustainable but can never be fully sustainable (or ever completely know what the condition is). It knows it cannot arrive without action or a community of thinkers and a culture of a critical institution. And it knows it has nothing in common with 'the world' of intellectual fashion, but rather is the constant building of a thinking in which to dwell, and upon which dwelling depends. This thinking was once philosophy. (If this statement were accused of 'essentialism' then the retort would be that philosophy, as thinking rather the academic discipline, is essential and that we are in danger because philosophy is no longer thought to be essential.)

## DESIGN'S LAST WORD

Design has been posited as neither lodged in the natural nor the artificial, but as that which has made these binary oppositions untenable.

Design has been made present as fields of effects, as process, rather than as the singularity — a reified designed and designing object. As this, it has been named as a certain kind of post-foundational formation and force whereby all that is designed remains open, on-going and active. All things designed are animatory (which is one of the reasons why humans so frequently attribute qualities of the living to them).

We act in and on our world through that which is designed, that which designs and through our designing, which is why a knowledge of Design is an essential knowledge that is basic to being informed and responsible. Thus it follows that we exist in an ecology of image (mind), which is to say that Design always lies between us and that which we name as image, place, environment, or world.

Design requires to be remade, and thereafter be seen to unfold, as both a theory of action in crisis and as a theory of the actor. In the face of dysfunctionality and directional crisis, we, in our intercultural differences, need to find ways to embrace a designing that has the ability to get nearer to an understanding of how to create a critical selectivity of what is to be designed. Especially relevant here is gaining an understanding of Design's powers of world making. As can be seen throughout this text, such a 'development' is not being presented as a call to a new breed of aware designers (although no doubt such designers are needed as a transitional agency) but rather it is the calling up and extension of an ontological designing — in short a shift in designing from what things are, how they function, and what they look like, to what they do. What this transformation of design means, in a fundamental sense, is not only a radical shift in the very 'nature' of how and what to design but of who designs and how function is understood. First of all, the degree to which we are all designers demands to be confronted in practical terms (as a responsibility), which in turn requires the application of responsible design. Besides the role of the professional designer being weakened in some respects, what this actually means is embracing the material, social or symbolic environmental consequences of the impacts of our actions. It means recognising that designing incrementally constructs a world that itself makes the world the 'natural' place of being. What is now being registered here is not some kind of proposed technological imposition — a giant 'biosphere' or a new utopia — but rather the form of our taking responsibility, in all our differences, for the relation between our presence, our actions, our mode of habitation, and impacts upon place and all the forms of others.

## WHERE DO WE GO FROM HERE? LAST WORDS

The answer to this question, irrespective of who or where we are, requires both going back and going forward. Going back implies a critical reflection upon, a learning from, and taking into ownership of defuturing. It has been offered as a fledgling method to appropriate, develop and transport into the vast space of the defutured, of which there is no outside or other. Going back thus leads to going forward.

Going forward is movement from where one is, as defuturing creates an informed awareness of the presence of one's own defutured circumstances. By implication, no matter what one does, the learning of defuturing has potential directional and ethical consequences for how one exercises one's mind and labour. If this is not the case then nothing has been learnt. Going forward means doing more, including bringing defuturing to more than has been presented in this book. It also means acknowledging that defuturing is but one critical element of a larger project of the development of 'redirective practices' that turn against the unsustainable in the service of sustain-ability.

However, there are also major overarching problems to confront. The one that this author has started to confront (which is the task of another thinking) is that democracy, as it is currently constituted, is unable to deliver sustain-ability. It lacks the means to overcome the 'freedom of choice' of the unsustainable — a freedom which is never individual or contained, as is often claimed. In common with Design, freedom for us can only ever be in a condition of limit. We are confined within the limits of our mortality, the law, and the structures of our socio-economic dependencies. Unless a politics that limits unsustainability arrives we will negate the essential negation of negation. From a position of anthropocentric bias, it can be said we will be nothing.

# SELECT BIBLIOGRAPHY

Adas, Michael, *Machines as the Measure of Men*, Cornell University Press, New York, 1989.
Aristotle, *De Anima* (trans Hugh Lawson-Tancred), Penguin Books, London, 1986.
Banham, Reyner, *Theory and Design in the First Machine Age*, The Architectural Press, London, 1960.
Baudrillard, Jean, *For a Critique of the Political Economy of the Sign* (trans Charles Levin), Telos Press, St Louis, 1981.
— , *Simulations* (trans Paul Foss, Paul Patton, Philip Beitchman), Semiotext(e), New York, 1983.
— , *America* (trans Chis Turner), Verso, London, 1988.
Beck, LW (ed), *Kant on History* (trans LW Beck, RE Anchor, EL Fackenham), Bobbs-Merrill, Indianapolis, 1963.
Benton, Tim *et al.*, *The New Objectivity: History of Architecture and Design 1890-1939*, (units 11–12), Open University Press, Milton Keynes, 1975.
Berman, Marshall, *All That is Solid Melts into Air*, Verso, London, 1982.
Cadbury, Deborah, *The Feminization of Nature*, Hamish Hamilton, London, 1997.
Carr, EH, *What is History?*, Macmillian, London, 1961.
Derrida, Jacques, *Of Grammatology* (trans Gayatri Chakravorty Spivak), John Hopkins University Press, Baltimore, 1974.
— , *Writing and Difference* (trans Alan Bass), University of Chicago Press, Chicago 1978.
— , *The Post Card: From Socrates to Freud and Beyond*, University of Chicago Press, Chicago, 1987.

Dreyfus, Hubert, *Being-in-the-World: A Commentary on Heidegger's Being and Time Division 1*, MIT Press, Cambridge (Mass), 1991.
Elliott, Dave, *New Worlds: Russian Art and Society 1900–1937*, Thames and Hudson, London, 1986.
Ellis, John, *The Social History of the Machine Gun*, Johns Hopkins University Press, Baltimore, 1986.
Falk, Pasi, *The Consuming Body*, Sage Publications, London, 1994.
Farrell Krell, David, *Daimon Life: Heidegger and Philosophy*, Indiana University Press, Bloomington, 1992.
Fry, Tony, *Remakings: Ecology, Design, Philosophy*, Envirobook Sydney, 1994.
Fry, Tony (ed), *RUATV?: Heidegger and the Televisual*, Power Publication, Sydney, 1993.
Fukuyama, Francis, *The End of History and the Last Man*, The Free Press, New York, 1992.
Fussell, Paul, *The Great War and Modern Memory*, Oxford University Press, Oxford, 1975.
Giedion, Siegfried, *Mechanisation Takes Command*, Norton, New York, 1948.
Gramsci, Antonio, *Selections from Prison Notebooks* (ed and trans Quintin Hoare, Geoffrey Nowell Smith), Lawrence and Wishart, London, 1978.
Gropius, Walter, *Scope of Total Architecture*, Collier Books, New York, 1974.
Hall, David and Ames, Roger, *Thinking Through Confucius*, SUNY Press, Albany (NY), 1987.
— , *Anticipating China*, SUNY Press, Albany (NY), 1995.
— , *Thinking from the Han: Self, Truth and Transcendence in Chinese and Western Culture*, SUNY Press, New York, 1998.
Haar, Michel, *The Song of the Earth* (trans Reginald Lilly), Indiana University Press, Bloomington, 1993.
— , *Heidegger and the Essence of Man* (trans William McNeil), SUNY Press, Albany, 1993.
Hegel, GWF, *Philosophy of Right* (trans TM Knox), Oxford University Press, Oxford, 1975.
— , *Phenomenology of Spirit* (trans Parvis Emad, Kenneth Maly), Indiana University Press, Bloomington, 1988.
Heidegger, Martin, *Being and Time* (trans John Macquarrie, Edward Robinson), Basil Blackwell, London, 1962.
— , *What is Called Thinking* (trans J Glenn Gray), Harper and Row, New York, 1968.
— , *Poetry, Language, Thought* (trans Albert Hofstadter), Harper and Row, New York, 1971.

— , *The Question Concerning Technology and Other Essays* (trans William Lovitt), Harper and Row, New York, 1971.
— , *The Basic Problems of Phenomenology* (trans and intro Albert Hofstadter), Indiana University Press, Bloomington, 1982.
— , *Early Greek Thinking* (trans David Farrell Krell and Frank A Capuzzi), Harper and Row, New York, 1984.
— , *Kant and the Problem of Metaphysics* (trans Richard Taft), Indiana University Press, Bloomington, 1990.
— , *Nietzsche* vols I–II (trans and ed David Farrel Krell); vol. III (trans Joan Stambaugh, David Farrell Krell, Frank Capuzzi; ed David Farrel Krell); vol. IV (trans Frank A Capuzzi: ed David Farrell Krell), Harper, SanFrancisco, 1991.
— , *Parmenides* (trans André Schuwer, Richard Rojcewicz), Indiana University Press, Bloomington, 1992.
— , *The Metaphysical Foundations of Logic*, Indiana University Press, Bloomington, 1995.
— , *Aristotle's Metaphysics-1–3* (trans Walter Brogan, Peter Warnek), Indiana University Press, Bloomington, 1995.
— , *The Principle of Reason* (trans Reginald Lilly), Indiana University Press, Bloomington, 1996.
— , *Hölderlin's Hymn 'The Ister'* (trans William McNeil, Julia Davis), Indiana University Press, Bloomington, 1996.
Heidegger, Martin and Fink Eugen, *Heraclitus Seminar* (trans Charles H Seibert), Northwestern University Press, Evanstone, 1993.
Heim, Michael, *Electric Language: A Philosophical Study of Word Process*, Yale University Press, New Haven, 1987.
— , *The Metaphysics of Virtual Reality*, Oxford University Press, Oxford, 1993.
Heraclitus, *Heraclitus Fragments* (trans TM Robinson), University of Toronto Press, Toronto, 1987.
Herf, Jeffery, *Reactionary Modernism: Technology, Culture, and Politics in Weimar and the Third Reich*, Cambridge University Press, Cambridge ,1984.
Hughes, Thomas P, *American Genesis: A Century of Invention and Technological Enthusiasm*, Penguin Books, New York, 1989.
Ihde, Don, *Technology and the Lifeworld*, Indiana University Press, Bloomington, 1990.
Jameson, Fredric, *The Prison House of Language: A Critical Account of Structuralism and Russian Formalism*, Princeton University Press, New Jersey, 1972.
Jullien, François, *The Propensity of Things: Towards a History of Efficacy in China*, Zone Books, New York, 1995.
Kojève, Alexandre, *Introduction to the Reading of Hegel: Lectures on*

the *Phenomenology of Spirit* (trans James H Nichols; ed Allan Bloom), Cornell University Press, Ithaca, 1969.
Kumar, Kirshan, *Utopia and Anti-Utopia in Modern Times*, Basil Blackwell, Oxford, 1987.
Levinas, Emmanuel, *Totality and Infinity* (trans Alfonso Lingis), Duquesne University Press, Pittsburg, 1990.
Leder, Drew, *The Absent Body*, Chicago University Press, Chicago, 1990.
Levin, David Michael, *Modernity and the Hegemony of Vision*, University of California Press, Berkeley, 1993.
Lloyd, GER, *Adversaries and Authorities: Investigations into Ancient Greek and Chinese Science*, Cambridge University Press, Cambridge, 1996.
Luhmann, Niklas, *Social Systems* (trans John Bednarz Jr, Dirk Baecker), Stanford University Press, Stanford, 1995.
Lyotard, Jean-François, *The Postmodern Condition: A Report on Knowledge* (trans Geoff Bennington, Brian Massumi), Manchester University Press, Manchester, 1984.
Margolin, Victor and Buchanan, Richard (eds), *The Idea of Design*, MIT Press, Cambridge (Mass), 1995.
Marx, Leo, *The Machine in the Garden*, Oxford University Press, London, 1964.
McLuhan, Marshall, *Understanding Media: The Extension of Man*, Routledge Kegan Paul, London, 1964.
Meikle, Jeffrey, *Twentieth Century Limited*, Temple University Press, Philadelphia, 1979.
Melzer, Arthur M, Weinberger, Jerry and Zinman, Richard M, *Technology in the Western Political Tradition*, Cornell University Press, Ithaca, 1993.
Miyoshi, Masao and Harootunian, HD (eds), *Postmodernism and Japan*, Duke University Press, Durham, 1989.
Mitcham Carl, *Thinking Through Technology: The Path Between Engineering and Philosophy*, University of Chicago Press, Chicago, 1994.
Merleau-Ponty, Maurice, *Phenomenology of Perception* (trans Colin Smith), Routledge, London, 1962.
— , *The Visible and the Invisible* (trans Alfonso Lingis), Northwestern University Press, Evanston, 1968.
Needham, Joseph, *Science and Civilisation in China* (vol II of *History of Scientific Thought*), Cambridge University Press, Cambridge, 1956.
Nobel, David F, *America by Design*, Alfred Knopf, New York, 1977.
Plato, *The Republic* (trans and intro Desmond Lee), 2nd ed of Penguin 1955 ed, Penguin Books, London, 1988.

Queens Musuem, *Dawn of a New Day: The New York World's Fair, 1939/40*, catalogue, Queens Museum/New York University Press, New York, 1980.

Rheingold, Howard, *Virtual Reality*, Secker and Warburg, London, 1991.

Rosen, Stanley, *The Question of Being*, Yale University Press, New Haven, 1993.

Roth, Michael S, *Knowing and History*, Cornell University Press, Ithaca, 1988.

Said, Edward, *Orientialism*, Pantheon, New York, 1978.

Scarry, Elaine, *The Body in Pain*, Oxford University Press, Oxford, 1987.

Schürmann, Reiner, *Heidegger on Being and Acting* (trans Christine-Marie Gros), Indiana University Press, Bloomington, 1987.

Smith, Merritt Roe (ed), *Military Enterprise and Technological Change*, MIT Press, Cambridge (Mass), 1985.

Stambaugh, Joan, *The Finitude of Being*, SUNY Press, New York, 1992.

Temple, Robert, *The Genius of China*, Simon and Schuster, New York, 1986.

Virilio, Paul, *Speed and Politics* (trans Mark Polizzotti), Semiotext(e), New York, 1986.

— , *War and Cinema* (trans Patrick Camiller), Verso, London, 1989.

— , *Popular Defence and Ecological Struggle* (trans Mark Polizzotti), Semiotext(e), New York, 1990.

Wheen, Francis, *Television: A World History*, Century Publishing, London, 1985.

White, Hayden, *Tropics of Discourse*, John Hopkins University Press, Baltimore, 1978.

— , *Metahistory: The Historical Imagination in Nineteenth Century Europe*, John Hopkins University Press, Baltimore, 1973.

Winograd, Terry and Flores, Fernando, *Understanding Computers and Cognition*, Addison-Wesley Publishing, Reading (Mass), 1986.

Willett, John, *The New Sobriety 1917–1933*, Thames and Hudson, London, 1978.

Wyschograd, Edith, *Spirit in Ashes: Hegel, Heidegger and Man Made Mass Death*, Yale University Press, New Haven, 1985.

Young, Iris M, *Throwing Like a Girl*, Indiana University Press, Bloomington, 1990.

Yovel, Yirmiahu, *Kant and the Philosophy of History*, Princeton University Press, Princeton, 1980.

Zimmerman, Michael, *Heidegger's Confrontion with Modernity*, Indiana University Press, Bloomington, 1990.

# INDEX

aboriginal cultures, 92
abstract machine, 279n
Adas, Michael, 55n
AEG, 152
aero-dynamics, 112
aesthetics, 35, 42
African crisis, 181
agricultural industry, 79
agricultural technology, 79, 214
*alètheia*, 237
alienation, 24, 31, 34, 260, 268, 277
America, American, 16
   army engineers, 83
   Civil War, 82
   Constitution, 76
   culture, 76, 77, 83, 117, 118, 123
   economy, 16, 75
   engineering schools, 83
   highway program, 44
   industry, 78, 93
   jazz, 117
   machine tool industry, 82
   philosophy, 84
   space program, 84
   system of manufacture, 81, 85, 87
   regional planning association, 122
   universities, 83
   way of life, 140
Americanism, 71, 84, 85, 89, 93, 156, 164, 211
Ames, Roger T and David Hall, 17, 104n, 215, 219, 133n, 224n, 226n

analytic engine, 259
Anaximander, 96
anthropocentrism, 10–12, 25, 31, 43, 53, 72, 76, 99, 137, 148, 155, 174, 177, 202, 209, 228, 238, 241, 253, 290
*Architectural Record*, 125
architecture, 151, 153, 155
Aristotle, 35, 57n, 100, 192, 206, 226n, 267, 280n
arms trade, 38
art deco, 118
artificial (the), 26, 27
arts and craft movement, 153
AT&T, 126
attunement, *see stimmung*
authenticity, 191
autonomic technocentricity, 276, 253–82 *passim*
autopoietic system, 192, 220

Babbage, Charles, 259
Bacon, Francis, 55n, 99, 133, 137, 144n
Baird, John Logie, 225
Banham, Reyner, 161, 165n, 168n, 169n
Baudrillard, Jean, 139, 140, 144n, 154, 159, 160, 168n, 249n, 250n, 272
Bauhaus, 118, 143, 149, 150, 151, 152, 154, 155, 156, 158, 159, 160, 161, 165n, 166n, 167n, 168n, 169n
Berlin, 165n

Dessau, 151, 152, 157, 167n, 168n
vorkurs, 152, 164n
Weimar, 151, 152, 157, 167n
Beck, LW, 57n
Bell Telephone Company, 126
Bellamy, Edward, 122, 138
Benedict, Ruth, 127
Benton, Tim, 169n
Behrens, Peter, 152
Berman, Marshall, 113, 122, 143n, 144n
Beynon, Huw, 102n, 140n
Bigelow, Jacob, 83
biocentrism, ix, 14, 179, 260
biological designing, 178
biology, biodiversity, 31, 35, 36, 172
Blumenberg, Hans David, 249n
body (human) 174, 175
  absent, 183
  biological, 180
  designing, 178
  image, 189
  mind, 185
  modernity, 189
  organic, 178
  performing, 192
  philosophies, 180
  reconstruction, 195
  sign, 190
  sustain-able, 195
Boeing Rocketdyne, 251n
Braun, Karl, 235
Breuer, Marcel, 166n
British Broadcasting Corporation (BBC), 235
Brown, Lester and Brian Halweil, 235
Brundtland Report, 8
Buchanan, Richard and Victor Margolin, 103n
Burke, Edmund, 68n

calculation, 26, 277
Callenbach, Ernest, 145n
Canguilheim, Geoges, 192, 203n
capitalist mode of production, 34
'care' 230
Carlyle, Thomas, 77
Carr, EH, 76n
causality, 63
Central Committee of the Communist Party, 163
Central Institute of Labour, 164
Century of Progress Exhibition (Chicago), 123
Chicage design culture, 157

Chicago School (of sociology), 36, 127
China, 213–21
  agricultural technology, 223n
  ancient, 13
  defutured, 217
  floods, 217, 225n
  Han, 223n
  identity, 215
  manufacturers, 218
  medicine, 202
  modern, 208
  people, 216
  philosophy, 258
  scholarship, 219, 280
  science, 214
  thinkers, 232
chronopolitical, 211
climate change, 92
cloning, 54
CNN, 198
Coca Cola, 147, 148
cold war, 123
colonialism, 45
communication, 13, 36
communism, 133
Communist manifesto, 134
community, 45
Colt, Samuel, 81
Colt revolver, 81, 88
command economy, 162
computers, computerisation, 270–77
  computer aided design (CAD), 272
  computer aided manufacture (CAM), 272
  computer aided planning (CAP), 272
  computer integrated manufacture (CIM), 272
Comte, Auguste, 137
Condillac, Etienne Bonnet de, 68n
Confucius, 220
  Confucianism, 102, 219, 220, 223n
  Neo-Confucian, 180
constructivism (Russian), 150, 166n
consumer (modern), consumption, 43, 64, 87, 191, 269
consumerism, 87, 120, 127, 154
Copernicus, 99, 232
Cornford, FM, 248
corporate sustainability, 288
cosmos, 37
Coxe, Tench, 76
crisis of crisis, 130, 244
critical (the), 253

critical distance, 254
cubism, 154
culture, 20, 23, 24, 36, 50
  consumer, 7
  industrial, 7, 74
  modern, 112
  planetary, 254
  popular, 31, 83, 117, 140
  post-industrial, 7
  post-modern, 11
cybernetics, 43, 45, 230, 246

D'Arcy, Eamon, 251n
Darwinism, 36, 193, 261
dead labour, 277
de Beauvoir, Simone, 187
deconstruction, 2, 3, 11, 72
defuture, defutured (the), 2, 20, 22, 41, 45, 60, 66, 87, 112, 147, 156, 172, 181, 182, 206, 208, 237, 238, 263, 266, 275, 277, 285, 286, 290
defuturing, ix, 2, 3, 10–14, 34, 62, 63, 284, 285, 286, 288, 290
Degler, Carl, 102n
democracy, 125, 208, 290
department stores, 87
Derrida, Jacques, 57n 62, 222n, 249n, 285
Descartes, Renè, 63, 76, 192, 201
de-severance, 269
Design (the capitalised meta category), 6, 7, 13, 14, 16, 22, 40, 73, 96, 110, 111, 113, 129, 133, 136, 147, 158–60, 164, 174, 176, 188, 194, 202, 231, 234, 236, 262, 270, 277, 285, 288, 289
design
  community, 45
  computers, 264, 277
  education, 4, 7, 158
  European modernist, 162
  history, 2, 3, 7, 16, 60, 149, 156, 158
  ontology (theory of), 25, 33, 39, 40, 73, 93, 95, 176, 201, 220, 231, 232, 234, 241, 260
  philosophy, viii, 2, 10, 172
  theory, 22
  total, 116, 120, 147, 148, 150, 154, 157, 163, 191
  unsustainable, 7
De Stijl, 151, 161n
developing ecological sustainment (DES), 8, 9, 29
development, developing, 206, 208, 289
  uneven development, 206
Dewey, John, 84
Deutscher Werkbund, 151, 165n
de-worlding, *see* world
difference engine, 259
DIN format, 169n
Dreyfus, Henry, 117, 119, 120, 125
Dreyfus, Hubert, 203n, 281n
Drummond, Bulldog, 203n
Du Pont, 126
Durkheim, Emile, 65
dwelling, 23, 24, 26, 28, 106, 107, 109–12, 197
dystopia, *see* utopia

Eco, Umberto, 272
EcoDesign Foundation, ix, x, 286
ecologically sustainable development (ESD), 8, 29, 257
ecology, ecological thinking, 10, 33
  of the image, 242, 245
  of mind, 260
  system, 55
economy, 266
Edo regime (Japan), 211, 222n
*eidos*, 100, 176, 235
*einbildungskraft*, 238, 240, 249n
Eisenstein, Sergei, 162
Elliot, David, 164, 170n
Ellis, John, 103n
El Lissitsky, 169n
Emerson, Ralph Waldo, 138, 139
enframing, 31, 34
Engels, Friedrich, 134, 144n
Enlightenment, 23, 26, 28, 48–50, 60, 61, 63, 66, 97–100, 111, 129, 130, 135, 150, 183, 192, 207, 214, 257, 258, 260
ethnocide, 259
entropic, 8
environmental impact statement (EIS), 91
environmental management, 262
environmental technologies, 254
environmentalism, 42, 287
ethnocentricity, 43, 49, 214
Eurocentrism, 42, 66, 92, 101, 140, 207, 208, 213
everyday life, 2, 272

Faison, Seth, 225n
Falk, Pasi, 203n

'Family of Man', 65
fascism (German), 123, 147, 149, 159, 165n
fascist imagery, 148
Fink, Eugen, 200
Firestone Tyre Company, 126
Fitzgerald, Scott, 124
Flores, Fernando, *see* Winograd *and* Flores
Flushing Creek/Meadow (New York), 123,
force, 206, 208–10, 215, 218, 219, 224n, 225n, 264, 267, 268
Ford, Henry, 85, 89, 109, 133, 142n
    Ford Motor Company, 89, 94, 210, 211
    Fordism, 84–86, 89, 210
    Highland Park plant, 85
    Model T, 85
formalism, 163, 210
    Russian, 174
fossil fuel, 91, 92
Foucault, Michel, 74, 268
Fournier, Charles, 134, 137
Frank, Andre Gunder, 221n
Franklin, Benjamin, 83
Frederick, Christine, 141n
freedom, 11, 28, 37, 63, 133, 184, 253n, 264, 290
Freud, Sigmund, 65
Fry, Tony, 103n, 104n, 248n, 259n, 281n
Fukuyama, Francis, 61, 67n
functionalism, 36–38, 40, 213
Fussell, Paul, 198, 203n
Futurama, 125, 208
futures, 11, 12, 65
Futurism
    Italian, 2
    Russian, 169n
futurists, 153, 154, 286.

Gabo, Naum, 162
Galileo, 99, 222
Gastev, Alexie, 164
Gatling, Richard Jordan, 88
Gatling gun, 88
General Electric Company (US), 235
General Motors, 86, 94, 125, 211
    Holden Motor Company, 95
    Sloan, Alfred, 86
genetics, 54, 172, 272
*gestalt*, 100, 238
Gestetner duplicating machine, 118

Gibson, William, 282n
Gilles, Peter, 135
Ginsburg, Moisei, 169n
globalisation, 206, 216, 240, 262, 288
God, 36, 37, 42, 54, 67n, 76, 77, 98, 192, 255, 258
Goetzmann, William H, 103n
Gramsci, Antonio, 70, 102n
Great Exhibition (Crystal Palace), 81
Greeks (the), Greek culture and thought, 57n, 98, 99, 100, 218
greenhouse gas, 91
Gropius, Walter, 143n, 151, 154, 155, 157, 160, 165n, 166n, 168n, 169n
Gulf War, *see* war
Guttman, Allen, 203n

Haar, Michel, 52, 201, 204n, 233
Habermas, Jürgen, 68n
habit, 184
habitus, 51, 110, 184, 188, 229
Hall, David L and Roger T Ames, 17, 104n, 215, 219, 223n, 224n, 226n.
Halweil, Brian, 225n
Hancock Hall, John, 80
Hare, Michael, 126
Harootunian, HD, 222n
Harpers Ferry Armories (US), 81
Hartnett, LJ, 103n
Hegel, GWF and Hegelian thought, 41, 48, 50, 51, 57n, 58n, 74, 134, 267
Heidegger, Martin, 52, 56n, 58n, 62, 102n, 110, 140, 142n, 188, 200, 201, 203n, 204n, 218, 221n, 226n, 230, 234, 238, 247, 248n, 249n, 250n, 251n, 255, 264, 267, 278n, 279n, 280n, 281n, 284, 285
Heim, Michael, 278n, 280n, 281n
Heinz foods, 126
Heraclitus, 38, 52, 56n, 200, 202, 233, 261
Herf, Jeffrey, 165n
hermeneutics, 242, 285
history, 48, 49
Hobbes, Thomas, 68n, 184, 202n
Hollywood, 117, 140
Homberger, Eric, 103n
home, 107, 108
household technology, 108
Hughes, Howard, 190

Hughes, Thomas, 77, 120n
humanity, 4, 10, 20, 24, 41, 71, 72
  anti-humanism, 50
  human being(s), 16, 32
  human rights, 9
  humanism, 47, 49, 51, 54, 130, 155, 209, 255, 260
  humanities, 4
  inhuman, inhumanism, 25, 44, 49
  post-human, 276
  species, 177
Husserl, Edmund, 285n
Huxley, Julien, 143n
hydroelectric generation, 115
hypertextuality, 271

*I Ching*, 280n
Idhe, Don, 30, 56n, 237, 249n, 281
information, information theory, 24, 259
information ecology, 25
inhuman, *see* human
Inkhuk, 162
Instrumentalism, 2, 33, 141
Irish Republican Army (IRA), 46
Ittens, Johannes, 152, 165n

Jameson, Fredric, 174, 202
Jesuits, 215
Jorden, R
Joyner, Florence, 197
judgement, 2, 11, 241
Jullien, François, 248n
Jünger, Ernst, 56n

Kandinksy, Vassily, 131, 162n, 168n, 169n
Kant, Immanuel, 17, 48–51, 60, 67n
Klee, Paul, 166n, 168n
Kodak, 117
Kohn, Robert, 124
Kojève, Alexandre, 211, 222n
Krell, David Farrell, 58n, 200, 203n, 204n
Krupps, 88
Kumar, Kirshan, 133, 135, 144n

language, 12, 13, 174, 175–76, 222, 228, 243, 260, 271
Lao Tzu, 226n
Lasch, Christopher, 131
learning, 14, 15, 25, 278
Le Corbusier, 107, 125, 133, 141n, 143n, 168n, 195, 203n

Leder, Drew, 180, 183, 202n
Lee, John R, 142n
*legein*, 239
Leibniz, Gottfried Wilheim, 17, 213, 224n, 255, 257, 279n, 280n, 281n
Le Quin, Ursula, 145n
Levin, David Michael, 249n
Levinas, Emmanuel, 110, 111, 142n, 200, 203n, 271
Lewis and Clark exploration, 74
life, 9, 10, 13, 33, 44, 266
life cycle analysis, 91
lifeworld, 28
Lilienthal, David E, 143n
limits, 93
  to growth, 9
Lincoln, George S and Company, 80, 81
Lingis, Alphonso, 202n
Littler, Craign R, 103
Lloyd, GER, 204n
Locke, John, 68n
Loewy, Raymond, 118, 119, 120, 124
logic, 255, 280n
logic machine, 279n
*logos*, 100, 101, 133, 176, 236, 237, 249n, 250n
Lovelace, Lady Ada, 259
Luhmann, Niklas, 15, 17, 36, 37, 56n
Lynd, Robert and Helen, 127
Lyotard, Jean-François, 61, 62, 67n

McAnemy, George, 122
Macauley, Thomas Babington, 30
McCormick Company, 80
McCormick reaper, 88
Macedonian phalanx, 39
Machiavelli, Niccolò, 68n
machine(s)
  aesthetic, 153
  farm, 79
  intelligence, 277
  learning, 277
machine guns, 88
  Browning, 88
  Gatling, 88
  Lewis, 88
  Maxim, 88
  Vickers, 88
McLuhan, Marshall, 231, 248n, 278, 282n
making otherwise, 17
Malevich, Kasmir, 162

Mao, Zedong, 219, 225n, 226n
Marc, Franz, 131
Marx, Karl/Marxism, 65,132, 133, 134, 138, 144n, 219
Marx, Leo, 75, 76, 102n, 103n
mass markets, 87
mass media, 87
mass production, 87
Massachusetts Institute for Technology, 83
Matthews, John, 282n
Maurier, George D, 235
Maxim, Hiram, 89
Mayakovsky, Vladmir, 106, 162, 163
Mead, Margaret, 127
measurement, 25, 255
Meikle, Jeffrey, 117, 143n
Melman, Seymor, 83, 103n
Melville, Herman, 139
Melzer, Arthur M, 56n
Merleau-Ponty, Maurice, 110, 142n, 179, 180, 181, 184, 187, 193, 202n, 234, 244, 250n
metahistory, 15, 172
metanarrative, 15, 71, 172
metaphysics, 5, 10 13, 35, 54, 95, 101, 187, 213, 219, 233, 237, 238, 241, 246, 258, 272, 285
  and technology, 28
Meyer, Adolf, 168n
Meyer, Hannes, 166n
military industrial complex, 122
millennium bug, 273
Mitcham, Carl, 56n
modern movement, 36
modern subject, 106, 108
modernisation, 63, 72, 127, 132, 207, 212
modernism, 63, 117
modernists, 157
modernity, 42–44, 52, 63, 64, 66, 67n, 70, 83, 106, 129, 139, 158, 163, 182, 198, 206, 207–209, 214, 215, 262
  American, 70, 121
  cultural, 63
  economic, 47, 63
  philosophical, 63
  political, 63
modular, 195
Moholy-Nagy, Laszlo, 166n, 167n
Mondrian, Piet, 131
More, Sir Thomas, 135, 137, 138, 144n
Morris, William, 131, 138

Moses, Robert, 122, 125, 143n
Mujahideen, 46
multiculturalism, 208
Mumford, Lewis, 122
Myoshi, Masao, 222n

NATO (North Atlantic Treaty Organisation), 245
'nature' 16, 26, 49–50, 55, 76, 110, 159, 210, 224n, 237, 243, 253, 254, 256, 262, 263, 273, 277
natura, 182
natural, 7, 287
natural sciences, see science
natural world, 99
technology, 32
Nazi, Nazis, 151, 155, 157
Needham, Joseph, 214, 223n, 280n, 281n
New Deal, 113–15, 122, 133
  Booker T, Washington Park (Tennessee)
  Conservation Corps, 115
  Tennessee Valley Authority (TVA) 114, 115, 143n
New York World's Fair, 16, 106, 120–25, 129, 131, 139, 208, 240, 267
Newton, Sir Isaac, 223n
Nietzsche, Fredrich, 58n, 62, 201, 226n, 264, 267, 268
Nipkow, Paul, 235
North, Simeon, 80
nuclear power, 29

O'Conner, Francis V, 124, 144n
ocularcentrism, 98
Olympic Games, 195, 195
ontology, ontological, 43
  learning, 35
  questions, 5
  structure, 254, 276
  theory, viii
Oud, JJP, 151
Orwell, George, 60
Owen, Robert, 134, 137

Parmenides, 96
Peoples Liberation Army (China), 216, 225n
perception, 244
philosophy
  American, 84
  eastern, 31

modernist, 148
phenomenology, 45
positivism, 84
pragmaticism, 65, 101
pre-Socratics, 196
post-Socratics, 101
poststructuralism, 101
   see also deconstruction, ontology, metaphysics
*physis,* electro-*physis*, 182, 233, 257, 275
Plato, 97, 98, 135, 136, 144n, 192, 234, 236, 249n, 260, 280n
Popova, Liubov, 169n
popular culture, *see* culture
postmodern culture, *see* culture
postmodernism, 64, 132, 206, 228, 267, 268, 272
practical reason (phronèsis), 35
productivism, 23, 25, 27, 42–44, 47, 52, 100, 148, 223n, 257, 259, 260, 261, 272, 278
progress, 2
proximity, 23, 32, 33, 38, 182, 231, 253, 278
Pythagoras, 96, 97

Queens Museum (New York), 124, 144n

RCA (records), 126
Reagan, Ronald, 246
realism, 210
reason, 133, 255, 257, 279n
reason machine, 254, 255, 279n
redirective practice, 290
relationality, 3, 13–17, 186
Remington Company, 80, 88
representation, representational forms, 26
revolutionary art, 210
Ricardo, David, 68n
Robbins and Lawrence Company, 80
Rodchenko, Alexander, 169n
Roosevelt, Franklin D, 113, 114
Rosen, Stanley, 248n
Roth, Michael, 48, 51, 57n, 58n
Rousseau, Jean Jacques, 68n
Russell, Jane, 190
Russian Revolution, 133, 162, 168n
Rybeznski, Withold, 142n

Said, Edward, 223n
Saint Augustine, 184

Saint-Simon, Henri, 137
Scarry, Elaine, 181, 202n
Schlemmer, Oscar, 168n
Schmitt, Carl, 268
science, 4, 25, 179, 185, 193, 206, 242, 258
   natural sciences, 100
   scientific management, *see* Frederick Winslow Taylor
seeing, 234, 239
Seimens process, 223n
sexual politics, 180
Shannon, Claude, 259
Sharps Rifle Company, 80
*shi*, 268
sign (the), 156, 159
   economy, 154, 156, 272
   management, 157
   political economy of the sign, 158, 160, 199
   weapon, 241
Sloan, Alfred, *see* General Motors
Smith, Merritt Roe, 81, 103n
Snow, CP, 84
social Darwinism, 193
Socrates, 124, 223n
Spencer, Herbert, 137
Spivak, Gayatri Chakravorty, 222n
Stalin, Joseph V, 163, 225n
Stambaugh, Joan, 238, 249n
Stepanova, Varvara, 169n
*stimmung* (attunement), 202, 204n
stirrup, 40
Straus, Erwin, 187
streamlining, 16, 106, 107, 112, 113, 116, 119, 124, 139, 150, 156, 162
Sullivan Louis, 36
Susman, Warren, 144n
sustain-ability, ix, x, 3, 4, 8–15 *passim,* 17, 22, 29, 34, 35, 40, 41, 47, 74, 92, 95, 107, 111, 112, 136, 180, 181, 189, 191, 104, 207, 209, 221, 241, 247, 253, 254, 263, 267, 277, 278, 285, 287
sustainments, 12, 256
symbolic logic, 255, 257, 258

tao, taoism, 13, 219, 220, 232, 261, 268
Taylor, Frederick Winslow, 85, 133, 141n, 164
Taylor, Mark, 272
Teague, Walter Dorwin, 117, 122

*technè*, 32
technology, 3, 17, 22–24, 26, 28–31, 33, 39, 41, 51, 54, 60, 76, 78, 99, 108, 134, 140, 164, 228, 230, 236, 253, 257, 264, 265, 267
  appropriate, 278
  autonomic, 266
  being, 53
  computer, 16, 263, 270, 274, 276
  cultural, viii, 140, 172, 269
  desire (of), 231
  determinism, 36, 54, 126, 215
  medical, 246
  meta, 273
  philosophy (of), 31
  sustainable, 29
  techno-ontological domain, 22
  technocentrism, technocentricity, ix, 17, 64
  time, 27
telescope, 42
television, televisual, 43, 46, 128, 139, 228–30, 233, 236–38, 240, 241, 243, 244, 245, 247, 264, 271, 272
  tele-dynamics, 241
  tele-logos, 240
  tele-presence, 255
*telos*, 48, 52, 132, 219
Temple, Robert, 223n
Tennessee Valley Authority (TVA), *see* New Deal
thinking, 110, 129
thinking machine, 278
Third Reich, 44, 148
Thompson, J Walter, 127
Three Gorges Dam (China), 225n
time, 206
Topographical Bureau, *see* United States of America
total design, *see* design
total mobilisation, 41
Trotsky, Leon, 133
Turing, Alan, 259
Turkle, Sherry, 281n, 282n

underconsumption, 113
unfreedom, 259, 269
United Nations, 8, 128, 209
  UNESCO, 65
United States of America
  Department of Ordnance, 81, 86
  navy, 44

Topographical Bureau, 52
*see also* America
unmaking, 277
unsustainability, viii, 3, 4, 8–15, 20, 22, 40, 46, 47, 53, 65, 66, 72, 89, 93, 101, 108, 109, 129, 150, 156, 183, 186, 194, 288
utopia, 121, 129, 130, 135, 241
  dystopia, 126, 138
  utopian, 138
  utopianism, 3, 129, 130, 132, 140, 149

value, 149, 150, 154, 155, 159, 160, 168n, 241, 242
van de Rohe, Mies, 169n
Van Doesburg, Theo, 166n, 168n
van Doran, Harold, 118
Vertov, Dziga, 162
Vesin, Alexander, 169n
violence, 51
Virilio, Paul, 52, 58n, 251n
virtuality, virtual reality, 2n, 259, 271
Vkhutemas (the), 149, 150, 161–63
von Neumann, John, 279

Walker, Timothy, 77
war, 16, 22, 38, 40–47 *passim*, 53, 198
  American Civil, *see* America
  eco, 42
  engines, 27
  Gulf, 198, 199, 245, 246
  machines, 38, 39, 46
  modern, 44, 46
  pure, 52
  total, 52
  Vietnam, 44, 46, 245
  warring, 22
  World War I, 85, 89, 112, 151, 153, 195, 221, 251n
  World War II, 167, 195, 250n, 259
waste, 191, 254
Watson, John B, 127
weapons, 46
Weber, Max, 65
Weinberger, Jerry, 56n
Wells, HG, 131, 144n
WGY Radio Station (New York), 235
Whalen, Grover, 122
White, Hayden, 61, 62, 67n
Whitehead, Alfred North, 279n
Whitman, Walt, 83
Whitney, Eli, 80
Willett, John, 161, 165n, 169n,

Wingler, HM, 165n
Winograd, Terry and Fernando Flores, 279n, 282n
Wolfe, Tom, 165n
word processing, 275
world, 16, 20, 26, 30, 31, 71, 72, 269
   being in the world, 20, 26, 34, 71
   deworlding, 22
   world development, 65
   worlding, 41, 244, 265
   world picture, 149, 208, 209, 238, 242
   worlds, 16, 25, 65, 239
Worldwatch Institute, 225
Wright, Frank Lloyd, 36, 167n

Wyschograd, Edith, 58n

Xiaoping, Deng, 225n

Yangtze River (China), 217
*Ying-yang*, 25, 224n
Young, Iris, 187, 188, 202n
Yovel, Yirmiahu, 50, 57n

Zeitgeist, 154
Zemin, Jiang, 225n
Zimmerman, Michael, 56n
Zinman M Richard, 56n